T0265550

EMILY MANN

EMILY MANN

Rebel Artist of the American Theater

ALEXIS GREENE

APPLAUSE
THEATRE & CINEMA BOOKS
Guilford, Connecticut

APPLAUSE
THEATRE & CINEMA BOOKS

An imprint of Globe Pequot, the trade division of
The Rowman & Littlefield Publishing Group, Inc.
4501 Forbes Blvd., Ste. 200
Lanham, MD 20706
www.rowman.com

Distributed by NATIONAL BOOK NETWORK

British Library Cataloguing in Publication Information available

Library of Congress Cataloging-in-Publication Data available

Names: Greene, Alexis, author.
Title: Emily Mann : rebel artist of the American theater / Alexis Greene.
Description: Guilford, Connecticut : Applause, [2021] | Includes
   bibliographical references, filmography, and index. | Summary: "Emily
   Mann: Rebel Artist of the American Theater is the story of a remarkable
   American playwright, director, and artistic director"— Provided by
   publisher.
Identifiers: LCCN 2021017477 (print) | LCCN 2021017478 (ebook) | ISBN
   9781493060320 (cloth) | ISBN 9781493060337 (epub)
Subjects: LCSH: Mann, Emily, 1952- | McCarter Theatre Center (Princeton,
   N.J.) | Women dramatists, American—Biography. | Women theatrical
   producers and directors—United States—Biography.
Classification: LCC PS3563.A5357 Z68 2021 (print) | LCC PS3563.A5357
   (ebook) | DDC 812/.54—dc23
LC record available at https://lccn.loc.gov/2021017477
LC ebook record available at https://lccn.loc.gov/2021017478

♾™ The paper used in this publication meets the minimum requirements of American
National Standard for Information Sciences—Permanence of Paper for Printed Library
Materials, ANSI/NISO Z39.48-1992

CONTENTS

PREFACE

I FIRST MET Emily Mann in 1983, during a theater conference in Minneapolis. She would sit in the audience, at any of numerous panels, a serious and attentive expression on her face beneath her head of dark-brown curls. She would listen and then she would ask challenging, in-your-face questions.

Already, by virtue of her art and her drive, she had made a statement in an American theater that was abysmally short on women seeing their plays produced or being hired to direct on the country's main stages. The Guthrie Theater, where Mann had worked her way from assistant stage manager to resident director, had begun life in Minneapolis in 1963. But no woman had directed on its glorious thrust stage until 1979, when Alvin Epstein, momentarily the Guthrie's artistic director, offered twenty-seven-year-old Emily Mann the chance to conceive a revelatory production of *The Glass Menagerie*. By the time she was twenty-eight, Mann had written a groundbreaking play, *Still Life*. An unvarnished expression of the human damage caused by the Vietnam War, *Still Life* brought Mann international recognition, and in the opinion of the revered South African director Barney Simon, had introduced a form of documentary theater that became known as theater of testimony.

In the 1970s and early 1980s, Mann was not alone on the front lines as a woman intent on making a career in the professional theater. She was particularly determined, however, to bring both her directorial skills and her dramatist's voice to American theater's most prominent stages, including Broadway, and she succeeded. In 1990 she became the first woman to lead the McCarter Theatre Center in Princeton, New Jersey, and for three decades she would be one of a minority of women heading a League of Resident Theatres (LORT) stage. The arc of her career is notable for challenging the patriarchal structure of American theater.

In the years since I first saw Mann in Minneapolis, I often interviewed her for books I was writing or editing and for feature articles, and during the course of writing a profile for the July/August 2015 issue of *American Theatre* magazine, I suggested embarking on a biography. Mann invited me to delve into her myriad private files, and that exploration informs this book, combined with background research, numerous conversations with Mann herself, and interviews with more than one hundred of her colleagues, friends, and family.

Events and political movements of the twentieth and twenty-first centuries have coursed through Mann's life and inspired the content of her plays. While a youngster, she learned about the Holocaust and the Civil Rights Movement in America. She came of age during the irreverent and often physically violent 1960s, and the Women's Liberation Movement that thrived during the late 1960s and the 1970s. As a director, playwright, the leader of an arts center, and especially as a woman, she has responded to and participated in waves of feminism and, since 2018, to the expanding Me Too movement, activated by women speaking up loudly and publicly about the sexual objectification and harassment they have endured. My approach as a biographer has been to integrate historic events and political movements with description and discussion of Emily Mann's life, her playwriting, her leadership of the McCarter, and examples from among the nearly one hundred productions she has directed.

But a biography is not solely a scholarly enterprise. It is a personal journey for both biographer and subject. From 2015 through 2019, I met and talked with Mann for close to one hundred hours, often for two hours at a time, and usually sitting at the round table in her miniature office at the McCarter, surrounded by photographs of her family and posters of her productions. Occasionally, in early summer, we met at her home, where she could recline on a chaise in her screened-in porch and look out at her lawn and its luxuriant trees. This is not an authorized biography. No topic was off limits, and she's had no approval of what I've written.

One of my goals in writing a biography of Emily Mann has been to show that resistance can reside in defying preconceived assumptions of what a woman of the theater can stage or write or, finally, achieve. I also hope to show how Mann's art and career can contribute to the discourse in the public square, a role that has become essential for American theater as it aims to be part of the cultural changes enveloping the country.

My chief goal, however, has been to write the life of a woman who has created unique art and along the way has wrestled with, learned from, and overcome personal trauma and illness. For centuries, the lives of women have been hidden: buried in diaries, letters, and in the day-to-day tasks that women undertook but few observed. This biography of Emily Mann brings one more woman's life into the light.

Alexis Greene
April 17, 2021
New York City

Prologue
Emilyville

One of Emily Mann's earliest memories is of being about seven years old and living in Northampton, Massachusetts, in a house with her father and mother and her ten-year-old sister, Carol.

Emmy, as her family and friends called her, is a skinny kid, with curly, frizzy, dark-brown hair cascading to her waist, smart brown eyes that look hard and long at people, and a serious expression on her face. But she is often locked out of the bedroom she shares with Carol, who does not want to play with her younger sister. So Emmy is given the guest bedroom for her very own private space. She is also given a set of bedroom furniture that her mother used when she was a girl, as well as a rocking chair and a vanity table, which Emmy uses as a desk. And along one wall and on the floor she arranges large, cardboard boxes, out of which she fashions stables and homes for a town she creates and calls Emilyville.

On one of her birthdays, her father gives Emmy a brown, soft, embrace-able teddy bear, with floppy ears and amber-colored glass eyes, and she names him La Guardia, because her father often talks about a mayor named La Guardia. She designates La Guardia the Mayor of Emilyville. There is also Bozo, a clown with a white face and an impish smile, a white peaked hat, and a long, red, flexible body. He is the spirit of Emilyville. And there is a stuffed octopus named Octi, who is the town's professor, and there are horses, which Emmy particularly loves, and numerous other creatures.

Sitting cross-legged on the floor, Emmy makes up stories about the citizens of her town. She invents conversations, sometimes in her head, sometimes

La Guardia and Bozo
COURTESY OF EMILY MANN

out loud. *There are laws for the town, and there is a city council, and town meetings.*

"An entire world," Emily Mann recalled years later. "I would go there and spend hours and hours and days and days, just happy as can be, away from everyone else."

She kept the history of Emilyville and the laws of Emilyville in her desk, along with her diaries. And no one could enter her room unless she let them.

1

Family

(1952–1955 and Before)

EMILY BETSY MANN was born on April 12, 1952, at Boston Lying-In Hospital. Her mother, Sylvia Blut Mann, and her father, Arthur Mann, were living at the time in Belmont, a Boston suburb; Arthur was about to receive his doctorate in American history from Harvard and was teaching in Cambridge at the Massachusetts Institute of Technology (MIT). Mann recalled being told that she was named for the American poet Emily Dickinson, a favorite of both her parents. As for the source of "Betsy," the story Mann heard while growing up was that Sylvia wanted to use the name of her paternal grandmother, Bertha—except Sylvia didn't have the heart to name any child Bertha.

Sylvia grew up in Paterson, New Jersey, the eldest of two children of Isaac Blut and Gussie Blum, Jews who had emigrated from Poland. Immigration records are contradictory, but it seems that each arrived separately at Ellis Island: twenty-one-year-old Isaac, known then as Isaak, in 1914 from Warsaw, the capital of the Kingdom of Poland, which was part of the Russian Empire; Gussie, or Gossie, Blum, who was seventeen, arriving from Ostrołęka, a shtetl, or town, in Poland's Bialystok region.

Once upon a time, late in the nineteenth century, Jews dominated the population of Ostrołęka. But with the onset of World War I, the Russians and then the Germans expelled the Jews, and shelled and burned the town. According to Gussie, her own mother insisted that she and her sister go to the United States, an arduous trek: overland across Europe, often to Hamburg, and then by ship to Liverpool and

Gussie Blut, Emily Mann's maternal grandmother
COURTESY OF CAROL MANN

at last America. Gussie did not want to leave her mother, but that decision undoubtedly saved Gussie's life. Twenty-five years later, in 1939, the Jews who had returned to Ostrołęka after the Great War, including members of Gussie's family, were annihilated when Hitler's armies invaded and occupied Poland.

The origin and fate of the Blum family, and the eradication of Ostrołęka and its Jews during World War II, would become the impetus for Mann's first professionally produced play, *Annulla Allen: The Autobiography of a Survivor* (1977).

How Isaac Blut and Gussie Blum met is no longer known, but they were married on June 27, 1920, in New York City and settled at first in Harlem, where, early in the twentieth century lived one of the largest Jewish communities in the world. There, at home on a cool, rainy, early spring day—April 16, 1921—Gussie gave birth to Sylvia. Family lore has it that Gussie went out to visit a relative and do some shopping, came back to the apartment, went into labor, and gave birth on the floor.

By 1925, Isaac, Gussie, and four-year-old Sylvia had moved to Paterson, New Jersey, for in that year Isaac established the United Shop Cap Company with several partners. Emily Mann never met her maternal grandfather (he died in 1949), but she knew Gussie, who kept a kosher home and was an outstanding cook, producing matzoh balls and potato latkes, stuffed derma and a splendid brisket. She spoke Yiddish—what the writer Isaac Bashevis Singer called "the jargon of exile"—and broken English, and many times Emmy would sit at a table in Gussie's kitchen, chin resting on her hands, mesmerized as she watched her grandmother chop vegetables, or deftly shape matzoh balls, or cut up a chicken, talking all the while. The intimate kitchen visits, and the pleasure Emmy took in them—they, too, would find their way into Mann's plays, into *Annulla Allen* and later into *Having Our Say: The Delany Sisters' First 100 Years* (1995).

"Some of the most profound wisdom came from older women in my life in the kitchen," Mann once told me. "The kitchen is where most people, male and female, used to go and put their little elbows up on the Formica table, smell all the food, and be in a very close and secure place, and learn about the world."

America offered Isaac Blut and his family a refuge from the wars that lay waste to European Jewry, and the freedom to live without fear of official persecution, but their new country was not free of prejudice against

Jews. Well into her nineties, Sylvia Mann spoke about the anti-Semitism she experienced as a child and also as a young woman, when, after graduating in 1942 from Paterson State Teachers College, with a B.S. in education, she tried to find a teaching job and often was passed over.

That firsthand experience of anti-Semitism was something Sylvia Blut and Arthur Finkelman had in common.

Sylvia was twenty, when, during the summer of 1941, she and her family vacationed at a resort in New York State's Catskill mountains, a popular destination for middle-class Jews from New Jersey and New York. The lifeguard at the swimming pool that summer was a young man with dark curly hair, a tapering waist, and muscular legs, who was sitting in the lifeguard's chair reading a Dostoyevsky novel. He and the slim, graceful woman with the heart-shaped face, tightly waved brown hair, and soft, warm smile became entranced with each other.

Arthur managed to get his hands on an old car and scraped together enough money for gas; fortunate, too, because after the United States entered World War II, in December 1941, hardly any new automobiles were manufactured, and gasoline was rationed. Still, whenever money, fuel, and his courses at Brooklyn College would allow, he drove to Paterson to court Sylvia Blut. As for Sylvia, whether talking with her children years later, or in private wedding anniversary notes to Arthur, she often said that her life really began the day she met him.

Like Sylvia's parents, Arthur's family had left Europe for the safer, democratic, and ostensibly more economically promising land of America. Sometime before 1900, Arthur's father, Karl Finkelman, not speaking a word of English, came to the United States from Sereth, a shtetl in the Bukovina region of Austria-Hungary. In America, Karl met and married Mary Koch, who also hailed from Bukovina, and the couple lived in Brooklyn. Arthur, the third of Karl and Mary's four children, was born on January 3, 1922.

But staying in one domicile for any length of time was difficult for Karl Finkelman. His business attempts rarely thrived, and so he moved his growing family around the borough, settling wherever he could afford the rent. Originally, Karl told his children, he and a brother were

Sylvia Blut at the Lakeside Inn, 1940. Possibly Lake Placid, New York.

Arthur Mann, probably 1943
COURTESY OF EMILY MANN

partners in a wholesale produce business. Arthur's youngest brother, George, who was born in 1926, remembered that "Pop used to talk about how, in the middle of the night, he and his brother Dave would get on a horse and wagon and . . . go out to the Polish farmers on Long Island and buy produce, come back home, and sell their produce," usually at a market that served the immigrant Jewish community of Manhattan's Lower East Side.

Finally, after what George understood to have been a nervous breakdown, Karl went into partnership with one of his wife's cousins, and they started buying and renovating dilapidated auto-repair garages. In an atypically successful venture, they bought a garage at Seventh Avenue and Tenth Street in Manhattan and, George recalled, "That's where the main living came from after a while."

Unlike Isaac Blut, whose cap factory did well even during the Great Depression of the 1930s, Karl, Mary, and their four children (Gertrude, Philip, Arthur, and George) and Gertrude's husband, Abe Rabinowitz, who lived with them, all struggled during the devastating economic crisis. George remembered with chagrin that he, Arthur, and Philip slept in the same room in at least one of the places they lived, and that he and Arthur had to share a bed. "But," said George, "we always had shoes, clothes, a roof, and food."

In George's memories of growing up in Brooklyn, Arthur always functioned at a higher level than his brothers and sister. He was studious, disciplined, and certain that, one day, he would be a college professor. "Serious as hell," is how George described him. "He always knew, whatever he would start, he would not only finish, but would finish well."

"When I was in grade school," George recalled, "Arthur would come home from high school—always shirt, tie, and jacket—sit down at his desk and do his work and study, like clockwork." Arthur was the first person in the Finkelman family to go to college, where he garnered A's in all his courses except physics and hygiene, according to his transcript, and graduated *summa cum laude*—with the highest distinction.

Arthur's competitive side also expressed itself through sports: boxing, baseball, basketball. But tennis was his game. Somehow, despite the family's tight budget, Karl Finkelman found enough money to buy Arthur a tennis racket. "Now, who played tennis on East Twenty-Fourth Street in Brooklyn?" George asked gleefully, during our interview. "But Arthur researched a tennis place on McDonald Avenue, where he could go and get lessons," George said, amused and admiring at the same time. "Then, typical of Arthur, he learned all of the strokes, and if you ever saw him on the tennis court, he was almost like a ballet dancer. The strokes were perfect." At James Madison High School, "Artie," as friends called him, was on the varsity tennis team, and at Brooklyn College, the Department of Athletics gave him its highest award, "By reason of scholarship, sportsmanship and exceptional skill in the sport of Tennis."

By then, Arthur Finkelman had changed his name to Arthur Mann.

The complete story of how and when Arthur changed his last name is not known, but at some point, according to George, Arthur wanted to go into the service, perhaps before the United States entered World War II, perhaps shortly afterward. He had heard that it was possible to receive military training from the Navy and finish college at the same time, and since he had entered Brooklyn College in 1940, the Navy's arrangement must have sounded appealing.

But his attempt to join the Navy's program taught Arthur a significant lesson. He believed that when the examiner saw "Finkelman" on the application, suddenly there was no more room in the program. Arthur's sister, Gert, furious when she heard this outcome, called the program and introduced herself with an Irish name. "Absolutely, send your brother down, there's plenty of room," was the response.

So Arthur went back, and the examiner, possibly hoping to eliminate this Jewish interloper, quizzed him on the capitals of what were then the forty-eight states. Studious Arthur easily passed that test, but the Navy rejected him anyway. So, Arthur changed his last name to Mann. As he would explain to his parents, to Sylvia, and years later to his two daughters, he realized that if he wanted eventually to go to graduate school and be hired to teach at a university, he would need a name that was less obviously Jewish.

The Finkelmans of Brooklyn had never been a religious family and, according to George, there was "a total lack of belief on our part in God." On Friday evenings before the sun set, when Gussie Blut in Paterson lit Shabbat candles to signify bringing peace and sanctity into her home, Karl Finkelman, in Brooklyn, would be setting a bottle of Schnapps on the table, and at dinner time, talk along a liberal bent would begin. But, as George put it, "the one thing we understood was, we are Jews." So when Arthur wanted to change his name, he first went to Karl and promised, "Pop, I will never, ever deny who we are." And Karl, according to George, said, "Okay. Ask your brothers. If your brothers say 'okay,' do it. I will not change my name, but I don't want your brothers having different names. Everybody must have the same name." Arthur's brothers changed their last names.

Arthur had told his family that he wanted to marry Sylvia as soon as he met her. And so it was that, on Saturday, November 6, 1943, Sylvia Blut and Arthur Mann were married at the Paramount Hotel in Manhattan. According to an announcement in a New Jersey newspaper, the Reverend Dr. Wexler performed the ceremony. Despite Wexler's title, which suggests that Sylvia and Arthur were married by a Protestant minister, it is likely that Wexler was a Jew and a cantor, and as a cantor, under Jewish law and legally in New York, he could perform the ceremony. Emily Mann is adamant that Gussie Blut would never have allowed her daughter to be married by a Protestant clergyman.

Sylvia Blut and Arthur Mann at their wedding, November 6, 1943, New York City
COURTESY OF EMILY MANN

The couple spent three nights at the Paramount and then lived for most of November with Sylvia's parents in New Jersey. Exactly a month after their wedding, on December 6, 1943, the War Department sent Arthur by train to the University of Indiana, in Bloomington, to study "Area and Language"—specifically Russian and Hungarian—in an Army Specialized Training Program, and Sylvia accompanied him. While in Indiana, Arthur received his BA from Brooklyn College on June 18, 1944, one of only three students, and the only man, to graduate summa cum laude that year. About two and a half months later, on September 2, 1944, he completed the army's program, and either in late fall of 1944 or early 1945, Private First Class Arthur Mann—a.k.a. Soldier #12127087, Company B-355th Infantry Regiment, 89th Infantry Division—was shipped overseas, and Sylvia returned to New Jersey to live with her parents and teach elementary school.

Arthur saw action, for Emily Mann remembered her father saying that he had been a radio operator "at the front" and that the bombing had damaged his hearing. Among Arthur's personal papers is a note written in pencil to Sylvia, dated March 25, 1945, from "somewhere in Germany." Indeed, histories of the 89th Infantry Division indicate that Company B-355th Infantry Regiment crossed the Rhine River on March 26, 1945, overcame German resistance, and continued apace through the crumbling Third Reich. At Ohrdruf, Arthur's regiment, along with elements of the 4th Armored Division, captured a concentration camp, the first to be liberated by American troops. Among the personal papers that Arthur left after he died are black-and-white photographs of emaciated corpses heaped in piles at the Buchenwald concentration camp, about thirty miles from Ohrdruf. But if Arthur entered any of the camps, he perhaps only confided in Sylvia. He did not speak about it to his siblings or his daughters.

Germany surrendered to the Allies on May 7, 1945, and Arthur's company was ordered to the French port of Le Havre. On January 14, 1946, he sent his wife a cable with news for which they both were longing: "Coming home."

Back in the United States, Arthur and Sylvia Mann moved to Roxbury, Massachusetts, about seven miles from Cambridge. Arthur took advantage of the G.I. Bill, which paid tuition and living expenses for veterans who had served at least ninety days and been honorably discharged, and in the fall of 1946 he entered Harvard's master's degree program in American history. Sylvia, during the 1947–1948 school year, taught first grade at the Lincoln Schools in Lincoln, Massachusetts. Twice she was pregnant and suffered miscarriages, but on July 23, 1949, she gave birth to Carol, and three years later, to Emily.

Perhaps changing his surname did help Arthur Mann's nascent career, or perhaps his customary discipline and application, combined with what students and colleagues always described as a charismatic presence and a sharp sense of humor, brought him early success. At any event, after earning his doctorate from Harvard in 1952 and teaching at MIT, as an instructor and then as assistant professor of humanities, he applied to be an assistant professor of history at Smith College, the elite women's school in Northampton, Massachusetts, and got the job.

In the summer of 1955, Arthur drove his family about one hundred miles from the outskirts of Boston to the considerably smaller city of Northampton, with Sylvia beside him in the front seat, and their daughters in the back. Carol was six, and Emmy was three years old.

2

Beloved Second Born

(1955–1966)

NORTHAMPTON IN 1955 was a picturesque, well-kept New England city. Its wide and winding Main Street was lined with plain but solid three-and-four-story brick buildings, many of which dated from the nineteenth or early twentieth centuries. There was a handsome court house and several churches; a movie house, the Calvin, which had been built in the 1920s; and an imposing, if weatherbeaten Academy of Music, all yellowed brick and neo-Renaissance in style—America's first city-owned theater.

The city was home to about 29,000 people, a number of whom worked or taught at Smith College, an island of formal, red-brick buildings floating near the center of town. There was a town-gown divide, with a kind of two-way snobbery prevailing between those who were not connected to Smith—storekeepers and the assembly-line workers at local factories such as Fuller Brush and Kollmorgen Optical—and the professors and their families.

It was the kind of place where boys and girls took swimming lessons at the YMCA and hung out at a soda shop after school. Kids rode bikes up and down residential streets, nobody locked their doors, and parents let their children walk to school by themselves. And almost everyone in Northampton was white. Mann recalled having only one African American classmate—a boy whose father was stationed at a nearby Air Force base—from the time she started kindergarten until she left Northampton at the end of the eighth grade. When Arthur's friend, the esteemed Black historian John Hope Franklin, visited the Manns with his wife,

Aurelia, and their son, John Whittington ("Whit"), who was Emily's age, they not only stayed with the Manns, they also ate all their meals at the Manns' house. Local restaurants, inns, and motels did not welcome people of color. "When the Franklins came to visit," Mann remembered, "they got such looks. It was terrible."

Northampton was the site of Mann's earliest encounters with racism and also with anti-Semitism. It was a city with a large Irish-Catholic population and, as in much of America, Jews were a minority. Carol Mann's childhood friend Marilyn August belonged to the largest and most prominent Jewish family in Northampton, and Marilyn estimated that there were only about one hundred Jewish families there during the 1950s and early 1960s. One Halloween, some person or persons wrapped her cousin Michael's house with toilet paper on which they had drawn swastikas. Opening up her school book in class one day, she found the words "dirty Jew," and once, when she was eight years old and riding her bike in Northampton, the mother of a classmate drove by, rolled down her window, and yelled "dirty little Jew."

Despite its picturesque exterior, Northampton possessed an ugly side.

Arthur and Sylvia Mann were mindful of the potential for anti-Semitism in their new community. After all, so far as they knew, Arthur was only the third Jewish academic to be hired by Smith. But as Mann said about her father, "he wasn't really an idealist. He was a realist. I think he saw a lot of America's faults, but he also saw that America was a place where, if you worked hard and had a great education, you could move up and out. Which is what he did."

Nonetheless, when they moved to Northampton, neither Arthur nor Sylvia went out of their way to announce that they were Jewish. "We were not part of the Jewish community in town," Mann remembered. "My mother and father were not comfortable with the Hadassah ladies and the merchants." Her parents "preferred the company of intellectuals and academics."

Mann was never called "a dirty Jew" in Northampton, but she did tell the story of how, one Friday night when she was in the sixth grade, she went to a girlfriend's house for a sleepover, and this friend, who was

Catholic, burst into tears and predicted that Emmy would "burn in hell" because she was Jewish. Soon both girls were sobbing, at which point Sylvia was called. She immediately drove over and told Emmy, "Say goodbye. You're not coming back." And she reassured her sensitive and impressionable daughter that the threat of burning in hell was "absolute rubbish."

In Northampton, the Manns at first rented a house on Paradise Road, near the Smith campus, where Emmy attended the Elizabeth Morrow Morgan Nursery School. Then in 1956, when Carol was seven and Emmy was four, the Manns took out a mortgage on a modest two-story clapboard house, with an attic, a shallow porch, and enough surrounding property to grow flowers. The house at 102 Crescent Street was in a different neighborhood from where most of the Smith faculty lived, but it was close enough to the campus that Arthur could bicycle to his classes. And when Emmy entered first grade, the house on Crescent was an energetic but doable walk or bike ride to the public school, several tree-lined blocks away on Vernon Street.

By American middle-class standards of the time, the Manns lived a privileged existence in Northampton. Unlike many fathers, Arthur Mann had relatively flexible hours, and when not teaching or advising students—or playing tennis or squash—he could be found in his study at home, sitting at his short, squat, oak desk, smoking a pipe and reading, preparing his classes or correcting papers. The only times he could not be interrupted were when he was writing a scholarly article or working on a book. Yet, when he was writing his biography of Fiorello La Guardia, he would often ask his wife and daughters to come in, sit on the hassock and a two-seater couch, and listen to him read the draft of a chapter, to make sure that what he had written could hold their attention.

Come summer, he would usually organize a car trip for the whole family, often arranged around a summer teaching assignment. Wearing slacks and a jacket and tie even on vacation, Arthur was organizer, driver, tour guide, and instructor, and each trip became a lesson in

*Left to right: Carol Mann, Sylvia Mann, and Arthur Mann, with Emily standing
in front, center. Arthur presents his biography of Fiorello La Guardia to Tom Bosley,
backstage at* Fiorello! *c. 1959.*
COURTESY OF EMILY MANN

history and geography. The excursions would be for a month or more,
and one that Mann particularly remembered took the family down the
East Coast and through the South to Miami, for a stay on the beach at
a grandiose brick edifice, the Roney Plaza Hotel. Stopping somewhere
south of the Mason–Dixon line to use the restroom, Emmy asked her
mother why there were "White" and "Colored" signs, and when her
mother explained that Emmy's friend Whit Franklin and his family
would not be allowed to use the bathrooms that the Manns used, Emmy
announced that she, too, would not use the "White" bathroom and got
so upset that she wet her pants.

After the births of her two daughters, Sylvia had chosen not to work,
although, according to Mann, Arthur encouraged her to do so. He also
suggested, as an alternative, that she type the manuscripts of the books
he was writing. She turned that suggestion down. Only during the last

three years that the Manns lived in Northampton, when Carol was in high school and Emmy in junior high, would Sylvia again have a paying job, teaching remedial reading two hours a day in a local public school. She started the Northampton Remedial Reading Program, a project that helped her earn a master's degree in education from Smith.

On the surface, then, Sylvia resembled the white middle-class women who were victims of what the feminist (and Smith graduate) Betty Friedan decried in her 1963 best-selling book, *The Feminine Mystique:* the false belief, encouraged by a paternalistic American society, that a truly womanly woman functioned primarily as a wife and mother, fulfilled by bolstering her husband's career and nurturing her family.

But Sylvia apparently did not feel she was sacrificing her intellect or skills by dedicating herself to her husband and children. She seemed to like being a faculty wife and gave memorable dinner parties, at which Carol and Emmy were employed to pass around hors d'oeuvres. She chauffeured her daughters to sleepovers and took Emmy, who loved horses, to a farm outside of Northampton, in order to ride. Sylvia did all the cooking, although someone else, a woman, came to the house once a week to clean. "I never saw my mother scrub a floor or clean the toilet," Mann recalled. "I've done that all my life, too. Always had someone come to clean, since graduate school. I'll even barter: 'I'll give acting lessons, if you would clean.'"

Beneath the externals of middle-class life existed the belief in family as the place for unwavering emotional support and loyalty. Family, and by extension the family's home, with its history, its private conversations and secrets, was to be guarded preciously. Nobody in the family was allowed to reveal that Arthur had changed his last name, and whenever grandmother Mary Finkelman came to visit, Emmy would squirm when introducing her.

At home, Arthur stressed the importance of thought-provoking inquiry and comment. "He loved organized thought," said Mann. "Sometimes he would say, 'Emmy, that's too emotional. What are the facts? Tell me the facts.' I used to hate that, because I would never remember the facts, I would remember the feeling."

The mid-to-late 1950s and early 1960s were tumultuous times for the Civil Rights Movement, and Mann recalled dinner table discussions about the "Little Rock Nine," Arkansas Governor Orval Faubus's ultimately unsuccessful attempt, in 1957, to block nine Black students from entering a local public school. She remembered conversations about James Meredith, the first Black student to desegregate the University of Mississippi, in 1962.

"Dinner," Mann remembered appreciatively, "was like a seminar. You talked about not only what was going on in your life, but what was going on in the world. My father didn't allow you your opinion unless you could back it up. He talked to us, when we were small, as though we were important people with real minds." Emmy and Carol never sat at a "children's" table, even when company came. They always ate with the adults, and Arthur expected both girls to speak up if they had something meaningful to say or a question to ask, and he expected his guests to listen and answer.

Arthur Mann set high standards for his children. "You sort of had to do your best at everything," said Mann. "I was a straight-A student. But I seemed to want to be, too." Yet, in Mann's memory, her father was not conventionally strict, in the sense that she or Carol would be grounded or spanked if either of them "did something wrong."

"The worse thing was, if you did something wrong, you had to go in and talk to Daddy. A horrible thing, because it seemed endless. He would usually take his swivel chair and turn it around, and I would sit on the hassock or the couch, and we would discuss what I had done wrong and all the ramifications of what that meant to others and to him. And you were never let off the hook. It was torture. I remember feeling really hot and having tears in my eyes, and squirming and hating it."

If family and education were preeminent values in the Mann household, organized religion was not. Arthur kept the promise to his parents that he would never forget he was a Jew, and the first book he edited, while still at MIT, *Growth and Achievement: Temple Israel, 1854–1954*, was a collection of essays about the evolution of New England's oldest reform Jewish congregation. But Emily Mann described her father as "a secular Jew" and "probably an atheist," and he never went to temple. Not that there was even a synagogue to attend when the Manns first arrived in Northampton; for decades the city's Jews had congregated in St. John's Episcopal Church, until the church was torn down. Finally, in 1963, the Jewish community built a conservative synagogue for Congregation B'nai Israel, on Prospect Street, a brief walk from the Manns' home on Crescent. Arthur and Sylvia became members, but mostly for Carol and Emmy. On Sunday mornings, Sylvia and Arthur sent their daughters to religious school at the synagogue, "to learn about who we were," said Mann, who joked years later that her parents probably wanted to have the house to themselves.

Emmy embraced one of the Jewish rituals to which her parents paid only lip-service. Every spring, Congregation B'nai Israel made a children's Seder, so that young Jews could learn the rituals and meaning of Passover. For Emmy, the experience was a revelation. "The whole idea that, because you were once slaves, you understand the plight of the oppressed, that you are not free if anyone else is enslaved and it's your duty as a Jewish human being to make sure that you help free others—it was huge for me. It marked me emotionally, politically, spiritually."

Already a storyteller, she found the saga of the Jews' exodus from Egypt to be dramatic, and the Seder a sensual event. There was the taste of the bitter herb—the horseradish—to remind Jews of their bitter servitude. Reclining while eating, as royalty used to do, signified that the Jews were no longer slaves but free people. "It's brilliant theater and brilliant storytelling," Mann declared years later. "All five senses are at play: taste and smell and feeling, visual and aural. You sing, and we learned dances. Reclining, pretending. It was just heaven for me."

And so much better than the Seders at her Uncle George's. At George Mann's home in Searingtown, Long Island, Emmy, sitting at the children's table, her curly hair pulled back into a kind of ponytail, used to get upset that the grownups, at their table, were making jokes and not taking the event and its rituals seriously. "It just wounded me that they weren't getting the bigger picture of why it was so important," Mann recalled, with good-natured mockery of her younger self. "I was a very serious child."

Her favorite place in the Mann home was her bedroom, with Emilyville. "It was my refuge," Mann said years later. Her favorite friend in elementary and grade school was Ruth Weinstein, whose father, Leo, was a professor of government at Smith.

"Ruthie was also a nerdy kid," Mann recalled, "and she and I would get together on Saturday mornings in the TV room, next to my bedroom, and we would have plastic telephones. We wore our leotards, and we would take Kleenex and make breasts. And then we had eyeglasses, because smart girls had glasses. We got frames at the five-and-dime. And we'd take our fathers' blue exam books and we would write books. We thought we were secretaries. We'd answer the phone and we'd say, 'Hello?'

"'We want a story about a flying horse.'

"'Right away!'

"We'd put down the phone and we'd write a story about a flying horse."

Weinstein, who eventually became a county judge in Florida, remembered she and Emmy sitting on the floor, "seriously writing," and then, "being proud of ourselves, and acting the stories out or reading them out loud to ourselves."

Sylvia seems to have been especially protective of her younger daughter. If Emilyville was Emmy's favorite place in all the world, her favorite time of day was the late afternoon, when she would cuddle with her mother on the living room sofa. "My mom and I had this ritual. We called it the magic hour, just about dusk. And everything would get all rosy red and beautiful, and I would put my head in her lap, and we would daydream together."

But Sylvia did not protect her daughter all the time. Carol and Emmy often didn't get along; the older girl picked on or ignored her younger sister. Also, when Emmy was about eight, one of the bigger boys at school began ambushing her as she walked home for lunch and punching her repeatedly in the stomach. "I tried going around the block once," Mann remembered, "and he found me." Her teacher said, "Oh, Emmy, it's just because he likes you." But Emmy was scared, and the punches hurt. Sylvia asked Carol to intervene, because Carol was bigger and older. "And my sister: 'Unh hunh, unh hunh.' Never." Then, Mann remembered, after the stomach-punching had been going on for a couple of months, maybe more, "We were all playing dodge ball during recess, and he bent down to pick up the ball, and he had just hit me so hard with it. . . . And he bent down to pick up the ball, and I took my hands and went 'Whomp,' down on his spine, and he collapsed and burst into tears. And I said, 'Don't you ever hurt me again.'"

Both parents recognized that their younger daughter was unusually imaginative, and they let her explore wherever her creativity led. At school she learned to play the soprano recorder and the piano (there was a second-hand upright in the Mann's TV room), and in 1961, when she was nine, Arthur arranged for her to take piano lessons with the celebrated African American composer and pianist George Theophilus Walker, who had just begun teaching at Smith and would become the college's first tenured Black professor. Later, in sixth grade, she joined the school's marching band and learned to play the flute.

According to Mann, it was her fourth grade teacher, Mrs. Deinlein, "who realized I was a writer," when she was ten years old.

"There were forty kids in our class, everyone from people who still couldn't read, to me and Ruthie. And Mrs. Deinlein would say, 'Okay, we're going to take the next half hour just to write.' She would have what we would call 'Free Writing' hours and she would give you a topic or an idea, and you just wrote. . . . So the one I remember is 'If I Were a Penny,' and how, like a penny, you would go from one person to the next person and the next, and all the things you would experience. And for some reason it triggered something, and I wrote and wrote and wrote and I wrote, and everyone else was finished and I asked Mrs. Deinlein, 'Could I just write a little more?' And she was thrilled and said, 'Of course you can.' So I wrote for another half an hour, an hour.

I don't know. And I wrote this long, long, long, long story. There was a monkey; somehow the penny got to Africa. And Mrs. Deinlein read it and called my mother and said, 'I think your daughter is a writer.' She started encouraging me to write, and I started writing short stories and showing them to her." Marilyn August recalled seeing Emmy sitting on her bed, "with her little knees up, writing in her notebook."

When Emmy was about seven, she saw a play for the first time: a Yiddish production in New York City of *Tzvishn Zwey Weltn–der Dibuk* (*The Dybbuk, or Between Two Worlds*) by S. Ansky.

The Dybbuk tells the story of Leah, who has fallen in love with a poor Yeshiva student. Leah's father insists that she marry a rich suitor instead, and shortly before the wedding, Leah's body is invaded by the wandering spirit, or dybbuk, of the student, who has died. Ultimately a rabbi orders the dybbuk to leave Leah's body, and she, too, dies, but her soul unites with the soul of her lover.

One of the most dramatic moments in any production of *The Dybbuk* occurs when the actor playing Leah, inhabited by the Dybbuk, speaks for the first time in her dead lover's voice. But no one had told Emmy the plot in advance, so she was listening to an English translation through earphones when, Mann remembered, she saw "this amazing woman, all in white, with a big black braid down her side, and all of a sudden a man's voice came out of her. And I screamed bloody murder. I was terrified. I loved it, but I was terrified."

"Emily was very gentle and extremely sensitive," Marilyn August recalled. "Carol, she's got a tougher side to her. Tougher than Emily. Carol and I, we played aggressively. Emily was more intellectual."

One sign of Emmy's intensity and hypersensitivity was the willingness, and the ability, to imagine what it was like to be in someone else's shoes, to have empathy for another person's situation, no matter how painful. This tendency emerged particularly strongly during the Manns' 1963 summer trip to Europe, the first European excursion for Carol, who was fourteen, and Emmy, eleven.

Mann considered the trip "one of the greatest educations of my life." Starting in June, and over the course of ten weeks, the family traveled from London to Scotland and then to the Continent, driving to a number of countries in Western Europe.

In London, Sylvia and Arthur had bought books for Carol and Emmy to read about the places they were to visit, and when they reached the Netherlands and were heading toward Amsterdam, Emmy began to read *The Diary of Anne Frank* in preparation for seeing the attic in which Anne and her family hid from the Nazis during World War II.

As Mann described the experience, "At that point in my life, I would become the characters I read. I would internalize everything. There I was, miles away from where Anne lived. But, reading her book, I thought we were the same people. She was a hypersensitive kid, I was a hypersensitive kid. She wrote a book. I just thought, that could be me, and this was happening to me. So by the time I got to the end of the diary, and she was taken away—and nobody had told me how it was going to end—Oh, god, I was unable to cope. I could see it happening, feel it happening. I could see my father—because my father was so fantastic, he would find us a place. I just totally felt it could be exactly our family, the same dynamics. My sister was having the same kind of fights with my mother that Anne was having with her mother. And as we came into Amsterdam, I was finishing it. I remember when we were in the car, it was like we were escaping, and there was no place to escape."

In retrospect, Mann called her reaction "a form of hysteria." The Manns never got to Anne Frank's attic: Emmy became ill with a kidney infection, and her parents took her to a hospital in Bruges, where she spent the night. Unfortunately that overnight stay only added to her fears, for she found the Belgian nurses "cold and mean" and, still wrestling with the trauma she had undergone when reading the *Diary*, she believed that, if the nurses knew she was Jewish, "they would be terrible." It was, Mann said years later, "quite a psychic wound." But her sometimes wrenching capacity to inhabit someone else's world would ultimately serve her when she became an actor, a director, and a playwright. The philosopher Martha Nussbaum has called this "the narrative imagination. The ability to think what it might be like to be in the shoes of a person different from oneself . . . and to understand the emotions and wishes and desires that someone so placed might have."

Back in Northampton in late August of 1963, sixth grade awaited her. That month, in an extraordinary display of peaceful togetherness, thousands of civil rights marchers gathered at the Lincoln Memorial in Washington, D.C., and heard the Reverend Martin Luther King Jr. memorably declare, "I have a dream that one day this nation will rise up and live out the true meaning of its creed: 'We hold these truths to be self-evident; that all men are created equal.'" Only one month later, however, members of the Ku Klux Klan planted sticks of dynamite at the Sixteenth Street Baptist Church in Birmingham, Alabama, and the resulting explosions killed four young Black girls.

On Friday, November 22, at twelve thirty in the afternoon, President John F. Kennedy was assassinated in Dallas, Texas, and the principal of Emmy's school, Mr. Moriarty, sent all the students home. It was the first time Emmy had seen an adult man cry.

The murders in Alabama and Dallas were opening salvos in a decade that would bring increasing violence across America and around the world. On March 2, 1965, the United States began bombing Communist North Vietnam, defending the American-supported government of South Vietnam in an offensive with the grandiose name of Operation Rolling Thunder.

On March 7, later known as Bloody Sunday, the Reverend King attempted to lead nonviolent protestors from Selma, Alabama, to Montgomery, the state capital, to support Black men and women's constitutional right to vote. In 1870, the 15th Amendment to the Constitution had granted Black men the right to vote, but for decades local and state governments, primarily in the South, had turned Black voters away from the polls with literacy tests and other invented ordeals. As the marchers crossed the Edmund Pettus Bridge out of Selma, state troopers and local posses attacked them with billy clubs, dogs, and tear gas. Two days later, on March 9, King, obeying a federal injunction, aborted a second march, but violence against the protestors continued. That night, white segregationists beat and murdered civil rights activist James Reeb, a white Unitarian minister who had come to Selma from Boston.

John Hope Franklin, in his autobiography *Mirror to America*, writes that Walter Johnson, the Preston and Sterling Morton Professor of American History at the University of Chicago, urged historians to participate in what would be the third march from Selma to Montgomery. Franklin, in Emily Mann's telling, called Arthur and told him to join them.

For Emmy, the tension between violence and safety was often a part of her private narrative, sometimes generating aggression, at other times fear. As a little girl, she had confided to her father about nightmares in which he and her mother both died (they assured her they would never die). And her experience reading *The Diary of Anne Frank* emerged in large part from fear. Now, on Wednesday, March 24, 1965, driving with her mother and father to Bradley International Airport in Connecticut, to see her father off for the third Selma to Montgomery protest, thirteen-year-old Emmy was again apprehensive.

U.S. Historians at third Selma to Montgomery March in 1965. From left, John Hope Franklin, John William Higham (with umbrella), and Arthur Mann.

Arthur flew to Atlanta, where, the next day, he and numerous American historians were taken by private bus to the outskirts of Montgomery. There they joined a march that had begun four days and fifty-four miles earlier in Selma, and along with 25,000 protestors, Arthur Mann and John Hope Franklin walked to the capitol building in downtown Montgomery to hear Dr. King and others speak. Someone (Mann believed it was her father) found a large piece of cardboard and wrote "U.S. Historians" on it in bold, black letters, and the actor and photographer Dennis Hopper caught an image of Arthur standing with Franklin and John William Higham of UCLA, while Higham hoisted the sign on the tip of his furled umbrella and held it high above the group. But Emmy's anxiety about potential violence was not unfounded. That night, after the historians had been driven back to Atlanta, they learned that Viola Liuzzo of Michigan, who was transporting marchers to the Montgomery airport, had been shot and killed by members of the Ku Klux Klan.

For some time Emmy had slowly been dismantling Emilyville, for her imagined town was less of a refuge now that she was older. She and Ruth Weinstein were still friends, but they were not so close as they had been when they were youngsters. In Mann's recollection, Ruthie "was into boys in a more advanced way than I was. She had become a woman a little earlier than I." The girls in Emily's class at Hawley Junior High ganged up on her and stopped inviting her to sleepovers. They made fun of her hair and her body, laughing about her "big butt." Arthur, in an April 1966 letter to his nephew Howard Rabinowtiz, wrote that his younger daughter was still recovering from "her operation" (a burst appendix) and also a "heavy grippe. She has had the worst year possible, poor thing."

Arthur had been considering leaving Smith for several years. In 1962, Washington University in St. Louis had offered him a position that would have given him a lighter course load and a higher academic rank than at Smith. But Arthur had been uncertain about whether to accept, and a letter from him to John Hope Franklin, who was a mentor as well as a friend, suggests Franklin dissuaded him. Then in 1964,

Franklin became a professor of history at the University of Chicago, and when fellow faculty member Walter Johnson announced he would be leaving the university at the end of spring 1966, Franklin recruited Arthur to join the faculty as a professor of American history. According to Mann, "John Hope called my father and said, 'Don't ask the girls. You should come here. It's time.'"

Arthur ultimately decided to take the offer. In February 1966 he wrote Franklin, "You must have divined that I was ready for a move and that I would seriously consider one now that my children were of an age to change homes. Once again I have reason to believe that you are without peer in reading the human heart." It would mean uprooting Carol, who was in her junior year of high school and would have preferred to finish her senior year with her friends. But Sylvia was apparently open to the change, and Emily, who would turn fourteen in April 1966, desperately wanted to get out of Northampton.

On June 7, 1966, Arthur and Sylvia closed on Walter Johnson's home at 4919 South Woodlawn Avenue in Hyde Park-Kenwood, on the South Side of Chicago—a three-story red-brick house built in 1910, when the neighborhood was attracting Chicago's wealthy business people. In mid-August, Arthur, Sylvia, and their daughters climbed into their Ford Falcon, and with Arthur behind the wheel, they headed for Illinois.

3

Living the Sixties, Discovering Theater
(1966–1970)

ON A HOT, cloudy Wednesday, the seventeenth of August, the Manns arrived in Chicago. Arthur stopped the car in front of what looked to his younger daughter like a mansion. "It was a bit dilapidated, but it was gorgeous," Mann recalled. Everyone in the family changed into bathing suits and went swimming in the cold, invigorating water of Lake Michigan, from where they could see the skyline of downtown Chicago in the hazy distance. Emily had her menstrual period for the first time. "That's when I decided I was no longer Emmy but Emily," Mann remembered. "I was starting new. I could be a real grown-up."

There is a color photograph of Emily from when she was in high school in Chicago. Sitting on a couch or a large cushion, she is wearing dark, loose, bell-bottom pants and a sleeveless, beige T-shirt. One leg is tucked under the other. Her hair is long and dark and falls somewhat messily along both sides of her face and across her breasts. She looks serious, but comfortable. At home.

By the time the family left Northampton, the city felt narrow and judgmental to Emily. In contrast, Chicago felt open and receptive, and tantalized her with the possibility of adventure. The Loop teemed with people and automobiles, and buildings thrusting ever skyward. Downtown were the renowned comedy club and improvisational theater company The Second City and the commercial theaters, where Emily and her mother caught a touring production of *Fiddler on the Roof.* Over at the Art Institute of Chicago was the Goodman Theatre's repertory company, for classical and contemporary plays, and on the South Side,

Emily Mann at the Lab School in Chicago
COURTESY OF EMILY MANN

about five miles from the Manns' house, were blues clubs like Florence's and 1125, where, if you were hanging with the right crowd, you could go to hear the guitarists and singers Hound Dog Taylor and Magic Slim. Emily believed she was often the only white woman in the place.

Chicago in the 1960s was a segregated city. Nominally Democratic when it came to local and national elections, Mayor Richard J. Daley's town nonetheless generally ignored its African American residents, many of whom lived in deteriorating neighborhoods where rats scurried in the gutters, through basements and apartments. Schools, overflowing with students, were desperate for teachers. On August 5, 1966, thirteen days before Emily and her family moved into their new home in Hyde Park-Kenwood, Dr. Martin Luther King Jr. had been stoned by white protestors in Marquette Park, on Chicago's southwest side. King had temporarily moved to Chicago to experience firsthand how most African Americans there were living, and he was demonstrating in Marquette Park to protest the deplorable housing and the overcrowded, run-down schools. "I've been in many demonstrations all across the South," he later told reporters, "I have never seen . . . mobs as hostile and hate-filled as I've seen here in Chicago."

Yet at the University of Chicago Laboratory Schools, where Emily and Carol, like most faculty children, were now enrolled, the political attitudes of many teachers and students moved toward the liberal end of the spectrum. In contrast to the all-white schools Emily had attended in Northampton, at the Lab School, where students were enrolled from elementary school through twelfth grade, African Americans comprised about twelve percent of the student body. Aurelia and John Hope Franklin's son, John Whittington Franklin, a year ahead of Emily, was among them.

All too often, however, white students and Black students seemed to self-segregate, a pattern that Emily resisted. After school, she and other students would mingle with African American young men and women from the Hyde Park community—sometimes at local hangouts, sometimes in the cafeteria at "U-High," as the University of Chicago Laboratory's high school was popularly known. "All the Black guys would come over after school to U-High, and we'd put on records and dance," said Mann. "I love to dance. They taught me how to dance the South Side Chicago Bop. Stormy, his name was. He taught me all the moves."

Socially, she was more comfortable in Chicago than she had ever been in Northampton. John Hope and Aurelia Franklin became a second family for Emily, and Mann always credited that closeness with fostering her engagement with Black art and politics. As for U-High, at the end of her freshman year she was named the most popular girl in her class.

The Lab School proved an ideal place for encouraging Emily's self-esteem and self-reliance, her imagination and empathy, and an independent way of thinking. Founded in 1896 by the American educator John Dewey, this progressive school believed in teaching students to research, to explore, and essentially to learn how to learn on their own. "You could study how you wanted to study," was the way Mann described it.

Significantly for a future writer of documentary plays that would present contrasting voices and opinions, the Lab School urged students to look at the world critically and from multiple perspectives. In Emily's humanities classes, there was no "right" or "wrong" point of view or response, no single correct answer. In fact, there might not be any "answer" at all. There were mainly questions and possibilities, and probing, open-ended discussions.

Most important for Emily, at the Lab School she discovered her love of theater.

As Mann often told the story, shortly after she entered U-High, in the fall of 1966, she developed a crush on a dark-haired, dark-eyed boy named Michael Rosenberg, who was playing the lazy young fisherman Nogood Boyo in *Under Milk Wood*. So she walked up three flights of a narrow staircase in neo-Gothic Belfield Towers, to Belfield 342 and what she described as "a tiny, awful, high proscenium" stage, and there was Rosenberg, rehearsing.

"He was miming being in a rowboat, and being very sly and funny," said Mann, "and I found out that if you worked on one of the productions, you could go to the cast party. So I decided to work on the production."

She started by sweeping floors, then graduated to helping with makeup and props. According to Rosenberg, Emily may even have acted in a play which he wrote, directed, and produced. Then, by the end of her first year at U-High (Mann's phrase), "The crush ended with Michael, but the affair continued with the theater." She took a few classes with Paul Sills, a founder of The Second City, who had left the troupe to spread the gospel of improvisational techniques and theater games. In the summer of 1967, Emily found her way to the Court Theatre, which at the time was an amateur, outdoor theater on the campus of the University of Chicago. There, Louise Grafton, who was in charge of building props, put "this thin, dark-haired kid" to work finishing one-piece scabbards and swords for *Macbeth*, a task that involved gluing tissue paper to wood, then painting the tissue paper so the weapons looked metallic. It was a task, Grafton said, which required patience, and Emily, she recalled, "did it right."

A high-school crush notwithstanding, it was really U-High's new drama teacher—a tall, thin, and somewhat mysterious individual named Robert Keil—who deepened a love of theater in Emily when he arrived in 1967, at the start of her second year of high school.

An entry about Keil in a U-High yearbook describes how he "was graduated from Northern Illinois University after seven years of switching majors and taking time off to lumberjack in Alaska," before settling on educational theater as his desired occupation. In the early 1960s, he had helped restore the famous Woodstock Opera House, northwest of Chicago, where Orson Welles had acted during the 1930s (among Keil's goals upon arriving at U-High was to transform Belfield 342 into a flexible theater-in-the-round). According to Loren Sherman, who graduated from the Lab School in 1971 and later became a scenic designer, Keil had also spent time working on highway construction crews. He'd been around.

In a 1987 interview with the theater scholar David Savran, Mann described Keil as "a rather brilliant guy," who "took a lot of emotionally churned up, smart, excited and excitable young people and turned all that energy into an artistic endeavor, making theatre."

Keil, for his part, thought Emily a talented young theater artist, although, when it came to acting, he used her in character parts rather than leading roles. Her splashiest assignment, in March 1968, was playing the Conjur Woman opposite Michael Rosenberg's Conjur Man in Howard Richardson and William Berney's perennially popular *Dark of the Moon*, about the doomed love affair between a human woman, Barbara Allen, and a Witch Boy in the mountains of Appalachia. A black-and-white rehearsal photograph shows Emily, hair streaming down her back, face scrunched in a kind of grimace, huddling and plotting with Rosenberg in a cave-like structure. Rosenberg remembered that, in performance, they were both "ludicrously made up and raggedy," to look like cranky oldsters who lived in a cave. But Emily recalled really being into the part, so much so that, at one performance, when her Conjur Woman suddenly screeched in the face of a girl in the audience, the girl threw up.

Emily played a butterfly in Karel and Josef Capek's satire of human behavior, *The Insect Comedy*, and performed in an outdoor production of Megan Terry's anti-war rock musical *Viet Rock*. She wanted to audition for the title role in Jean Anouilh's *Antigone*—understandably, as it was an ideal part for a smart, articulate, and emotional teenager, who at five feet, five and a half inches, would have looked imposing in the role. But Keil, who was directing, said he couldn't have an Antigone with braces on her teeth, or so Mann recalled. Keil did not remember making that comment. Ahead of his time in terms of non-traditional casting, he gave the role to an African American student. Emily ended up understudying the part of Antigone's younger sister, Ismene.

"The thing I remember most," said Keil, "Emily was very outspoken. She and I had a great dialogue about working with students in various roles. For *Insect Comedy*, which was not done in the theater—it was done in a stairway and several hallways near the theater itself—I remember often asking Emily to take the animals and insects and go off in a room and rehearse various sections, and then bring them back into the rehearsal. What Emily told me about what a student could tackle, I listened to."

Whether as a result of working with her on *Insect Comedy*, or observing how she interacted with the other students, Keil perceived that Emily might have the inclinations and instincts to direct, and he suggested that she try her hand at it. Thus it was that she made her first excursion into directing in June 1969, shortly after turning seventeen,

lucation and the U-Higher

science classes as "teaching ig and worthless" because "already knew the facts of

: school does have a respon-ty to provide sex education, of the students questioned d. Several students pointed that not all parents discuss with their children, and the ol needs to make sure stu-: know more than just "fool-ss and stories.)ST OF those questioned also that 6th grade was the earliest

level at which sex education should begin, though a few said 2nd or 3rd grade was not too early.

The students who endorsed the 6th grade plan said that at that level sex could be considered with-in the context of its social impli-cations, such as dating behavior.

Some students felt sex education should be required, while others said, "You can't force a student to learn about sex if he doesn't want to."

ONE SENIOR thought that a doctor or similarly qualified per-

son, not a teacher, should teach sex education to remove any sense of embarrassment from the class-room atmosphere.

Though a few students thought sex education could be completed at the Middle school level, many said it could be carried into high school with frank discussions of v e n e r e a l disease, illigitimate births, pregnancy, abortion and birth control.

If sex education classes included informal discussion groups, films, question and answer periods and

"no homework," they would be popular, one student noted.

ONE JUNIOR emphasized that in such classes teachers should be honest and frank, but express no moral viewpoint on behalf of the school or himself.

A few of the students questioned said it is a parent's responsibility, not the school's place, to explain sex.

Of the 40 students interviewed, 14 learned the facts of life from their friends, 12 from parents and 14 from parents and friends.

J - HIGH MIDWAY

Vol. 43. No. 15
Tuesday, March 5, 1968
University high school
1362 East 59th street
Chicago, Illinois 60637

Photos by Edith Schrammel

FOUR WITCHES try, and finally succeed, in getting John the Witchboy to return from a mortal state to his supernatural status in Drama Workshop's "Dark of the Moon." The witches are from left, Ellen Irons, Brenda Williams, Sarah Lincoln and Gloria Rogers.

A REFLECTIVE MOMENT between Barbara Allen, played by Ann Bunting, and John the Witchboy, played by Mat Saidel, gives little evidence of the tragedies they will face as a result of their love af-fair in Drama Workshop's production of "Dark of the Moon."

Designer helps students

Play getting professional setting

Drama Workshop is taking no chances with lighting and sets, an important part of its winter play, "Dark of the Moon."

It has secured the services of Mr. Leo Yoshimura, a lighting design-er from Second City.

Although Mr. Yoshimura has not designed sets for "Dark of the Moon" before, he has worked on productions of "The Glass Menag-erie" at the Arena Fair theatre, "The Devils" at Hull House thea-tre and "Cherry Orchard" at Sec-ond City.

MR. YOSHIMURA came to U-High at the request of Drama Teacher Robert Keil, to whom he was introduced by Sophomore Mike Rosenberg.

"When I was at the Arena Fair theatre," Mr. Yoshimura ex-plained, "Mike was working there as one of my assistants. I suppose you see the connection. He talked to Mr. Keil and then I came in for this one show."

"Dark of the Moon" will be pre-sented at 4 p.m. Friday, March 8, and Tuesday, March 12; 2 p.m. Sunday, March 10; and 7:30 p.m., Saturday, March 9, Wednesday, March 13, and Thursday, March 14, in Belfield 342.

Tickets are $1 for adults and 75 cents for high school students.

THE PLAY is about John, a witchboy who falls in love with a

mortal, Barbara Allen, thereby defying the laws of separation be-tween supernatural beings and hu-man beings.

In featured roles will be Junior Mat Saidel as John and Senior Ann Bunting as Barbara Allen.

Juniors Ellen Irons and Brenda Williams, Seniors Sarah Lincoln and Gloria Rogers will share the spotlight as the witches.

The cast includes 35 students.

ATMOSPHERE of the play is rural and demonic, Mr. Yoshi-mura said. To sustain this mood, he decided to surround the audi-ence with walls, rafters and plat-forms of unfinished wood.

According to Mr. Yoshimura, the resulting effect will conform to the concept of total theatre. "It keeps the audience involved in the play and eventually they feel a part of it," he said.

"The only problems we encoun-tered designing this set was getting wood. We found it in the garage in Scammons gardens and the jani-tors gave us some," he added.

To set the mood of the play, Mr. Yoshimura decided to "light for shadows.

"The shadows are the dark things happening in this play," Mr. Yoshimura said, "like the burning of a baby and the assault on Barbara Allen."

Photo by Roger Miller

BEGGING John the witchboy not to be changed into a mortal for a year because of his love for Barbara Allen, Mike Rosenberg as Conjur Man tries to counteract the taunts of Emily Mann as Con-jur Woman in Drama Workshop's production of "Dark of the Moon."

Lower right-hand corner, Emily Mann and Michael Rosenberg rehearse a scene from Dark of the Moon, *at the Lab School in Chicago* and selected the existentialist philosopher Jean-Paul Sartre's *Huis Clos* (*No Exit*), which she had been assigned to read for French class. "I hadn't read many plays," Mann later explained, "and there was this four-character play. I just liked it."

Emily asked her twenty-five-year-old French teacher, Karl Bortnick, to play the cowardly Garcin, who has recently died, as have the other main characters: the adulterous socialite Estelle, who has murdered her infant; Inez, who is attracted to Estelle. The trio find themselves together in a locked room, where they have no free will and will be in each other's company for eternity. In other words, in Hell. Emily's friends and classmates Gina Heiserman and Polly Bruno played Estelle and Inez respectively, and their fellow student David Kovacs took the small role of the Valet.

Heiserman and Bruno recalled rehearsing on the third floor of Emily's home in Hyde Park-Kenwood, in what originally was a ballroom but now functioned as a kind of attic space. Bruno remembered that, "We used to separate and go into these closed-off areas on the third floor of Emily's house, sit in the dark and go into character. Our version of Stanislavskian preparation to inhabit the role. We talked about motivation and talked about emotion, and really tried to build characters."

Possibly because his schedule was less flexible than the students', Bortnick remembered having to bear down on learning his lines and rehearsing only a few times in the theater prior to the production's two late-afternoon performances, at four o'clock on June 4 and 5. Emily, he recalled, "was interested in the shifting alliances between various characters, who often were paired off two at a time against the third one." The staging, he said, was "very deliberate." He described two benches on which the actors sat at various times—one bench stage left, the other stage right—and he recalled standing between Inez and Estelle, who were motionless in the obscurity of a darkened stage, while Garcin was "bathed in a shaft of light from above" and "remembering and disclosing and enacting" his cowardice and cruelties. Bortnick interpreted the lighting to be a metaphor for each character's visualization of his or her life.

In the Lab School tradition of encouraging students to find their own ways through a project, this was a students–only endeavor, despite the presence of a teacher in the cast. Students ran lights and sound, worked props, did makeup, and helped find the costumes Emily wanted: a dumpy-looking pleated skirt, a blouse, a sweater, and Oxford shoes for Bruno; a cocktail dress for Heiserman. Bortnick supplied his own black turtle neck and "dull-colored" pants.

"The play was an ambitious choice," in Bortnick's estimation. "I remember how impressed I was at the audacity of it, because this was not a play with action, although it's not static. It's philosophical, and yet literary. It was a challenge for everyone doing it."

By the time Emily directed *No Exit*, in June 1969, the world within and beyond Chicago seemed to be consumed by violence and war. More than a year earlier, on January 30, 1968, North Vietnam had shocked American and South Vietnamese troops with the strength of its Tet Offensive, undercutting President Johnson's public assertions that a successful end to the Vietnam War was in sight. In February 1968, a Gallup poll revealed that nearly half of the American populace was against the United States continuing to fight in Vietnam. Anti-war protests abounded across the country, and many students at U-High, Emily among them, were fiercely and vocally against the conflict.

Then on April 4, 1968, in Memphis, Tennessee, James Earl Ray shot and killed the Reverend Martin Luther King Jr. as he stood on a motel balcony. Around the country, African American neighborhoods, including the neighborhood near U-High and Emily's home, erupted in grief and fury. Throughout the weekend following King's assassination, Mayor Daley's police, along with army units and the Illinois National Guard, patrolled the city, guns and rifles at the ready, as though the city, like the country being bombed thousands of miles away, had become a war zone.

Almost exactly two months later, on June 5, Senator Robert F. Kennedy, who had decided to seek the Democratic nomination for president of the United States, was assassinated by a Palestinian named

Sirhan Sirhan as Kennedy was leaving the Ambassador Hotel in Los Angeles. Kennedy, Sirhan later told television interviewer David Frost, deserved blame for supporting Israel in attacks against the Palestinians. And in late August 1968, Chicago seethed again during the Democratic National Convention, underway from August 26 through August 29 at the International Amphitheatre on the South Side, near the Union Stock Yards.

This time, however, the violence that occurred was between law enforcement, represented by the Chicago police and the Illinois National Guard, and mostly white demonstrators from the Youth International Party (Yippies), Students for a Democratic Society (SDS), and the National Mobilization Committee to End the War in Vietnam. As Todd Gitlin would note astutely in *The Sixties: Years of Hope, Days of Rage*, "violence also became the threat and the temptation around which the whole movement, whatever its actual disinclination to pick up stones or guns, revolved." Emily, who was in Mexico with her family for a vacation, watched on television as the police beat demonstrators with billy clubs in Grant Park and demonstrators, in turn, threw rocks and chunks of concrete at the police. Like a number of her classmates, Emily had once been roughed up by Chicago cops and shoved up against a police car, in her case for being on the street after a city-wide curfew. "When they were clubbing kids at the convention," Mann said to me, "we were that same group to them. They hated us. We had long hair, we were running around with Black kids. They were just ready to kill us all."

Is it any wonder, when Emily Mann later began writing documentary plays, that she dramatized the damaging effects of warfare and physical violence on men and women? Or that, by extension, she indicted an American society which gravitated to violence? Again, here's Gitlin: "It was as if the assassinations, the riots, and the war distilled all the barely suppressed violence seething through American life."

Despite the gratification of working in U-High's theater program, life at home during her junior year of 1968–1969 had become increasingly tense. Emily and her father were often on the opposite sides of the changes that were driving the sixties (Carol, away at college as of fall 1967—back in Northampton at Smith—escaped much, but not all, of the tension). The students at U-High had voted to allow women to break a long-standing tradition and wear jeans to school. But at home Arthur Mann insisted that Emily wear a skirt to the dinner table, and he did not want to hear her use "bad language." So they argued, with Emily rebelling against his dictums.

Emily admired Fred Hampton, the bearded, charismatic leader of the Black Panther Party's Chicago chapter (and, later, the entire Illinois chapter), who was trying to organize a Free Breakfast Program, work with the BPP's People's Clinic to provide free health care, and generally steer away from the images of armed Black citizens that had drawn unfavorable FBI attention to the San Francisco chapter formed by Bobby Seale and Huey P. Newton. But Arthur Mann, who had marched in Montgomery, Alabama, in 1965 and had always supported the Civil Rights Movement, believed Black Nationalism would set that movement back decades. And so he and his daughter argued some more.

But what most unsettled the relationship between Emily and her father were their opposing views about the war the United States was waging on the government and people of North Vietnam: Emily passionately against it; Arthur firmly supporting it. "He actually believed the [U.S.] government," Mann explained years later. "He believed the domino theory, that if one country in a region fell under the sway of Communism, others would topple. He couldn't believe that the [Johnson] administration was lying."

Martin Luther King Jr., in a remarkable speech at New York City's Riverside Church on April 4, 1967, had forcefully pleaded with his "beloved nation" to seek peace in Vietnam, affirming that "the Good News was meant for all men—for communist and capitalist, for their children and ours, for black and for white, for revolutionary and conservative." Arthur Mann must have known about King's speech, for it made headlines across the country. But King's fervent plea for "nonviolent coexistence" instead of "violent coannihilation" could not dissuade Arthur from siding with the government for which he had once fought, and which had repaid him by sending him to graduate school and giving him a profession.

Sylvia usually supported her husband's views, according to Emily. "Every now and then she would stand up for me," Emily recalled. "She would say, 'Arthur, listen to what Emily is saying' or, 'explain to her why that isn't valid.' She would protect him from me if I got too wildly emotional and started screaming at him, which I did occasionally, I'm sad to say. She would say, 'How dare you talk to your father that way?' I did sometimes get way out." But her father, who, Mann observed, could be "cool" and "rational" was also "prone to seething tempers."

That Arthur Mann was undergoing an ordeal of his own, at the University of Chicago, contributed to the tension at home. In January 1969, sparked by the firing of a popular assistant professor of sociology named Marlene Dixon, a feminist and a Marxist, the radicalization that had been growing within a section of the student body culminated in some 400 students occupying the Administration Building for sixteen days, though their numbers fell as the days of the occupation wore on. The occupation ended when Dixon was offered a one-year contract (which she turned down). But other issues came to the fore: anger among some students and faculty about the small number of tenured women at the university; the perception that the university cared more for its ivory tower reputation than the quality of its students' experience, in and out of the classroom; and the university's apparent tendency to ignore the nearby African American community.

Mann remembered her father being dismayed when the school's new president, Edward H. Levi, asked him to be on the University Disciplinary Committee, whose members were appointed the very day that students took over the Administration Building, on January 30, 1969. But Arthur ultimately agreed to be on the committee and, as a member, he participated in the expulsion and suspension of more than one hundred students, disciplinary actions that only aroused more student activism, including student strikes and a hunger strike. Faculty members who appeared to have done President Levi's bidding did not emerge unscathed. Ralph Austen, a young colleague in the Department of

History who occasionally played squash with Arthur Mann, opined that Arthur had been "besmirched by having been on this committee." Emily said her father went from being one of the "best-loved" history professors to one of the "most hated." He stopped writing, became depressed and irascible, and she always believed that the experience destroyed his health. Indeed, from Arthur's correspondence in the months following the student occupation, it is clear that he continued to have no tolerance for students who, in his view, were harming an educational institution which he believed they were privileged to attend. In April 1969 he wrote to a friend in Massachusetts: "We are dealing with a very tiny minority that is grabbing the headlines and convulsing the campuses because faculties and administrators don't as yet have enough self-confidence in their own good sense and their own good intentions to take a firm stand against disruption."

Not surprisingly, Emily was eager to stay away from home as much as possible, if only to avoid arguments with her father and remove herself from his anger, control, and unhappiness. On her own, she attended Temple Kehilath Anshe Maarav (KAM), the oldest Jewish congregation in Chicago, where, in her sophomore year, she had confirmed her commitment to Judaism, learning Hebrew phonetically for a confirmation ceremony. She participated in U-High activities and committees, continued to draw A's in her classes, and study the flute. And she spent hours in the Belfield theater, where Keil would let students hang out late into the night, to work on sets, or simply talk and smoke.

In the summer of 1969, between her junior and senior years, she and John Whittington Franklin, who had just graduated from U-High, traveled to France, where Emily studied flute at the American School of Paris. There she realized that, despite her musical talent, she was not at the professional level, nor did she have the commitment to a career that a number of the other music students possessed. Her passion and instincts were for theater. "I stepped into a theater class [at the American School] and knew just what to do. The ease I had in theater was the ease my friends and colleagues had as instrumentalists. I remember the moment I made the switch in my mind."

But violence followed her to Europe. After hiking in the mountains of Yugoslavia with a group from the school, she returned to the town where the group was staying, near Split on the Adriatic Sea, to find a letter waiting from her parents. A close friend of Emily's, a young U-High actor named Richie Booth, had died in a car crash. "Dear Mommy and Daddy," Emily wrote back, "the news was such a shock that in front of everyone, I sat down with my head between my knees and screamed. . . . I can only remember running away from everyone. . . . I could only sob and sob and sob." Grief, she wrote her parents, aroused her fear of dying. "Ever since I was little, you remember, I've been petrified of death, not for me but for those I love."

A boy whom Emily had met in town offered to console her, and they went off to a beach, where he raped her. Hurt in body and spirit, she nonetheless did not reveal the assault to anyone. Not to her mother, not to a friend. No one until college, when she confided in a lover. She did not reveal the rape publicly until she was in her sixties, although her fear of sexual and physical violence would become an undercurrent in her playwriting and directing.

Emily's summer away did not quell the tension in the Mann household, or the fights with her father, or the emotional turmoil aroused by America's, and Chicago's, political conflicts. On October 8, a group of about two hundred to three hundred Weathermen—the self-styled revolutionaries who wanted to destroy what they labeled U.S. imperialism—trashed a wealthy Chicago neighborhood and ignited a battle with the police, who considerably outnumbered them during what became known as "Four Days of Rage." One week later, on Wednesday, October 15, U-High closed so that students could demonstrate in the first nationwide Vietnam Moratorium against the Vietnam War, and Emily joined a peace vigil on the Civic Center plaza (now Daley Plaza) in downtown Chicago. On Saturday, November 15, more than half a million anti-war demonstrators congregated on the Mall in Washington, D.C., for what was, at that point, the largest protest march in United States history.

In Chicago that November of 1969, a gun battle between Black Panthers and the police resulted in one dead Black Panther Party member and two dead cops, and on December 3, the police retaliated. Acting on a tip from an FBI informant, police raided Fred Hampton's house and shot and killed him. Emily and a number of friends who believed that Hampton had been a compassionate and skilled community organizer were both furious and deeply saddened.

Sitting nearly fifty years later in her office at the McCarter Theatre, Mann reflected on the tumult during which she came of age. "I no longer trusted or believed in the government. I didn't believe we were doing the right things in the world. I questioned authority at almost every turn. . . . I found refuge in the theater. That's where I kept sane. It saved my life. I would have been out on the street, but I wasn't. I was in theater. Theater gave me a place to put all these feelings and this sense of mission and this sense of idealism, and the need to connect and create and make change."

Her 1969–1970 school year was her last at U-High. She acted in *Viet Rock* and directed *Riders to the Sea*, John Millington Synge's wrenching one-act about a widow, Maurya, who lives with her two daughters and her son Bartley in the Aran Islands, off the western coast of Ireland. Maurya has lost her husband and five sons to the sea, and by the play's end she will learn that Bartley, too, has drowned.

As with *No Exit*, Emily seemed to work on her own, without faculty guidance, and once again the cast rehearsed in the attic at the Mann home on South Woodlawn Avenue. Emily's classmate Lorraine Ann Bowen played Maurya, the pivotal role, and she remembered that Emily had the cast "do family sorts of improvs, to help everyone get to the part where they would grieve at Bartley's death. What was tough was the arc of the play, and letting it happen. Something Emily worked on with all of us, letting us be carried along by the wave of the play."

"The humorous part of it, to me," Bowen recalled, "was that I had listened to Siobhan McKenna, the great Irish actress, and obviously I totally mimicked Siobhan's voice. But Emily never said an unkind word. Up in the attic, she locked me in a closet and said, 'I want you to practice keening.' I must have done all forms of wailing for about an hour. Whatever came out of me. I trusted her." Gina Heiserman, who played one of Maurya's two daughters, remembered that Emily had the entire cast practice keening, so they would sound authentic in performance.

A rehearsal schedule extending across four weeks indicates that Emily set aside a couple of three-hour time periods for blocking, and hour-long meetings for one-on-one "conferences" with particular actors. A sketch of the stage arrangement shows a curved thrust, with only a few set pieces: stage right, a fireplace and stairs to a loft; a spinning wheel downstage right; a table, used for laying out the body of her last son, upstage left. The audience out front. Heiserman remembered that each woman had a large shawl, as well as long skirts and red petticoats, which Synge calls for in his script. "By the time we got onstage," Bowen recalled, "it was one of the more intense experiences. I kind of remember eyes in the first rows bugging out of people's heads. Emily really had her finger on pacing, even at that time. And all of the audience was drowned by the end of the performance." Toward the end of the play, Maurya has a celebrated speech, during which she laments that, "They're all gone now, and there isn't anything more the sea can do to me." Bowen recalled playing the lines "to the audience and myself. It ended up focused out to the audience and the sea, and myself–my own soul."

In her senior year of high school, Emily was accepted at Radcliffe College in Cambridge, Massachusetts. She had yearned to go there since she was in junior high. The summer before eighth grade, her father had taught at Harvard, and Emily had not only adored Cambridge but, in true young-teen fashion, had also fallen in love with a pair of "fabulous, really cool" wine-colored suede boots worn by the daughter of one of her father's colleagues, the historian and feminist Barbara Solomon. As Mann put it during one of our conversations, "Smart, cool women went to Radcliffe. I wanted to have those boots, walk down Brattle Street. I also knew that the Radcliffe–Harvard relationship was beginning to change, and I wanted to be part of that change." Just as importantly, "I wanted to go to a place where I could find out what I wanted to do without people telling me what to do. I've always had a problem with people telling me what to do."

During her junior year at U-High, Emily had interviewed with Solomon, who by then was associate dean of Radcliffe (in 1970 she would become the first woman to be dean of Harvard College). Emily had hoped to skip her senior year of high school and get out of her father's house, but Solomon advised her to keep up her grades and wait another year.

Emily's last months at U-High in 1970 were filled with a tangle of emotions: pride about her production of *Riders to the Sea*, which was presented in high schools throughout Chicago; eagerness to leave home and be on her own; anger in response to Ohio National Guardsmen shooting at unarmed, protesting students at Kent State University and killing four of them, an event that sparked a "screaming match" with her father at the dining room table. Arthur, while horrified that four young people had been killed and others wounded, nonetheless, so Mann remembered, declared that the students had acted "stupidly" and "were not innocents."

Yet it was a proud Emily Mann who, at graduation on Thursday, June 11, 1970, at two o'clock in the afternoon, sat in Rockefeller Memorial Chapel, playing the flute for two pieces composed by her classmate and boyfriend, Stuart ("Skip") J. Sherman (Loren Sherman's older brother): "Processional: Beginning of a Certain End" and "Thursday Farewell." She had learned a great deal about herself during her four years in Chicago, including, she once said, "how angry I could be." But of greatest consequence, said Mann, "I discovered the theater. I discovered my life's work."

4

Radcliffe Days, Harvard Plays
(1970–1974)

IN CAMBRIDGE, Massachusetts, during the fall of 1970, Emily bought a pair of wine-colored suede boots like the ones she had admired some years earlier on Barbara Solomon's daughter.

It was, in a way, an expression of her newfound personal freedom. Nearly 1,000 miles from home, she could dress and behave and talk as she wished. She could wear cool, sexy boots, and wear them with tights underneath short, flowery, diaphanous dresses and stride down Brattle Street, in the heart of Cambridge, whenever she wanted, her dark hair tossing below her shoulders. She could study all night, sustained by many cups of black coffee, and she could drive with friends to Woods Hole on Cape Cod for the weekend, to read or walk on the beach. Boyfriends became lovers.

Soon after the semester began, she wrote her parents that "really the work here is not any more difficult or time consuming than U'high's, only more stimulating. . . . I read two hundred pages of Chinese history last weekend at Wood's Hole and sixty pages of Montaigne. That is heavy stuff, but somehow there I want to study so I do. It's the wu-wei idea of work (pardon me as I show off my new-found knowledge and love of Lao-Tsu, that ancient Taoist seer).Wu-wei means non-action— one does nothing yet there is nothing left undone. One accomplishes things naturally, one flows with it all. That's how I feel now about my work."

A trunk packed with sheets, pillows, and towels arrived at her dorm several weeks after Emily did, but she coped. Who cared about sheets and towels when she had auditioned for the freshman acting seminar taught by George Hamlin, the producing director of Harvard's Loeb Theater Center, and was one of only four women out of seventy to be accepted? She "loved" her history course with Edwin O. Reischauer and a course in dramatic literature with William Alfred, she wrote her parents. In fact, she was beginning to write a play, in the hope of submitting it to Alfred for his spring playwriting seminar.

At first Emily lived in Barnard Hall, a staid, rectangular, red-brick building overlooking Radcliffe Yard, which was an open, grassy expanse in the spring and white with snow during the Massachusetts winter. Radcliffe had done away with parietals, those *in loco parentis* regulations of an earlier age, which required men to sign in before visiting a woman's dorm room and restricted said men to daylight hours. Now, Radcliffe and Harvard dorms and residences housed both men and women, an arrangement that allowed for the sexual freedom to which many colleges had bowed since the sexual revolution of the 1960s. Jamie Bernstein, the daughter of the composer and conductor Leonard Bernstein, lived in Adams House, to which Emily would move in her sophomore year, and Bernstein recalled that Radcliffe and Harvard students lived wherever they wished, freely moving in with boyfriends or girlfriends. "We were in this magic zone," said Bernstein, "where we all had the pill but didn't yet have AIDS, so everybody slept with everybody."

But with freedom came risks. Cambridge, and the Harvard and Radcliffe dormitories, turned out to be unsafe places for women. On October 21, Emily wrote her parents that, in one week alone, three women in other dormitories had been raped, apparently by a man who disguised himself as a student. On October 27, she wrote that "the rapist was in our dorm" that very day. "He was disguised in a wig and wore black rimmed glasses without the lenses," Emily wrote her parents. "One of the girls was in the hall, and he pulled a gun on her and told her to get into a room. She told him her boyfriend would come back to the room in about ten minutes so he took her for a walk around the dorm looking for a room that was empty and open. They didn't find it. I found them in the hall. He asked me where a girl who doesn't exist was. I told him I didn't know. All the while the girl was making signs at me, but I couldn't figure out what she was referring to. He seemed very funny to me. I left, then he pulled the gun again and made her not say anything or he would shoot and all that. Then he left and she told me what happened and I called the police."

Arthur and Sylvia were doubtless alarmed by Emily's proximity to an ordeal that could have ended catastrophically. Yet Emily seemed surprisingly calm: "Nervous, but certainly in control," she scribbled at the end of her typed letter.

As when she was a youngster, and now as a young woman of eighteen, Emily was a mixture of strength and vulnerability, take-charge coolness and heated emotionality, self-confidence and self-doubt, anger and loving affection. She could be elated about her projects and herself one day, despairing the next. And despite the desire to be on her own, and away from the furious arguments with her father, she still turned to her parents for solace and sought her father's advice when she felt overwhelmed by work, or by uncertainties and fears.

Two weeks after the incident with the gun-wielding intruder, the composure she had exhibited vanished in an emotional explosion. She confided to her parents that she was "crying now," because, "Since last year, I've felt a real withering of emotion and warmth inside of me; it's all an act." Except for a few close friends, "Everyone else is kept at arm's length." Also, Emily wrote, she did not want "to play the happy, stable, in-control daughter for you anymore because I know you want to see me as I am. It's too much of a strain for you and for me to not be me. And I'm afraid the real Emily is not sweet Emily B." She described herself as "goddamned scared" and, referring to a spurt of "furious anger" that she had recently experienced, she called herself an "ugly person" who never comes up to anyone's expectations.

Arthur Mann responded quickly in a letter. "It's nonsense for you to think that you are essentially 'an ugly person,'" he assured her emphatically. "This is not to say that you're all sweetness and goodness. I know your faults, daughter of mine; the worst of them are my very own. But don't hate yourself for them. Cope with them, after first recognizing them . . . see yourself whole and clear, then do what, concretely, needs doing."

She went home to Chicago for Thanksgiving that November and talked at length with her father, whom she thanked profusely for his gentleness and perception. By early December, she was again feeling that school was "wonderful" and writing Sylvia that "I like my life and work here. I like to live alone and live my own life, sharing what I want to with those I love, but free to keep to myself what I want." She was playing her flute. She planned to go hiking with friends in January, during winter break. And whatever her academic problems earlier in the semester, she apparently overcame them, for she made the Dean's List.

Adding to her renewed optimism about school and about herself, she learned when she returned to campus in February that William Alfred had admitted her to his playwriting seminar. She had also been cast as Alison Porter, the upper-class, pregnant, abused wife in English playwright John Osborne's 1956 drama *Look Back in Anger*, scheduled to open in March 1971 at the Loeb Drama Center.

"I loved the Loeb," said Mann one day during an interview in her office. "I loved that you could make your own theater without being graded, and by that time I knew I wanted to do a lot of theater. At Radcliffe and Harvard, theater wasn't a course. You made your work. And I was already doing that."

For decades, Harvard's theater activity had relied on a slew of semi-professional theater groups and clubs, which often operated in cramped quarters with miserable equipment. Then in 1953, Nathan M. Pusey, Harvard's twenty-fourth president, encouraged the building of a state-of-the-art university theater. John L. Loeb '24 donated one million dollars to spur the project; the architect Hugh Stubbins, a member of the Harvard faculty, designed a two-story, rectangular, modernist building; and the innovative theater designer George C. Izenour consulted on the main stage and auditorium. The main theater sat 542 people and could be converted from a proscenium to a thrust by moving two banks of seats at the front of the house. The theater building, at 64 Brattle

Street, in the heart of Cambridge, also housed a flexible space called Loeb Ex, for so-called experimental productions, as well as a scene shop, a costume shop, space to store props, and rehearsal rooms.

The Faculty Theatre Committee and the Loeb's administrative staff functioned fairly amicably with the students' Harvard Dramatic Club, which had its own executive board. A student like Emily could bring the board a script she wished to direct, and the board would say yea or nay. Graduate and undergraduate students produced the shows, with advice from consulting designers and technical people on the Loeb staff. Professional directors were often on hand, hired for a semester or two to give classes, and local actors, as well as students, could audition. Theater critics from the Boston newspapers often reviewed main stage productions. Ed Zwick, who entered Harvard in 1970 and, like Emily, was intoxicated by the Loeb, affectionately called it "a ten-million-dollar sandbox," in which "to make all the mistakes an amateur could make . . . be bold and fail hugely."

Zwick was assistant director for *Look Back in Anger* in March 1971, when Radcliffe sophomore Liz Coe staged Osborne's play in the Loeb Ex, updated to the present and set in the United States. Coe cast Emily as upper-class, submissive Alison Porter, who has married Osborne's angry, working-class anti-hero, Jimmy Porter. "I remember [Emily] being very emotionally available as an actor," said Zwick, who became a theater and television director. "It's a very vulnerable woman that is being portrayed, and I remember Emily being able to capture that aspect of the performance."

Look Back in Anger seems an odd choice for the decade of the Women's Liberation Movement. At one point, Alison walks out on her bullying husband, but she returns to him at play's end, having miscarried their baby, possibly unable to conceive another, and now lavishing her maternal feelings on Jimmy. The British feminist Michelene Wandor, in her critical study *Look Back in Gender*, wrote that "Alison finally capitulates to Jimmy on his terms . . . the dynamic of their relationship—and, indeed, that of the play—is predicated upon Jimmy's needs."

Perhaps Coe intended the production as a warning about gender inequality, of which Radcliffe women were certainly aware: Radcliffe fresh (women) numbered 300, while 1,200 men entered John Harvard's college, with the result that men's voices outnumbered women's in the majority of lectures and seminars. In the event, the production was a "hot ticket" according to one reviewer, who also wrote, with what feminists might have called patriarchal condescension, that "Emily Mann . . . is great as the sweet and sensitive young thing who falls under Jimmy's spell."

Emily's acting brought her praise and attention, but her most significant theatrical accomplishment that freshman year was revising her first play in William Alfred's playwriting seminar, and crafting a vivid, stage-worthy script.

William Edward Alfred was forty-nine years old in the spring of 1971 and something of a Harvard legend. A gentle scholar who went about in a three-piece suit and always wore a hat—a fedora in winter, a straw boater in summer—Alfred had taught English literature at Harvard since 1954 and still lived on Athens Street, near the Charles River, surrounded by the myriad clocks he collected. He also wrote plays and had garnered one New York success, a blank-verse tragedy called *Hogan's Goat*, which Wynn Handman produced off Broadway in 1965 at the American Place Theatre. In the cast was a young actor named Faye Dunaway, and she and Alfred became lifelong friends. Dunaway always credited Alfred with offering calming advice, encouragement, and sympathetic guidance.

"He was a magical man," said Mann. "He had a spiritual energy around him that you shared. An energy that just made you find your best self and your best mind."

All the other students in Alfred's playwriting seminar that spring were either juniors or seniors. But Emily wanted to take the class, so she had written an intermission-less three-act play called *Amy*, based, she said, on a confused and unhappy high school friend. Emily believed she was the first freshman ever to be admitted to the course.

Professor William Alfred in his study in Cambridge, Massachusetts
PHOTO COURTESY OF BROOKLYN COLLEGE ARCHIVES. THE PAPERS OF PROFESSOR
WILLIAM ALFRED

Amy "poured" out of her, Mann recalled. "I remember writing it in long-hand . . . and then typing it. I used to think with my hand." Listening to the reel-to-reel recording she made that spring, acting all the parts, one hears the emotion and intensity with which she wrote her first play.

The play opens in a cramped, dark apartment in New York City's East Village. It is five o'clock in the morning. An eighteen-year-old woman named Amy and an older man are in bed; they have just made love and are smoking cigarettes. But Amy is restless and uncomfortable; she gets up, dresses, argues with her lover, who wants her to come back to bed. She is angry; she wants to be a writer, she wants to do *something, anything*, but doesn't know what or how. And soon she walks out.

That exit takes her to Chicago, where her upper-middle-class mother and stepfather live with Amy's half-brother and her deaf, five-year-old half-sister, Leisha.

The first scene of Act II takes place in Amy's bedroom, between Amy and Leisha, who can only speak with her hands and her body, or make sounds. This allows Mann the freedom to have Amy say whatever she wishes, and Amy talks about herself in the third person to Leisha, knowing that the child cannot hear her: "Once upon a time there was a very miserable girl. She had a father who lived in California and a mother who lived in Chicago with a man who hated this very little girl." She tells the unhearing Leisha about her dreams and nightmares, and her misadventures. Like the time she was raped by a Frenchman in his villa: "And his hand went to the robe and undid it, and they fell back on the bed and he started getting on top of me and pumping. I didn't know what he was doing. And then he hurt me and he wouldn't stop. . . . and I was screaming."

At other times Amy berates Leisha, then feels abysmally guilty and embraces her. Throughout, there is a stream-of-consciousness flow to Amy's words, as she unburdens herself of her thoughts and needs and unhappiness.

As Mann recalled, Alfred particularly praised the second scene of Act II, in which Amy is at breakfast in a formal dining room with her stepfather, mother, and half-brother. The stepfather, Phil, is characterized as a punitive, domineering man, who uses the occasion to take for himself a piece of toast that the cook has specifically prepared for Amy. Mann remembered that the scene impressed Alfred because of the way she used an object (the toast) to illuminate the ongoing war between Phil and the stepdaughter he hates, who loathes him in return.

There is an impassioned scene during which Amy accuses her mother of weakness for staying with the despotic Phil, and a third act in which Amy tells a woman friend that Phil has ordered Amy to get out of his house. At the end, Amy sits on her bed alone. Emily's final stage directions describe "Clothes around her. Cold spot on her. Stares straight ahead. Dead look on face. Slow fade. Blackout."

Students in Alfred's playwriting seminar had to read their work aloud, and the playwright Christopher Durang, then a Harvard senior in Alfred's class, remembered the expressiveness with which Emily acted the roles in her script. Mann's memory is of reading it aloud and "thinking it was no good." As with almost any playwright's first script, there are places in *Amy* where scenes could be tightened with rewriting and editing. But overall, the characters are distinctive; the realistic dialogue authentic, evocative, and actable. *Amy* is quite different from the documentary plays with which Mann would eventually be recognized as a dramatist. Yet her skill at creating emotionally stirring scenes is already evident, as is her affinity for creating portraits of women and drawing on autobiography when making her work. She created two women who are under the control of one man, but left open the possibility that Amy, by leaving her stepfather's house, will save herself.

Alfred became Emily's advisor (she majored in English and French literature), and she met with him once a week at his home. They would sit in his study, with Alfred nestling in a battered, leather wing chair, and they would discuss the work of an array of playwrights and novelists, from Aeschylus and Euripides to Shakespeare and Shaw, Virginia Woolf to Elizabeth Bowen. "It was Alfred who harnessed what I was good at and what I loved, and made me understand that I was a wonderful interpreter of the written text," Mann said. "He understood how mean the environment could be for women at that time. At the university especially. I never had a woman professor, so there was a sense that women were intellectually inferior. We felt that all the time, and it would make me alternately angry and then cause me to lose confidence in myself." Alfred, she recalled years later, "encouraged me as a writer and encouraged me in the theater."

Yet she did not think of herself as a playwright at this point in her life. Her aim was to direct. Letters to her parents indicate she had planned to direct in the Loeb Ex that spring, but her lifelong inclination to take on as many projects as possible, especially if they were scheduled at the same time, affected her health. Midway through casting, she was temporarily felled by gastritis and ended up at the college's health services, which prescribed "her old-time friends" Maalox and Donnatal; apparently she had suffered bouts of severe gastritis before.

Adding to the tension, a man stalked her in downtown Cambridge. "He left a note on my bicycle," Emily wrote her parents, "saying that. . . he wanted to love me. If I didn't call him, he'd steal my bike. The next day my bike was stolen. I feel so invaded and hounded and I feel silly for letting myself be bothered by it."

She reported the incident to the police, but as too many women before and since have discovered, the police "were no help." Instead, "They kept joking about me asking for it or having boyfriends who have decided to play jokes on me. Very funny." Not surprisingly for women who have experienced sexual assault or harassment, Emily questioned her own role in the episode, although she seemed to realize that blaming herself was off the mark. "I keep wondering what I do," she wrote her parents. "I haven't worn a dress since it's happened. And that's just not me. Why can't people leave me alone? It isn't flattering, it isn't humorous, it's just weird, a little frightening, and very aggravating."

What with fatigue and anxiety, she postponed directing at the Loeb and enjoyed what, for her, was a less arduous schedule. In addition to her academic courses, she took an acting seminar at the Loeb with the Shakespearean director Stuart Vaughan. She handed in a revised script of *Amy* to William Alfred, although, self-critical as always, she now felt that it seemed "shallow, transparent, self-indulgent, and shrieky." Her next play, she was determined, would be about "strong, real people" with "beliefs in themselves and people they love." For Father's Day, June 20, she gave Arthur her taped recording of *Amy* and a tender letter. "I want to give you what is most a part of me, what means the most to me, and what I hope will give you both pleasure and a sense of me. . . . you give me courage, hope, and a sense that in a world where 'the devil never goes to sleep' there is grace . . . and gentleness."

For much of the summer following her freshman year, she remained in Cambridge, in Quincy House, a Harvard residence where she and her friend Joanna Lu were paid to be "housewives," as Emily described it with a mixture of good humor and sarcasm; they cleaned and cooked for five visiting businessmen. (Honoring her friend, Mann would give the name Joanna Lu to the character of the TV reporter in *Execution of Justice*.)

Emily also worked part-time in the Loeb box office and assistant-directed a production of *As You Like It* across the street on the arena stage in Agassiz House, one of Radcliffe's oldest and most beloved theaters. "I am . . . realizing that directing is really what I want to do," she wrote her parents, "and that theater really can be alive, that once timid, deadly theater is realized for what it is, a pretentious, empty. . . bore, an exercise for egotistic minded actors who realy [*sic*] hate drama except when it's used for personal therapy, theater will come back as the medium it is—a living telling of a story communicated <u>live</u> from actor to audience."

Emily's first directing turn at the Loeb came in the fall of 1971, when she staged Tennessee Williams's *Suddenly Last Summer* in the Loeb Ex, the first of several Williams's plays she would interpret during her career. She had written her parents during the summer that she wanted to explore ideas she had been mulling for a while, "and this is the perfect script to work with."

Set in a wild, overgrown private garden in New Orleans, Williams's intense one-act play focuses on the conflict between young Catharine Holly and her elderly, rich aunt, Violet Venable. Catharine had traveled to Spain with Mrs. Venable's gay son, Sebastian. But as Catharine recounts graphically in the play's climactic scene, one blazing hot afternoon Sebastian was set upon at the beach by a band of starving, naked children, who "had torn bits of him away and stuffed them into those gobbling fierce little empty black mouths of theirs." Catharine's mother and brother want her to stop talking about the horrific event, lest they lose an inheritance. Mrs. Venable wants to commit Catharine to an asylum and have a lobotomy performed, "*to cut this hideous story out of her brain!*" Toward that end she has invited a doctor to observe Catharine, hear her tale, and, Mrs. Venable hopes, declare the young woman insane.

During most of her career, Mann would fill pocket-sized notebooks with ideas about the plays she was directing or writing. But with *Suddenly Last Summer* she wrote a paper about the production for the Modern American Drama course she was taking. Her concept began, she explained, "by seeing the core of the play as a confrontation with ritual—ritualistic sacrifice." Cannibalism, whether literal, monetary, or psychological, was, she believed, the play's theme, beginning with Williams's description of the garden setting: *"massive tree-flowers suggesting organs of a body, torn out, still glistening with undried blood."* Inspired by Antonin Artaud's writings about ritual theater in *The Theater and Its Double*, she wanted to use "symbols, intonations, and spectacle to create the mystery and terror which Tennessee Williams evokes in his play. The actual terrifying acts to which [Williams] constantly refers are always talked <u>about</u>," she stressed. "I wanted to <u>create</u> them, make them live in all of their immediacy on the stage. I envisioned a 'masque' or stylized, symbolic portrayal of the crucial images and memories in the play."

Emily conceived three major areas on her stage: a central circle, for the patio where Mrs. Venable, Catharine Holly, and the other characters sit or stand; what Emily called "the mountain, the memory area"; and the garden, which joined the two areas. The so-called mountain and the garden were created by an outer circle of platforms of varying heights, widths, and colors, surrounding the patio area. On these platforms, dancers often performed stylized movements supposedly based on the martial art "gung fu" [sic]. But, Emily emphasized in her paper, the movements did not "illustrate" what the characters were describing or remembering; rather, they "showed the interior images of the characters' minds."

Emily's concept reflected the influence of Artaud's theory of theater, which explicitly rejects psychological and socially relevant theater in favor of what he called "essential theater." This theater, Artaud wrote, "like the plague . . . releases conflicts, disengages powers, liberates possibilities, and if these possibilities and these powers are dark, it is the fault not of the plague nor of the theater, but of life." Words, especially the everyday language of human interaction, were paltry things compared to "the physical knowledge of images" and "the communicative power and magical mimesis of a gesture."

The Loeb, as Ed Zwick said, was a place to follow one's inclinations, wherever they might lead. So why not add evocative, even ugly, gestures to this play about cannibalism in its several forms?

Suddenly Last Summer opened on November 11, 1971, and Emily's staging experiment was rewarded with enthusiastic reviews. Richard Bowker, for the *Harvard Crimson*, wrote that "Director Emily Mann's idea to counteract the static nature of the play is to have dancers above and beside the stage mime some of the crucial events the characters are describing. . . . This kind of device is dangerous, but here it works, because the director has sense enough to use it sparingly, and never lets it get in the way of what's happening on stage." He called the production "brilliant" and the direction "ingenious."

Emily was less successful at corralling Liz Coe's three-act play about a female comedian, *The Bull Gets the Matador Once in a Lifetime*, which she directed in March 1972 at Agassiz House. The event was less notable for its artistry than for being the first "full-scale" Radcliffe-Harvard production written and directed by women. Emily acknowledged in a letter to her parents that the play was "shallow" and "conventional," and vowed that, "If I must slave for a hope for mediocrity at best, I will not do it."

In the fall of 1971, Emily had moved out of Barnard Hall, with its memories of violence and threatened sexual assault, and into Adams House, which occupied an inviting red-brick building on Plympton Street and was one of the oldest and, in the early 1970s, more politically activist of the colleges' residential houses. The residences had their own dining rooms and often their own theaters, and while Adams did not have a stage, it did have a Drama Society and a sizeable lounge on the first floor, where students could perform, play music, or simply hang out.

In September 1972, Irene Dische, who was new to Radcliffe, joined Emily at Adams in a two-bedroom suite. "She was very vivacious," said Dische, "and a fantastic dancer. At parties, she always commandeered the dance floor. Everyone waited for her to come and dance."

Dische, the daughter of Jewish refugees, and Emily Mann, whose maternal great-grandparents perished in the Holocaust, became close friends. They were like sisters, is how Dische described it, "but not similar." For one thing, blonde, slim Irene had lived a more unstructured life than Emily. When still a teenager, she had ended up in Libya during the revolution that put Colonel Muammar al-Gaddafi in power and subsequently she had backpacked to Kenya, where she met and worked with the anthropologist Louis Leakey, who had helped her apply to Radcliffe.

And of course, Emily was a theater person, which Irene was not. Dische liked to tell the story of how, on her first afternoon in the suite, Emily answered the phone and, after listening a few seconds, gasped, "Oh my God! Oh God! Oh no!" Irene, overhearing the conversation, was sure that someone in Emily's family had died. But as it turned out, somebody at the theater had sprained their ankle, potentially a challenge if an actor is supposed to perform that night, but not a cataclysmic event in Irene's experience. Emily, Irene noted to herself, "was very dramatic."

But aside from Irene, most of Emily's close friends were theater people: Liz Coe; an opera singer named Peter Kazaras, lean and dark-eyed, with wavy, enticingly strokable dark hair; Ed Zwick; Lee Abraham, a young actor and director whom Emily had met during the production of *As You Like It*; and tall, thin Stephen Zinsser, later known professionally as Stephen Wadsworth. Although Wadsworth was not part of the Loeb cohort, he would become a distinguished opera and theater director, and when Mann headed the McCarter Theatre Center, he ignited a Marivaux revival with his translations and lively productions of that eighteenth-century French playwright's comedies.

Wadsworth believes he first met Emily one autumn night in 1972, when he and Kazaras and Emily were among a group of friends streaming along a street in Cambridge. Emily announced that she needed actors to play "brain impulses, dressed sort of like eyeballs" in her upcoming production of Robert Montgomery's *Subject to Fits*, her directing debut on the Loeb's main stage. As Wadsworth remembered it, Kazaras turned to him and said, "'You should do that.' And I said, 'Okay.' Emily turned around as she was walking and looked directly at me and went, 'Really?' And I thought, 'Okay. . . Registering Intense Person.' I said, 'Sure. What do I have to do?'"

Subtitled a "response" to Dostoyevsky's novel *The Idiot*, Montgomery, in an Author's Note to the published script, describes his play as "neither adaptation, dramatization nor translation of Dostoyevsky's inimitable novel. . . . It is its own work – smacking of *The Idiot*, dreaming of *The Idiot*, but mostly taking off from where *The Idiot* drove it."

The script calls for a chorus, which speaks and sings on occasion. But a chorus of eyeballs was Emily's invention, fitting for the darkly comic nature of Montgomery's play and for the action, which takes place inside Myshkin's epileptic brain. As Wadsworth soon discovered, he and the rest of the chorus were encased in light-colored spandex costumes and stood on a platform upstage behind a scrim, responding, so the *Crimson*'s reviewer put it, "to the contortions of the Idiot's mind." Wadsworth put it more bluntly: "Whenever Myshkin had a fit, we would contract dramatically. We were sort of eyeballs standing on end and just being part of his frying brain." Ed Zwick described the chorus as "corpuscles filled with blood."

Peter Agoos had designed what he called "a collection" of irregular, six-sided platforms that connected to ramps and bridges and appeared "to float" on their supports. "The form of the platforms was a deliberate allusion to both beehive and brain cells," was how he described his design during our interview. In this skewed environment, Prince Myshkin, child-like and well-meaning, encounters numerous figures seeking to entangle him in their worldly schemes: a man who barks like a dog; sundry drunks and hangers-on; and the wild, seductive Natasha, played by a tall, dark-haired young actor named Marianna Houston. When the virginal Myshkin embraces Natasha, he has a grand mal seizure, and by play's end, he has been sent to a "mental clinic." There he lives forever in a catatonic state, an innocent's only defense against a nightmarish world.

Fits was a more heightened play stylistically than Emily had previously directed, but she apparently met the challenge. *The Crimson* reviewer wrote that "Mann . . . sends [the play] off with the balletic theatrics and vivid emotionalism needed to give it effect."

Because this was a main stage production, the critic William A. Henry III reviewed it for the *Boston Globe*, and he compared it to both the original 1970 production at the Yale School of Drama and the critically praised 1971 production directed by A. J. Antoon at the Public Theater in New York City. The Loeb version, Henry wrote, was clearer than either of the previous outings. He believed that the contrast between those who would corrupt the "pure, smiling, guileless" Myshkin—the contrast between "the blemish and the beauty it reveals"—was starker in Emily's production. But with the production's clarity, Henry wrote, came the dispiriting realization that Montgomery's play was less than profound.

That slight put-down did not dampen Emily's and her cast's pride in their work. They relished the positive reviews and the enthused applause of their audiences. "We were euphoric," said Houston. "We thought we were the coolest people in the world."

Stephen Wadsworth kept his spandex eyeball costume and occasionally teased Emily by wearing it when he met her at an airport.

During their daughter's four years at Radcliffe, Emily's parents would fly in from Chicago, attending practically every production she directed, and Carol, who was now living and working in New York City, would occasionally join them. As much as possible, the Manns tried to maintain their closeness. Emily continued to seek her parents' advice about her health and sought her father's counsel about her career. Arthur continued to encourage his beloved second-born. The United States was still mired in Vietnam and also in Cambodia, so Emily avoided discussing the wars with her father. But they agreed that the 1972 burglary and wiretapping of Democratic National Committee headquarters, in a Washington, D.C., building called the Watergate, was morally repugnant, especially when it became evident that President Nixon helped cover up the break-in. She went home for holidays or special birthdays, such as turning twenty-one in April 1973. But she reserved weekends and college breaks for herself or to be with friends or a lover. And she kept her summers for travel, or theater, or both.

In that vein, Emily flew to England in mid-June 1973, to use archives at Stratford-upon-Avon in preparation for her fall production of *Macbeth* at the Loeb. She studied John Gielgud's promptbook for the *Macbeth* he had directed at Stratford in 1952, with Ralph Richardson playing the Thane as a vulnerable twentieth-century man with a conscience (to the disdain of most critics) and Margaret Leighton as a deeply insane Lady Macbeth. During a side trip to London, Emily saw the Royal Shakespeare Company perform *uMabatha*, South African playwright Welcome Msomi's adaptation of *Macbeth*, set among the Zulu of South Africa in the early nineteenth century. "I still think nothing comes close to [Akira] Kurosawa's *Throne of Blood*," she wrote her parents, citing the Japanese movie director's 1957 film. "His rearranging of the script, additions, deletions, and order, using the performance idiom, is very powerful, improving, I think, on the original."

At the Criterion Theatre, Emily took in Patrick Garland's production of *A Doll's House* starring Claire Bloom and Anthony Hopkins, and her opinion of Bloom's performance presaged her own directorial interpretation more than a decade later. "She is lovely but I cannot stand her Nora. . . . I had little sympathy for her great reversal and much compassion for Torvald. If she had had any guts at all she would have gone back to her husband. Faulty play or production? I don't know."

Then, at the end of June, a delighted Emily surprised her parents, and herself, with news. "You may not believe this," she wrote, "but I have, as of today, become the assistant to Tony Richardson at the Bankside Globe on <u>Antony & Cleopatra</u> with Vanessa Redgrave & Julian Glover."

It all came about when wealthy friends of her parents took her to lunch in London with Sam Wanamaker, the American actor and director who was raising funds to rebuild the Globe Theatre near its original site along the Thames River. As Emily told the story, Tony Richardson was slated to direct Redgrave, his former wife, in the first major postwar production of the play, and in the spirit of you-don't-get-what-you-don't-ask-for, she asked Wanamaker if Richardson had an assistant. If not, could *she* be his assistant?

"I don't know how I had the nerve," Emily wrote her parents, "but I went to speak with Sam Wanamaker and at the end he said he had no money but if I were willing to be 'exploited' in order to learn something, I could work for Richardson." Emily told him that really she wanted "only to be able to watch a great cast and director do a great Shake-speare." That was Friday, June 29. She had to find a place to stay and report to Richardson's offices in Mayfair the following Monday, July 2. Rehearsals began Monday, July 9, for an August 9 opening. "Basically," Mann said years later, "I got a job because I was with big donors."

Perhaps to protect her parents and herself from disappointment, she acknowledged that the arrangement with Richardson was risky. "Luck certainly has been w/me," she wrote Arthur and Sylvia. "Not 2 weeks and I am being allowed to work myself to the bone for the very best! I must be crazy. It seems almost too good to be true. I hope it is not a disaster. I can see a lot of crying in the privacy of my own room (if I have my own room), but I can also see a lot of joy and learning."

She was right on both counts. The office work she had been assigned was "boring," although she was "learning a lot" about how casting agents work. "Richardson still has not looked me in the face or said two words to me," she wrote her parents. And even when rehearsals started, they had little contact; she described him as "distant." But Julian Glover was friendly (he even took her to a cricket match), and the rest of the cast "was super," with the possible exception of Redgrave. One of Emily's assignments that summer included baby-sitting Redgrave's daughters, Natasha and Joely Richardson, a task that did not make Emily happy. "I was barely an assistant director," Mann recalled.

Yet for the time being she felt more peaceful than she had for a while. "I have finally reached a human rhythm," she wrote her parents. "I am doing what I want to be doing, and I want to be doing what I'm doing. I feel no panic . . . I don't feel that at every 'free' moment I should be doing something else."

Emily did learn by watching. A few days into rehearsal, she wrote her parents that "V. Redgrave . . . is a fantastic actress, very lovely woman–absolutely beautiful. Huge performer–gives grandeur to an already magnificent script." At the start of rehearsals, when the actors were sitting around a table reading the play, Redgrave already knew her lines and, Mann recalled, "[The work] was so simple and so pure and so connected. And then she got on her feet and started doing tricks. And what she thought were radical, brilliant ideas—weren't. She ruined her own performance."

Rehearsals progressed, Mann remembered, and there was no controlling Redgrave. Richardson set the production in the 1920s, and Redgrave, sporting a red wig, orange sunglasses, and a white pants suit adorned with epaulets, played Cleopatra as a spoiled imperialist who gets drunk and throws Coca-Cola bottles at her servants. Richardson apparently could not say no to her.

Ultimately Richardson did begin to take more notice of Emily, largely, she thought, because Julian Glover was supportive; he and a few of the other actors were taking notes from her. At one point Richardson really did turn to Emily for assistance, asking her to take over briefly for an ill stage manager. But then it was back to carrying coffee. Still, in the program for the Bankside Globe Playhouse she was listed as Assistant to the Director, and for one brief, shining moment "Tony" asked Emily to assist him in making a film of *Antony and Cleopatra*. In the end, however, that project evaporated for lack of funds.

Mann always contended that she essentially taught herself to direct by directing, but also by watching other directors and deciding what she wanted to adopt or, alternatively, what she promised herself to never do. "From Tony Richardson I learned to just be quite daring," Mann recollected. "I also learned that you can lose a production through headstrong actors."

Returning to Cambridge in the fall of 1973, she set about casting *Macbeth*. She had hoped that Julian Glover would come to the Loeb and play the title role. They had discussed this in London, and Glover had apparently agreed. But to Emily's disgust, the Loeb's administrative staff botched the arrangement, either because of poor follow-through or, she suspected, from jealousy of her summer assignment with Richardson. "I returned to a building ranting about who does Emily Mann think she is anyway bringing in some guy we don't even know," she wrote her parents. "They all assume he is my lover and that I am using the building for my own selfish purposes. (My welcome was less than cordial.)"

Eventually she cast the strapping David Gullette, who had acted a variety of parts while a Harvard undergraduate and, now in his early thirties, was an English professor at Simmons College in Boston. For Lady Macbeth, Emily again used Marianna Houston, her tantalizing Natasha in *Subject to Fits*. But Emily was "terrified about *Macbeth*," she admitted to her parents: "I am not confident in my cast nor am I confident with myself."

In October, Arthur's mother, Mary Finkelman, died, and Emily drove down to New York for her grandmother's funeral.

She found the experience of mourning her grandmother "strangely life confirming. . . . There was so much love and support in that room in Grandma's apartment Monday night that even when I got home and was alone, all alone, I felt strong enough to cope with the very deep sorrow I felt. . . . I was struck by the very deep family commitment there."

The calm that Emily experienced may have transferred to the rehearsal room, for her initial concern about the project was now largely gone. "The play is going superbly," she wrote her parents. "Mimmie," as Houston was known to friends, "is magic, Macbeth is beginning to spark, the witches will be something you have never seen before, and a few of the minor parts are very solid." During one rehearsal of the Three Witches, Emily threw a piece of raw meat at the actors and urged them to lunge for it. In performance, before the action of the play begins, Emily staged a beheading and directed the Witches to cross toward the severed head and claim it for themselves. Then, during the third scene of Act I ("Where hast thou been, sister?" "Killing swine."), the First Witch holds the head out to the other two, and they eat of it.

Perhaps inspired by Tony Richardson's daring, or the sexual tension created onstage between Glover and Redgrave, or by her own sexuality, Emily directed Macbeth and Lady Macbeth to be a highly sexualized pair. Houston recalled that Emily wanted the couple to be "a sexualized team." But they had lost a baby, "so she's compensating," is how Houston viewed Lady M's behavior. In other words, "'If I can't have children, let's be king and queen, something we can call our own.'"

"She seduced [Macbeth] into it," is how Mann described the pair's relationship in her production. "When I looked at the dark side of the moon with the Macbeths, I had a really interesting set of tools in my tool box that I didn't have before I was the assistant on [*Antony and Cleopatra*]. At one point Vanessa jumped on [Julian] and straddled him, and the guy did that, too. . . . I just said, look, this is a very sexy relationship [between Lady Macbeth and Macbeth]. . . . We got really into quite a thing with it. And being young, we were all juiced up anyway, so we understood what that was."

"Juiced up" they may have been, but for Mann, the sexuality she brought forth in the Scottish play was prelude to the eroticism she would instill in a number of her later productions, notably *Miss Julie* (1993) and *Meshugah* (1998), both at the McCarter Theatre Center. Although hardly discussed in scholarly analyses of her work, let alone in mainstream reviews, Mann herself has always been aware of this aspect of her directing. "That's my card," she said. "I guess I'm a passionate woman, and it drives me. And I think people like to see an erotic charge. Because it's human. And so often, when things are way too polite and that's covered up or tamped down, I feel sad . . . it's important to look at women fully, especially their sexuality."

Gullette recalled that his Macbeth was supposed to be less grasping at the start, that Lady Macbeth was "the pathological one" from the beginning, creating a "Frankenstein monster." Eventually the sexual bond disintegrates, and Gullette remembered playing Macbeth "as someone who pays less and less attention to his wife as he gets steeped in blood and in paranoia about the people around him."

"I come to know our awful president's mentality a little better after each rehearsal," Emily wrote her parents at the end of October, referring to Richard Nixon, who was using any contrivance to forestall his political demise. Emily added that "the statesmen and people of this country react just as any people reacts when under the rule of a madman and a tyrant—ineffectually, despairingly, cynically."

Houston and Gullette both experienced Mann as empathic but tough. "You could tell this was her life's work," was how Gullette described

Emily's approach. "I remember her being charming but a tough-as-nails director. She was a perfectionist."

"She was available if you needed extra help," was the way Houston expressed her working relationship with Emily. Even after the reviews came out, Houston remembered walking with Emily along the Charles River to talk about the performance, for Houston felt the need to make adjustments in her portrayal. But she did not depict Emily as "this cozy director who was there for you. She was a toughie. I was a strong person, but I was amazed at seeing Emily operate: 'Sure, give me the Loeb Theater. I'm going to do this.' She did not think small."

Photographs of the production reveal a handsome, if conventional, set, designed by Edward Stauffer. Upstage, on a raised level the width of the stage, stone-like columns braced a stone-like arch, suggesting an edifice in an eleventh-century Scottish landscape. A wide, curved staircase dominated stage right, from the upstage level to the deck, and during Lady Macbeth's sleepwalking scene, Houston descended those stairs, hair unfastened, candle in hand. Macbeth's floor-length cape of feathers and furs was a striking costume, and one photograph shows him embracing and caressing Houston, who is costumed in a clinging burnt-orange gown.

Macbeth opened on November 29, 1973, and reviews mingled compliments with correctives. The critic for the *Christian Science Monitor* wrote that "Director Emily Mann undoubtedly made great strides bringing this show to what it is. There are some splendid moments in the production. But, it lacks that final polish, that pulling together of the show as a whole which only comes after long rehearsals, severe criticism, and strong demands on individual actors."

A *Harvard Crimson* reviewer particularly admired Gullette's portrayal, calling it "bold and strong but careful and considering nonetheless . . . liable to fear—but fear of things within." Houston, the reviewer thought, did not match Gullette in terms of characterization or stage presence. Finally, he found the setting "not particularly inspired," but he liked certain "special effects," especially the ghost of Banquo "in a green light, posed behind Macbeth's chair like Christ in *The Last Supper*."

"It was such a different feeling than after *Subject to Fits*," recalled Marianna Houston, "where we all went, 'We rock, we're the best.' It was sobering. Obviously *Macbeth* is very tough for any director. And a big monster to take on at a young age."

William Alfred, supportive as always, tried to get permission for Emily's production to be accepted as her senior thesis. But the English department, which just the year before had awarded Emily the annual Lucy Allen Paton Prize, which came with fifty dollars and was given to the junior "who shall be deemed by her instructors to have manifested the greatest promise in the Humanities or Fine Arts," rejected that idea. The department also rebuffed Alfred's attempt to submit Emily's research and director's book in lieu of a thesis. Mann, in fact, never wrote a thesis, and as a result she graduated with honors but not Summa Cum Laude. She did, however, make membership in Phi Beta Kappa, the liberal arts and sciences honor society.

"I guess I could have written my senior thesis on the play, or the history of the play," Mann reflected years later. "But I was not interested in doing that. I remember my father was disappointed. But I think he understood. He thought it would be more important to my life than of course it was."

Senior year, and the pressure was on to decide what to do with her life. Emily's friends did not doubt that she would overcome whatever challenges arose. Emily herself was not so sure.

"Everybody says I always knew what I wanted to do," said Mann. "It's a bunch of crap. I was as confused as everyone else. I mean, I knew what I loved, but I didn't even know if I could do it as a living. I didn't get many good answers, either, to my questions. I did a lot of my own research, meeting with people, tracking people down." It did not help that the Loeb's producing director, George Hamlin, told Emily in her senior year that a woman could not have a career directing in the professional theater and that the best she could hope for was staging children's theater.

At one point Emily was even unsure if she wanted to continue in the field. "[T]heater is terribly narrow," she wrote her parents at the beginning of her final semester. "I am beginning to admit I do not see its value anymore." She considered being a journalist. She also thought about training to be a psychologist, because of her fascination with how human beings think and behave. "I wasn't sure that theater mattered enough," Mann said about the future she was contemplating. "I was brought up to think that you have to make a difference. You have to make the world a better place than when you came into it. So I wasn't sure you could do that with theater."

She did not want to be an English professor. "This was absolutely not of interest to me," Mann confirmed. "How academics looked at literature, I found anathema." To be sure, teaching at a university would offer advantages: she could have both a fulfilling intellectual life and raise a family, and Emily wanted to have children. "Academia would have been a very nice rhythm for me, if I had wanted just to be a writer," said Mann. "But when I discovered how much I loved directing, and how much I loved being connected to literature in that way, there was no going back."

She concluded that, through directing, she could tell stories that would affect people's attitudes and behavior, and increase people's acceptance of their fellow human beings. The actor Jack Gilpin, whom Emily had directed in *Subject to Fits*, said that "her belief in theater as a powerful voice in human life and not a chamber concern, or pastime, was inspiring and confirming to those of us who decided to give our professional lives to it."

What, then, to do after graduation? Receiving a Master of Fine Arts degree sounded like a smart, practical move, and the Yale School of Drama, the most prestigious graduate school for theater on the East Coast, seemed a logical choice at first glance. Under Robert Brustein, dean of the school since 1966, a resident professional company now existed with which graduate students could presumably work. But Emily had heard that Yale was awful for women directors and crossed it off her list.

She applied instead to the St. Paul–based Bush Foundation for a Fellowship in directing, a grant that would provide $10,000 to cover tuition and fees for a twelve-to-eighteen-month period ($10,000 in 1974 was the equivalent of about $52,000 in 2021). During her first year as a Fellow she would take graduate courses at the University of Minnesota in Minneapolis and earn a small salary as a teaching assistant. In her second year, she would be an assistant stage manager at the renowned Guthrie Theater, which meant she would be in the rehearsal room with the Guthrie's esteemed artistic director, Michael Langham. She would also receive an Actors' Equity Association (AEA) union card, a precious symbol of professionalism entitling her to earn an Equity salary as either an actor or stage manager. At the end of the Fellowship's second year, the University of Minnesota would award her a Master of Fine Arts degree.

While waiting to hear from the Bush Foundation, Mann passed her last months at Radcliffe engaged in two of the most creative and enlightening undertakings of her time in Cambridge. Vesna Neskow, who had played the First Witch in *Macbeth* and had experimented with clown work in Paris the previous year, asked Emily if she would like to help organize a clown troupe. Emily was intrigued and, according to Neskow, brought in twenty-five-year-old Cheryl Gates McFadden, who had been giving movement classes at the Loeb and had studied with famed mime and theater teacher Jacques Lecoq at his International Theatre School in Paris. McFadden created a class for five emerging clowns, all women.

In his book *The Moving Body*, Lecoq wrote: "We are all clowns, we all think we are beautiful, clever and strong, whereas we all have our weaknesses, our ridiculous side, which can make people laugh when we allow it to express itself. . . . This discovery of how personal weakness can be transformed into dramatic strength was the key to my elaboration of a personal approach to clowning, involving a search for 'one's own clown', which became a fundamental principle of the training." He called a clown's red nose "the smallest mask in the world." And, he wrote, "When the actor comes on stage wearing a small red nose, his face is in a state of openness, entirely without defence."

Emily found her clown: a nurse who went around healing everyone, equipped with a doctor's stethoscope and a small bag of bandages. "I am quiet, stupid, (dense, shy, obsessively anxious to please–open, warm.)," she wrote in her notes from the class. The notes suggest that she found her clown through "1 - singing - I have always been ashamed of my voice but they kept liking it - - I got more courage until I was belting it and dancing wildly around the stage as I thought of my singing "Maria" in W.S. Story. I would dance – all Jerome Robbins leaps. The human came from gaining more & more confidence for no reason."

"We did exercises as our clowns," Emily wrote to herself. "I did somersaults as well as I could. I would shyly, softly ask Cheryl to watch me. She would say 'that's very good.' I beamed." Everyone in the class did walks as their clowns, told stories as their clowns. Emily's clown told the story of Little Red Riding Hood and got "so lost" and "confused."

Finally, one Saturday night in March, the troupe gave a performance, probably, according to Neskow, in a ground-floor space at Currier House on the Radcliffe Quadrangle. Emily's costume was a torn, white, knee-length skirt and "a red top w/ a yellow knit corsetty kind of shirt top worn from breasts to below waist"; a blue blazer that was too small for her; knee-socks rolled down to her ankles; sneakers with red shoe laces, and a floppy hat. And of course, a red nose: "(small)."

"Succés!" Emily divulged to her notebook. "I was the funniest & learned the most. My clown was absolutely terrified of the crowds and the entire ordeal." Her clown shrieked to people in the audience, "I'm so scared." She looked out at everyone and froze. "The rest of the clowns dragged me off. My walk got fast, frantic, and my right arm shook." Someone blew a whistle, the cue to leave the stage, and Emily's clown made for the nearest exit, upstage center. Another whistle, and she and the rest of the clowns had to enter again. But Emily's clown peeked at the audience from backstage and "freaked" and "froze" until the final whistle cleared the playing space. Exeunt all. In her notebook, she put an asterisk next to one particular discovery: "I was funny because I just stood there paralyzed."

Remembering her clown, years later Mann confided, "I'm always taking care of people. That's the side of me people don't know. Taking care of all the actors. I could put up a shingle: Shrink. Therapist."

Despite what Mann learned by observing other directors, she averred that "the person who really taught me" was a thirty-year-old acting teacher and director named Peter Frisch, with whom Emily took both an acting seminar and, in the spring of her senior year, a directing seminar at the Loeb.

In the directing sessions, Frisch talked with the students about finding the thematic resonance in a play, or as he put it years later, "something you want to explore, that means something to you personally. So it becomes a personal cause. Rooted in your humanity." He discussed taking a concept and using it as the basis for a production's design, manifesting the concept in colors and materials and textures (students had to bring in photographs, drawings, and materials for a play they might want to direct).

He talked about casting. There was the bad way—what he called the Hollywood way—in which "they have this idea of a person in mind and wait for someone to walk through the door." And then there was the way he encouraged a theater director to engage with casting: "If this person were to play the role, how would that affect the play and the concept, the balance of the piece and the meaning of the piece?"

Frisch talked about staging for three different theater configurations: proscenium, modified thrust, and full round, and urged his students to believe that the working rehearsal, during which a director and her actors dig beneath the surface of a text, exploring and experimenting, is always more important than the rehearsal showing results. "The work yields the result," he stressed. "You want to see the process."

Emily worked on a scene from James Joyce's only play, *Exiles*, and filled a small brown notebook with Frisch's suggestions. Among her scrawled notes for "Rehearsal Process" is the following breakdown, one that she tended to follow throughout her career: the first third of rehearsals is devoted to "playing intentions, elements. Non-directional blocking";

the second third is dedicated to firming up blocking, "intensive beat & intention work. Scene work. Digging & playing," and during the last third, "Polish, integrate."

Frisch, who went on to became Head of Drama at the Carnegie Mellon University School of Drama and subsequently opened an acting studio in California, described Emily as being "hungry for two things: learning and what was true. She was very present. I remember those eyes so well: a little bit tired, but intense. Absorbing all the time."

"What she had then," he said, "and what she's had going forward, was an incredible amount of vulnerability coupled with a lot of fight."

"NEWS: I got the Bush Fellowship!!!!!! NEWS: I am taking the Bush Fellowship. NEWS: I want to go."

Emily announced the award to her parents in March of 1974. Indecision about her career had vanished. "My life is ecstatic," she wrote. That April, Irene Dische threw Emily a party for her twenty-second birthday, and then, in a private celebration, Emily cut her hair and replaced the waist-length tresses with a head of tight, dark-brown curls, which accentuated her high cheekbones and full lips. "I feel great," she reported afterward to her parents. "It is very curly just like when I was little." She played tennis and softball, and performed in clown shows at street fairs in Cambridge. She set about forging summer plans, helped by a $450 Radcliffe Fellowship to study theater in England. Even preparing for her last final exams could not douse her spirits.

On June 13, 1974, Mann graduated from Radcliffe College. The Commencement speaker was Elliot L. Richardson '41, Nixon's former attorney general, who eight months earlier, on October 13, 1973, had resigned when Nixon ordered him to fire special Watergate prosecutor Archibald Cox. The choice of speaker did not thrill the Radcliffe women, but the Class Day committee thought Richardson a better selection than others on the list, one of whom was the comedian and filmmaker Woody Allen. Susan G. Cole '74, Radcliffe senior marshall and a Class Day committee member, presciently told a reporter for the *Crimson*, "I didn't want Allen because I knew he'd be sexist. Asking Woody Allen not to be sexist is like asking Richard Nixon not to lie."

In the spirit of commencement, Emily took part in a demonstration supporting equality for women, and a photographer for the *Boston Herald American* captured Emily in her cap and gown, smiling and carrying a banner proclaiming "Equal Opportunity for Women" in capital letters.

In the spirit of surviving four years of rigorous work, there is a black-and-white photograph of Emily sitting on a window sill in Adams House, still in her cap and gown but also wearing her clown nose, and sharing the sill with a mostly empty bottle of Scotch.

5

Annulla Allen
(1974)

HER VOICE IS LOW and shaded with a slight Central European accent as
she talks about the people and events that have formed her life: rescuing
her late husband from Dachau during World War II; the tribulations
of taking care of her invalid younger sister, Ada; the "bloody Negro"
chauffeur with whom she got into a swearing match one day in London, when, driving behind him in her Jaguar, she became irritated that
he was driving too slowly. On the two audiocassettes that have survived
among Emily Mann's papers from the summer of 1974, from when
Emily and Irene Dische recorded Dische's aunt Annulla Allen, the older
woman's words occasionally sound muffled. Time and poor storage con-
ditions have degraded the tapes. But it is possible to hear why Emily
believed Annulla could be the central figure of her first produced script,
Annulla Allen: The Autobiography of a Survivor. And it is testimony to
Emily's imagination that she was able to convert the bits and pieces of a
disordered life into a compelling portrait, preserved in a play.

Emily broke free of the intensity of her four years at Radcliffe by
returning to Europe after graduation, for a trip that stimulated her to
write *Annulla Allen* and became a reservoir of subjects and themes to
which she has returned as both a director and a dramatist. The Holocaust forms the background of the entangled, sometimes desperate love
affairs in *Meshugah* (1998) and is the horror at the forefront of *The
Pianist* (2021). The dire effects of hatred of "the other" emerge clearly in
Execution of Justice (1985) and *Greensboro (A Requiem)* (1996).

Mann's recollections about how she came to meet Annulla Allen have been told and retold, have merged and been elaborated over the years. But it seems likely that, at some point during her junior or senior year at Radcliffe, she was home in Chicago, browsing among her father's papers in his study, and she came across the transcript of an oral history conducted by the daughter of a Holocaust survivor. Moved by the interview, Emily asked her father, who was then heading the oral history project of the American Jewish Committee, if she could edit and shape the document, with the aim of directing it. He said no, that it was the property of the interviewer. But he suggested she take a tape recorder and find her own subject.

As for whom that subject would be, Emily probably did not have an inkling until she and Irene Dische arranged to visit England together during the summer of 1974, Emily to study theater, and Irene to pursue an interest in oral history. "We may develop a script out of an oral history we plan to do together with her aunt in London," Emily wrote her parents. The previous summer, when Emily was in London observing the rehearsals of *Antony and Cleopatra*, Irene had introduced her to this favorite aunt, and now they returned, hoping to record Annulla's memories of being a young Jewish woman in Austria at the beginning of World War II.

And so, early in July 1974, Emily and Irene climbed the stairs to Allen's flat in Hampstead, a relatively affluent North London neighborhood, and sat in her kitchen, drinking tea and watching Annulla make chicken-in-the-pot for Ada. At first, Mann recalled, she and Dische were unsure about whether to ask Annulla if they could record her and, like silly schoolgirls, hid the recorder under the kitchen table while taping. But eventually Emily and Irene brought the machine into the open, and over the course of several visits, supposedly with Annulla's consent, taped hours of conversation. In the two audio cassettes in Mann's possession, it is often Dische who talks with her aunt, sometimes in English, at other times in German, and Irene asserted years later that she, in fact, did most of the interviewing. But at a couple of points Emily herself engages Annulla, and one of the more humorous exchanges occurs when the older woman describes how she once wanted to be an actor, only to be told that, at four feet and eleven inches, she wasn't tall enough, a story that would amuse audiences when the diminutive Barbara Bryne originated the role at the Guthrie Theater.

Annulla Allen was not a completely sympathetic figure. She was racist (Mann did not include the altercation with the Black chauffeur in any versions of the play). She often found caring for her sister to be an unpleasant chore. But, said Mann, "she was a kick as a character. . . . not all sugar and molasses. . . . a tough broad, and lots of her relatives didn't like her at all. But she's a great theater character."

Talking with Annulla held personal meaning for Emily as well as artistic possibilities. That summer of 1974, visiting Annulla was the first step in a search to learn about the world in which her parents' ancestors lived and died. After London, she intended to travel to Poland, to the town of Ostrołęka, where her grandmother Gussie was born, and where pogroms and then the Nazis had decimated Gussie's family. Emily's grandmother could not understand why two vibrant young women would want to see such a place. "Why do you want to go there?" she asked Emily and Irene, when they visited her in Clifton, New Jersey, to talk about their planned trip. "They killed us there." Still, at Emily's request, seventy-seven-year-old Gussie drew a map of the town as she remembered it, and Emily had the map with her when she and Irene flew into London's Heathrow Airport on June 30, for the start of their adventures.

In a diary from that summer, Emily wrote about finding London drearier than she had remembered from the previous summer. Yet she was happier than she had been the previous summer. "I am not in the rain going to Elephant & Castle for a rehearsal of A&C," she wrote. "I am me, now, happy, older, on a trip abroad." After concluding their meetings with Annulla, Irene took off for Paris, and Emily followed, taking a boat across the channel shortly after July 9. In Paris, she wrote in her diary, she couldn't go anywhere without being "accosted" by "fiendish skinny Frenchmen," even when she wore the baggiest jeans in her knapsack. And while Irene traipsed to parts unknown with a new love,

Emily sat in cafés and started to transcribe, by hand, their recordings of Annulla, and she began organizing the transcript into sections. She also made preliminary notes for a play, imagined at this point to be structured conventionally, with scenes and flashbacks and several characters in addition to Annulla.

Then it was off to Germany, where Stephen Wadsworth had parked his orange Volkswagen bus, nicknamed Isolde, for Emily and Irene to borrow and drive to Czechoslovakia and on to Poland. This portion of the trip might well have been called "Travels with Emily and Irene," for despite their often contradictory recollections, clearly the two women encountered and relished several adventures, emerging mostly unscathed from all of them. Lodging was usually outside their budget, so they often parked for the night on a street, near a hotel. They would sleep in Isolde and then wash up at the hotel in the morning. It turned out that Wadsworth had not updated his license plates, and so, he later heard, at border after border in what was then Communist Eastern Europe, the women "did a giggly we-don't-speak-the-language act" for the guards, who usually grinned and waved them through. According to Irene, who was even more of a fabulist than Emily, on at least one occasion Emily cried on cue and begged a guard to let them across. Irene recalled that the tears worked; Emily, that they didn't.

In her diary from that trip, Emily mentions an "amazing 12 hr. drive thru Czechoslovakia" (Irene did not drive at the time), which she accomplished despite Irene directing her onto the wrong roads. They arrived, exhausted, in Upper Silesia, probably toward the end of July, and visited for a few days with elderly members and friends of Irene's family. Then they proceeded to Ostrołęka, in northeast Poland.

For Emily, the visit was illuminating and disturbing. Shops from earlier in the century still remained, but which one had belonged to her grandmother's family? The ride through town was like "a tunnel to the past," she wrote in her diary. Carts, horses, peasants, children, everywhere. She imagined Gussie as a youngster, more than sixty years earlier, riding on carts very much like the ones the citizens of

Ostrołęka were still using in 1974. But there were no records to help her find where the family's shop once stood, and no Jewish graves. "The memory of slaughtered Jews wiped out—forgotten," she wrote. They followed Gussie's map to where the synagogue should have been, but found nothing there. Soon she and Irene realized that the towns-people were watching them, and when Irene, who spoke Polish, asked about where to find family records, people stared back at her icily. Writing about the experience afterward, Emily described how at some point she began to wonder what the older citizens of Ostrołęka had been doing during the war, and she retched and vomited. "I just got sick and sick and sick." When she reconceived her play about Annulla in 1985 to include her own voice, these sensations and reflections would become part of the script.

Before leaving Poland, Emily and Irene stopped in Warsaw, where they attended the meeting of a literary bund, a sort of writers' union. There, under the cover of a dimly lit room, Irene, by pre-arrangement, smuggled in a bag that contained at least one copy of Aleksandr Solzhenitsyn's 1973 opus *The Gulag Archipelago*, illegal in the Soviet Union and its bloc countries (the Soviet government had expelled Solzhenitsyn in 1974). It was an audacious exchange, for which both women could have been severely punished had Irene been caught. "I put the bag of books between my legs," Dische later recounted when driving us from New York City to Princeton, New Jersey, "and I pushed the bag with my feet over to one of the two people we were meeting. And one set of legs or feet met my feet and took the bag. And then it was under their legs, and they left with it, after we had cake and coffee and conversation."

In Warsaw, Irene became ill and could not continue on. Emily drove back through Czechoslovakia by herself, got lost, was rescued by a Czech family who fed her and let her bathe and gave her directions to the Austrian border. Somewhere in Austria she returned Isolde to Stephen Wadsworth, and she, Wadsworth and Peter Kazaras headed to the Bayreuth Festival in Germany to hear Wagner. Wadsworth and Mann's memories differ, but she is certain that, because of the license plate problem, the trio could not enter Germany. Stalled in Salzburg, Mann sat in the orange VW bus, intently transcribing the taped conversations with Annulla.

She flew home to Chicago on August 23, transcriptions of Annulla Allen's words stowed protectively in her knapsack.

6

Portrait of a Survivor

(1974–1978)

In 1974, the resident not-for-profit theater movement, while still young, was flourishing artistically. From Baltimore, Maryland, to Louisville, Kentucky, from Providence, Rhode Island, to Costa Mesa, California, professional theater companies were offering seasons of classic European and American plays, sometimes in rotating repertory. Seasons of Shakespeare and Molière, Eugene O'Neill and Tennessee Williams, were becoming welcome alternatives to nonprofessional community theater, dinner theaters, and touring productions of Broadway hits.

The 1960s, the decade that had witnessed violence in numerous American cities, and more than two million American troops serving in Vietnam, had paradoxically also seen the U.S. Congress, in 1965, establish the National Endowment for the Arts (NEA), to support creativity and bring artistic innovation to American audiences. The resident theater movement was also benefiting from the financial sustenance of the Ford and Rockefeller Foundations, and the proliferation of state arts councils. In Minneapolis–St. Paul, corporate leaders, who wanted to raise the Twin Cities' cosmopolitanism and visibility, generously supported the growing not-for-profit theater community.

The Guthrie Theater, as Emily soon discovered, was a very patriarchal institution. This was ironic, since it was a woman, the pioneering English designer Tanya Moiseiwitsch, who, collaborating with Tyrone Guthrie, had designed the theater's somewhat asymmetrical, multisided thrust stage, with steps leading down to the audience and the two voms (vomitoria, or tunnels), underneath the raked seats. The theater sat as many as 1,441 people, in a space that was surprisingly intimate. Moiseiwitsch had also been the Guthrie's principal designer from 1963, when the Guthrie produced its first season, until 1966. But the theater's founders and first managing director were men: eponymous British director Guthrie; American theater producer Oliver Rea; and Peter Zeisler, a former stage manager who envisioned a national theater beyond Broadway.

By 1966, Guthrie and Rea had left, and Zeisler followed in 1970. In 1971, when the Guthrie board hired British director Michael Langham, who had led the Stratford Festival in Ontario, Canada, from 1956 to 1967, the Guthrie had shed audiences and was deep in debt. But together with managing director Donald Schoenbaum, Langham brought the Guthrie back from the fiscal edge, and as far as Guthrie audiences were concerned, he possessed a magic touch.

By the time Emily arrived, the Guthrie was still largely producing classic European, Russian and American plays, with a nod to contemporary playwrights such as LeRoi Jones and Lanford Wilson when the Guthrie dallied with a second space during three seasons prior to Langham's arrival. More than ten years after its founding, only one play by a woman had been produced on the main stage: *I, Said the Fly*, a two-character item about the demise of vaudeville, written by and starring former vaudeville luminary June Havoc. *Fly* had been a resounding flop, artistically and at the box office. Barbara Field's lively adaptation of *A Christmas Carol* for the 1975–1976 season would be only the second play by a woman to be produced on the main stage, but at least it became a stalwart among Guthrie productions and led to more Field adaptations. One of several playwrights who started the Minnesota Playwriting Laboratory (later the Playwrights' Center) in Minneapolis, Field was the Guthrie's literary manager and the sole woman in Langham's upper tier of artistic staff.

As for two seasons when the Guthrie had also presented plays at the Crawford Livingston Theater in St. Paul and produced so-called experimental work for three seasons in what was called The Other Place, on Harmon Place in Minneapolis—no play by a woman had been staged in those venues at all. And no woman had directed at the Guthrie, whether in St. Paul, The Other Place, or on the main stage.

Emily drove with her mother from Chicago to Minneapolis at the end of August 1974, and together they found an apartment for Emily on the fourth floor of a bland but affordable brick apartment house at 330 Oak Grove, near Loring Park, within walking distance of the Guthrie at Vineland Place. In Emily's mind, the Guthrie was her destination, even though she was supposed to spend much of her first year as a Bush Fellow at the West Bank campus of the University of Minnesota. Sylvia bought furniture for the apartment, and Emily moved in and decorated it with reminders of home. "What has <u>made</u> the apartment," she soon wrote her parents, "is the little Mexican vase, the candlesticks, the grandma doilies, the lamp. (All the little things.)"

The Minneapolis in which Emily lived and studied had less ethnic diversity than the city in which she had come of age. In Chicago, the middle-class Hyde Park–Kenwood neighborhood was comparatively multiracial, as was the Lab School. The African American neighborhood of North Minneapolis was far removed from the largely white worlds of the Guthrie and the MFA program at the University's West Bank campus.

The area around Oak Grove, where Emily's apartment was located, was considered a bit rough. However, the violence that Emily would experience and hear about when she lived in the Twin Cities did not take place in the street, but in supposedly protective realms likes theaters and homes. According to Mann, "everyone knew" that John Clark Donahue, the artistic director of the Minneapolis Children's Theater, was sexually abusing boys who acted in his productions. The Vietnam War veteran who became the central figure of Mann's play *Still Life*, in 1977, brought that war's violence home with him to St. Paul, to the woman who became his wife.

For now, Emily's new environment felt welcoming and almost rural, with parks, numerous small lakes, and the broad ribbon of the Mississippi River, which flowed between the Twin Cities of Minneapolis and

St. Paul. "Minneapolis is a marvelous city," Emily wrote her parents toward the end of September 1974. "I keep discovering new things here and I am quickly finding <u>more</u> than enough to do."

MFA courses kept her busy, although they did not always meet her standards, which had been honed by the Lab School, Radcliffe, and the Loeb. As she wrote her parents:

1. Excellent voice [class]
2. Terrific movement class
3. Mediocre at Best directing class but I will be directing 2 one-act plays
4. Playwrighting [sic]–Hope to finish Annulla & give it to a Guthrie actor by end of quarter

At the university, she found friends and advocates in several teachers: Mark Lamos, who was a member of the Guthrie's acting company and gave an acting class at U of M; the dancer and choreographer Robert Darrell Moulton, who taught the "terrific" movement class, called Dance and Prance; Charles Nolte, a stage and film actor turned playwright. After a moderately successful acting career, in which Nolte had played the title role in the 1951 Broadway production of *Billy Budd,* he had earned a doctorate and now taught playwriting courses to which some students (Emily not among them) were devoted.

Overall, Emily attended as few classes as possible and wrote her parents that most of the students "are mediocre at best as are the faculty. I hope to get skills and <u>leave</u> the place alone." After seeing her directing projects in class, the graduate faculty conceded that she really did not need to go to class very much, at least not for directing.

Her first encounters with the Guthrie proved a challenge. If Emily had been unaware of the Guthrie's patriarchal attitudes before she arrived in Minneapolis, she soon became educated. Each Bush Fellow had to meet with Langham, who informed her that women do not direct professionally and insisted that she do an acting audition for him. "I said, 'No, I've come here as a Bush Fellow in directing. I want to be a director.' And he said, 'Well, I still want you to audition for me.'"

Mann remembers she prepared the conventional duo, a classical soliloquy and a contemporary piece, and auditioned for Langham in one of the two large rehearsal rooms in the Guthrie's basement. She stood and performed; Langham sat in a chair in front of her, watching. Afterward, the artistic director said, "Well, you're an actress," at which point Emily declared, "'No, I might be, but I don't want to be an actress. I want to be a director.' And he said, "Well, you know, women directors are either hysterical or dykes. Which are you?' And I said, 'Both.'"

Her ability to summon a retort to Langham's provocative comment, and her determination to use the platform of the Bush Fellowship to create her own directing opportunities, are indicative of the ways in which Emily stood out that first year in Minneapolis.

At the Guthrie she had an advocate and admirer in David Ball, then in his early thirties, who described his Guthrie role as "sort of a combination dramaturg and assistant director." Ball had been instrumental in selecting Emily for a Bush Fellowship.

"When we were looking at applications," he remembered, "we hardly ever got to meet the applicants. We were just going by recommendations. So it was quite a surprise when I met Emily; she was unlike the girls that I had grown up with. The times were such that it was almost foolhardy for a woman to say she wanted a career as a director. It's not like she came from a lot of money. She had a lot of guts, or maybe she was too stupid to see the odds against her. But she knew what she was doing. There was an energy force there. I can't remember her sitting down. I can't remember her not forcefully moving into something, whatever the task was. And it was not just that she was a woman, but for somebody that young to move with that much self-possession, surrounded by a lot of the top people in the business—she was at home in it."

Lean, dark, angular David Feldshuh, a young actor and director who worked at the Guthrie in the late 1960s and early 1970s (later to become a playwright, teacher of theater, and a practicing physician), found Emily "beautiful. She was charming and funny," he remembered. "She was supportive. She was easy to be around." And as David Ball had noted, even at twenty-two, her affect was one of self-confidence. Michael ("Mick") Casale, whose mass of shoulder-length dark hair, along with a mustache and beard, marked him as the hippie in the room, had received a playwriting fellowship, and he remembered observing Emily at the first meeting of all the Fellows. "You had to say your name," Casale recalled, "and some guy from the Guthrie was writing the names down. So Emily says, 'Emily Mann,' and the guy writing it down says, 'M-a-n?' And the look–I can still remember the look she gave the guy. And she said . . . 'n.' And I remember liking her right from that moment. That one little beat."

Undeterred by Langham's appraisal, in the fall and spring of 1974–1975, Emily dove headlong into her classes and her pursuit of the professional goals she had set for herself: to create a performance using the transcripts of Annulla Allen's recollections; to make a career as a director; to support herself financially. As at Radcliffe, and with help from her usual diet of cigarettes and black coffee, she juggled numerous activities, often, as at Radcliffe, overcommitting herself.

One of her first actions upon arriving in Minneapolis had been to attend Michael Bawtree's production of *Tartuffe* at the Guthrie.

She had never seen a production at the Guthrie and was entranced by Tanya Moiseiwitsch's thrust stage, smaller than she had imagined, and by the electricity between the actors and the audience that surrounded the thrust so tightly. Playing Molière's savvy servant Dorine was Barbara Bryne, a short, plump, spirited actor whom Emily immediately believed would be ideal for Annulla Allen. Hastening backstage after the performance, Emily asked if Bryne would consider acting in a play about a survivor of the Holocaust. Bryne said she would be interested in reading the script, and Emily returned to her apartment, assembled her transcripts, and spent the next several days and nights shaping a monologue out of Allen's rambling recollections. Bryne read the result and told an ecstatic Emily that she would perform it.

"When I read a play, I see pictures, if it means anything to me," Bryne said during a telephone interview, years after she had left the Guthrie but was still living in Minneapolis. "And I saw lots of pictures. It sprang alive to me. I saw conceited, brave, argumentative, garrulous. An opinionated woman. And that seemed very intriguing to me."

Emily spent some of the fall of 1974 trying to edit what she was then simply calling *Annulla*, helped by the gift of a new electric typewriter from her mother. She also read scripts for David Ball; embarked with a fellow student on a video adaptation of William Hanley's *Mrs. Dally Has a Lover*, a one-act play she had directed in class at the University of Minnesota; worked as a teaching assistant at the University's Rarig Center, a new campus building that contained four performance spaces; and looked for directing jobs.

The writing was challenging. "Annulla is going nowhere," she wrote her mother in October, though she had given the beginnings of the script to David Ball to critique. "I really am undisciplined and lazy with my own material. I find my editing skills are very well-developed for other people's scripts. But I am unable to get the distancing I need for my own."

Her search for a directing opportunity, however, proved successful. Barbara Field (then known by her married name, Barbara Nosanow) had finished one act of a play called *Matrix*, which takes a mixture of fictional and Biblical female characters, including Donna Anna, Elvira, and Zerlina of Mozart's *Don Giovanni*, and Esther of the Old Testament, and puts them in a palace room—a kind of harem for discarded women—to share thoughts about sexuality, their bodies, and the men they have bedded who may or may not desire them anymore. Women are both willing and unwilling sex objects in this brief, sometimes clever play, and they talk and argue and tease each other about the advantages of feminine subservience versus the power of independence. Donna Anna is pregnant, goes into labor, and gives birth to Don Giovanni's child, who, to the dismay of some of the women in attendance, is female.

Emily was slated to stage the play for the Directors' Series at Theatre in the Round, a long-time community theater largely fed by aspiring playwrights, actors, and directors in the University of Minnesota's graduate theater program. "The first act is really brilliant–very difficult and challenging but I think a stroke of real genius on Barbara's part," she wrote her parents in early December. "I have found a good style to put it in, I hope," she added, although she admitted letting exuberance run ahead of artistic judgment, for her letter suggests she had not even read the first act when she agreed to direct, and Field had not yet written a second act. "But it is still a bit scary to cast a play which is only half-written. Point of fact—until I received the play yesterday I was set to place it in a totally different style, place, and design with a very different cast. Then I read Act One. Just in time. Let us hope that Act Two does not demand as big a readjustment in thinking!"

Then in January 1975, David Ball told Emily that the Guthrie was once again planning to open a second space, called Guthrie 2, but this time mainly for new plays. Not only could *Annulla* be produced there, but, as Emily recalled, he promised she would be able to direct other plays there as well. Eugene Lion, who had recently staged Samuel Beckett's *Waiting for Godot* at the Guthrie, would be the artistic director; Ball would be second-in-command.

As soon as possible, Emily called her parents and gave them the news.

"I'm so happy for you," Arthur Mann wrote his daughter that same day. "The opportunities are falling your way, big and all of a sudden. That's the way it often is with breakthroughs." Aware that his second-born had a tendency to try to do too many things at the same time, he urged her to concentrate on immediate tasks rather than plan now for Guthrie 2. "Too much of <u>anything</u> in one's future calculations is bad business," he cautioned. "The business of life is: one thing at a time."

Field did turn in her second act, and taking her father's suggestion for the moment, Emily focused on directing *Matrix*, set to open February 20, 1975, for six performances. Arthur and Sylvia were in the audience on a wintry Thursday night, when Emily staged what Peter Altman, arts critic for the *Minneapolis Star*, called "her first major local assignment." Barbara Field had attended rehearsals, but she did not remember much about Emily's process except that it "wasn't conventional" and "she was so open to letting the actors work their way into the characters. She was a dream of an actor's director." Altman, in his review, dismissed the script as "a lopsided work of female subject and sensibility," but he praised Emily's work. "Her direction," he wrote, "has authority, good variety of intensity and use of space, and about as effective a blend of comedy and didacticism as probably was achievable."

Mike Steele, the theater critic for the *Minneapolis Tribune*, was more attuned than his colleague to feminist issues. He called *Matrix* "a provocative chamber play that probes the female experience" and complimented Field on a play that "confronts women with, among other things, the nature of sexual politics, the choices open to women and the way they're tempered by women because of their need for men, security, identity and sex." He considered Emily's production "sensitive, extraordinary really."

Despite her father's words of caution, it is hard to imagine Emily putting Guthrie 2 out of her mind, for not only was she in contact with Ball, who would be the new theater's literary director, but also, as 1975 progressed, Minneapolis newspapers kept up a regular drumbeat of coverage about the proposed second stage. In one interview, Guthrie 2 artistic director Eugene Lion told a journalist that "we see this as a place where there can be greater freedom for the unknown." For Guthrie 2, he stated, "either the play has to be unfamiliar or the approach has to be" and, somewhat mysteriously, he more or less quoted Edgar from Act 3, Scene 6 of *King Lear*: "We're going to be anglers in the lake of darkness."

And yet, by the end of July, the team of Lion and Ball had not found a satisfactory performance space for Guthrie 2. From Ball's comments to the press, the men sought an open space, "unbroken by walls or pillars" and near the university, whose students and faculty they envisioned as their primary audience. They were hoping to open Guthrie 2 amid the darkness of November, but increasingly that seemed an unrealistic target.

Emily could not have felt reassured by these developments. In fact, something about the Guthrie 2 project must have alarmed her, for back in May she had written her parents that "I have finally come face to face with power on a professional level (Guthrie 2) . . . anti-feminism on a professional level coupled w/ intense reading of Virginia Woolf and feminism and realizing that my thinking from a young age and our home has better equipped me to deal with these issues than any kind of new found political awareness ever could." Whatever prompted her thoughts about withstanding anti-feminism in the theater, the provocation was serious enough that, in the same letter, she stated dramatically that "No woman ever has nor will she in the near future direct a play on one of the great mainstages in America." Actually, in the 1940s, Margo Jones and Nina Vance had both founded substantial resident theaters in Dallas and Houston, Texas, respectively, and had directed on those stages. In Washington, D.C., Zelda Fichandler was directing plays at the Arena Stage, over which she had held sway since 1951. Yet they were the exceptions that proved the rule of severe gender disparity.

While the artistic heads of Guthrie 2 continued their search for a venue, the frigid Minneapolis winter departed, making way for a brief spring. Emily finished her spring quarter at the university and celebrated by moving out of her drab apartment building to a late-Victorian house not unlike the one in which she grew up in Northampton. She shared a two-bedroom attic apartment, first with Susan Galbraith, who would play Lulu in Mann's fall 1975 production of *The Birthday Party*, and then with Karen Landry, a young actor in the Guthrie's resident company. Eventually Emily and Karen shared two floors in the house.

Sharing living expenses eased the state of Emily's finances. Supporting herself was proving harder than she had hoped, for the Bush grant apparently did not cover all her expenses. In December of 1974, she had over-optimistically written her parents about "awaiting a big money job this summer, $2800 for directing two children's shows. I want it very badly—I would like to do clowns and mask shows for children—form a company, train, develop new scripts out of improvisations." But the job did not materialize, nor did $400 for working on the still-ephemeral Guthrie 2; to her annoyance, the university did not allow her to take the assignment, for reasons that, at this distance, are unclear. Emily wrote her mother, to whom she regularly confided budgeting challenges, that she was having a "money mess" and asked for help paying her car insurance and the fee at a health club, where she was now lifting weights to keep up her stamina. "I will be fine financially if I watch everything very closely," she promised. She offered to repay her mother as soon as possible and apologized for causing any difficulties at Sylvia's end, although Sylvia never questioned her daughter's need for financial help.

Emily did earn money that August of 1975, acting the small role of a music teacher in Charles Nolte's production of *The Magistrate*, Arthur Wing Pinero's 1885 farce involving a wife who pretends to be five years younger than she really is. This was the first and only time Emily performed on a showboat—the Minnesota Centennial Showboat—a cheery, red-and-white paddle wheeler once known as the *General John Newton*, which docked during the summer on the St. Paul side of the Mississippi. Peter Altman in the *Star* described her characterization as "sly and sweet."

David Ball had considered Emily poised and confident, and certainly a sense of her own intelligence, attractiveness, and talent lent her self-assurance, even at times a feeling of privilege. But in truth she was less experienced in certain ways than she appeared or even recognized herself. In her enthusiasm for creating a play based on Annulla Allen's life, she wrote Allen in September 1975 what she thought was a gracious letter, informing her about the play project:

> Dear Annulla,
> I want you to know that I have developed a play, <u>Annulla</u>, based on your life taken from the tapes Irene made. You have deeply affected my life. I feel what you have experienced should be shared. I hope you see that the work is a tribute to you: you are one of the most beautiful women I have ever met.

I cannot send you a script of the play since it is still in the process of being developed with the actress. If you would like to see a script when it is finished, I will be glad to send it to you.

I hope you are pleased and honored that you have inspired this work because I feel it a rare honor to have met you. I remain forever your admiring

Emily

But Allen quickly wrote back that she was neither pleased nor honored and had given neither her niece, Irene, nor Emily permission to use the tapes. In fact, in her page-long, single-spaced, typed letter, she asked why Emily had not told her about the play before starting to write it. She wanted to see a copy at once, finished or not, and indicated that she would be writing to her late husband's cousin, an assistant professor of law at Columbia University, presumably to ask about her legal rights.

Given the somewhat furtive way in which Emily and Irene had initially taped their conversations with Allen, Emily perhaps should not have been surprised by this reaction. But she was hurt by Allen's response, and by Irene, who angrily took her aunt's side. Emily telephoned her father for guidance, and they talked at length. "I can well understand— more, I can feel and did feel—the pain you went through," he wrote his daughter afterward. Whether as a result of speaking with her father, or through self-examination, or both, Emily soon wrote him that "A person is more important than a play. If I cannot do this without consent on her side, I will not do it. . . . I made a mistake handing her a fait accompli. I should have realized her life has been led on rules of survival & that she trusts no one, because of this. Therefore, extreme care & tact must be used."

Emily sent what she called a "rough monologue" to Allen, accompanied by an apologetic letter that was more considered than her first approach. In addition to assuring that the play would only be done with Allen's consent, Emily also offered her the chance to "revise the manuscript, add sections or delete sections, and tell me whether you want names changed or to use your own." And at the end she added: "Your feelings mean more to me than a play, I cannot be more clear. I respect you. I leave it in your hands."

Allen did not make any changes in Emily's script, and in her next letter to Allen, Emily described what she intended to create through Annulla's words, both in the script and ultimately onstage. "I have left the transcript anecdotal and chatty," she wrote. "Sometimes humorous, so that people will not feel threatened as they do in didactic theater. The feel is of having a cup of tea with someone who has a stimulating mind and a humanity. One feels free to think about the issues being raised."

Emily's year at the University of Minnesota culminated with her production of Pinter's *The Birthday Party*, a directing assignment required for her MFA. The opening was slated for November 13, 1975, in the Rarig Center's 200-seat Arena Theatre.

Emily had selected *The Birthday Party* in part because Pinter's 1958 script evoked for her the fearsome knock-on-the-door which had terrified European Jews during World War II. Set in a decrepit, seaside English boarding house, the action centers around the arrival of two threatening men named Goldberg and McCann, who interrogate and torture a longtime boarder named Stanley, the object of the birthday party. Goldberg and McCann reduce Stanley to a compliant, gurgling shade of himself and take him away. "It rang the Holocaust bell for me," Mann said, "The Jewish theme just hit me."

It is fair to assume that, in addition to admiring Pinter's writing and discerning a theme that resonated with her, Emily chose a literate script which would not only please her advisors at the university but also appeal to the power players at the Guthrie. In May 1975, when Emily had to choose the play she wished to direct, Pinter's *The Caretaker* was in rehearsal for a June opening on the Guthrie's main stage. Consciously or not, Emily was leaving herself and her production vulnerable to comparisons and putting herself in competition with *The Caretaker*'s director, Stephen Kanee, the Guthrie's associate director.

Correspondence with her parents during rehearsals indicates that at first Emily was pleased with how the production was coming together. Then, late in October, with the opening about two weeks away, she wrote that she was struggling. David Ball attended a rehearsal and, according to Mann, "put me straight & back on the track." But he returned during dress rehearsal and, in Mann's description of what took place, gave her notes which she passed along to the actors, to her regret. Ball, when interviewed, recalled only that "there was a maturity to [Emily], and that was reflected in how she did *The Birthday Party*." Emily, however, believed these last-minute changes, which she blamed herself for incorporating, ruined the production and resulted in the negative coverage.

The reviews were not as universally catastrophic as Emily felt, but she was sensitive to negative criticism and had wanted to end her year in the MFA program with a public success. Instead she read complete failure in the reviews and, as 1975 turned to 1976, went home for a few days to Chicago for solace. Upon returning to Minneapolis, she felt more in control of herself and her work, but she wrote her parents that, "I felt clubbed in the stomach, stunned, all clarity gone and I cannot afford that personally or professionally. . . . I learned from this experience w/ David some crucial things about my work: when you see something potentially dangerous, grab it, examine it, question it."

Guthrie 2 opened on the night of Wednesday, January 14, 1976, a freezing night in Minneapolis, with snow on the ground.

David Ball and Eugene Lion finally had discovered a space that they liked: the Southern Theater on Washington Avenue South, which was built in 1910 as a combination vaudeville house and legitimate theater for the local Scandinavian community. Time and an erratic economy had not treated the Southern kindly, but the building was vacant, and Ball and Lion believed they could transform it into a flexible performance space. They left the proscenium arch as they found it: "funkily unrestored," according to one article. And they left the auditorium walls encrusted with its decades of paint and patched plaster. The stage became the scene shop, the auditorium floor became the playing space, and a battalion of interns outfitted the auditorium with bleachers, which a director could arrange however he or she wished. Like its parent on Vineland Place, Guthrie 2 would operate as a rotating repertory house and have a permanent company of actors. And when Guthrie 2 was not using the space, other groups, or individual performers, could, ideally, rent it. The bleachers sat about two hundred people.

The new theater opened with *The Collected Works of Billy the Kid*, which Michael Ondaatje, a Sri Lankan–born Canadian, had adapted from his novel about the notorious American outlaw. *Kid* was joined in February by Scottish playwright Menzies McKillop's *The Future Pit*. Eugene Lion directed the inaugural play, and David Feldshuh staged McKillop's dark comedy.

Emily's turn came in March, when she directed Mick Casale's *Cold*, the last one-act on a bill that included *Waterman* by Frank B. Ford, and *Glutt* by Indiana native Gladden Schrock. At the same time, she was also rehearsing David Ball's adaptation of *Summerfolk*, retitled *Summerfolk (through October 16)*, at Theater in the Round (Emily had apparently overcome any residual tension with Ball). *Cold* opened March 17, *Summerfolk* two days later. "I have never had such an artistic load before," Emily wrote her parents. "I am excited and very scared."

Cold is a dreamlike play, in which the action takes place on the day the movie star Marilyn Monroe commits suicide. There are three Marilyn Monroes in the script, all onstage at the same time, often sitting at a long dining table but each, nonetheless, in her own world. One is Norma Jean, who is Monroe as a young girl, wearing dungarees and a red blouse and on occasion receiving an injection from a mysterious Man. Another is simply Marilyn, drab but motherly, watching out for Norma Jean and for MM, the star, who wears a tight, sparkling dress, smokes cigarettes, and keeps up a stream-of-consciousness patter: about herself as a kid, then as an object of male desire, and finally, as the film star whose unhappiness drowns her career. She is catered to by a butler who continually brings her coffee, which she downs along with many aspirin.

"I had studied Asian literature," said Casale. "That was my undergraduate major. And there's an Asian literary theory which involves attaining a perfect burst of beauty. And that's what I was trying to get. That one moment at the end where the woman is remembering all these things of her life. All the pieces come together, and it would be the peak. It would be beautiful."

The budget for sets and costumes was limited, but Maurice Palinski's design conjured the dreamlike nature of the script. There was "a drape of this gorgeous crimson velvet on the floor," said Mann, "and it was lit by candles." Casale described a stage area in a corner of the auditorium, with the audience sitting around the playing area on chairs and bleachers. Palinski had put pieces of broken mirrors at the edges of the stage floor, with candles on top of the mirrors, and at one point the Butler made his way around the entire area, lighting the candles. Then, toward the end of the play, he made his way back, blowing them out.

"I think Mick has gotten to the essence of a woman beyond this particular woman," Emily told a reporter for the *St. Paul Sunday Pioneer Press*. "A tiny moment, that last moment. Marilyn Monroe has a chance to finally say to an audience how she feels about herself and them."

"Emily had a real feel for the play," Casale remembered. "The casting was good. Anita Gromish, playing Marilyn, was beautiful, while Irene O'Brien, the woman playing the MM character, was way overweight. She was, like, poured into that dress. . . . Beautiful-ugly, beautiful-ugly. The production did what it was supposed to do, for sure."

Emily went into rehearsals believing that *Cold* could be a career breakthrough. This was her first Equity production in Minneapolis and had the imprimatur of the Guthrie, no small accomplishment for a twenty-three-year-old director. Not just local critics would be reviewing, but *Variety*, the national bible of the entertainment industry, would be covering the show as well.

But at the dress rehearsal, Mann recalled, one of the actors had "an off performance. I was a little concerned, but thought I could get her back to it. And Eugene [Lion] called me out and said, 'That's a piece of shit.' He pulled me outside, into the empty lobby. I was so upset that I said, 'No, I can do it, I can do it,' and then I started to cry. So he pushed me up against a wall and said, 'No woman director can cry. Do you want to be a housewife or do you want to be a director, because clearly what you're showing me is you're really a housewife.'"

Along with the physical shock of being manhandled to the point where her head banged hard against the wall, Emily felt assaulted psychologically. "I had no tools to handle this," Mann recalled. Sitting in her office at the McCarter and recounting the experience, she said that she believed Lion did her a favor by "toughening her up," and she remembered that "I finally pulled myself together and went back in and directed. But," she said, "it was horrible."

"Mick was a young writer, and it was his first play and it had its flaws," Mann added. "But the play was also quite beautiful. And I think I gave it the best production I could have."

The much-awaited *Variety* review dismissed all of the one-acts as "an unmemorable evening of theatre," although the critic thought Irene O'Brien as MM was "effective." Local reviews of *Cold* tended to damn the play but compliment the direction and the acting, particularly O'Brien. As for David Ball's adaptation of *Summerfolk*, Emily had written her father in January that Ball had crafted "a brilliant script." The Minneapolis critics respectfully disagreed. Peter Vaughn at the *Star* liked neither the play ("heavy-handed") nor the direction, and Mike Steele at the *Star Tribune* volunteered that Ball had "missed on this one." But Steele thought the production "superb": "Ms. Mann," he wrote, "formed a taut ensemble and moves it with a wonderful flow and a real commitment."

One month after the one-acts went up at Guthrie 2, Michael Langham fired Eugene Lion. Not because he had pushed a director up against a wall; Emily never told anyone at the Guthrie about the assault, nor did she tell her parents when they came to see *Cold*. "When someone throws you up against a wall and says, 'You're going to end up being a housewife,' you're not going to tell anyone," said Mann. "That's part of the insidiousness of that kind of violation. So I was quite typical that way. I'm sad I was, but I didn't want anyone to know that I wasn't just acing it."

Langham fired Lion primarily because Guthrie 2 was not drawing enough of an audience. The choice of plays had been poor, Langham said. The bleachers were uncomfortable. All together, the productions had played to 3,989 people, or about fifty-two at each performance, a paltry number in the Twin Cities, where, according to Mann, "People went to the theater the way Bostonians went to the movies." Langham declared that the Guthrie would not put more money into its second stage unless more appealing plays were selected.

Lion retorted publicly that Langham had approved all the scripts, had not even attended the Guthrie 2 opening night, and had seen only one performance. He called a press conference and talked about taking over Guthrie 2 himself, and he sued Langham, the Guthrie Theater Foundation, and the president of the Guthrie's board for $4.8 million for breach of contract. The suit was settled out of court in 1978 for an undisclosed amount. By then, Lion had left Minneapolis.

Emily was not sorry to see him go.

Barbara Field had called Emily "an actor's director," and the more Mann worked in the Minneapolis theater community, the more she became known for the trust she engendered in actors, and the unguarded, risk-taking performances she usually elicited in her productions. Tom Dunn, who, with Field, was one of the founders of what became the Playwrights Center, and its first director, said that whenever Emily was free, she would join the Lab for what he called "nonperformance workshops." Said Dunn, "Playwrights would sit in, to see how she worked with actors." Said Mann about her directing, in a 1988 interview with Nancy Erhard at the University of Minnesota, Duluth, "I get in and it's as if I've written [the play] and I'm acting every part . . . I just completely inhabit a piece."

Throughout Mann's career, actors and playwrights, dramaturgs and stage managers—anyone who observed Mann in the rehearsal room or in the theater during a performance—would see that she seemed to absorb the actor's performance into her own body and let it course through her, so that she often moved in rhythm with the performance as she sat in her chair, in response to emotions being expressed onstage. Janice Paran, who functioned as Literary Manager, dramaturg, and Director of Play Development at the McCarter for fourteen years, beginning in the 1991–1992 season, ascribed this to Mann's "empathic nature" and her "uncanny ability to enter the play through the skin of every one of the characters in it. I saw her transform in a rehearsal hall, as she lived through whoever was speaking at the moment. That's always given her a great facility with the emotional core of a play."

The "empathic nature" Paran cited arose in part from Mann's accessibility to her own feelings, which were often at the ready, both in daily life and when she herself was acting. Listening to the recording she taped of her first play, *Amy*, in which she acts all the parts, one hears how readily she inhabits the emotional world of each character. Yet if Mann's empathic approach emanated from her naturally, she also nourished it consciously, after observing and working with directors to whom she responded positively, like Bob Keil at the Lab School in Chicago, and directors whose approach to actors she did not wish to emulate, like Michael Langham.

By all accounts, Langham was a complicated individual. Born in England in 1919, he grew up in England and Scotland, studied drama, then law, and in 1939 enlisted in the British army, in a Scottish regiment. After being captured by the Germans in 1940, Langham spent five years in prisoner-of-war camps, staging plays to keep himself and his mates sane and teaching himself to direct. He was a perfectionist who could be cruel to an actor one minute and behave the next as though the unkindness had never occurred.

Even David Feldshuh, who admired Langham as a director, acknowledged that he "had that quick, sarcastic wit that could be extremely biting. . . . He's not the first director I've ever met that would pick somebody out from a cast, and that person would become [a] scapegoat."

Mark Lamos, who left acting for directing and eventually became artistic director of the Hartford Stage Company in Connecticut, thought Langham had "An intimidating intellectual grasp of the plays" and was "Ceaseless in pushing himself. No one worked harder." But

Lamos also recognized that Langham's way of working with actors, especially women, could be "difficult." He recalled that Langham "made them cry. And I'm talking about women who had worked with him for season after season after season. Mature actresses. . . . He could intimidate you with a horrifying precision, pick out something about you."

In June 1976, at the start of the Guthrie's 1976–1977 season, Mann embarked on the Assistant Stage Manager segment of her Bush Fellowship. She had the opportunity to be in the rehearsal room when Langham was directing Thornton Wilder's *The Matchmaker* and Shakespeare's *The Winter's Tale*, and observed Langham's style.

"He was extremely difficult to actors," Mann said during one of our interviews. "Barbara Bryne, for example, was always better at first readings than later. And I thought, 'There's something wrong there.' One of the things he would say to actors—and I remember he did this with Barbara, who was playing Dolly Levi in *Matchmaker*—he said, 'What are you doing? What are you doing? You're killing it.' And she froze. And she never really found that moment until the second week of the run. So I said (to myself), 'That's not the way to go.' I wanted to know how to stage beautifully and understand conceptually . . . and do great moment-to-moment work where you're getting the best out of actors." In retrospect, Mann observed, "I do the opposite of what Michael did when I direct. Over many years of work, I've learned a different technique. Because I couldn't bear what he did to actors' psyches. And it didn't help the work. If he had just been gentler, if he had just used all the ideas in the room, he would have had better productions. I just knew it."

"She sculpts," is how stage, film, and television star Mary McDonnell described Mann's approach. McDonnell originated the role of Cheryl in Mann's *Still Life*, and Mann subsequently directed her in Kathleen Tolan's *A Weekend Near Madison*, Mann's *Execution of Justice* on Broadway, two productions of Ibsen's *A Doll House,* and Mann's biographical play about Gloria Steinem, *Gloria: A Life*, when Mann staged her play at the McCarter Theatre. "Emily is more like a sculptor as a director. As an actor you feel complete confidence as you're building this role, because it's coming out of you, and she's sculpting it. I think a lot of actors don't understand that it is direction."

"By the time I was at the Guthrie," said Mann, "I really had pretty much developed how I work. Very actor-centric. Very deeply, emotionally based. Really pushing people to go to their limits and strip quite bare. And by then I have hopefully given them a safe place to do that. Then, working rigorously in the discipline of the moment-to-moment work."

James Morrison, who played Brick at the McCarter in Mann's 1992 production of *Cat on a Hot Tin Roof*, and acted in her McCarter productions of Marina Carr's *The Mai* and Sam Shepard's *Fool for Love*, described Mann's directing approach as "a lack of technique, because she knows how to address the humanness of a situation within the context of rehearsal and serving the play. In other words, when she talks to you as a director, she doesn't talk to you about acting, she talks about the story. She puts the story before everything else. It's always a note to Brick, not a note to James. She's talking to a human being, and the human being is within the context of the story."

"It's a child's game, acting," said Morrison. "It's a game of make-believe. And Emily facilitates that world of make-believe."

While Mann repudiated Michael Langham's way of directing actors, she did admire his way with Shakespeare. "Worth two years of graduate school for me," she recalled. "How he ripped apart a text. How he did it word by word, syllable by syllable, consonant by consonant. He looked at the punctuation. Extraordinary text work. He choreographed scenes. He was choreographing scenes to illustrate text, which is not what we do anymore. We do much more of taking deeply from the text and then, through the actor, out. That's how I direct."

Despite the educational benefits of observing Langham, in Mann's memory her season-long excursion into stage management at the Guthrie was a miserable journey. She recalled being in the rehearsal room with Mark Lamos, who was playing the title role in Marlowe's *Doctor Faustus*, Guildenstern in *Rosencrantz and Guildenstern Are Dead*, and the vagabond Autolycus in *The Winter's Tale*, and apparently she always looked so unhappy that Lamos would come over and ask if he could cheer her up (Lamos does not remember this). She was a Bush Fellow in directing, yet there she was, sitting in the rehearsal room following a script and making notes more for herself than for the directors. "I was not a good assistant stage manager," Mann conceded. "I was very messy with my book. But I learned a lot about discipline and staging and explicating text."

An unwelcome accompaniment to her drudgery as an ASM was a spinal tap performed at Abbott Hospital in Minneapolis in August 1976, in response to what Mann described as "weird symptoms." The hospital "botched it," she remembered. "It was the most painful thing I had done in my life." The technicians apparently neglected to tell her to keep her head down during the procedure, and she suffered migraines for weeks afterward.

But there were pleasurable antidotes to her ASM assignment: giving an acting class (the Guthrie let her use a rehearsal room); directing a Guthrie tour of the masks and mime entertainment *A Party for Two*, created by Dominique Serrand and Barbra Berlovitz and slated to go on the road in January 1977; and collaborating with Barbara Bryne on what was now called *Annulla Allen: The Autobiography of a Survivor*.

During the year since Emily first told Annulla Allen about the play, the two women had signed an agreement. Allen had asked for and been granted joint copyright and 50 percent of whatever payment Emily received if the Guthrie or any other theater produced the script. Emily wrote her parents that Mark Frost, a playwright with whom she had fallen in love, and with whom she was living, was "going to help me to do the final editing and structuring of the script." The immediate objective was to perform the play for Langham, who would decide whether or not to produce it at Guthrie 2 in March 1977.

In the fall of 1976, according to Barbara Bryne, she and Emily were given a rehearsal room at Vineland Place, complete with running water and a working stove so that Bryne's Annulla could boil water for tea and cook the chicken which she takes to her sister. Bryne marveled, in retrospect, that she found the time to rehearse, given a season in which she was playing demanding roles in *The Matchmaker*, *Cat on a Hot Tin Roof*, and *The Winter's Tale* in rotating repertory.

"Emily and I got together on scattered occasions and at odd hours, like ten o'clock in the morning," said Bryne. But finally she performed the play for Langham in the rehearsal room and, Bryne recalled, "He was very intrigued by it."

It was an ironic coda to Langham and Emily's relationship. "Michael Langham has told me that my stamina (lack of it) was a great disappointment to him," she wrote her father with a degree of sarcasm toward the end of December 1976:

"Never having stage-managed or having had to keep to a rigid seventy-hour a week schedule, also drunk, so drunk that he had to cancel a rehearsal, [Michael] told me that in the theater, one had to have a tough ego—that perhaps I was ill-suited to the profession, but that he thought I was a real artist anyway. I just hadn't lived up to expectations, that's all. . . . He hadn't spoken to me in months and when we finally did talk, he was nearly under the table from scotch, depression, and all the rest of his problems. Making me look like a model of stamina and responsibility, I thought, in comparison."

But unlike the previous year, when the negative reviews of *The Birthday Party* felt like a wrenching public attack on her work and on her personally, Emily survived Langham's drunken scolding with her self-esteem intact. "Hard as it is to be a disappointment to one's mentor," she wrote her father, "I find I am not disappointed with me, and when I leave my place of apprenticeship I think I will have left with more than I even knew I wanted to learn. And yes, I think one must leave one's place of apprenticeship. That is the start of self-respect and autonomy I think. I hope."

Annulla Allen: The Autobiography of a Survivor opened at Guthrie 2 on Wednesday evening, March 16, 1977.

"No one was running Guthrie 2," recalled Barry Robison, who designed both the set and Bryne's costume. "It was basically an empty stage," said the designer. "Productions were being done on an ad hoc basis, and *Annulla* was one such production." Lion had been fired, and David Ball had left the Guthrie of his own volition. Emily essentially was in charge of making her production happen.

Robison had been at the Guthrie as a milliner and had also shadowed the Guthrie's scene designers, to learn from them. When Emily asked him to design *Annulla Allen*, he was eager to begin his own design career. He and Emily, with Bryne's input, configured the floor space as a thrust with the audience on three sides, much like the Guthrie's main stage (the crippling bleachers had been replaced by about 170 conventional theater seats). "I was able to do a door and a back wall," said Robison. "Up center was a vestibule area that had a door that let out to a landing. The houselights went down, the stage lights came up, you heard some-one at the door, [she] comes in . . . and there is Barbara and applause. And she basically begins. An area for her to cook, sets a kettle on for tea, goes to cupboard for cup, saucer, biscuit, and she sets it on the table. She sits down and begins to remember." It was "scenery as backdrop," said Robison. There was no money for props or wardrobe, but the Guthrie allowed Robison and Emily to rummage about in stock and pull what they needed; Emily supplied a china teapot that had belonged to her grandmother Gussie, who had died in August 1976. Bryne wore a tai-lored suit under her coat. Set and costume, according to Robison, were "drained mostly of color, to give them a more timeless quality."

The set freed Emily and Barbara Bryne to use the entire performance area. Annulla enters her kitchen from the outdoors in a rush, shaking off an umbrella and carrying more packages than she can comfortably hold. She dumps her parcels on a counter near the stove, turns on the gas and puts a tea kettle on, all the while addressing the audience—her "visitors"—who are there to take tea with her. She tells about how she passed for Aryan and extricated her husband from the Dachau concen-tration camp, became political, and fled to England. She has written a play, and its disorganized pages lie on the kitchen table and sometimes on the floor. And while talking, she cuts up vegetables and a chicken, puts them in a pot, and exits at one point to go shopping for the special bread her sister demands (at this point in the performance at Guthrie 2 there was an intermission). At the end, she places the cooked chicken in a container, puts on her coat, collects her pocketbook and bags of groceries for her sister, and says a longing good-bye to the audience that has spent an hour or more with her.

"I would write little notes to myself" during rehearsals, Bryne recalled. "On the kitchen table, on the stove, on whatever it was, at

Barbara Bryne in the 1978 Goodman Theatre Studio production of Annulla Allen: The Autobiography of a Survivor
PHOTO COURTESY OF THE GOODMAN THEATRE

various points when I moved around. I rehearsed like this, so that I was thoroughly used to the activities: 'Poking around with the cooking'; 'Cross to table on so-and-so.' Sometimes I used the notes and sometimes I didn't. With regard to her accent, Annulla was born in Galicia, in Austria, then it became part of Poland, so her accent is up for grabs. Annulla didn't think she had an accent, but of course Emily said that she did have one, but it was slight. I didn't want too much of an accent."

"One thing about Annulla," said Bryne, "she was brave in what she did, as well as being conceited and argumentative and garrulous, and that appealed to me, because it made for variation. She's always going on about her sister Ada and then finally ends up taking the cooked chicken to Ada and the loaf of bread, complaining all the time, but really caring about her, too. And Emily, having met her, was able to describe all this to me and illuminate it."

The play's appeal at this point in its growth lies first in the vagaries of Annulla's conversation, her speech rhythms, her Annulla-isms: "I am a woman who has never any time"; "they bored me to extinction." Her conversation moves swiftly from the "disorder" of her life, to complaints about her sister, to a youthful attempt to float on massive water-lily leaves, to passing for Aryan in 1938, when her husband was imprisoned in Dachau. "Either or. Either they will find me out and kill me or I would survive," she tells her new friends in the audience.

Here, Mann's playwriting purposely mirrors the disorder of Annulla's life through the disorder of her conversation. Yet while the conversation seems to roam chaotically from one topic to another, it is not aimless. For the Annulla of this script, and for the actor playing her, there are underlying connections between one subject and another. A tale of surviving a childhood accident leads eventually to the memory of surviving the risk of posing as an Aryan. Reminiscing about her husband, whom she married because she was "bedazzled" by sex and with whom she ultimately falls in love, takes her to stories about her indifferent father, a pressuring mother, and then to her sister Ada's failed relationships with men. As with many people when voicing their recollections, Annulla begins by talking about one subject, veers to another, then returns to the first, but with a difference.

The script conveys a political message, although not, perhaps, the one an audience would expect at a play about a Holocaust survivor. Yes, Annulla expresses anger "at what was happening" to the Jews and rages that "nobody did anything about it." But that, she concludes with her typical realism, "is normal human nature." Three decades after the end of World War II, Annulla theorizes that, "If the women would start thinking, we could change everything within a year. But the women are not thinking. And that is the trouble."

Annulla has been writing a play called *The Matriarchs*, which posits that "women thinking" is the solution to the world's problems. Annulla's play will never be finished, let alone produced. The enormous manuscript, half typed, half written by hand, lies on the kitchen table or on the floor in disarray. But—and one can grant Emily a bit of well-earned schadenfreude here—the play Emily Mann imagined and shaped *is* being staged, and by a thinking woman. Through its existence in a theater, *Annulla Allen: The Autobiography of a Survivor* confirms that women are thinking, creating, and changing the male-dominated cultures into which they have been born.

The form is a monologue, but Bryne grasped that Mann intended a conversation with the audience, which Bryne evidently delivered vivaciously, with the illusion of spontaneity. Twin Cities theater reviewers considered her performance remarkable, and a couple were inclined to praise Bryne more highly than the play.

"This is supposed to be a review of 'Annulla Allen,' a new, one-woman play running through April 2 at Guthrie 2," wrote Mike Steele. "And indeed, with solemn objectivity I will try to organize my thoughts and analyze this interesting little work, but if it all turns into a love letter to Barbara Bryne, don't blame me." Nine paragraphs later, he writes that "a measure of the play's success is that we'd like to know more about [Annulla Allen]. The weakness of this form, however, is that it tends to journalism, to a brief reporting of events and thoughts without the kind of detailed description we'd like. We lose a sense of the stature and richness of Annulla Allen's experiences."

At the *Pioneer Press*, John H. Harvey wrote that, "If Miss Mann has skillfully distilled some of the essence of Annulla [Allen] into her play and equally skillfully directed the production, Barbara Bryne has fleshed her out uncannily, down to the tiniest gesture, fleeting expression and injection of Central European-accented English. One need not have met Annulla [Allen] in the flesh to know her in the person of Miss Bryne."

The underwhelmed critic at *Variety* tepidly complimented Mann for "faithfully recording both recollections and digressions," but complained about her "failing to shape the material into a cohesive stage vehicle" and concluded that "Much of the monolog is fascinating, thanks to a convincing performance by Barbara Bryne." He suggested that Mann drop the "contrived" intermission, especially since the running time was just slightly over an hour.

By contrast, Philip Weiss, in a lengthy review for *Metropolis* magazine, recognized that Bryne's performance was connected organically to the staging. Watching Bryne's Annulla move back and forth in her kitchen, he wrote, "It's as if you broke the ground with a shovel to discover a fieldmouse scurrying about in its suddenly-exposed burrows. . . . So minute is this staging that you wonder just what's in the small brown bottle Annulla Allen pours into her chicken soup." Unlike his colleagues, Weiss thought Annulla's stories "both antic and powerful."

Annulla is Mann's first effort to make theater solely from a person's own words, using those words to draw a portrait of a sometimes sympathetic, sometimes insensitive woman who has survived a traumatic time in the world's political history. What the play lacked at this point in its evolution is the playmaker's point of view about what she was presenting. It lacked authority, in the sense of authorial confidence and attitude, which a more seasoned dramatist would have supplied and which Mann brought to her next play, *Still Life* (1980), and to a 1985 version of *Annulla* titled *Annulla, An Autobiography*. In the revised version, she introduced the voice over of a young woman—Mann herself—describing her own experiences and perspectives. Absent that weight, the authority critics readily identified belonged to Barbara Bryne, who owned the role.

Arthur, Sylvia, and Carol came to Minneapolis to see the production, and Arthur praised it for being "superb theater. . . . suffused with your humanity, your artistry, your empathy, your humor, your insight."

Emily, for her part, sat in the audience, letting Bryne's performance flow through her body and feeling that maybe, in addition to directing plays, she could write them. "I thought, 'Yeah. I want to keep doing this.'"

"It will be hard to have this show close," Emily wrote her parents at the end of March 1977. "Everyone keeps saying it should go on, it cannot stop here." She did not yet have an agent, and the Guthrie, she wrote, "has been altogether unhelpful about helping me along professionally." But Emily knew Gregory Mosher, whom she had met in 1972 at the Harvard Summer Theater in Cambridge. Mosher was now Associate Artistic Director at Chicago's Goodman Theatre and Director of the Goodman's Stage 2, and when Emily was in Chicago in October 1977, directing Mark Frost's play *The Nuclear Family* for the St. Nicholas Theatre Company, she met with Mosher. The meeting was "positive," she wrote her parents. "I would like to do the show in Chicago."

On March 16, 1978, the Goodman opened *Annulla Allen: The Autobiography of a Survivor*, by Emily Mann and Annulla Allen, at the Latin School of Chicago, which had a proscenium theater with a raised stage that the Goodman used as a second stage.

"[In Chicago] it was a bigger space," said designer Barry Robison. "We were able to embellish the set, there was a lot more ceiling. But it was never a three-walled set. We always were playing to the thrust idea as much as possible." Reviewers described a purposefully fussy and cluttered kitchen.

Chicago's theater critics wrote more perceptively about *Annulla Allen* than their Twin Cities' colleagues. Richard Christiansen, the chief critic on the *Chicago Tribune*, described it as "a shrewdly constructed stream-of-consciousness monolog [sic]," although he also wrote that

"Without Bryne, the evening would probably evaporate, its moment of touching sorrows outweighed by interminable stretches of family gossip and philosophical nonsense. . . . Bryne is able to convey through her own person this endearing, engaging, all-embracing female the play obviously wants us to see."

David Elliott at the *Sun-Times* recognized Annulla's sometimes "half-baked" ramblings to be part of the play's style and Emily's intention. "Remarkably, and rather bravely, [Mann] lets Annulla speak as a person rather than a spokeswoman. Her dealings with the Hitler terror . . . are simply woven into the ragged fabric of her reminiscences." For Elliott, Mann evoked Chicago's beloved author and broadcaster Studs Terkel, who for years had regaled readers and radio listeners with oral histories of so-called ordinary people. "This is a very small play," Elliott concluded in his review, "with the modesty not to push. It works because of a fine actress, shrewd staging and the fascination of a human voice that is true to the story—the sort of thing that has made Studs Terkel's reputation."

Ironically, the legendary Chicago theater critic Claudia Cassidy, who in 1944 had defended the greatness of Tennessee Williams's *The Glass Menagerie*, volunteered in her weekly broadcast on WFMT Radio that she had walked out of *Annulla Allen* at intermission. "Acidy Cassidy," as she was known, opined that she just did not like monologues.

Two months after the Chicago opening, Earplay Radio Drama, a program of National Public Radio, carried a version that Emily had adapted for an hour-long broadcast, again with Bryne as Annulla. John Madden, a friend of Emily's whom NPR had lured from BBC Radio to Minneapolis to advise and run Earplay, directed the broadcast, which was also carried one year later by the Australian Broadcasting Commission.

The radio script, titled *Annulla Allen: an Autobiography of a Survivor*, is tighter than the stage version. Its underlying story is the love of Annulla for her husband, and Annulla's particular feminist message stands out more clearly. Atrocities such as Hitler's would never occur, Annulla believes, if women had more political power. "Men have strong feelings," she says, "but they are violent. They should not be allowed to rule. A woman's *natural* instinct is loving."

The recording offers a tantalizing hint of what Bryne's stage performance must have been like. Her high, clear voice is a little breathless as she chatters away while chopping carrots and cutting up the chicken. Her accent is slightly Eastern European, with a touch of British inflection. And her varying rhythms and inflections bring humor and compassion to her portrayal of a woman who, despite losing her country and most of her family, has survived.

7

Woman of the Theater
(1977–1979)

THE PRODUCTION of *Annulla*, rather than *Cold*, was Emily Mann's break-through in the Twin Cities. If theater people in Minneapolis–St. Paul had not heard of Emily Mann previously, they knew about her now.

To her frustration and anger, however, the powers at the Guthrie—Langham, Stephen Kanee, and Donald Schoenbaum—were not step-ping forward to offer the post of resident director which she believed she deserved, especially now that her Bush Fellowship had ended so positively.

Langham and company wrote "To whom it may concern" recom-mendations instead, as though ushering Emily on her way. Langham's letter was a mere seven typed lines, but at least he described Emily as "a gifted and dedicated artist with an enviable future." Kanee, however, began his letter by stating that he had been "highly critical of Emily's tal-ents when she first came to Minneapolis. She had a taste for the esoteric and showed a tendency to make obscure what was already difficult." He then added that "she has consciously addressed herself to these and other problems and has proven herself to be a director of professional stature and great potential."

It was a letter that no self-protective, ambitious director would ever share.

In the year between the productions of *Annulla* at Guthrie 2 in March 1977 and the Goodman, in March 1978, Emily coached actors privately to earn money and looked for directing work. She had once explored At the Foot of the Mountain, the women's theater collective where Martha Boesing was artistic director, but radical feminism did not attract her. Boesing put it bluntly: "I was an ardent, left-wing feminist," she said. "Emily was not. She wasn't there on the streets with us. Which is not to say she wasn't for women. But it's like anyplace a path diverges: weeds and woodlands for some, and others to a main road."

Boesing confessed to being "a little envious" of what she saw as Emily's upward trajectory as a director, even if Emily herself did not always feel she was progressing. "Emily was doing her own thing," said Boesing, "and that's kind of remarkable. She might have been the only visionary woman who created her own thing inside of the establishment. Emily's *Annulla* was just lovely and absolutely her foot into that world. Her obvious next step was the Guthrie."

Langham and Kanee may have been reluctant to help Emily professionally, but she persevered. The Guthrie reactivated Guthrie 2 in September 1977, and Emily's production of *Ashes*, the British playwright David Rudkin's haunting drama about a man from Northern Ireland and his English wife who try unsuccessfully to conceive a baby, opened on September 14 to laudatory reviews. Then she headed for Chicago and the St. Nicholas Theatre Company, which David Mamet had started in 1974 with the producer Patricia Cox, the actor William H. Macy, and the director Steven Schachter, and there she staged Mark Frost's *The Nuclear Family* to middling reviews (Frost would ultimately gain recogniton in film and television, notably for co-creating the 1990s television series *Twin Peaks* with David Lynch). After returning to Minneapolis Emily took what amounted to a respite for a woman who tried to fill each moment of the day with activity. She taught acting, worked out three-to-five times a week, and took weekly hikes with Frost and friends, although her affair with Frost was disintegrating. And despite Langham and Kanee's lack of support, Emily wrote her father in November that she was not yet ready to leave Minneapolis. She wanted "to try to get a season from the Guthrie with a good steady position at Guthrie Two before I make the move. I feel I have paid my dues and want the fruits of that labor before I move elsewhere."

January 1978 found her staging the Mamet one-acts *Reunion* and *Dark Pony* at Guthrie 2, to reviews which praised her ability to give Mamet's language "the right timing and space," and specifically in *Dark Pony*, bringing forth "the communion between father and child." In February she directed David Storey's *The Farm* at the newly established Actors Theatre of St. Paul. Then it was off to Chicago to direct Barbara Bryne in *Annulla Allen: The Autobiography of a Survivor* at the Goodman and participate in its recording for Earplay. She returned to Minneapolis to mount an April production at Theatre in the Round, of Charles Nolte's *The Roads in Germany*, a tender drama about three generations of a family who spend the summer by a Minnesota lake, probably for the last time, while World War II looms in Europe. Reviewing the production for the *Minneapolis Star*, Peter Vaughn wrote that "Mann's direction is relaxed yet sure in its gentle approach to the play. The moments of crisis burst out of the dreamy summer and assume frightening intensity. She always emphasizes character and doesn't seem to worry about imbuing the drama with great meaning. It succeeds very well on its own human terms and she sensibly realizes this."

The winter was rewarding artistically, but it had challenged her physically; she suffered with migraines through much of it, she told her parents. After *Roads in Germany* opened, she felt less pressured and took time off to drive with Karen Landry to Los Angeles and help her move there. While in L.A., Emily reconnected with her Harvard friends Ed Zwick and Liz Coe, both of whom were establishing television careers. She had just turned twenty-six.

At the Guthrie, the 1977–1978 theater season that ended in February was Michael Langham's last as artistic director. Fifty-three-year-old Alvin Epstein, a respected actor and the associate director of the Yale Repertory Company in New Haven, had been hired to replace him.

Epstein's hiring heralded something akin to a revolution at the Guthrie. He would be the first American to head the company; he believed new plays belonged on the main stage; he was only partially wedded to the concept of a rotating repertory; and he intended to act in the Guthrie's productions as well as direct them and run the theater. He brought with him the dramaturg Michael Feingold, who headed Guthrie 2 and became literary director, overseeing Barbara Field, who remained the literary manager.

The change in artistic leadership seemed at first to bring Emily the recognition for which she had been reaching since arriving in Minneapolis. She and Epstein shared a rapport that she had not enjoyed with Langham, and when Epstein opened the main stage season in June 1978 with his production of Henrik Ibsen's *The Pretenders*, Emily finally was listed in the program as the Guthrie's resident director. She was also associate director of Guthrie 2.

But the titles did not confer the responsibilities, or the advantages, they promised. Mann recalled that, at the beginning of the 1978–1979 season, in June, she asked the managing director, Donald Schoenbaum, for an office, a phone, and a salary, and he retorted that she should be paying the Guthrie. She believes that she did eventually receive a desk, in a corner of a rehearsal room, and a salary of sorts.

It was Feingold who chose the entries for the season at Guthrie 2, which would now offer a "Studio Series": an amalgam of staged readings, work-shopped plays, cabaret performances, and the occasional fully mounted, if spare, production. In her diary, Emily scrawled several versions of a resignation letter addressed to "Don and Alvin," noting that her job at Guthrie 2 had become merely "a coordinating position" and that her directing would entail only one staged reading and one production at Guthrie 2. The Guthrie was resisting the logical next step for a resident director: asking Emily to direct on the main stage.

In frustration, she wrote her parents that "I . . . look forward to wrapping up my Minneapolis chapter, and on to a new adventure. I think I will be moving to New York in the coming year." In the middle of June she flew east, to interview for a directing job (that did not materialize) at the Arena Stage in Washington, D.C., where Zelda Fichandler had handed the artistic reins to David Chambers for two years. She then rode the train north to spend a couple of days at the Eugene

O'Neill Playwrights Center in Waterford, Connecticut, before returning to Minneapolis, where she held separate, lengthy interviews with a Vietnam veteran, his wife, and his lover, interviews that would form the basis of her next play, *Still Life*.

She did not resign, but her status at the Guthrie did not change. When Guthrie 2 opened for the season on October 4, Emily was on the bill with a staged reading of Canadian Michel Tremblay's *Surprise, Surprise*, a slight piece involving phone calls and absurdist cacophony among three women, two of whom are planning a surprise birthday party for the third. Her only other directing assignment for Guthrie 2, also in October, was a fully staged if minimally designed production of West German dramatist Tancred Dorst's *On Mount Chimborazo*, which, despite its title, did not take place in Ecuador but atop a mountain near the border between West and East Germany. She returned briefly to acting in January 1979, when Bruce Siddons cast her as Rita in Ibsen's *Little Eyolf* at Guthrie 2, and she suffered such stage fright during one performance—Mann described it as a "panic attack"—that the experience convinced her, in case she had lingering doubts, that she could not be an actor. Nonetheless, in a production that received lukewarm reviews, the *Star Tribune*'s critic singled her out for giving "the most consistent characterization, a woman repressed and grasping hard for completeness rather than the bitchy, possessive woman so often seen."

Mike Steele wrote that *On Mount Chimborazo* "has been directed with quiet dignity and humor by Emily Mann." He had followed Emily's career in the Twin Cities since *Matrix*, in 1975, and now he wrote that "She's become an excellent naturalistic director, letting things evolve in a natural pace in an arena of quietly casual reality. Things emerge organically."

If Steele was trying to nudge the Guthrie's new artistic regime into using Emily's directing talents more frequently, he was not successful. In her diary she continued to confide her discontent and the pros and cons of staying at the Guthrie and in Minneapolis or going elsewhere. The jottings were a dialogue with herself:

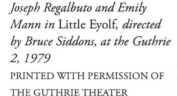

Joseph Regalbuto and Emily Mann in Little Eyolf, *directed by Bruce Siddons, at the Guthrie 2, 1979*
PRINTED WITH PERMISSION OF THE GUTHRIE THEATER

"Is this what I am worth? No. . . . I don't like it here. I have to leave."

"Look for other opportunities but not as a way to 'escape'–just to enrich–not to feel trapped. Positive–to feel free w/options."

"Work on Viet Nam project."

"My writing is crucial to my sense of well-being."

"Find a way to deal exclusively w/ Alvin - <u>not Don</u>."

And one Sunday she wrote: "<u>For myself</u>: Know I have mainstage show by Nov. 1 or leave for good."

By the end of November, however, she still had not resolved her situation. "My health is shakey [*sic*]," she wrote her parents, "a good indication that there is alot [*sic*] of stress in my life that I am not protecting myself from." Yet, she added, "Something good has come out of this battering few months. I know that my work is good. I know that my integrity is intact and that the following of people I have here love to do work with me not only because it is good work, but because they are treated with respect and dignity, and human, good feelings come through."

Soon afterward, Emily apparently presented Epstein with a request to direct on the main stage. He offered her the third production of the 1979–1980 season and asked if she would like to direct Tennessee Williams's *The Glass Menagerie*.

Not surprisingly, Emily was ecstatic. She was a passionate devotee of Williams's play, with its characters, theatrical yet so human, and its family entangled by love and anger and poverty, all in the context of a world heading toward war. Also, as Epstein must have recognized, and Emily knew instinctively, the play was an ideal choice for her particular directorial skills, her personality, and background. She also knew that she was on the verge of achieving a breakthrough in Guthrie Theater history. As a February 1979 article in the *Minneapolis Star* duly noted with a corny headline, "Mann to be 1st woman directing at the Guthrie."

For *Glass Menagerie*, Epstein and Emily selected a trio of skilled designers: Jennifer von Mayrhauser on costumes; Duane Schuler, the Guthrie's resident lighting designer; and Ming Cho Lee, whom Epstein knew from Yale and whom Bruce Siddons had also recommended to Emily, to design the scenery. "Ming Cho Lee and I have been wrestling for two days with GLASS MENAGERIE," she wrote her father in December, "and it is nothing short of inspiring. . . . I still find my deepest creativity in collaboration. There are pros and cons to this. The hardest is knowing that I have to rely on others to do my work, but the joy is when I find someone or a group of people and the chemistry is magic."

"You, Ming, made me an artist," Mann would tell him publicly at a celebration for the designer in 2018: "you smiled your beautiful warm smile and encouraged me to calm down and just tell you what the play meant to me, and I did. I had no idea if I was talking nonsense, but I did know I was speaking from my heart. . . . You told me to come back in a week. I did. You had drawn one of the most beautiful designs I have ever seen for any play."

It was the first time Lee had worked at the Guthrie and he built out the Guthrie's thrust stage, changing the shape of the stage and the interior of the theater. Mike Steele would write in his review that "Duane

Schuler's calculatedly unrealistic lighting . . . creeps on, slowly illuminating first the forestage, then the rest of the stage." Lee, he wrote, created "not only a vast playing area, but an island surrounded throughout by blackness."

On this vast playing area, isolated pieces of furniture atop flower-patterned linoleum demarked what Lee called "centers of reality": the table where the Wingfields—Amanda, Tom, and Laura—eat and argue; the bed/sofa on which Laura and Jim O'Connor, the gentleman caller, sit and share their memories of high school; the chair in which Amanda sits when chattering on the telephone. But between each sparsely furnished area the stage floor was bare, suggesting, in Lee's conception, the distance we traverse when shifting from one memory to another, or one image in a dream to another.

Upstage left and upstage right of the thrust, Lee placed narrow, vertical panels of scrim that ran all the way to the flies and, under Schuler's lighting, resembled shards of glass. Further upstage, the walls of the Wingfields' St. Louis tenement were painted scrim—flower-patterned again—and during Tom's memory scenes they seemed to disappear, so that the apartment, with its few pieces of furniture, appeared to float, dreamlike, in an immense darkness. The fire escape from which Tom addresses the audience, offering "truth in the pleasant disguise of illusion," was situated in the stage left vom, and Tom could walk onto it from the stage.

Mel Marvin composed the music, of which there was a goodly amount in the production. "I used harps and glockenspiels and a number of percussion instruments to create a kind of soundscape," he remembered, "and underneath that I put a cello that played a thematic piece at various times throughout the show. The Guthrie had speakers that went around the house, and in the sound booth they had what they called a joystick, which could be used to make the sound swirl 360 degrees."

Sitting in the darkened house, as the performance was about to start, "you saw shapes on the stage that revealed a setting with furniture," said Marvin, "but in a dark, bluey-gray miasma. There was no light on the stage. The play began in darkness, and you heard silvery bell-like sounds. . . . I used a Mark tree—slender pipes that are tuned, and you can brush them with your fingertips and make a rolling, silvery noise. The sounds appeared from different places. They played for seconds, and then all of a sudden a big swipe of silvery sound started house right and floated all around you. . . . Ultraviolet light came up on the set, creating the effect of a revolving starscape, and then gradually other lights came up, shapes took form, and the cello started playing underneath the silvery bell-like sounds and played this thematic piece that said 'and now we are in memory.'"

Emily cast unconventionally. Barbara Bryne was a tiny, stout Amanda, far more matronly than the Southern belle of her longed-for past, and more pitiable as a result. Cara Duff-MacCormick, at thirty-five, was an older, less fragile Laura than audiences were used to seeing in the part. But her age made Laura's shyness and dependence appear even more desperate. Although Williams describes Laura as "crippled" from a childhood illness and calls for her to wear a brace, Emily chose another approach. "I let the limp come and go," Mann said, "because I'd remembered that my mother's cousin Rosalind had multiple sclerosis, and my mother told me that it would be exacerbated when things were emotionally upsetting. So the limp came and went." She did not have Laura wear a brace.

John Spencer, playing Jim O'Connor, the gentleman caller, whom Laura adored when they were in high school, was appropriately a little rough around the edges yet capable of deep emotional engagement. "An emotionally fearless actor," said Mann. "Never a false moment. He didn't know how to lie on stage." As for Jeffrey Chandler in the role of Tom (not to be confused with the film star Jeff Chandler, who had died in 1961), Mann said that "for the first time in his life, he had permission to play more of what he was himself, a gay man who had to work very hard not to look it . . . I encouraged him to be his own physical self and not put on the Guthrie-classic-theater poses that I always hated. I encouraged him just to be." Bryne, Duff-MacCormick, and Chandler were already members of the company; the Guthrie brought Spencer from New York.

"Yes, this is my play," Emily wrote her parents in May 1979, during rehearsals. "It's deep in me and coming out in the most wonderful way—through the actors, designers, composer. I feel inspired and alive, not really sure where we will end up, but confident so far in the life it has of its own."

According to many of the theater artists with whom Mann has worked over the years, one of her special skills was her collaborative ability. "Emily is always involved with all of the ideas," said Mel Marvin. "She was always pushing everybody forward, and that's why we ended with something so unusual . . . where all the design elements came together to make something coherent. That was Emily conducting and orchestrating."

She was understandably nervous. "This was the biggest production of my life," Mann said years later. She had watched rehearsals in that theater, seen performances, but as a director, she had to learn the Guthrie stage. She discovered that "You had to keep actors moving. . . . Or find the sweet spots on the stage where they could be still." Once, during rehearsals, Spencer spent the entire night alone in the theater, with only a ghost light onstage for company, running lines by himself and exorcising his fear of the hallowed Guthrie hall. Bryne, by contrast, knew exactly how to play that stage and the house. "As soon as she entered," Mann said, "the audience roared. They adored her."

Barbara Bryne agreed that normally she would not have been cast as Amanda, but she recalled that "Emily and I talked together about her and decided that Amanda was constantly changing. Williams meant her to be laughed at, and a lot of times she was silly, and also infuriating. But she loves her children. That's what attracted me to her. One minute you want to wring her neck and the next minute you want to comfort her. I got laughs, and I think they were intentional, but I could also break the laughter."

"What made Barbara's Amanda so rich," said Mann, "was the combination of the deep love she had for her children—deep, deep love—and the humor Barbara saw at every point. She's a very funny actress. She was also a little dumpling, and she hopped around and saw herself as the most beautiful thing, and there was something so dear and funny and tragic about Amanda's delusions. It was just captivating."

Emily saw Amanda's need to save her children as "the huge arc of the play." But Emily's way into the play was through Laura, and the production's emotional impact was fiercest during the scene in which Tom brings his friend Jim O'Connor home for supper, and Amanda purposefully leaves Jim and Laura together in the living room.

Rehearsing with Duff-MacCormick had been challenging, because, Mann put it delicately, "Cara wasn't in reality a lot. . . . she just saw things differently." But ultimately the actor's state of mind worked for the role and for the scene. "Everyone was in an altered space, and John used it, to let himself become altered. So Jim was a regular guy who suddenly saw magic and fell deeply in love." Von Mayrhauser dressed Duff-MacCormick in an ankle-length white dress for this scene, and Jim in a white suit. "Their dance was like her wedding dance," said Mann, "and he felt it too." During their waltz, Laura's slight limp disappeared completely.

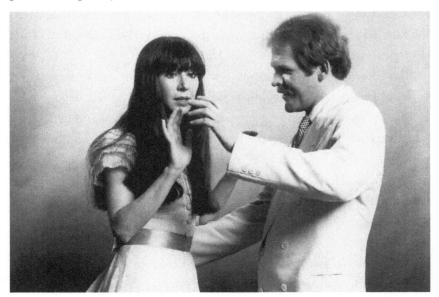

Cara Duff-MacCormick and John Spencer in The Glass Menagerie, *directed by Emily Mann at the Guthrie Theater, 1979*
PHOTO BY BOYD HAGEN

Mann was convinced that Williams wrote the scene to be played as a love scene. "If the gentleman caller doesn't fall in love with Laura—if it isn't mutual and if it isn't hard for him to leave and go back to his fiancée—then there isn't enough at stake. Then it's just pathetic. This was not pathetic. It was wrenching."

After Jim leaves, Amanda berates her son for bringing home a man who is already engaged to another woman, and her tirade finally drives Tom out of the house and out of his beloved sister's life. "Tom is not a fool for having invited Jim over," said Mann, telling the story of the play's ending as she interpreted it. "Tom was actually being a good brother and a good son. When it's all thrown into his face . . . it hurts more. It's just an incredible ripple effect, how deep the play goes. He loves his mother, adores his sister, and this destroys him. So he goes. During the last monologue, Tom's monologue, people in the audience were just wracked with sobs."

"This [is] an unforced and airy production," wrote Mike Steele, "leading inexorably, quiet moment upon quiet moment, to the play's thunderclaps of passion and emotion as the yearnings and loneliness, the false hopes and fading dreams of the lacerated Wingfield family are slowly exposed."

The actor Gerry Bamman, who was at the Guthrie that season, and with whom Emily was having an affair, said that he fell in love with Emily's work after seeing *Glass Menagerie*. Arthur Mann wrote his daughter that "in depicting the fragility of their lives, you reminded the audience of how vulnerable all our lives are. This last you did ever so delicately, . . . Here again your life-giving view was contagious. All of us who saw the play felt enlarged by it, chastened but glad to be human . . . . Tennessee Williams has found in you his kind of humanitarian (and artistic) director."

Tennessee Williams's younger brother Dakin came to a performance and reportedly called this production of the play the finest he had seen. Nearly two years later, Emily met Tennessee Williams for the first time, at a birthday party that the Goodman threw for the seventy-year-old playwright in Chicago. Mann recalled that they were sitting together on a couch, and Williams asked her to help with what turned out to be his last full-length play, *A House Not Meant to Stand: A Gothic Comedy.* Dakin had told him about Mann's extraordinary production of *Menagerie*, he said. They would live at his home in Key West, Tennessee promised, and work on the script together. He put his head in her lap and wept, "because you understood my mother so well," Mann remembered him saying. She held him and sadly declined the invitation, and never forgave herself for what she considered her cowardice. But she just could not muster the will to wrestle with Williams's depression and addictions, or with a script that, in her opinion, needed more repair than she knew how to provide.

The Glass Menagerie opened on Wednesday evening, June 20, 1979. During intermission, Emily went to look for Epstein in his office. Someone had turned on a television, high on a wall, and suddenly Emily was watching her artistic director being interviewed on a local newscast. He had just "resigned," a euphemism, one journalist wrote, "that should fool no one."

"It was devastating," Mann recalled, "and I had kept warning him. Because I had been around the Guthrie enough to know the Byzantine, subterranean way they plotted and planned, like some old, corrupted court. He didn't know the knives were out. He had walked in with his little white fluffy dog, and he looked like a gay man coming to work, and I thought Don Schoenbaum would take out a knife then. I knew Schoenbaum was trying to get him fired. I heard it, I knew it."

The Twin Cities' theater community and the journalists who covered it had heard for months about staff and audience dissatisfaction with Epstein. Subscriptions and single-ticket sales were down. Critics were less than enchanted. As Emily learned later when she was hired at the McCarter Theatre Center, a new artistic director's first season can be a precarious thing. Subscribers comfortable with one artistic director's taste have trouble adjusting to another's. Longtime staff resent a new regime. A board becomes nervous. Epstein never had the internal support that might have protected him during a first, rough season.

In July, Mike Steele wrote a profile of Emily for the *Star Tribune* and focused on her position as the first woman to direct on the Guthrie main stage and "one of the first to enter the halls of regional theaters anywhere." Adopting a jaunty style, Steele wrote that, "The heavens thundered, of course, and there were tremors, but when things calmed down, Mann's production of Tennessee Williams's 'The Glass Menagerie' was clearly the first strong production of the Guthrie season."

At Radcliffe and in Minneapolis, Emily had championed feminist causes, brutally aware of how sexism affected her profession and her place in it. But for Steele's article she resisted the mantle he was placing on her shoulders, although, later in her career, she would proudly cite her status as the first woman to direct at the Guthrie.

"I don't consider this a symbol," she told Steele, referring to breaking the Guthrie's particular glass ceiling. "On the other hand, I don't want to minimize the problems of women directors. They're real. If this in any way helps other women, I'm happy, but I want to be judged as a stage director, not as a woman director. It has been hard being a woman and a director," she continued. "It's hard getting a job. Management doesn't like to hire women except for 'women's plays.' I want to direct 'Richard II,' 'King Lear,' 'The Tempest.'" As the feminist and activist Gloria Steinem famously declared, "Whoever has power takes over the noun - and the norm - while the less powerful get an adjective." With admirable, if naive, optimism, Emily told Steele that "In 10 years we won't even discuss these problems."

In part, Emily was using the interview to respond to patronizing reviews that had taken her status as a woman and a director into account when critiquing the production. Peter Vaughn in the *Star Tribune* lamented that Emily "had pushed aside Tom's centrality" in the play and he concluded that "Mann's message, of course, is that nobody, least of all a man, will take [Laura's] hand . . . if Laura is to escape, she must, like her mother, move her own mountains."

Don Morrison, writing for the same paper, took an opposite, but similarly stereotypical, view. Morrison had hoped that Mann, because she was a woman, "would explore some unexamined focuses on the women's side of this long-popular play, thus lending it a reawakened impact." He averred that "a fascinating feminist case could be made" because "in many of Williams' texts . . . men historically have the power to victimize women, who classically have the greater sensitivity." He wished Mann "had given it a whirl."

An editor with a wry sense of humor ran the two pieces on the same page.

"Of course I'm a feminist," Emily told Steele. But she also told him, "I don't want to get into the feminist director category. I'm really a humanist, not just a feminist. I don't think there's a particular women's view anyway, just different persons' views."

Sitting in her office at the McCarter Theatre Center, forty years after her conversation with Steele, Mann took back her statement about there not being "a particular women's view . . . just different persons' views."

"I totally don't agree with that. But I know why I said it then," Mann explained. "I kept being asked what made my interpretation of *The Glass Menagerie* feminist. And I said, 'Well, I don't think it is.' It's just that I'm a woman and I can't separate myself from my sexuality and my gender. So I am a woman directing *The Glass Menagerie*. But I'm not just a *woman* directing *The Glass Menagerie*. I'm a particular individual. Artists are unique. If they're any good. So you bring all that you are to that play and interpret it and unearth it and try to commune with the great Tennessee."

"It wasn't that I didn't want people to know that a barrier had been broken and that this was an important barrier to break. It was more that I thought, 'Would it be good for the cause, and for other women and myself, for people who had never experienced a woman's direction before, to be spending all their time trying to figure out what made this a woman's production? It's that I directed it. And there might be a way that I come at it that might be different from a man, but every single director will come at it differently. . . . you're seeing a play directed by Emily Mann. That means a woman has directed it, yes. And I would go on to say, 'I'm also a mother, I'm also a wife, I'm a Jew, I'm also a daughter, I'm also an American. There are a lot of labels you can put on me. A lot of ways you can describe me. And 'woman' is certainly intrinsic.'"

Underlying Emily's responses to Steele was also the personal issue of whether she could have a profession that demanded long hours and might take her anywhere in the world, and still have a partner and make a family. Emily, whose letters to her parents during the 1970s express the longing for a committed relationship, made a point of telling Steele that "I want to hold on to femininity. I want to have a family and think I can do both. How can I espouse this great humanity in theater and not want to have children?"

"How I would articulate it has definitely changed," said Mann during the interview in Princeton. "But I'm not sure I have [changed]. I was being told that you had to make a choice between being a theater director and playwright, and having a family. I was told that you really couldn't do both. And I worried about that a lot. . . . It scared me then to go to New York, it scared me to again have to position myself to go where I thought I belonged. And I had a rather high opinion of myself. I thought I was going to be one of the most important directors in the country. . . but I also wanted to be in love, and I wanted to have a husband, and I wanted to have children . . . and I was constantly being told I couldn't do all that." Defending her language, she noted that "'Feminine' had become a dirty word" in the feminist lexicon, "and I decided to retrieve it. As something beautiful and wonderful and mine."

One more woman was scheduled to direct on the Guthrie's main stage during that 1979–1980 season: Rae Allen, who directed Samuel Beckett's *Endgame*. After Allen, the Guthrie reverted to its old ways, as though the Women's Liberation Movement had never happened. No woman directed on the main stage again until Mann returned in October 1985 to stage her own play, *Execution of Justice*.

After Epstein was fired, the Guthrie made it clear that there was no role for Emily on the main stage or at Guthrie 2, which in any case vanished from the Guthrie's agenda. The Guthrie terminated its lease on the old Southern Theater and closed the doors in 1979. Only after Garland Wright became artistic director, in 1986, did the Guthrie again use a second performance space.

In July, Stephen Wadsworth drove from New York to see *Menagerie*. He made a point of seeing as many of Emily's productions as he could, but *Menagerie* was special because Emily had dedicated the production to his twenty-year-old sister Nina, who had died the previous May in an automobile crash.

He also helped Emily finally move from Minneapolis, a leave-taking that she mourned but had decided was necessary both personally and professionally. She had sold her car, so they crammed Wadsworth's with five years' accumulation of belongings and drove to Chicago for a visit with Emily's parents. Then they continued east to New York City.

8

Still Life

(1979–1981)

THE NEW YORK CITY to which Emily Mann moved late in the summer of 1979 was emerging fitfully from a turbulent decade. The city of Times Square and Greenwich Village, Yankee Stadium and the Brooklyn Bridge, had nearly gone broke, and Gerald Ford, who became president on August 9, 1974, after Richard Nixon resigned to avoid being impeached, declined to provide federal help. As the *New York Daily News* famously announced on October 30, 1975, with its famously succinct headline: "FORD TO CITY: DROP DEAD."

Mann arrived in New York City determined to make a career as a director, whatever the odds. At first she moved in with her sister in Brooklyn. The two women were getting along somewhat better now that they were older (Carol was thirty and had started her own literary agency; Emily was twenty-seven). Photographs from that time show the two sisters cavorting on the sidewalks of New York, making faces for the camera, and apparently enjoying each other's company. But soon Mann began searching for her own place, and when the actor Gerry Bamman asked her to live with him, she moved into Bamman's ground-floor apartment at 317 East Sixth Street, between First and Second Avenues in Manhattan's East Village—an apartment that Bamman described as "kind of a loft space," with a galley kitchen and a garden out back. It was a neighborhood of antiquated buildings and tenements, offering affordable apartments; of Ukrainian eateries and mom-and-pop stores; art galleries and bars and clubs: Pyramid, World's End, C.B.G.B. Drug

Emily Mann on the sidewalks of New York, 1979
COURTESY OF EMILY MANN

addicts held sway in Tompkins Square Park, but punk-rock musicians, visual artists, and theater folk owned the streets.

Bamman was an exceptional cook, and he and Emily often invited friends over for informal dinners and parties. Through Bamman, Mann met a coterie of New York theater people, notably the actor and playwright Wallace Shawn; playwright Michael Weller and his wife Kathy, who lived nearby; and the playwrights Charles L. Mee and Kathleen Tolan.

Mann had seen Bamman perform at the Loeb Drama Center, when she was at Radcliffe, and then in Minneapolis at the Firehouse during the fall of 1974, in both cases when André Gregory's theater company, the Manhattan Project, of which Bamman was an original member, staged its iconoclastic *Alice in Wonderland.* According to Bamman, he and Emily had met once, briefly, introduced by the actor Laura Esterman. But they had begun an affair during the Guthrie's 1979–1980 season, when Bamman was there on a three-play, six-month contract.

Not all of Mann's friends understood her attraction to Gerry Bamman. The lawyer Nadine Strossen, a Radcliffe alumna whom Emily had met in Minneapolis and considered a good friend, found the actor "not particularly welcoming and warm." Strossen believed he was not really interested in anyone outside of the theater. Stephen Wadsworth described Bamman as "extremely taciturn" and "a very internal person," while Emily was "always turned outwards."

But unlike other men with whom Emily had had relationships since leaving college, Bamman was not dependent on her, either psychologically or, at the outset, for money. Eleven years older than Emily, he was a working actor and had a reputation for being a skilled, if demanding, performer. He and Emily were united in terms of resolutely pursuing careers in the theater and helping each other succeed. And Bamman was besotted with her.

The couple first worked together for the British director David Jones, who had been hired in 1979 by Harvey Lichtenstein, president of the Brooklyn Academy of Music, to form the BAM Theater Company, to perform plays in repertory. With a company of at least thirty actors, and the need to fill BAM's 1,000-seat Helen Owen Carey Playhouse at each performance, this was an ambitious, expensive project. Yet in David Jones, who had been the artistic director of the Royal Shakespeare Company at London's Aldwych Theatre, Lichtenstein had someone with a British imprimatur, positive advance press, and now a three-year contract.

Mann had met Jones briefly in Minneapolis, and in September 1979, her newly acquired New York agent, Ellen Neuwald, or perhaps Mann herself, followed up by sending Jones a résumé and reviews of *The Glass Menagerie*. Jones wrote back that he had talked with Alvin Epstein, who praised the *Menagerie* production highly, and while Jones could not assure her of a slot during the first, short season, which would begin in February 1980, he thought there might be an opportunity during the second season. In the meantime, he would try to see some of her work.

The American playwright Richard Nelson also recommended Mann to Jones. Nelson had met Emily in 1978 when Guthrie 2 produced his play *The Vienna Notes*. He was now literary manager for the BAM company, tasked with finding rarely performed but stimulating scripts from which Jones could choose a first season. Among the plays that Nelson suggested was Rachel Crothers' three-act drama *He and She*, which was first tried out on the road in 1911 under the title *The Herfords*. A revised version, now titled *He and She*, was ultimately produced at Broadway's Little Theatre, where it opened with Crothers playing the lead on February 12, 1920, nine months after Congress passed the Nineteenth Amendment to the Constitution, granting American women the right to vote, and six months before the Amendment was ratified, on August 18, 1920.

Nelson recalled, "The discussion was, if we were going to do this, we were going to do it with a woman director. There was no question, that was part of the fun and the interest in it, because the play asks [feminist] questions and then it veers seemingly to the wrong answer." In 1979, according to Nelson, the list of women who were directors was short, but "I said I have met this woman at the Guthrie Theater . . . David, I'm sure, called her in."

Jones hired Mann to make her New York City directing debut with Rachel Crothers' *He and She*, slated to open in May 1980.

Of the BAM Theater Company's four directors that season, Mann was the only woman—a position, she was aware, that drew favorable attention to her. That a young director, and a woman, would garner such visibility so soon after arriving in New York City was unusual. What is more, in a rider to her contract, BAM agreed to give Mann's name the same size and prominence in programs and publicity as David Jones would receive for his BAM debut, directing *The Winter's Tale*. Richard Nelson was correct that the list of women directing in the theater was short, but only in comparison to the list of men. During the 1979–1980 New York season for which Jones hired Mann, two African American women, Glenda Dickerson and Vinnette Carroll, were each staging a musical on Broadway (Carroll, in 1972, had been the first African American woman ever to direct on Broadway when she staged Micki Grant's musical *Don't Bother Me, I Can't Cope*). Off Broadway, numerous women were trying to make careers as freelance directors, artistic directors, or both, among them Sue Lawless, Elinor Renfield, Judith Martin, Nancy Rhodes, Elizabeth Swados, Susan Schulman, Mary B. Robinson, Dorothy Lyman, Lynne Meadow, and Carol Rothman. A former actor named Julia Miles, who was associate director of the American Place Theatre at 111 West 46th Street, was intent on bringing women who wrote plays into the theatrical mainstream, and in 1978, with an $80,000 grant from the Ford Foundation, Miles had launched the first season of the Women's Project at the American Place Theatre. During the first two years of the Women's Project, Miles presented seven productions in what was called the "SubPlot" at the American Place, and each production was written by and staged by a woman.

He and She is set in a comfortable New York City house in 1911 and primarily involves a married couple, Tom and Ann Herford, and their sixteen-year-old daughter, Millicent, who comes home unexpectedly from boarding school. Both the Herfords are sculptors: Tom more famous, Ann more talented. Tom supposedly believes in a marriage between equals, until both submit designs for a $100,000 commission, and Ann wins, to Tom's and her elderly father's annoyance.

Crothers, who never married and always supported herself by acting, directing, and writing for the commercial theater, juxtaposed first-wave feminist views of women as independent and self-reliant with nineteenth-century assumptions of women as home-bound, maternal, and self-sacrificing. But Ann Herford follows a different route from her creator. When Millicent reveals that she has fallen in love with a chauffeur at school and wants to marry him, she blames the seduction largely on her mother, whom she believes would rather make art than attend to her daughter's loneliness. And so, painful though the decision is, Ann refuses the award, lets her husband win, and gives up sculpting to take her daughter abroad and tend to the girl's needs. "There isn't any choice, Tom," Ann Herford tells her husband; "she's part of my body—part of my soul."

Structurally the play is of its time: three acts with an end-of-second-act surprise. Yet despite its early twentieth-century vintage, *He and She* can feel contemporary. Gender conflicts then were still gender conflicts in 1980. There is the husband who seems to support his wife's creativity, only to become unhorsed when her artistry outpaces his. There is Ann's insecurity about her talent, and her disappointment when her husband is not as joyous about her win as she hoped he would be. Ann, not Tom, gives up her chance to be an artist, believing that her truly important creation is her daughter and that it is her role, not her husband's, to come to the rescue. Crothers lets the women and men in the audience ponder if Ann's decision is the best decision and implicitly asks women if they would do better to follow their own stars and not marry at all.

But the play's period ambience can be an obstacle for a contemporary audience, and Mann's private notes suggest that she wrestled with how to reconcile "Old New York cliché buttressed against absolutely modern people"; "They are living the ideal life everyone wants . . . buttressed against 1911 feminism or probs of men & women." How to make that relevant for 1980 audiences? "UNIVERSAL—not period. Modern, today! US" was Mann's answer in jottings she wrote to herself.

Her early notes for *He and She* also demonstrate the kind of research she often embarked upon ahead of a production. Focusing on New York City during the first two decades of the twentieth century, she cites, "Race for skyscrapers. Rapid transit. Automobiles! 1910. 1911—Gibson girls. Armory Show 1913; Edward Steichen. Alfred Steiglitz." Also, "City going thru constant changes. Backdrop for personal changes," and "Act One: This is how life should be," Mann wrote, "as exuberant as the image of New York itself. Exuberance. Dreams. Crash."

Mann cast Bamman as Tom Herford (when Jones hired Mann, part of the arrangement was for Gerry to become a BAM Theater Company member). Laurie Kennedy was cast as Ann Herford. The company did not have an actor who could play sixteen-year-old Millicent, so the casting director, Elizabeth Woodman, brought in numerous young women who could conceivably portray an early-twentieth-century teenager. Among them was a twenty-four-year-old actor named Cherry Jones, who had never worked in New York before. "After Cherry's audition," said Woodman, "we all went, 'Well, she's so tall.' And then we said, 'Well, but Gerry's tall.' And then everybody at the same time went, 'Who cares?'" And so Cherry Jones made her New York acting debut in *He and She*.

At the first read-through, according to Mann's private notes, she encouraged the actors to "PERSONALIZE. 1) Natural speech—make it our own . . . 2) Talk to each other cannot be 'acted'—universal to today." She told the cast that Crothers thought *He and She* her most important play, and that the play is "Still import. today."

The first reading, according to Mann's notes, was "superb - alive, fun; the play works." The only actor about whom she had any concerns was Kennedy as Ann. "Day Two: Laurie still blocked." Then, "Day Three: L. breaks through. G. with her." On "Day 4 . . . get on our feet. Major excitement. Staging, relationships, life."

Laurie Kennedy probably had no inkling that Mann was concerned. She remembered the rehearsals being "very fluid. Sitting on the floor, doing whatever you wanted. . . . [Emily] would try anything, or go with the flow about it. If things began to feel too rigid, she'd suggest doing something else. You never felt that you were doing something wrong, though, and that she was correcting it. She kept things loose." Kennedy recalled that Mann even asked the actors to meet with the costume designer, Jennifer von Mayrhauser, to discuss "what *we* wanted to wear, which I'd never experienced."

Mann had worked with von Mayrhauser on *The Glass Menagerie* and trusted her. Mann was less confident about scenic designer John Jensen; she thought his first model did not capture the sense of "old/new" that she wanted. Other than the model, all Mann had received from Jensen as she went into rehearsal was a raw floor plan. She wanted drawings "Now," she wrote in a note to herself, "or I think we may have to part company."

Except for worries about the set design, Mann felt confident in the work. Her direction became more specific as rehearsals moved toward opening night. "Big scene: L/G work at table & then up. Allow no denial, soul-search—no block to reality"; "Act 3: Laurie/Cherry: Discuss the fear of sex/disgrace. Also—their intimacy, manipulation"; "Bamman—still conflict at end—don't rat on artist in you." She staged the Herfords' quarrel about the prize money so that they were at opposite sides of the stage, and Steve Lawson, in his review for the *Soho Weekly News*, described women on the stage "wandering silently at the start of the second and third acts."

Photographs indicate that Mann finally got the "old/new" combination she had wanted for her set, at least in Act I, which takes place in the Herfords' sculpture studio. Jensen designed a spacious, high-ceilinged room with faux-wood beams, a skylight above, a tiled floor below, and electric lights with half-shades dangling from the ceiling. Minimal furniture included a planked wooden table and one of Ann's sculptures, of a reclining nude woman, on a pedestal. For Acts II and III, Jensen gave the Herfords' living room selective pieces of formal period furniture.

He and She opened on a Thursday evening, May 29, 1980, to a deluge of conflicting reviews. Marilyn Stasio in the *New York Post* called the production a "triumph"; Edith Oliver in *The New Yorker* called it "soggy." At the *Christian Science Monitor*, David Sterritt wrote that "the

Far left: Gerry Bamman. Right of center: Laurie Kennedy. He and She, *directed by Emily Mann at the Brooklyn Academy of Music, 1980.*
BAM HAMM ARCHIVES. PHOTO: © KEN HOWARD

production sparkles from beginning to end," but at *New York Magazine* John Simon dismissed everything: play, acting, direction. To Steve Lawson in the *Soho Weekly News*, *He and She* was "BAM's most successful ensemble production yet," and he praised Mann's direction, which "nicely underscores the play's meanings with memorable images." In the *New York Times*, second-string critic Mel Gussow described Mann's direction as "busy" and the play as "conventional and repetitious," while Erika Munk in the *Village Voice* blamed "The guys at the BAM Theater Company" for selecting "such a lame chunk of three-act parlour realism." She surmised that the company's leadership just wanted to "round out the season with a play by a woman, something relevant, something that touches on present experience, something that gives us a reason to use a woman director."

In short, Mann had met the New York critics, and some were not kind.

The day after the opening, she flew to Tokyo on a grant she had received several months earlier from the Japan–U.S. Friendship Commission, to observe and learn about traditional and contemporary forms of Japanese theater. Bamman sent her the *He and She* reviews, and in her diary she wrote that, while "jolted" by the unfamiliar environment of Japan, "more than anything I feel jolted by reviews! . . . I wonder if I have no eye, no vision, whether I can really direct at all. Whether the vulgarity of NY & its reviewers will ever understand me." She chided herself for not having "a commercial eye – I am amazed at what sells & what fails here." Maybe, she concluded, "I'll be able to go back & put it all together."

She gave herself encouragement by returning to her own writing and temporarily returning to the Midwest to direct. There, in October 1980, Chicago's Goodman Theatre produced the world premiere of *Still Life*, which, Mann often said, "formed me as an artist."

Mann's play *Still Life* was born in the Twin Cities. Nadine Strossen had seen *Annulla Allen: The Autobiography of a Survivor* at Guthrie 2 in March 1977, and sometime afterward proposed that she, Emily, and a friend of Strossen's go out to dinner. Strossen's friend had a story to tell about a former Marine with whom she was having an affair, a veteran of the Vietnam War. He was haunted by his experience, and perhaps, Strossen suggested, his story could be the basis for a play.

Emily was intrigued, but she did not meet with the man immediately; from spring 1977 through spring 1978, she had been directing one play after another. But during the summer of 1978, she met with the former Marine in a conference room at the Guthrie to hear his story firsthand.

The pages and pages of transcript from subsequent recorded interviews testify to the man's pain and guilt, and his plain need to talk. He spoke about experiences he found both frightening and inexplicably exciting: operating with his unit one day in a booby-trapped area; walking along and tripping wires connected to grenades; being so scared he shit his pants; competing with his best friend to be the one who could set up the most and best ambushes and get the most kills. Emily was both shaken and mesmerized by the torrent of words, by the ugliness of what this man saw and did, and told about in a detached, odd monotone. Raw descriptions of his relationships to his fellow Marines, his parents, and his wife were searing.

Mann elicited the Marine's accounts without pressing him or pushing for answers, an ability that would serve her again when talking with strangers for *Execution of Justice* (1984) and *Greensboro (A Requiem)* (1996). "I think I went in with questions and quickly put them away, because he wanted to tell me what he wanted to tell me. And then I would listen and I might ask another question, and he would go on for ten, twelve, fifteen minutes. It was just astounding. I left there shell-shocked. I was just so numbed by it. It was so awful, all the things he was telling me, that I couldn't absorb it all."

Asked years later by Michael Bigelow Dixon and Liz Engelman about her interviewing technique, for their book *The Playwright's Workout*, Mann described her approach as searching for "the spill," that moment when the subject drops protective shields and tells all. "If you are really listening and really participating," she told Dixon and Engelman, "eventually you will ask the right question for your subject to break and let it all out." On the transcripts of her interviews with the Vietnam veteran, her questions are hardly even questions: "What's a Marine?" "Ever do that when you were angry?" Her comments, interjected after long passages when she was listening, are really more prompts than questions: "You talk about how good you felt and then you talk about destroying yourself."; "There are so many contradictions."; and, during one interview with the Marine, "I feel like crying." The Marine talked and talked, and talked some more. About six months after their first meeting, he told Mann that he had murdered an entire North Vietnamese family, a revelatory spill that became The Confession, the climactic moment of the play. "I . . . I killed three children, a mother and father in cold blood."

Mann recalled feeling unsure if she could face the emotional turmoil that a play about a veteran of the Vietnam War would arouse.

Arguments with her father about the war had bruised her and stirred rage at her father she had not known she possessed. She was reluctant to reopen wounds that were not completely healed, even ten years later. But the Marine urged Emily to talk with his wife, who was six months pregnant with their second child. And one day Cheryl, as she is called in the script, visited Emily at her apartment in Minneapolis, while the Marine (Mark in the play) waited for his wife outside. Sitting in Emily's rocking chair, the Marine's wife described her husband as a man who repeatedly got drunk and hit her. She considered leaving him, she told Emily, except then she would be alone with two kids to raise. By contrast, Mark's lover (Nadine in the play) told Emily that Mark, who, like Nadine, had become a photographer, was sensitive, considerate, and artistic, and the gentlest man she'd ever known.

As Mann recalled her process, it was the two women's radically different experiences of the same man, combined with the Marine's personal, horrific war, that finally stimulated her to write the play. The Vietnam vet in fact encouraged Emily to tell his story and thought a woman would be the ideal storyteller:

> I want it to come off the way it is, the way I am; the only way it can is to give it to a woman. Number one, there's nothing you have to question about it in terms of glorifying it in any way. And number two that eliminates a lot of the bull-shit. That eliminates the war story type of thing. It's a tragedy is what it is. . . . The time is right to blow apart that whole male mythology of what war is, for the bull-shit it is.

Initially, Emily constructed the play as a series of three separate, lengthy monologues, an approach based on how she had created *Annulla Allen* and also on the force of these three people's words. During the summer of 1979, after *The Glass Menagerie* opened in June, she directed two readings of the new script, one of them at the Walker Art Center, which was adjacent to the Guthrie. John Spencer read Mark; Barbara Bryne read Nadine; and an actor named Nancy Bagshaw, who was eight months pregnant at the time, read Cheryl, the Marine's pregnant wife. The characters did not speak to each other, but in Bagshaw's recollection, "we were directed to react to each others' monologues, so there was unspoken 'dialogue.'" The actors sat in chairs, facing Emily and a small group of friends. Said Bagshaw, "John and I fell into step quickly and I remember how powerful our scenes were—the writing jumped off the page. I also remember Emily's girlish gasps at regular intervals during our scenes." In Mann's typed notes prior to the reading, she wrote in capital letters, as though underlining the note's importance or perhaps her own discovery, "THEY COME ALIVE__THEY NEVER TALK TO EACH OTHER__STRAIGHT OUT TO AUDIENCE. BUT THEY SEEM TO UNDERSTAND WHAT HAS BEEN SAID__RESONANCES IN THE AIR AND BETWEEN THEM. THEY SENSE EACH OTHER."

Gerry Bamman attended that reading, and Mann always credited him with suggesting that the script would be more dramatic if she broke up the three monologues so that the three characters' words were intercut, as though the three people were responding to each other. "I can't tell what made me think of this notion of intercutting and splitting it all up," Bamman said. "I think I just felt it needed more variety than three monologues. And it wasn't so ingenious an idea. It just brought them into contact with each other a little bit more." He joked that, later on, Mann was not always so receptive to his ideas as she had been to this one.

Another reading took place that summer of 1979, somewhere in the Minnesota countryside, and Steven Marcus, who had studied acting with Emily in Minneapolis, read Mark. "The play blew everyone's minds," Mann recollected, "and I called Greg Mosher in the middle of the night, woke him up and said, 'You have to do this.'"

Mann worked on the script during her last days in Minneapolis and after moving to New York, breaking up the monologues into brief comments and observations and revelations, forming them into rhythmic, poetic lines, and interweaving them so that they seemed to bounce and reflect off each other. There were still extended passages, but nothing like the monologues Mann had originally transcribed and edited. The most recognizable remnant of Mann's original dramatic structure was that the play contained three "acts," and each act belonged more to one character than the others.

Gregory Mosher was now the Goodman Theatre's artistic director and he scheduled a production in the Goodman Theatre Studio, a 135-seat proscenium house, for October 1980. Mann offered the role of the Vietnam veteran to John Spencer and cast the other two parts with actors who auditioned in New York City: Mary McDonnell as Cheryl, Timothy Near as Nadine.

Near remembered thinking that Emily looked like "a hippie Bridget Bardot," with "that sort of wonderful Bardot poutiness." She also remembered that the audition was the longest of her acting career. "I think she cast me because the three of them—John, Mary, and Emily—were just like electric wires," Near said, interviewed in California, where for twenty years she was artistic director of the San Jose Repertory Theater. "There was energy that just sizzled in the room, and I think she needed somebody who was a little calmer. That's kind of a joke, but maybe has a bit of truth. We were sort of a gang, the four of us."

They all wanted to work on the play together before heading to the Goodman, Mann remembered, and the choreographer Twyla Tharp, with whom Gerry Bamman had once worked, loaned the group her Manhattan studio for about ten days.

Mann recalled,

> We just dived in. Using the words. But no rules. And all this shit came out. Oh my God. That ended up being part of what made this production so amazing. We would do all these different exercises. Mary one time wanted to do it blindfolded. Why? None of us could ever figure out. But it cracked John up so much he could barely stop laughing. Whatever works for her. So we put Mary in a blindfold. We rehearsed some days when they could hear everything the others said and they could respond to it, and days when they heard nothing. Days when they didn't hear but they felt what

the other was saying. So Mary began to feel the sexual chemistry between Timi and John for Nadine and Mark. They found all kinds of things to be working with, all kinds of tools that were truthfully found. And undirectable. You have to set up a space where the actors can find those things. We wanted to work with each other for the rest of our lives.

For Mann, *Still Life* proved both painful and exhilarating. She was revisiting a time when she was filled with anger, yet she felt she was breaking through to new levels as a playwright and director. When staging *Menagerie*, she had urged the actors to look uncompromisingly within themselves for the needs and desires that motivated Williams's characters. For *Still Life* she pushed the actors and herself "to vibrate at a level of truth at every second. . . . I had decided that audiences should believe the people on stage are the real people. It was a documentary, but you can't lie, you can't fake it . . . Also, it was different every performance, because I built it like a piece of jazz. And like jazz, where you are really creating it every time you play it, you might riff it differently one night than you do another night. That's what we were doing."

As a playwright, "I found a form," she said. "I found a way to work that thrilled me. I loved the idea of making plays from the words of real people and helping give voice to them. I started it with *Annulla*, but it went [to] another level with *Still Life*."

Part of that other level was the conveying of a point of view. In *Still Life*, more than *Annulla*, Mann took thematic control of the testimonies. One result of the interweaving is that Mann places Mark's stories about war near Nadine's stories about physical fights with her husband, near Cheryl's accounts of living with a man who, she fears, might kill her, near stories of sexual arousal. The juxtapositions are not blatant, but neither are they accidental. Mann interweaves the three peoples' words with a purpose. "Domestic violence in relation to war. That's really what the play is about," Mann said. "Why do men really want to go to war? Because they get off on it. Not all men do. The warriors do. And that's a disturbing concept to hold in one's mind and grapple with, and that's what the play made me do. Go to the dark side."

There is no single definition of a feminist play; however, if one criterion is to portray women's marginalization within, and subsequent resistance to, a society where men dominate in public and private realms—*Still Life* qualifies. But the resistance is Mann's, in the form of what could be considered a red alert. Cheryl continues to live with a man who abuses her. She expresses how exploited and mistreated she feels—physically, psychologically, sexually, financially—yet her only resistance is, on occasion, to lash out at Mark in anger. Nadine claims to understand Mark's physical violence and refers to her lover as though he were a warrior-artist, who has returned home from a treacherous journey and must be cared for. Each woman, Mann implicitly warns, focuses on the man in her life, fulfilling a centuries-old pattern of women welcoming men who return from the killing fields, even when the men bring demons home with them. In a culture that endorses war and often regards physical violence as a masculine rite, women are marginalized. And so ingrained is that ideology, Mann suggests, that these two women have marginalized themselves.

The American novelist and critic Roxane Gay, who has written fervently about the scourge of violence against women, has said that such violence is "a symptom of a much more profound malaise." Mann the dramatist essentially agrees. Beginning with *Amy* (1971), violence, both psychological and physical, is a theme that courses through her plays. Whether in *Still Life*, or in subsequent documentary plays like *Execution of Justice* (1984) and *Greensboro (A Requiem) (1996)*, Mann demonstrates that violence is emblematic of a virulently angry society, in which all of us are victims, although those who are not heterosexual, white, Christian, or male are usually the primary targets.

In one of her earliest visions for *Still Life*, Mann called for a stage with three areas. One area was Cheryl's living room, "with her bottle of bourbon, her TV, and her second-hand neat but dilapidated couch." Another was Mark's photography studio, "with his screen for showing his slides, his art work on the walls, . . . In front of him, a framers mat and table for cutting mats and glass." And a third area was "Nadine's dining room in front of her huge oaken table," with her photography equipment all around. Mann also wrote, however, that "A director may envision other means of communicating this story. It could all be done around a long dining room table with different kitchens at either end."

Thomas Lynch, the production's set and costume designer at the Goodman, suggested a spare look, more appropriate for the confessional nature of the play and for an audience that needed to concentrate on the characters' words. He provided two card tables, placed end to end, behind which sat Nadine, Cheryl, and Mark. The tables were equipped with water pitchers and glasses, ashtrays (Mark smoked continuously), and a slide projector, creating the look of a symposium about to happen. The only other decor was a screen upstage, behind the table, on which Mark projected his photographs—of his wife, of wounded children, of the maimed and the dead in Vietnam, and finally of the photograph he calls "Still Life": fruit and eggs, one of which is broken, and a grenade, all on a white plate that sits on a dark surface. Mann decided against a table cloth on the set's table, for she wanted the audience to see the actors' legs and feet. In a production where the characters rarely looked at or addressed each other, and where Mark was really the only one who stood and walked around, each actor's slightest movement, whether tapping their fingers on the table or crossing their legs, drew focus and became significant. The set design supported the form of the script, in which each character kept to his or her story to tell.

Timothy Near recalled that in rehearsal, "Emily talked a lot" about abusive relationships. "We all did. Cheryl certainly hadn't experienced trauma in the way Mark had. Two different wars. But women at home were warriors, too, and did suffer from parallel traumas."

McDonnell had memories of Mann talking to each of them privately about their character's self-knowledge. "Because that's all each of us really talked about in the play—our self," said McDonnell. "Emily and I only talked about what applied to Cheryl. Emily didn't want Cheryl to know where she was in the world, because Cheryl did not know how to help herself. The tragedy of being a very angry, abused, alcoholic. She was a woman of that time, a working-class American girl who was victimized by the war. And what she and her husband and her family had been through, she did not know how to articulate."

Near recalled that one of the things the three actors explored in rehearsal was where each should sit at the table. "Should Mark be between the two women? Was that a little sexist in some way? These were questions that we were asking. What did that say about. . . the power of the relationship? Should I be in the middle, because Nadine was kind of the calmest person, wasn't deeply, emotionally crazy from the whole situation? Or should the wife be there?"

They switched around in rehearsal, to see how they felt. "John and I felt sometimes we really wanted to be next to each other, and Mary would have none of it," Near remembered. "We ended up with Cheryl in the middle, which seemed the way it had to be."

Another question the actors had to answer for themselves was the nature of the event. Why were these three people sitting behind a table, telling about their loves and hates and fears, and in the case of Mark, ultimately confessing that he murdered five people?

"For me personally, they were an audience," said Near. "They were an audience that wanted me there to talk about this. So I just played the truth of the situation as much as I could. And I wanted to be there, to talk about a Vietnam vet and to talk about the war and about being a woman. That worked for me."

She and McDonnell recalled that Spencer sometimes engaged directly with the audience, especially at the intimate Goodman Theatre Studio and in New York at the American Place Theatre. During one performance—Near thought it was at the Goodman, McDonnell at the American Place—a man stood up and walked out after Mark's confession, and Spencer, apparently thinking he had disgusted the man with Mark's brutal story, stepped off the stage and followed the man, defending himself.

The actors had to decide if they were listening to each other, if they were present, if they were lost in their own thoughts. McDonnell recalled rehearsing at times with her fingers literally in her ears, because initially "I could not find Cheryl" or her journey while hearing the other characters' stories.

By the time the three actors performed *Still Life* in Los Angeles, in May and June of 1982, "I think we all felt that we were present all the time, that we heard everything," said Near, "and that we were very much in the same room with each other. Otherwise we would have been lying. You just had to play the truth of it, and the truth was we were all in the same room talking about this. The rules, the boundaries, were that we couldn't talk to each other, although maybe John and Mary broke that boundary once or twice."

Still Life had its world premiere at the Goodman Theatre Studio on October 23, 1980 (there were eleven performances, including previews). Mann sat at the back of the theater with her father, and at a certain point he took her hand and gripped it. In her diary, she wrote that the whole rehearsal period was "an emotional & physical trauma the intensity of which I have never experienced. . . . We walked around as the walking wounded, which we were. j. became deathly ill—great for him on an opening. I followed suit."

With few exceptions, the Chicago critics gave effusive reviews to both the play and the production, and good word-of-mouth preceded Mann's return home to New York and Gerry Bamman. But the most precious comments were her father's, who wrote, perhaps by way of healing their mutual wounds, "I recognized that [*Still Life*] was, in part, an attempt to purge yourself of the Sixties by writing about them. . . . the outcome for you was dazzling, thanks to your honesty and sensitivity and discipline and intelligence and craftsmanship." The play did not, Mann conceded, change her father's belief that the United States was right to have waged war against the Communists of North Vietnam, although the play did make Arthur respect her point of view.

In what had become her way of dealing with the intensity of work, at the end of October she and Bamman took a post-production trip to rest and recuperate, in this case to Greece. David Jones had invited them both to return to BAM for the company's second season, and Mann, slated to direct Sophocles' *Oedipus the King* in the spring of 1981, wished to immerse herself as much as possible in the archaeological remnants of ancient Greek theater. She also needed to recuperate physically and mentally. She returned in time to be assistant director on Jones's *A Midsummer Night's Dream*, which opened in January 1981, and on February 2, under the auspices of the Women's Project, Mann directed a rehearsed reading of *Still Life* at the American Place Theatre. There, in the SubPlot, the production opened on Thursday, February 19, 1981.

As in Chicago, the New York critics generally praised both the play and the production, which, in its realistic look and feel was very much like the Goodman premiere. If critics did not make the connections Mann intended, between violence on the battlefield and violence in the home and by extension the country, certainly *Still Life* caused them to question war's aims and devastating effects. "Are we talking about a traumatized victim of socialized insanity, or about a brute whose sickness pre-dated the war, which simply licensed it?" asked Marilyn Stasio in

Left to right: Timothy Near, Mary McDonnell, and John Spencer in Still Life, *written and directed by Emily Mann, the Women's Project at the American Place Theatre, 1981*

PHOTO BY: JAMES HAMILTON

the *New York Post.* "Even if we recoil from this killing man, can we rationalize the war machine that exploited his sickness?" Jeremy Gerard, in the *Soho News*, wrote that "The characters . . . become increasingly compelling, increasingly complex, in their inexorable growth toward a grievous unity."

There were, of course, those who did not respond to the play at all. Frank Rich, who had become the *New York Times*' chief theater critic in 1980, ventured to this subterranean level of the American Place and did not like what he saw. He called the writing "fuzzy-headed," claimed the play "leaves the audience cold," and opined that *Still Life* "tends to trivialize such issues as the plight of the Vietnam veteran, war atrocities and feminism."

Fortunately for Mann, Michael Feingold, in *The Village Voice*, counter-punched. He called *Still Life* "a jagged and arresting chunk of dramatic shrapnel." In a direct rebuttal to the *Times*, Feingold wrote that "the point which seems to have bypassed some of the daily reviewers is that . . . the contradictions which Emily Mann has arranged and intercut to such terrifying effect are the contradictions of human beings, not clever little droplets of character writing; the critic who sneers at them—sorry, Frank—is giving a bad review, not to the writer, but to God."

On June 1, the 26th Annual *Village Voice* Obie Awards would recognize Mann and *Still Life* for "Best Production," and Mary McDonnell, Timothy Near, and John Spencer would receive Obie Awards for their performances.

The good press and the awards helped propel *Still Life* to Los Angeles in May 1982, at about the same time that Theatre Communications Group published *Still Life* in a collection called *New Plays U.S.A.* Spencer, McDonnell, and Near performed the play for one last round as part of the Mark Taper Forum's New Theater for Now Festival, at Hollywood's old Aquarius Theater.

Near considered the Los Angeles production the best of the three. The set, once again designed by Lynch, was sleeker; the lighting more artful; the whole effect more presentational, she believed. The Aquarius had been built in 1938 as a legitimate theater for the *Earl Carroll Vanities*, and Lynch framed the set, adapting his design to the stage-upon-a-stage that the Taper had constructed and to an auditorium that sat several hundred. In addition, Near thought that "Emily stepped back from being a writer and was really a director. She was maybe more of a playwright the first two times, and when she came back to the play, she came as a director. We all felt she took charge. In my memory, Emily grew in her ability to pick and choose what we should do and what we shouldn't. Her hand became stronger."

McDonnell agreed, but phrased it differently. In her memory, the production started out in Chicago as "newly alive, raw, fragile—like a new flower. And then we did it again, and it fully bloomed. And the third time, we had learned about mistakes that we wanted to avoid. It was no longer as fragile a piece, because the actors weren't fragile, and [Emily] wasn't fragile as a writer."

One of Mann's memories from the L.A. production involved John Spencer, during a read-through of the script for Gordon Davidson, the Mark Taper's artistic director. Davidson apparently had a habit of falling asleep during read-throughs, but no one had warned Spencer about this disconcerting tendency. Mid-reading, Davidson was dozing, and Spencer leapt from behind the table where the actors were sitting and started screaming Mark's lines in Davidson's face. Davidson woke up.

But Mann's strongest recollection of the L.A. production was giving each actor "a huge emotional adjustment" on opening night, in reaction to what she believed was a poor preview but in defiance of one of the theater's unwritten rules about not giving actors radical changes, or even notes at all, on opening night. "A play that had been one hour and thirty-five minutes became one hour and fifty-five," Mann recalled, laughing a bit at the memory. "Because they trusted me and they did it. And I thought, 'Oh, my God. We're dead.' John was sobbing and moaning, and Mary was screaming. And it got this huge, standing ovation and rave reviews. John used to brag about that: 'Oh, you can't imagine what an amazing director she is, even on an opening night, she'll give you an adjustment that changes it all, and it's so much richer.' Thank God we got away with it."

One of the most valuable outcomes of the L.A. production for Mann professionally was that she met the South African director Barney Simon, who had co-authored and directed *Woza Albert!*, the festival's third entry, right before *Still Life*. She also met the South African composer and lyricist Mbongeni Ngema, and Mannie Manim, who would produce *Still Life* in 1983 at Johannesburg's Market Theatre, with Simon directing. Through these men she came to know the South African dramatist Athol Fugard, whom she would invite to the McCarter to direct (and perform in) his own plays.

Barney Simon was the source for deeming *Still Life* a form of theater that was essentially "testimony." A few reviewers had referred to the play as documentary drama, a term Mann deplored as "a bad mix of fiction and truth"; most had avoided any label. The printed programs had simply noted that "for the most part, these are the people's own words as told to Emily Mann during the summer of 1978." By 1983, however, in a program note for Simon's production at the Market Theatre, she did refer to the play as a documentary.

Simon proffered the concept of "testimony," he told Athol Fugard, because that element of Mann's play—the Vietnam veteran bearing witness about the war; the women in his life bearing witness about the effects of that war at home—felt especially significant in the Republic of South Africa of the 1980s. "We can't be silent!" Simon told Fugard, according to Fugard's notes of their conversation. "We must give evidence! We are witnesses!" Indeed, the Market Theatre's 1985 play *Born in the RSA*, subtitled "A collaborative effort by Barney Simon and the Cast," reads as though it were partially modeled on *Still Life*. The white and Black South African characters are based on actual individuals, and, as in *Still Life*, they mostly talk at length to the audience in interrelated monologues, describing, in personal terms, their backgrounds, their love affairs, and, finally, the racism, arrests, and incarceration that they either instigate or endure.

Mann embraced the concept of theater of testimony. Testimony is, after all, a form of storytelling. Testimony also has a strong confessional component, and because the testifying person/actor often speaks directly to the audience, ignoring any fourth-wall assumption, their testimony, rather than distancing us, reaches us viscerally. This emotional engagement, Simon believed, can arouse an audience to action. In the case of *Still Life*, to action against war and domestic violence, or at least to heightened awareness of the damage they inflict.

Still Life would bring Mann national and international attention. There would be productions at the Arena Stage in Washington, D.C., and the Eureka in San Francisco, at the Empty Space in Seattle and the Repertory Theatre of St. Louis, and at less widely known companies such as Lost Nation Theater in Vermont. Mann's new agent, George P. Lane at William Morris, negotiated productions in France and East Germany, Greece, Israel, Canada, and Great Britain. The British production was actually born in April 1984 at Utah's Salt Lake Acting Company, from where the Vietnam Veterans' Ensemble Theatre Company took it to Edinburgh for that city's beloved Fringe Festival. The production, directed by Molly Fowler, with James Morrison as Mark, garnered awards and went on to London.

Among the productions staged outside the United States, one of the more inventive was Jean-Claude Fall's French interpretation, translated by the French playwright Pierre Laville as *Nature Morte* and produced first in Avignon in southern France. There, in July 1984, Mann became the first American playwright to have her work performed at the renowned Avignon Festival, an arts festival that had been held every summer since 1947.

Mann described the production as "very French, very fashionable, New Wave staging," or as the critic Melinda Guttman wrote: "Red-lit palms flash outside the basement windows of Minnesota. . . . The front of the stage is covered with sand to represent tropical beaches. Sound effects consist of animal noises, confused radio transmissions, dark rock music." Behind the sand beach, Fall's scenic and costume designer, Gérard Didier, placed a row of theater seats, and behind them, steps running the width of the stage led to a platform backed by a high, textured wall. Above the wall was a chain-link fence and an open expanse through which one could see the palm trees. Unlike in Mann's productions, Nadine, Cheryl, and Mark frequently walked around, and sometimes Mark sat downstage, cross-legged, on the sand, at a distance from the two women. Silences were filled with deafening Algerian rock music and the sounds of wailing Algerian women, evoking the Algerian War, which ended in 1962 with Algeria finally winning independence from France.

After its acclaim in Avignon, the production opened in Paris in January 1985 and ran through late February, then gave an encore in March at the Théâtre de la Bastille. Mann flew to Paris, where she met France's Minister of Culture, Jack Lang, made several radio and television appearances, and became a darling of the French theater critics, who praised "L'incomparable talent d'Emily Mann."

Thirty-three years later, in 2018, the play was again produced in Paris, in a version titled *Still Life Today: La Guerre* à *Domicile*, translated once more by Pierre Laville, who also directed. Mark's war is now in Afghanistan, and Mann pointed out that the elements of the play which reawakened the passions of the 1960s, particularly "what it was like to be against the war . . . the split the war caused in the nation," are absent. What endures are the three characters' personal traumas, and the implicit political statement that war, any war, can annihilate relationships and destroy compassion.

For Mann in February 1981, the generally positive response following her New York production of *Still Life* was heartening. The spring, by contrast, proved challenging. The BAM Theater Company's artistic mission had shifted. For the first season, Jones had emphatically told a columnist for *The New Yorker* that "I do *not* believe in museum pieces." But audiences had not flocked to see *Johnny on a Spot*, a Charles MacArthur effort that had failed on Broadway in 1942, or the American premiere of Gorky's *Barbarians*, or *He and She*, or even *A Winter's Tale*, several of which seemed the very definition of museum pieces. Supposedly part of the difficulty was that Manhattan audiences were wary of that unfamiliar territory called Brooklyn, which was hardly the trendy destination it would become twenty-five years later (during the company's second season, BAM reinstated a bus service to transport Manhattan theatergoers to BAM's front doors). There had also been a transit strike for eleven days in April 1980. Jones, for his part, grumbled to Jerry Adler of the *New York Daily News* that "It is taking critical opinion a while to catch up with the concept of a repertory company."

There could be any number of reasons why audiences had not made the BAM Theatre Company their destination, but the bottom line was that attendance during the first season was somewhere between 50 percent to 60 percent of capacity. Jones decided to program recognizable classics for the second go-round, and according to Mann, it was he who suggested that she direct *Oedipus the King* for an opening in April 1981.

For *Oedipus*, Lichtenstein and Jones gave Mann the Lepercq Space, originally a long, narrow, high-ceilinged ballroom that, by 1981, had been converted into a long, narrow, six hundred-seat theater. Ming Cho Lee was hired to design the set, Jennifer von Mayrhauser the costumes, and Arden Fingerhut lit the production. David Jones's English wife, Sheila Allen, was Jocasta, and Mann cast Bamman as the Chorus Leader. Joe Morton would be playing Oedipus, a bit of unconventional casting in 1981, for New York audiences and critics were unaccustomed and, as John Simon revealed when reviewing *Midsummer*, not always welcoming to actors of color in traditionally white roles. Simon objected to "the verbally and kinetically stiff and stilted Lysander of Joe Morton (perhaps in a vain effort to act white)."

According to her private notes, Mann wanted a human, accessible production of *Oedipus the King*. She wanted to "break the Greek museum theater cliché" but "retain mystery, magic" and "a more modern look so that there is a bridge to the audience." She told Roger Oliver, in an interview for the BAM magazine *INSIDE*, that she spent the first three months of her preparation "working on the problem of the chorus, making them individual people with real needs." Playwright Richard Nelson, the company's literary manager, was not enthusiastic about the translation Mann had selected, by the American poet Stephen Berg and the classical scholar Diskin Clay. Yet he remembered liking her concept: "She talked about this as a very, very human story . . . the relationships being at the center."

But after Mann's trip to Greece, Nelson recalled, "she came back with a very different view of the play and with what she wanted to do with [it]." Nelson thought the white, raked slab that Mann and Ming Cho Lee agreed upon for the set was "monumental. . . . and seemingly very far away. It was presented so you were in a Greek theater." The production, Nelson said, "just became not about the characters or the relationships. . . . It came across as trying to do a Greek play in a Greek style . . . declamatory. Arch."

Mann herself told Roger Oliver for *INSIDE* that the trip to Greece had an impact on her direction. "I had to understand the Greek society, because the universal is best reached through the specific," she said. "And in Greece suddenly the gods made sense. . . by going to that country Apollo was real! And it's so much Apollo's play. Also the light in Greece is different from anywhere else. It sheds a clarity on the landscape. And going to Delphi was a spiritual experience. All these things add up to an experience of the play that I've brought back to the company."

Her comments suggest she was now looking at the play less as a family drama than as a play about an ailing civilization. "I found that Oedipus was a searing self-examination play," she told Oliver, "a play about people having to look into themselves. Something is desperately wrong. The city and the society are dying and we have to find out why. And we go from what begins as an examination of the society to an examination of the king. And after we find out who he is, then the people have to think about the nature of mankind. . . . I believe if you go to a New York audience and say, our city is dying, they can relate to that."

Joe Morton had a positive recollection of Mann's approach. He remembered sharing what he understood to be her enthusiasm for the play's mythical sources and recalled bringing in "all these books" and doing a great amount of research. As for Ming Cho Lee's white raked stage, "I loved the set," Morton said, "because it was so simple.

Emily Mann with Joe Morton in rehearsal for Oedipus the King *at the Brooklyn Academy of Music, 1981*
BAM HAMM ARCHIVES.
PHOTO: © KEN HOWARD

Straightforward." He liked his costume, a sleeveless white toga that went to the floor. Morton seemed to think that Mann had not abandoned her initial impulse to concentrate on the humanity of the characters. While his overall objective as Oedipus was "figuring out the mystery of what was going on and how to solve it," he remembered "dealing with the men and women in the play as a family structure."

When David Jones first proposed that Mann tackle *Oedipus*, "I was terrified," she told Roger Oliver. "I panicked. I said no one knows how to do this play, no one knows really how to do the Greeks." But if Mann felt unsure of herself, Morton said he was not aware of it in rehearsals. "That was the nice thing about Emily," he remembered. "You didn't feel you were working with a director who was kind of guessing at what she wanted. In hindsight, she may not have known things, but she didn't let on. Even if she wanted to experiment with something, it was always with confidence." Morton's main regret was that his opening night performance was not as good as it could have been. "I think I was just really nervous opening night, and I'm sure the performance was tight. After opening night, I was just flying. I just felt freer."

Oedipus the King opened on Thursday, April 23, 1981. Morton received generally favorable reviews; the production did not. Eileen Blumenthal, in *The Village Voice*, called it a production "to be pitied and condemned . . . at no point are any two actors on stage in the same play." Veteran critic Walter Kerr, reviewing for the Sunday *New York Times*, wrote that "Emily Mann's treatment of the Greek wonderwork needs much too much saving," and Marilyn Stasio wrote in the *New York Post* that "Emily Mann's production is a ragged creation . . . made particularly threadbare by the absence of a strong Chorus to point the way out of confusion." But Stasio began her review with "NO USE pretending that it isn't disconcerting to discover . . . that the King of Thebes is black, that his wife/mother and children are white, and that the ancient Thebans are a variety of black, Caucasian and Oriental races," so perhaps her judgment, on this occasion at least, was problematic.

More than three decades after the fact, it is hard to know what Mann intended as a director and what went awry, or to what extent critics (and audiences) brought preconceptions of how Sophoclean tragedy should look and sound. Walter Kerr had also written in his review that "[Oedipus the King's] not a domestic play, . . . It's a public play, a social one," so perhaps some of Mann's original intention, to focus on the play's human and familial relationships, came through after all. Her friend Bruce Siddons felt "there was an intimacy" to the production. Sitting in her office at the McCarter, she spoke deprecatingly about the whole experience, including unusual displeasure with Ming Cho Lee's set: "Ming had designed this really difficult set that looked more like a sculpture in an opera than what I had wanted for the set. And I had David Jones's wife playing Jocasta . . . which was really bad casting. And Gerry in the chorus, and he had no sense of what I was trying to do and was very grumpy. . . . It was just the wrong people in the wrong time, and the wrong chemistry in the room with the wrong designers, and I felt like I was speaking Greek. . . . I just did not yet have either the producer or director skill set to really pull it off."

Soon after the opening of *Oedipus*, Mann and Bamman left for Chicago, where Mann was rehearsing the world premiere of Michael Weller's *Dwarfman, Master of a Million Shapes* for the Goodman's main stage (Bamman was in the cast). While in Chicago, she received a letter from Jones regretfully alerting her that the BAM Board had decided against a third season for the theater company, which was in sore financial shape: the deficit, Jones reported, was at least $350,000 and could go as high as half a million dollars. *Variety* pegged the shortfall at nearly one million. The following November, Harvey Lichtenstein inaugurated BAM's Next Wave Festival, a mixture of innovative dance, opera, and performance art that would prove more attractive to audiences.

Dwarfman, which opened on May 28, 1981, did not fare well critically either, as a play or as a production. Richard Christiansen in the *Chicago Tribune* thought this play "about a cartoonist in crisis" to be "over-wrought," and the production "ill-conceived." But Mann recuperated from a trying spring, first by attending the 26th Annual Village Voice Obie Awards on June 1, at the Roxy roller-skating discotheque on West Eighteenth Street. Then it was on to Portland, Oregon, where she staged a well-received production of Athol Fugard's *Hello and Goodbye* for the first season of the Oregon Contemporary Theatre (OCT), founded by her friend Bruce Siddons. Gerry Bamman had accompanied Emily on this assignment, even though he was not in the cast, and after the production opened on July 31, 1981, they gave themselves a brief excursion to Jackson Hole, Wyoming, before returning east.

On August 12, 1981, Emily Mann married Gerry Bamman at Mohonk Mountain House, a resort situated atop the cliffs along the western side of the Hudson River. Mann was twenty-nine, Bamman nearly forty. A Justice of the Peace performed the ceremony outdoors in the resort's Rose Garden, a wild-looking enclosure of brick paths, wooden gates, and climbing rose bushes. Mann wore an antique white blouse, a gift from a friend, above a white satin skirt and a belt made of ribbons, and she wore a white veil. Her wedding clothes, she estimated, "cost all of a hundred bucks."

They had most likely decided to marry around the time of their trip to Greece, in November 1980. That December. they had visited Emily's parents, and Arthur and Sylvia's subsequent letters allude to a formal union, or as Arthur put it, "Once the tension of mounting <u>Midsummer</u> winds down, let's talk again about the details involved in making your twoness oneness." Bamman actually asked Arthur for Emily's hand in marriage. "I went to him and asked for his approval," the actor recalled. "We went out. I don't know why I thought that was a good idea, but I did. And I think he was flattered and happy that I did."

Probably it was a good idea, for Arthur was the kind of father who researched the background of the man his younger daughter planned to marry. On a 3x5 card, Arthur had written where "Gerry Bamman" was born (Independence, Kansas); where he had gone to school (Xavier University, Wayne State University, New York University); how many siblings he had (four) and their marital status. But even if Arthur's opinion of his future son-in-law had been less than positive, Gerry Bamman was not about to be deterred. "If he had said no, I wouldn't have obeyed."

The days after the wedding were filled with celebrations: a dinner given by Sylvia and Arthur for family and close friends; a party in the Lepercq Space at the Brooklyn Academy of Music. The couple flew to Egypt for their honeymoon and then went on to Israel.

"My father and I were especially close," Arthur wrote to his beloved second-born and her husband, "and I therefore feel confident in saying that were he alive on this gorgeous but also solemn occasion, he would say, as he said to my bride and me, 'This marriage is clearly made in heaven.' And he would be right for the second time."

9

The Dan White Project
(1978–1984)

NOVEMBER 27, 1978, was the Monday following Thanksgiving, and all over the country people were returning to work after the long weekend. In San Francisco that morning, a one-time cop and former member of the Board of Supervisors named Dan White went to City Hall with a loaded Smith and Wesson Model 36 .38 caliber revolver, and ten additional bullets. He entered the building through a first-floor window to avoid the metal detector at the front entrance. White, who was thirty-two, had recently resigned from the board, but he wanted to be reinstated and had learned that Mayor George Moscone was not going to reappoint him. White also knew that Supervisor Harvey Milk, California's first openly gay elected official, had lobbied against his reappointment. White walked to Moscone's office, pleaded to be reinstated, and when Moscone denied the request, White shot him four times, twice in the head. He reloaded his gun, located Harvey Milk, and shot him five times, twice in the head. Both men died. Moscone was forty-nine, Milk was forty-eight.

White was arrested and six months later, in May 1979, he stood trial for first-degree murder. But the prosecuting attorney was weak, the defense attorney charismatic, and a psychiatrist testified convincingly that White's high sugar intake had resulted in "diminished capacity"—the infamous "Twinkie defense." Instead of premeditated murder, the jury found Dan White guilty of voluntary manslaughter, and when the verdict was announced, late on the afternoon of Monday, May 21, San Francisco's enraged gay men and women took to the streets. In what

Harvey Milk
GARY FONG/*SF CHRONICLE*

George Moscone
SAN FRANCISCO CHRONICLE

became known as the White Night riots, they were met with tear gas and blows and arrests by equally furious police, retaliating for what they considered the desecration of San Francisco. The judge sentenced White to seven years and eight months in prison, the maximum sentence for voluntary manslaughter.

Three years later, in 1982, San Francisco's Eureka Theatre commissioned Emily Mann to write a play about the assassinations, the roots of the violence, and the aftermath.

Mere hours after Moscone and Milk were murdered, Tony Taccone, the artistic director of the Eureka Theatre, joined thousands of people on a candlelight march for the slain men. He had particularly admired Harvey Milk. "If you were on the left," said Taccone, talking with me one afternoon at the Public Theater in New York City, "you couldn't help but love the guy. He was a bit of a showman, had that showman's energy, but he understood how City Hall worked. Harvey represented a powerful bloc of people, people moving to San Francisco. To come out. Like a Mecca. And we at Eureka were in the heart of that."

But three years had passed since Dan White shed blood at City Hall, and Taccone and his dramaturg, Oskar Eustis, both of whom aspired to forge a political identity for their theater, had still not presented a play about the assassinations. In fact, they had mostly produced British plays. But they were eager to delve into American work, and with that goal in mind, in April 1982 the Eureka produced *Still Life*, which Taccone directed. "[*Still Life*]," he said, "was a very powerful experience for our audience, and for us." A play about the murders of Moscone and Milk could be an even more potent experience. What followed, Taccone recalled, was "a kind of tumble event"; things moved quickly. Mann and Taccone sat in his house in Berkeley, "jammin' on the idea" of her writing a play about the Dan White case. Taccone, Mann, and Eustis consumed Randy Shilts's new book, *The Mayor of Castro Street: The Life & Times of Harvey Milk*; Mann gravitated toward using the trial as a framework for the play; and the Eureka commissioned her. "We paid her probably twenty bucks," said Taccone. "It wasn't a lot of money."

In fact, he said, "Emily was ahead of us in her career. We had a good, strong local reputation, but we were pretty early in our work life."

For Mann, the murders in San Francisco were another example of the American violence she had witnessed and experienced. In a 1983 interview with costume designer Michael Murphy in Seattle, when she was directing Franz Xaver Kroetz's *Through the Leaves* at the Empty Space, Mann said that "There is a real connection between what the Gay Community goes through and the kind of oppression that women have gone through. And the kind of fears that we all walk around with. . . . to be an obvious target, as women are late at night, or a lone Gay man is in many areas of San Francisco. I understand that. I understand that terror and that rage."

Mann felt she was at a crossroads. Her drive to direct had been unswerving in Minneapolis and had steered her to New York. "The career side," she wrote in her diary in November 1981, has "been my life so completely." And while she had no intention of giving up directing, that particular ambition felt, for the moment, less enticing than her marriage and the rewards of writing. At times she felt depressed: she was concerned about her health, for she was prone to headaches and stomach aches, which she blamed on "cigarettes, coffee and liquor." But at other times she was "elated, refreshed and loving rediscovering my love for the art of writing."

Also, Mann wanted a child and, she wrote her mother, so did Gerry. But as she confided to Sylvia Mann seven months later, in May 1982, "I feel I am not ready yet for children or childbirth and then I think: well, 'ready'—what does that mean? And then I think about how creative I am feeling again—writing, directing, being with Gerry . . . and I don't know. Of course, I think, too, about how wonderful it would be to have a baby with Ger and the joy of bringing up a person together, but it seems as if it would also stop the flow of something magical that is happening right now."

She did not forgo directing completely. In May and June of 1982 she staged *Still Life* in Los Angeles. In July and early August, at Bruce Siddons' Oregon Contemporary Theater in Portland, she directed

Christopher Hampton's adaptation of *A Doll House,* on which she and Gerry made their own textual adjustments. Mary McDonnell played Nora, according to the critic Roger Downey, as a "lovable dimwit," and Bamman was "explosive" as Nora's husband, Torvald Helmer. In a bit of casting that delighted Portland's movie buffs, Wallace Shawn and André Gregory played Nils Krogstad and Dr. Rank respectively; their popular film, *My Dinner with André,* had been released the previous year. Gregory played Dr. Rank, Downey wrote, like "an almost campy old bachelor," and Gregory, years later, recalled that he visualized Dr. Rank "as somebody in the closet who absolutely loves women, and women like to confide in him." At one point, so Gregory remembered, Mann asked for a "more masculine" interpretation, and "I did Arnold Schwarzenegger, and she was delighted to go back to my original concept." Gregory decribed Mann "creating an environment of fun and safety."

But alongside directing assignments, what Mann and the Eureka were calling *The Dan White Project* absorbed her attention and her intensity. While in Portland, she requested as much material about the assassinations and the people involved as the Eureka's small staff could supply. She and Oskar Eustis exchanged names of individuals to be interviewed, some by Eustis and others at the Eureka, some by Mann whenever she could return to San Francisco: politicos, reporters, and newscasters; police, lawyers, relatives and friends of Moscone and Milk; people who lived in San Francisco's so-called working-class neighborhoods, and people in the gay neighborhood known as the Castro, where Milk had lived. "It was almost like we were doing the initial auditions, and she was doing the call-backs," said Taccone.

Eustis sent a stack of newspaper clippings and the huge trial transcript to Mann in Portland. Of course, there were no "thumb drives" for storing files in 1982, not to mention personal computers or laptops, and Mann remembered lugging around a duffel bag filled with pounds of Xeroxed court testimony. She even dragged it with her to Thailand, where Gerry Bamman was filming *Saigon: Year of the Cat*, a low-budget but well-cast Thames Television film about the collapse of South Vietnam and the final days of the Vietnam War. Directed by Stephen Frears from a script by David Hare, the movie starred Judith Dench and E. G. Marshall, and featured Wallace Shawn, Roger Rees, and Pichit Bulkul. When an actor failed to make it to Thailand, Frears enlisted Mann to act the small part of an American left behind with the South Vietnamese after U.S. Embassy personnel flee the country. The last frame of the movie has Mann, alone, in silhouette.

"I don't think I read through the [trial] transcript more than once," Mann recollected about the beginnings of *Execution of Justice*. "I think I read through the transcript and I highlighted and underlined those things that popped out at me, that were funny, weird, brilliant, important. . . . When I read those psychiatrists' testimonies, I just was amazed. . . . I also was very moved by Mary Ann White [Dan White's wife]," whom White called immediately after the murders, asking her to meet him at a church. Mann's first assignment to herself, as she phrased it, was to figure out "how do you tell just the story through the transcript?" One approach, explored in Mann's early private notes, was to have "Trial on stage - audience is audience in courtroom w/ actors/characters in audience." Her notes suggest that she contemplated putting "Mrs. Dan White front row - Reporters, etc." and "during 'trial breaks' do 'news coverage' -." The play would be written in "Hyper-real style - performance documentary but we are distilling and making electric in 2 hours what was a year long building up to this event & the trial itself. And its repercussions." Among her jottings, "The big question: Why was justice not done? A man murdered/assas'd 2 public officials in cold blood & will be out next year. WHY?" She experimented with possible titles: "Getting Away with Murder." "THE TRIAL of Harvey Milk or The Twinkie Defense." Even, perhaps in a lighthearted moment, "Trial by Twinkie." As she delved more intensely into her subject, the notes became more specific, until at one point, possibly weary of overthinking, she wrote, "I go to sleep dreaming it. It's time to write it. I know what I'm writing now."

In October 1982, Mann paused from *The Dan White Project* to direct for the first time at the Actors Theatre of Louisville (ATL). Jon Jory,

THE DAN WHITE PROJECT

ATL's artistic director, had invited her to stage two one-act plays in the theater's November festival, "82 Shorts." She directed *A Tantalizing* by William Mastrosimone, in which a woman brings an elderly homeless man back to her apartment because he evokes memories of her father; and she staged Jeffrey Sweet's *The Value of Names*, about two former show-business friends who meet again years after one publicly named the other a Communist during the red-baiting 1950s. Somehow Mann also found time to co-supervise "An Evening of Entertainment" in New York City with film producer Joan Micklin Silver, in support of the National Abortion Rights Action League (NARAL).

But when not directing, Mann continued to grapple with the material Eustis had sent her and by the beginning of November 1982 had mailed him a first draft of *The Dan White Project*. "First draft done," she wrote Liz Coe that December, "and that awful first draft completion feeling. It's good, needs tons more work, and I'm not sure yet how to do it. I wish I had a brilliant structure person looking it over. I think I have my first act wrong and don't know how to make it really work without sounding didactic. So I am putting it aside for a while."

The Dan White Project was considerably more complex than *Still Life*. In *Still Life*, Mark's photographs, projected on a screen upstage, had provided silent visual testimony in support of Mark's story. Now Mann was calling for film and video clips and even live video to function as additional layers of narrative. But in this early draft, words ultimately overtook visuals, as if Mann were still working through how to tell the story. The script at this juncture included extensive, verbatim excerpts from the trial (one reason the draft ran to more than 150 pages). Dan White and his actions were the apparent subject, but the play's spine was the duel between defense attorney Douglas Schmidt and prosecuting attorney Thomas F. Norman, or as Mann put it concisely in her private notes, "brilliant lawyer opposite bad lawyer." Accurately by all accounts, she selected transcript excerpts that revealed Norman to be an overly intellectual prosecutor, while Schmidt, with his parade of psychiatrists and friends-of-Dan testifying to White's instability, was a canny, passionate defender. Norman used legal terms that even his few witnesses had trouble comprehending, while Schmidt talked a language the jurors easily understood. Norman stressed what he believed was proof of intent to kill: the number of shots fired; White reloading his gun. Schmidt rendered Dan White a true-blue, moral American.

When she wrote to Liz Coe "I think I have my first act wrong," Mann may have sensed that she had not yet found a theatrical solution for the assassinations' political context or a way of dramatically weaving that context among the trial excerpts. Act I, originally called "Set Up for Murder," began with the sound of Mary Ann White's high heels clicking on a floor, as though on the marble or hard-wood floor of a church, then quickly shifted to film clips—of singer and gay rights opponent Anita Bryant; of an anti-gay California state senator; of Milk and Moscone and others—as Mann sought to present the political environment, the "set up," out of which Dan White and the assassinations emerged. Then the script moved to the trial testimony. Carlotta Schoch, an actor and close friend, remembered walking into Emily and Gerry's apartment in New York and seeing "little cards and pieces of paper and dialogue, like, everywhere." Mann cut strips of dialogue from interviews, clippings, and especially the transcripts, and scotch-taped them horizontally to form new pages of script. "Possibly start layering or juxtop. or intercut testimony mid-first act and then rapidly intercut to a mid-position 2nd Act, culminating in shrinks," she wrote to herself. The result of the cutting and pasting was energy and excitement, also clutter and confusion.

In New York, she organized a private reading at La MaMa Experimental Theatre Club (La MaMa E.T.C.), and afterward, she recalled, the playwright Charles Mee objected that the script was overly sympathetic to Dan White and Mann needed to give the other side an opportunity to be heard (Mee did not recall this conversation). At some later point, according to Mann, the designer Tom Lynch, who had also attended the reading, suggested adding "uncalled witnesses," which she always considered her most significant change to the script. Her notes suggest that Taccone and Eustis may have proposed a "chorus idea. Way to divide up uncalled witnesses," the "voice of the people." The people who make up the Chorus of Uncalled Witnesses are citizens of San

Francisco, who would eventually appear throughout the play, express-
ing their reflections about violence, about the trial and the verdict, and
about the future of their city.

"The spine of the play is the trial," Mann later told Michael Murphy at the Empty Space. "And the thing about the trial is, it's a complete portrait of Dan White and what a great guy he was. And how you
understand why he did what he did. When you put that forth, I thought
that was the end result. How ludicrous it was, and how justice was not
done. But, in fact, what happens when you read the play, the way it is, is
that you feel for Dan White, which is wrong. There's no rebuttal, there's
no prosecution. No one is ever challenging what the defense is saying.
. . . So, what I'm doing [is] picking up the un-called witnesses, the
people who were not called by the prosecution, to come in and testify."

With the Chorus of Uncalled Witnesses, said Oskar Eustis, the play
became "a courtroom drama playing out in the collective consciousness
of San Francisco. Reliving the trial, but bursting out of the bounds of
the trial for all the testimony that didn't happen. In a way, exposing the
limitation of the courtroom."

Mann and the Eureka were aiming to go into rehearsal on May 20,
1983, for a June 23 opening, and she was feeling the pressure to make
substantial edits to the first draft, which ran to hundreds of pages, and
submit a second draft by the beginning of April. In addition, she wanted
to do more interviews and incorporate the "uncalled witnesses." But she
had also returned to her intense directing schedule. On January 9, she
was contracted to start rehearsals for *Through the Leaves*, which would
begin performances at the Empty Space in Seattle on February 9. She
needed to return to the ATL to remount *A Tantalizing* and *The Value of
Names* in March, for the 7th Humana Festival of New American Plays,
and also stage Kathleen Tolan's *A Weekend Near Madison*, about several
thirtysomething college friends who gather for what turns into a stress-
ful reunion.

Yet she made time to go to San Francisco for a January 8 reading
of *The Dan White Project*, which, she announced during a brief speech

beforehand, "I am calling (today) *Execution of Justice*," a title adapted from the testimony of one of the defense attorney's several psychiatrists, who told the court that Dan White "was upset about how justice was executed in San Francisco." The actors read only about a third of the piece, or two hours' worth of a six-hour script, but the audience responded appreciatively, opening the door for an additional round of interviews during a weekend later in January.

Sometimes Mann struck out when on the trail of an interview. She wanted to meet Goldie Judge, who ran a sweet shop in District 8, Dan White's district. Judge had been White's campaign manager when he was running for supervisor, but she quit after learning that White was hiring Black gang members to disrupt other candidates' meetings. Mann and Eustis, who sometimes accompanied Mann on these searches, showed up at the sweet shop and explained why they wanted to talk with Judge, who was not there. They even bought ice cream cones. They were told to get out.

But others were eager to talk. Mann met Harry Britt, a gay activist who was elected to the Board of Supervisors the year after Milk was killed. "Where to start with Harry?" Mann told Murphy during their interview. "He moves me. He is a feminist. . . . He started out in the ministry, in the South. He was a great follower of Martin Luther King. When King was killed it totally changed his life. He left the church, went to San Francisco. He met Harvey and suddenly there . . . was a cause that made sense to him."

She talked with Gwen Craig, the lesbian African American president of the Harvey Milk Democratic Club, and she spoke with Harvey Milk's lover and archivist, Scott Smith, and their friends. She met at length with Joseph Freitas Jr., the (former) District Attorney responsible for selecting a losing prosecutor.

"[Freitas] wanted to spill his guts," Mann told Murphy. "He wanted to be exonerated. I think he wanted us to show that [the trial] ruined him, and that he tried to do the right thing. He was as shocked as anyone at the verdict." She described Freitas as "a Kennedy type, real attractive." But his good looks were not serving him well now. The trial had quashed his political career, and in the play, Freitas's lengthy monologue reveals a man searching for reasons why the District Attorney's office lost "an open-and-shut case."

Craig, Britt, and Freitas became figures in the Chorus of Uncalled Witnesses. Anita Bryant and the anti-gay state senator went into the wastebasket, and Mann moved a homophobic cop wearing a "Free Dan White" T-shirt from the end of the script to a place near the beginning, where she also put the drag queen Sister Boom Boom in his nun's habit. The antiphony of contrasting testimonies from the cop and the drag queen established two of the opposing worlds of San Francisco.

"The play is about a war," said Taccone. "It's a war for San Francisco. You have these different factions that are actually fighting, and it finally erupts in this event. You want to think it's an aberrant event, but how do events like that take place? Something else is bubbling up from underneath."

On the day Emily interviewed Freitas, she constantly felt sick to her stomach. To her and Gerry's delight, a test revealed she was pregnant. She was often physically uncomfortable during her pregnancy, but did not curtail her schedule, and she and Eustis talked and met whenever and wherever they could.

For Mann, Eustis, and Taccone, the year following the commission had been a remarkable journey. Mann spent the year amassing material and building her play. For her, the process was an immersion: in the trial, in communities she visited and learned about for the first time, in a theater piece that expanded with each new voice and perspective. Despite the pressures of scheduling interviews, making deadlines, and fulfilling directing assignments, the process had been luxurious. She had received a Guggenheim Fellowship to help support her research and writing. She had had the logistical and creative support of a theater's artistic director, dramaturg, and staff, who had encouraged her to paint as large a theatrical canvas as she wished. *Still Life*, by focusing on three people's intimate relationships, had raised the issues of war's destructiveness and women's victimization, set in the recent American past. *The*

Dan White Project allowed Mann to expose social and political conflicts being fought not only in San Francisco but also throughout President Ronald Reagan's America: conflicts between gay and straight, liberals and conservatives, secular Americans and religious fundamentalists, the so-called working class and those whom they denigrated for being the elite.

Her probing into the worlds of both Dan White and Harvey Milk had deepened her sense of a society gone awry. "I am still examining why I need in my plays to face this injustice I see all around me," she wrote Harry Britt after meeting with him. "Perhaps as a woman and a Jew whose family was effectively destroyed in the last World War, I have been conscious of what can happen when people are allowed to express through murder their hatred of what they don't understand or most fear in themselves. I constantly ask myself the question whether people destroy their opposites, the beings they least understand or whether it is a mirror—that they destroy what they see in themselves that they most hate (or do not understand). . . . I have an undying need to present what I know about this."

Oskar Eustis had not known that working with a playwright could be so rewarding. "There was no aspect of the play that was out of bounds for us to discuss," he said about collaborating with Mann. "When she would defend herself, it was because she thought she was right; her ego was never on the line."

Taccone recalled being pleased, but a bit amazed that the Eureka had embarked on a project which he privately doubted they or anyone else in the American theater could produce. For one thing, Eureka no longer had a theater. Two years earlier, in 1981, an arsonist had bombed Eureka's funky, black-box space in the basement of Trinity Methodist Church, and the church had burned down; the company had mounted *Still Life* at the People's Theater in the Fort Mason Center. But the arrangement with the People's Theater had expired. "We were doing all this research, and to be honest," said Taccone, "I thought, no one's going to do this play. It's too many characters. It's like, come on. Who's going to do this thing? But let's write it, let's make it happen. See what happens. I know that Oskar and I looked at each other a couple of times and thought, good luck to us."

Indeed, the June 1983 Eureka production did not happen. As Taccone said, the Eureka did not have a space, and a planned new theater was not ready. Also, the company simply did not have enough money to stage a play that required at least twenty actors. "There was no way we could afford to put this on," said Eustis. Judging from Mann's correspondence, her script was not yet ready either.

During the summer of 1983, Mann continued to rewrite and edit her play. She also took on new projects. Joseph Papp asked Mann to help with a problematic musical that Ntozake Shange had been creating with the Public Theater, for which Mann, who was almost nine months pregnant, attended a reading in August. Also that August, Mann began rehearsing *A Weekend Near Madison* for a commercial, off-Broadway production. The producer Dasha Epstein had seen the play at the Humana Festival, had loved it and optioned it. *A Weekend Near Madison* opened at the Astor Place Theater on a cool, damp Tuesday night, September 13, and at the opening night party Emily suddenly felt trickles of wetness running down her legs, saw a puddle at her feet, and realized her water had broken. She went home, and then she and Gerry walked uptown to Beth Israel Medical Center, at Sixteenth Street and First Avenue. There, on September 15, after a labor that lasted thirty-six hours and finally a Caesarian section, Emily brought Nicholas Isaac Bamman into the world. "Nicholas," after the late film director Nicholas Ray, who had been a good friend of Gerry's; "Isaac," after Emily's maternal grandfather. Stephen Wadsworth would be Nicholas's godfather, Irene Dische his godmother.

"I am just now coming up out of the haze of child-birth and starting to think about this project again," Emily wrote her father in October. "I do feel we must reexamine our notion of justice and our system of administering it if we are to have a future and with little Nick in my arms I care more and more about our future." She sent a draft of *Execution of Justice* to Jon Jory at the Actors Theatre of Louisville (ATL), and he scheduled a production for the 8th Humana Festival of New American Plays, in spring 1984. Taccone and Eustis would co-direct.

The birth of their son brought Emily and Gerry both happiness and change. For one thing, they decided to move from New York City. The apartment on Sixth Street was essentially one long room, and even before Nicholas was born, Emily often borrowed a friend's studio when she needed quiet to write and a floor on which to spread out her research or the pages of a script. "If she were in her space, writing, you did not bother her," said Bamman. Now they needed extra rooms, for Nicholas, and for grandparents and friends who wished to visit, and for Mann when she was writing.

Another reason for leaving the city was Emily's fear. In a diary entry from 1981, she wrote about having just seen the film *Body Heat*, and images in that film of a mutilated woman had remained with her. "I realize I am afraid of being murdered," she wrote. "My terror of violence—of people's capacity for it & my fear of it happening to me invade my every waking hr." One day, soon after Nicholas was born, she was walking in the East Village with Nicholas in her arms, and a man, possibly drunk, lunged at them. Emily kicked and kicked the man until he fell, and she rushed home and told Gerry they had to leave. By the end of November they had found a new place to live: a white, three-story clapboard house at 508 South Broadway, in Grandview, New York, a sliver of a village on the western side of the Hudson River. And they were just a forty-minute drive from Manhattan.

There were lingering, apparently inexplicable after-effects of the pregnancy and the Caesarian. Emily experienced what she later described as "a huge memory deficit. I really could not remember big things." At times, she also suffered relentless spinal pain. The discomfort had not interfered with her attending the first read-through of *Execution* in January. But at the beginning of February she started rehearsals at Hartford Stage Company for *The Value of Names*, which Jeffrey Sweet had expanded to a full-length play, and she was in so much pain she could barely walk. Mark Lamos, Hartford's artistic director, remembered that they set up a bed for her in the rehearsal room. "She was coping,"

Emily Mann with her son, Nicholas Bamman (n.d.)
COURTESY OF EMILY MANN

he said, "she was directing. She just couldn't get up and run around." Lamos worried that he might have to take over the staging.

The Value of Names opened at Hartford Stage on February 27, 1984; the first preview for *Execution of Justice* was scheduled for March 7, and Mann apparently was well and mobile enough to spend the intervening week in Louisville, with Gerry and Nicholas. Over the years, when women have asked how she managed motherhood and a theater career, Mann replied that she took her infant son on the road whenever she could and carried him to rehearsals, even nursing him there, and if that was not possible, then Gerry looked after him or they hired a babysitter.

As with any rehearsal, there was some tension in Louisville. ATL had a resident company, but Mann insisted on bringing in John Spencer to play Dan White.

"He was fabulous," said Mann. "That's where, in a lot of ways, Tony and Oskar and I diverged when it came to *Execution of Justice*. For me, it's a very raw show. At its best. And John, when he did [White's] confession, snot was flying every night, and tears, and rage."

Julie Crutcher, ATL's literary manager, believed that the three-act script was "crazy long." One run-through early in February had taken three hours and twenty-one minutes, including two fifteen-minute intermissions, and the stage manager, Benita Hofstetter, reminded Taccone and Eustis that artistic director Jon Jory had a less-than-three-hour rule. Crutcher recalled sitting with Mann for hours, "with index cards and half pieces of paper, and retyping pages. . . . I'd edit, edit, edit, and then in rehearsal it would be all back in there." On opening night, Crutcher remembered, Emily's present to her was a pair of scissors with "really long blades."

Taccone and Eustis claimed they had no difficulty directing in tandem. Taccone remembered both of them "doing everything"—blocking, giving notes to actors—although Crutcher, in her contacts with the two men, considered Taccone to be "kind of the background person, the quiet person," while "Oskar was the lead, the head honcho." Mann, of course, was also a director, and her directorial side emerged when she came to Louisville during the last week of rehearsals. "We'd do a run-through," said Eustis, "and Emily would come in with new pages, and absolutely nothing had changed in the dialogue, but what she had done was change the descriptions of the characters' moods . . . Emily clearly had a directorial point of view." Eustis, in fact, believed that what he called Mann's "heightened emotionality" occasionally "got in the way of the argument of the play. I know that she always thought the way Tony and I approached it was a little too cool and a little too classical."

Jory assigned the play to the Pamela Brown Auditorium, ATL's largest theater, which sat more than 600 and had a thrust stage. Paul Owen, ATL's resident designer, created a basic design that could accommodate several productions in repertory for the festival, so the set for *Execution* was functional and not elaborate. On the highest level of a dark, multi-tiered set were platforms for the actors, who could step down to a tier containing a chair for Dan White upstage center, a table with two chairs downstage right of White and another table with two chairs downstage left of him. A judge's desk and chair occupied the next tier down, and the lowest level, nearest the audience, was bare of furniture, but populated on occasion by the Uncalled Witnesses. Projections onto a scrim at the top of the set identified characters or announced significant moments in the trial, such as "the Twinkie defense."

"It was pretty stark and hard-lined," Paul Owen recalled, with "no color involved." The critic William Kleb, writing in *Theater* magazine, approved of the classical ambience: "On a dark grey, nearly circular stage, with stepped tiers flanking a black 'skene' at the back, the cop and the drag nun could be two malignant Euripidean gods, come out for a moment to set the scene."

The Humana Festival's three-day critics' weekend at the end of March 1984 attracted reviewers, agents, and producers from around the world. San Francisco's leading newspapers sent critics, who presumably wanted to cover the production of a play that had been commissioned by a San Francisco company, about notorious murders committed in their town. In what could be construed as either an ironic coincidence or perfect timing, Dan White had been released from Soledad State Prison on January 6, after serving only five years of his sentence, and was living, secluded, in Los Angeles. That real-world plot twist only heightened interest in Mann's play.

There were nine premieres that year at the Humana Festival of New American Plays, including John Patrick Shanley's *Danny and the Deep Blue Sea* and Lee Blessing's *Independence*. But *Execution of Justice* was the only play by a woman, an imbalance noted by Mel Gussow, who had cited Mann the previous year in a feature article for the *New York Times*, "Women Playwrights: New Voices in the Theater."

Judging from reviews, *Execution* was the play that the majority of critics considered the most stimulating. Gussow wrote from Louisville, "'Execution of Justice'. . . is not about families, the only tables are in a courtroom and it is concerned with public, not domestic, crises. It is, in fact, the most challenging and provocative play in the festival." Even critics who had reservations tended to offer suggestions for making a complicated, charged play additionally compelling. Whatever the flaws that some critics found in *Execution* at Humana—the play's length (still three acts), trouble identifying the many characters, and an overabundance of trial testimony were the most frequent objections—Mann's documentary exposed disturbing levels of fear and anger among the citizens of San Francisco and by extension, America.

10

Execution of Justice
(1984–1986)

JULIE CRUTCHER HAD called ATL's production of *Execution of Justice* "a kind of out-of-town try-out." But which theater or producer would option it for a major regional or commercial production? Correspondence during the summer of 1984 between Mann and Gordon Davidson indicates that she was eager for the Mark Taper Forum in Los Angeles to produce the play. But in the meantime she had given production rights to M. Burke Walker, artistic director of the Empty Space in Seattle, and to the Eureka, although she assured Davidson that these would be small productions.

After she returned from seeing *Still Life* in Avignon in July 1984, she and Davidson spoke on the phone, and the Taper's artistic director apparently raised the possibility of an "interim" instead of a "full" production, which Mann declined. But three days later, she wrote Davidson that she would consider a production on the scale of *Still Life* at the Aquarius, if that was what he had in mind. Significantly, she also declared that "I do very much want to direct the play myself. I think it's time. I think it's right for the further development of the play. . . . I think the Eureka directors did a splendid job and I learned a lot from their excellent production, but I can go further. I want to go further. I'm not sure I will feel it is realized without that." She asked Davidson "to see if a slot opens up for us this season," but if not, she hoped for the first slot the following season. "I would like to commit to each other on this play. I don't need to 'look further.'"

But the Taper did not schedule a production for 1984–1985, or for any season; financial pressures that made such an expensive show unfeasible was the explanation. So Mann did look further, to the Guthrie, which announced in November 1984 that it would produce *Execution* approximately one year later, in October 1985, with Mann directing (Houston's Alley Theatre scheduled a production to be directed by Pat Brown at the same time). And early in 1985 Arena Stage in Washington, D.C., announced that their Associate Producing Director, Douglas C. Wager, would stage the first major regional production in May 1985.

At Arena Stage, the artistic staff had carefully weighed the decision to produce. In fact, Arena had been considering the play at least since January 1984, when James C. Nicola, at that time producing associate, directed an in-house, four-hour-and-fifteen-minute reading. Planning a season at Arena was complicated, explained Nicola, with four performance spaces to program and a resident company of actors to be shared among the venues. Wager, for his part, wanted to direct the courtroom drama *A Class "C" Trial in Yokohama* by Roger Cornish, about the 1948 trial of a Japanese physician accused of mistreating wounded American prisoners-of-war. But Arena's co-founder and producing director, Zelda Fichandler, read *Execution* and liked it. "Think it hits a good note with the idea of relative (historically–rooted) justice," she mused in a handwritten note to Wager and David Copelin, Arena's Director of Play Development. She wondered with a mixture of doubt and amusement, "What does one do with the million+ people in the cast? The visuals?" Nicola, who considered Fichandler "my spiritual artistic mother," believed that Fichandler was uncomfortable with the play's gay context. She "was struggling with issues of the gay community," said Nicola. "[It was] not an easy subject for her to put forward under her banner."

Nicola believed he was the strongest advocate for the play among his colleagues. In addition to directing the *Execution* reading, he had staged a production of *Still Life* at Arena in 1983 and admired Mann's writing. Also, he said, *Execution* "really interested me as a gay person at the time." Despite Wager's mixed feelings about Mann's script, he recalled being "excited" about a production and finally telling Fichandler that

Execution was better for their resident company than *Class "C" Trial,* and that "from a social-conscious point of view, it was equally if not more compelling to deal with." Then, in December 1984, David Copelin alerted Fichandler and Wager that Center Stage in Baltimore was presenting a minimally rehearsed production to launch their Playwrights 85 series, and that other regional theaters were standing by to produce *Execution of Justice.* Indeed, with the Taper out of the picture, M. Burke Walker's production at the Empty Space in Seattle would be the play's West Coast premiere and in fact would open before the Arena's production. But Arena Stage had in mind something much more ambitious than what the Empty Space's smaller budget and capacity would present.

Fichandler gave her approval, and in February 1985, Arena Stage sent Mann a contract.

When Mann was creating what she initially called *The Dan White Project,* one criticism had been that the script dwelled on Dan White to the exclusion of "the other side. " Mann agreed and added the Chorus of Uncalled Witnesses.

But Douglas Wager had the opposite reaction. "My first response, when I read the original draft: I got really angry," said Wager, discussing Arena's production thirty-two years later during a lunch in Philadelphia. In 2004, he had joined the faculty of that city's Temple University and was now associate dean of the Division of Theater, Film and Media Arts. "I had this awful sensation of what I would call 'theater for registered Democrats.' It was completely one-sided, complete diatribe and condemnation of Dan White in the way that it was organized." He was angry, he realized, because he believed that "the real story of the play for an audience is not to confirm their prejudices," but to bring the audience "into this difficult place where, for at least the time that they are living and breathing in the theater, they can get to the end of the play and realize how complex this idea of justice really is, and why justice is blind."

Wager said he discussed this interpretation with Mann and understood that she "was open to what I meant by that and how that would be expressed in the way the show would be produced, directed, and edited." She edited the script down to two acts, and as Wager wrote in a prepared description of his vision for the Arena Stage company, "The play presents events of the past, present and future surrounding the story, and to accentuate that, the playing space is finally a trial room, a conference room, a convention hall, an American public space, a mind space."

Ming Cho Lee designed a stark set: the flat stage floor covered in blue industrial carpet; a polished, red, eight-foot square in the center of the playing space; numerous black chairs scattered about; and suspended above it all, a large cube with screens displaying film and video, so that audiences on each of the four sides of Arena Stage's playing space could watch the transmitted images. Wager aimed to make film and video integral to the theatrical event. "What I intend to do to make this event exist the way I hope it can," he told the company at the outset, "is to have it exist with actual video documentary footage taken from the time of the event, fictionalized documentary images which we will produce, simultaneous broadcasts at certain points of live stage action so if there is a reporter onstage making a news report you see the reporter in the environment but you see the report on the screen happening simultaneously." Sometimes, he explained, the live image might be of someone listening to a scene. "The wide range of possibilities that this presents us is a grand experiment." He planned to station video cameras in two of Arena's four vomitoria, or voms.

The production began with aerial shots of San Francisco, intercut with sequences involving George Moscone and Harvey Milk. Then the audience viewed images of people milling about on the streets at rush hour, at the same time that actors entered from the voms and crossed the stage, to create a sense of San Francisco street life. Suddenly, the screen images cut to Supervisor Dianne Feinstein announcing the assassinations, and onstage, the actors/citizens of San Francisco stopping to watch.

One of Wager's aims was to use the cast to create what he called "an ensemble emotional landscape" and give "emotional velocity" to what was happening in the filmic and verbal texts. Film of the Candlelight Vigil in San Francisco played alongside audio of Harvey Milk famously telling "Gay brothers and sisters, . . . You must come out. Come out," and at the same time, actors holding lighted candles came onstage from the voms, a moment in performance during which members of the audience would sometimes flick on their cigarette lighters, or light matches, or just sob. Toward the end of the play, when the jury announces its verdict, "chaos sort of ensued" onstage, said Wager. "We used expressionistic and choreographic effects to demonstrate the riots . . . turning chairs over, at the same time that there was documentary footage of actual events playing."

With a couple of exceptions, local critics were enthusiastic to the point of sounding delirious with praise. "Landmark production of consummate artistry" and "Emily Mann has created a powerful drama" raved one reviewer. "It's absorbing, it's riveting, it's thought provoking

Left to right: Stanley Anderson, Gina Franz, Gerry Paone, and Casey Biggs in Douglas Wager's production of Execution of Justice *at Arena Stage, 1985*
PHOTO: JOAN MARCUS

and it's based on truth," wrote another. David Richards at the *Washington Post* called the play "deeply disturbing" and a "sweeping drama," and the production "a stunning multimedia staging." Fichandler took her copy of the *Post* and scribbled a note: "Doug—congratulations on your superlative production. You have illuminated the Truth in a profound personal way—using the tools of the theater for revelation. It makes me feel honest, whole, grateful." To Mann she wrote, "You are a Treasure. As playwright, woman/person, listener, asker-of-questions, seeker-of-Truth, you are an original. I look into my crystal ball and see such a large contribution you will make to the world's insight! Thank you for this play. And things to come. Love, Zelda." And Mann, in Seattle at the Empty Space, wrote back, "Thank you. Thank you for the honor of producing Execution of Justice at the Arena Stage. Thank you for believing in it, seeing it clear, and demanding its full clarity. And also, thank you for your belief in me and in the work for the future. Your interior sight has been a great inspiration to me for many years."

Judging from the reviews, Wager succeeded in his original goal of asking audiences to consider the murders and the verdict, the people of San Francisco and the American system of justice from not one but several angles. The play now gave him that foundation. "What is extraordinary about this work," wrote David Richards, "is that it doesn't take one side over another. It takes *all* the sides and forces you to do as much. Just when you believe you've got your feelings in hand and your thoughts sorted out, Mann suddenly introduces an angry voice from the streets, a cry from the heart, a plea of utter bewilderment, and all your certainties are swept right out from under you." Richards thought Wager's staging, with its multiple visual perspectives, echoed the many voices and viewpoints in Mann's script. And while Richards sometimes found the plethora of characters confusing, he concluded that Mann's play "will leave you with worrisome questions—not about White's guilt, perhaps, of which there is no doubt, but about a society that can produce such profound fissures." *Execution of Justice* won the Helen Hayes Award for Outstanding Resident Play. Wager received the Helen Hayes Award for Outstanding Direction of a Resident Production.

Arena Stage, wishing to draw as much attention to the production as possible, had invited theater critics and journalists from around the country. *American Theatre* magazine slated the script for its November 1985 issue, the first script to be published in the barely two-year-old magazine. *The Village Voice* obliged by sending theater critic Elinor Fuchs, who called the play "a riveting journey into American law, social values, and moral life. Harvey Milk is quoted as exulting 'The system works!' when he became the first openly gay candidate to be elected to public office in the nation. The terrible question Mann's play asks . . . is not just whether the system works, but what exactly it is that 'works.'" Praising Wager's concept for the production, Fuchs wrote that the dual focus—closed-circuit images above, actors on the stage below—was "a powerful metaphor for the American social confusion to which this play so eloquently attests."

Mel Gussow traveled to D.C. for the *New York Times* and wrote a dry but encouraging review, which complimented Mann for making improvements to "structural problems that were intensified by the skeletal production" in Louisville. "Since then, the author has distilled and sharpened her drama. In an imaginative production by Douglas C. Wager at the Arena Stage, the play is well on its way to becoming a most compelling act of political theater."

That June, the Eureka Theatre, in a co-production with Berkeley Repertory Theatre and the San Jose Repertory Company, finally staged the play it had commissioned three years before, on which it had bestowed so much thought and so many resources. Once again, Oskar Eustis and Tony Taccone co-directed a low-tech production, and Vicki Smith's austere, three-tiered set was reminiscent of the classical design at ATL. Reviews of both the production and the play were mixed, but Eustis and Taccone were pleased that so many of the people who figured in Mann's play came to see it: Schmidt, the defense attorney, arrived with Frank Falzon, the Chief Inspector of Homicide; Freitas, the former district attorney, was there; Sister Boom Boom; Harry Britt; Supervisor Carol Ruth Silver. On opening night at Berkeley Repertory, said Taccone, "a significant portion of the people in the audience were in the play," along with many whom Mann and the Eureka had interviewed for background. "The emotion of the evening was overwhelming," said Taccone. "When the candlelight vigil happened, the audience burst into tears. So many people recapturing their experience." The play received the Bay Area Theatre Critics Circle Award.

With reviews such as those from Washington, D.C., and the *New York Times*, Broadway producers ordinarily would have clamored for the rights. Possibly the play's political nature was a drawback, not to mention a cast of twenty-three. The impetus for a commercial production finally came from an Arena Stage board member named Mortimer Caplin, a lawyer who had been an IRS commissioner under President John F. Kennedy. Decades earlier, Caplin had roomed at the University of Virginia School of Law with one Lester Osterman Jr., who, in the late 1950s, had embarked on a career owning and operating commercial theaters and producing Broadway plays and musicals. When Caplin asked his former roommate to invest, Osterman suggested instead that they co-produce, along with Osterman's wife, Marjorie. Osterman had a reputation for producing literate plays (Edward Albee's *The Lady from Dubuque*; Michael Cristofer's *The Shadow Box*), but he had not had a commercial success since 1978, when he produced Hugh Leonard's comedy *Da*. An August 16, 1985, article in the *Times* announced that *Execution* would arrive on Broadway early in 1986, with Wager directing.

Yet it was Mann who was directing the Guthrie production, which began seven weeks of rehearsals on August 27. Most of the actors were members of the Guthrie company, but Mann brought in others: Suzy Hunt, playing Cyr Copertini, Mayor Moscone's broken-hearted appointment secretary, had been in the Empty Space production; Bamman played the excessively cerebral prosecutor Thomas F. Norman; and John Spencer, as at the Actors Theatre of Louisville, played Dan White. Ming Cho Lee again designed the set.

The Guthrie's dramaturg, Mark Bly, had been one of the play's most fervent supporters and he had flown East to see Wager's production, in preparation for the Guthrie rehearsals and also at Mann's urging. "Emily kept saying, 'Mark, you have to see it. I'm really happy with this production.'" But while Bly appreciated that Wager had staged "a big, sweeping epic" and had taken the script beyond the "chamber versions" generated at other regional theaters, privately, he recalled, he was disappointed by what he saw.

"This very contemporary, hot, cold, play, that was very epic and Brechtian, somehow had devolved into a bunch of people walking around the stage without their coats on, holding onto their suspenders," he recalled. "I felt I was watching *Inherit the Wind* or *Anatomy of a Murder*. It was not the *Execution of Justice* that was in my brain, that was in a modern courtroom with cold, metallic chairs and men and women in very chic-looking suits." Wager had incorporated film and video to dynamic effect, but the cameras for the live television feeds were lurking in the Arena's voms, and Bly thought they should be onstage, hand-held, and shoved in the actors' faces, "intruding into the lives of these people . . . like they had been in the world of Dan White, of Harvey Milk, of Moscone."

During the months preceding the Guthrie rehearsals, Bly remembered talking with Mann regularly, earning her trust and slowly bringing her around to his view that the production should look cool and contemporary. He remembered sitting practically every day after rehearsals started and giving her written notes, as specific as possible, about the script and the staging.

"You have to have courage with Emily, to be as courageous as she is," said Bly. "You have to start from a point of saying, 'Emily I agree with you.' You have to share with her your tremendous admiration for something. Her play, a starting point. And then she looks at you and says, 'This person I want next to me.' She got that from me. She trusted me. And then I slowly took the time to say, 'Now you know I'll go anywhere with you. I will spill blood for you. But this is not as good as you think it is. It's actually a seven and your play is a ten. How do we get this up to that ten?'

"There was this wobbly transition period, but I kept at it and I stayed with it, and even when she was looking at me cross-eyed, I didn't waiver.

Left to right: Jay Patterson, John Spencer, and Kurt Schweickhardt in Execution of Justice, *written and directed by Emily Mann at the Guthrie Theater, 1985*
PHOTO: JOSEPH G. GIANNETTI/GUTHRIE THEATER

Because she saw how much I believed in that play. And that was my putting in day after day after day of time with her. And that's what counts with Emily. Because she's all about trust. She's all about loyalty."

Reportedly the production was even more startling visually than at Arena. Ming Cho Lee replaced the blue carpet with what the critic Mike Steele described as "a shimmering, plasticized" blue floor, which could also reverberate with the sounds of Mary Ann White's clicking, high-heeled shoes. "The high heels," Mann said, "are the sound that I always hear when I think of Mary Anne White running to meet her husband in the cathedral. I knew he was alone there, waiting for her. I knew he must have heard her running to him, and I heard that sound in my sleep." The chairs, as Bly had envisioned, were largely of metal. Mann and Ming Cho Lee set up bleachers across the back of the Guthrie's thrust stage, in effect turning the thrust into an arena configuration and enabling members of the audience to sit onstage amid the action, often side-by-side with actors also sitting on the bleachers. And in case any-one doubted where the action was set, or somehow missed the theme, a replica of the stone facade of San Francisco's Hall of Justice loomed over the bleachers.

View of the stage in Emily Mann's production of Execution of Justice, *Guthrie Theater, 1985*
PHOTO: JOSEPH G. GIANNETTI/GUTHRIE THEATER

A credit in the Guthrie's program thanked "Douglas C. Wager, Guy Bergquist [Arena's production coordinator] and the Arena Stage for their invaluable assistance in the development of the audio and video." As at Arena, one cube, its screens visible to spectators in the theater and on the bleachers, hung above the red rectangle where the witnesses sat and testified. Two cameras on the thrust stage captured live close-ups. "At the end of the first act," wrote Mark Kasel for the *Twin Cities GAZE*, "we see a re-enactment of White's pitiful confession hours after the murder which reveals, with his hard-lit video image projected on a white cube above his chair at center stage, a man who tried to emulate masculine American responsibility."

Robert Breuler as the Cop, and Peter Francis James as Sister Boom Boom in Execution of Justice, *written and directed by Emily Mann, the Guthrie Theater, 1985*
PHOTO: JOSEPH G. GIANNETTI/GUTHRIE THEATER

The script received little in the way of substantial rewrites during rehearsal: a few cuts, a few lines rearranged. The antiphony between the Cop (Robert Breuler) and Sister Boom Boom (Peter Francis James) set up the polarization between Dan White's homophobic supporters and the gay men and women of San Francisco, and as at Arena Stage, the play was in two acts. Act I was simply called "Murder"; Act II, "In Defense of Murder."

Act I was intricate, but two main stories unfolded: Schmidt (Peter MacNichol), White's defense attorney, giving his opening statement to the jury, was intercut with Norman (Gerry Bamman), the prosecuting attorney, questioning his witnesses. And interspersed throughout both unfolding actions were the comments of the Uncalled Witnesses. The act ended with Dan White (John Spencer) being interrogated by detectives at the police station and confessing to the murders, and then, along with Mary Ann White (Katherine Leask) and several jurors, collapsing in tears.

Act II was similarly intricate, except here it was Schmidt who questioned witnesses, including the string of psychiatrists, which provided a bit of comic relief as one after the other assiduously testified to White's emotional instability. The stage action then shifted to the attorneys' closing statements and the jury's verdict, interwoven with the on-camera reactions of Uncalled Witnesses and on-camera news reports from Joanna Lu, the sound of explosions, film images of police cars in flames, rioting onstage, and a few sarcastic words from Sister Boom Boom, who raises a Twinkie in her hand and eats it.

The play's closing words belonged to White: "I was always just a lonely vote on the board. I was just trying to do a good job for the city." That comment was followed by the sounds of Mary Ann White's clicking high-heeled shoes, Sister Boom Boom silently confronting police carrying riot shields, "Execution of Justice" on the cube above the stage, and the echoes of a gavel.

Mann relished directing again on the Guthrie's thrust stage, and the Twin Cities critics welcomed Mann like a daughter whose career they had nurtured, with Mike Steele highlighting that Mann had written both of her previously produced plays while in Minneapolis. "I've watched several productions [of *Execution of Justice*] and learned from them," Mann told Steele, "but now, directing it myself for the first time, I've discovered new power in it. It's obvious that society was on trial and the questions were tough ones: How do we judge our fellow man? Have I ever been mad enough to kill? How confident can we be of a system that, up until now, we've always believed in? How fragmented is our society? There aren't any simple solutions."

Bly thought that one of the features which distinguished Mann's production at the Guthrie was its rough kinetic energy. Actors frequently moved back and forth from the bleachers to the thrust stage. The anger of the White Night riots erupted onstage and was captured live by cameras and projected onto the cube's screens. Actors surged in and out of the voms. Mann's production was not a restrained aesthetic object. The point was to arouse the audience emotionally as well as intellectually. Suzy Hunt, playing Cyr Copertini, remembered the force Mann wanted in the production. "She used the expression, metaphorically, that she 'wanted to see blood on the stage.' She wanted it life or death. She wanted the issues to be poignant and raw. An urgency to tell the story. An absolute from-the-gut kind of response. . . . I felt like every night was a life or death thing."

Execution of Justice opened on October 18, 1985, a cool Friday evening in Minneapolis, and received a round of cheers from local critics. Steele wrote, "This is Bertolt Brecht taken into the electronic age and it's very powerful. And like Brecht, Mann can't subjugate her own political feelings to documentary objectivity. She ultimately wants us to see Dan White's side but certainly not side with Dan White. The victims, their politics and their sexual orientation, were ultimately on trial more than the defendant. The jury, supposedly representing the community, was made up of white, straight, middle-class people. Mann can't quite hide her anger." In the *St. Paul Pioneer Press Dispatch*, David Hawley lauded "a stunning piece of epic pyrotechnics, a state of the art performance extravaganza that also gives the impression it is wrestling with some fundamental questions about the American social order." Tim Campbell, writing for GLCVoice, called *Execution* "a superbly crafted" morality play. His only real complaint: "The Guthrie did not advertise in the gay press. Could it be that some white males at the Guthrie do not want the play to be their biggest hit of the season? It deserves to be." Donald Schoenbaum, one of Mann's nemeses at the Guthrie in the 1970s and still its executive director, had reportedly warned the current artistic director, Liviu Ciulei, that the show would be too big, too expensive, for the Guthrie's budget. But by the end of the production's thirty performances, the Guthrie announced that *Execution* drew 38,642 people, or 89.2 percent of capacity, exceeding projections.

Mann did not stay in Minneapolis to digest the reviews. Her father had suffered a heart attack in Chicago and was in the hospital. There, on Monday, October 21, Mann learned that thirty-nine-year-old Dan White, who had moved back to San Francisco, had committed suicide. He was discovered in his yellow Buick Le Sabre, apparently having run a garden hose from the exhaust pipe into the car. He had rolled up the windows, stuffed towels around the hose and turned on the engine. "I was in my father's hospital room," Mann recounted, "and I was so sad to hear it, and I remember thinking, 'Huh. He finally got the justice he felt he deserved.' He knew he shot both of them in cold blood. He knew that he went there to do it. I think he believed in the death penalty and I think he gave himself the death penalty."

Mark Bly called Mann in Chicago. The Guthrie was being deluged with phone calls from journalists wondering how this would affect the production. The actors were distressed—John Spencer especially. In addition they wanted to know if there would be a new scene. Finally, after much back-and-forth between dramatist and dramaturg, at around one o'clock on Tuesday morning, October 22, Mann dictated a single line to Bly over the phone, for TV reporter Joanna Lu (played by Lynn Chausow). The new line went into the show that night: "Dan White was found dead of carbon monoxide poisoning on October 21, 1985 at his wife's home in San Francisco, California." Mann inserted the line after Sister Boom Boom sarcastically reads from the "Book of Dan" and eats the Twinkie, and right before the judge sentences White and states that the punishment is too lenient. The suicide announcement, with its considerable irony, comes about nine lines from the end of the play.

"In the context of the documentary style," said dramaturg Mark Bly, "it's one more fact. Make of it what you will. It's the final piece of evidence in the execution of justice. Did he feel guilt, did he not feel guilt? Was this a result of his getting out and saying, 'Can't face it anymore, can't face this world?' It will always be a mystery, that gesture. . . . You just leave it there. It's like any of the Greek plays. Like *Oedipus Rex*. The final revelation, the final piece of the puzzle reveals a greater mystery."

Since Louisville, Mann had desired to put her own directorial signature on the play, so it was perhaps not surprising that, in addition to pursuing a regional theater for the opportunity, she wanted to direct *Execution of Justice* on Broadway. Osterman's planned Broadway production dangled an opportunity that might not come her way again soon, especially as a woman in the theater. And after all, it was her play. At some point, possibly even before she went into rehearsals at the Guthrie, Mann and

Osterman agreed that she would direct the production at the Virginia Theater.

The decision came as a surprise to Wager, who said that he did not learn about the change until the end of October 1985, when he was supposed to fly to Minneapolis and see a performance. "I heard from a secretary in Osterman's office that my trip to Minneapolis had been cancelled," he said, "because Emily had decided to direct the play herself, and I was no longer the director." Tara Rubin, now a flourishing casting director but at that time assistant to the producers and the general manager ("my very first job"), explained that she "would have been the secretary," since "it was only me, Osterman, and [General Manager] Al Francis in the office" (the office being Osterman's Sutton Place living room). Rubin had no recollection of making such a call.

In whatever way Wager learned he had been replaced, he averred years later that "I had signed a contract, and they told me that my signed contract was technically null and void, because Lester had not received SEC [Securities and Exchange Commission] certification to raise money." He remembered vividly being "furious. . . . I was furious about how it happened."

On November 9, Wager flew to Minneapolis at his own expense to see a matinee of *Execution of Justice* and afterward talk with Mann in person. According to a letter Wager wrote that December to his attorney Benjamin Zinkin, in Minneapolis he may have offered to direct the Broadway production and incorporate the ways in which Mann's interpretation differed from his, even though he did not agree with her interpretation (Mann did not take him up on the offer.) In that same letter to Zinkin, Wager reported that Osterman subsequently asked him to come on board as co-director; Wager declined. He did, however, want financial compensation for the loss of directing jobs which, he wrote Zinkin, he had turned down in order to clear his schedule for Broadway, and he wanted a share of Mann's director's and author's income for his directorial and conceptual contributions, that he believed had been used or might be used in productions or published versions of the play.

Mann's lawyer, George Sheanshang, sent a letter to Zinkin, dismissing Wager's claims.

It was, in short, a behind-the-scenes show-biz rumpus that left nobody looking very swell.

For Mann, who was now thirty-three years old, the prospect of directing *Execution* on Broadway provoked both anxiety and elation. Ming Cho Lee adapted his design—video cube, bleachers, and all—to the proscenium stage at the huge, 1,149-seat Virginia Theater (later the August Wilson Theater) on West Fifty-Second Street. Jennifer von Mayrhauser and Pat Collins, who had designed costumes and lights, respectively, at the Guthrie, were also on board. But according to Gerry Bamman, the producers did not want to bring the Guthrie cast to New York.

"My feeling," said Bamman, "is that the producers forced [Emily] into a corner. They didn't want to bring in a Guthrie production. So the people they didn't hire were David Hyde Pierce, who played Harvey Milk's friend (that's a great judgment) and Peter MacNichol, and both those people were so much better than the actors in New York that it just left gaping holes. She had to fight like a banshee to get them to accept John [Spencer], because he wasn't a name. That was the big battle. They just hated the idea. I know that she had some struggle about me, too, but she spared me the details." (If so, this apparently was the only time a producer objected to Mann casting her husband in one of her productions.) Mann's new cast included a few actors well-known from theater, films, or television, such as Donal Donnelly, Nicholas Kepros, and Earle Hyman, who had a recurring role on *The Cosby Show*. Others, such as Mary McDonnell, who was playing Mary Ann White; Peter Friedman, playing Dan White's charismatic defense attorney; and Wesley Snipes, who was cast as Sister Boom Boom, were still comparatively new to Broadway audiences.

Suzy Hunt recreated her Guthrie performance as Moscone's appointment secretary, Cyr Copertini, and remembered that Mann again wanted "blood on the floor." Susan Letzler Cole, who sat in on the New York rehearsals for her book *Directors in Rehearsal: A Hidden World*, wrote about John Spencer, hands cuffed behind his back, "crying so profusely" while rehearsing the scene of Dan White's confession to Frank Falzon, the Chief Inspector of Homicide, that Jon DeVries, playing Falzon, left the scene to find tissues so he could wipe Spencer's face. Mann, "visibly moved," in Cole's account, told Spencer "it's wonderful" and rubbed his shoulders and back to comfort him.

But as rehearsals went forward in February 1986 for a March 13 opening, problems arose. For one thing, Bly could not be there to give dramaturgical or emotional support; he was needed at the Guthrie, which in any case refused to pay his airfare to New York. He paid his own way for a few rehearsals, and then for tech week and previews. By that time, Bly recalled, Mann and Gerry were quarreling, and Mann's stress and exhaustion were palpable. So palpable that almost everyone except Bly shied away from giving her notes. It undoubtedly did not help that, two days before the first preview, co-producer Mortimer Caplin sent her suggestions for cutting the script (the running time was two and three-quarter hours with an intermission).

The producers had drawn up an $800,000 budget for rehearsing and mounting *Execution of Justice*, but even with the addition of associate producers Richard C. North and Christopher Stark, they apparently had not raised their target amount. "My understanding," said Tara Rubin, "is that Caplin covered for investments that never came through." Osterman, she observed, "was like an old-time impresario," with "old-fashioned optimism: 'It's all going to work out.'" Except there was not enough money to ride out the previews (only 1,674 people actually paid to watch the first four previews, according to *Variety*) or counter the effect on the box office of a dispiriting critical reception. *Variety*'s final tally was twelve pans, five favorable reviews, and three mixed. In the *New York Times*, Mel Gussow gave an intelligent, positive appraisal. But his review of the Arena production, which he occasionally cited favorably in his Broadway coverage, had been more of an endorsement. His latest critique would not have encouraged anyone to rush right over to the Virginia Theatre.

Bly recalled Mann begging him to get in touch with James H. Binger, a Minnesota philanthropist and Guthrie board member whose Jujamcyn Theaters owned the Virginia, and ask for an infusion of cash to keep the show open. But much as he wanted to help, Bly would have had to clear the request with the Guthrie's executive director, Donald Schoenbaum, who was unlikely to agree. "She was protecting her baby," said Gerry Bamman. "Emily, she's a tough cookie. And she was pulling every string she could to keep that show going."

Mann, when discussing attempts to save the show, did not remember trying to approach Binger, although she did recall the producers asking her to "give up any money" she was supposed to be paid. A letter to Mann signed by Lester Osterman and dated March 27, 1986, indicates that in order to persuade Mortimer Caplin to underwrite the production for the week after the March 13 opening, she agreed to loan $14,000 of her $22,800 author's advance to the producers' Limited Partnership. Mann was not the only potential lender called upon.

These efforts could not stave off the inevitable. On March 22, 1986, four years after Mann began *The Dan White Project*, *Execution of Justice* closed on Broadway after eight previews and twelve performances.

Mann felt devastated. She was also angry. "I felt a lot of the New York notices were unintelligent. I don't want to give up on Broadway, but plays like this will have to be subsidized," she told Richard Hummler, *Variety*'s long-time theater critic and reporter. "The critics here can't go on saying 'where are the new American plays?' and then kill them when they appear. This will make producers think 1,200 times before taking this kind of risk."

"We're all really proud of the work. It's a good piece," she told journalist George Richardson III at the *St. Louis Post-Dispatch*. But she urged "serious playwrights" to "avoid New York as long as you can . . . the great national theater of America is outside of New York—it's in our non-profit theater circuit around this country." As if to bolster her claim, the following year saw two more regional productions of the play: an award-winning conception from Chicago's Bailiwick Repertory Theatre and, in the City of Angels, a Colony Theatre Company production at the ninety-nine-seat Studio Theatre Playhouse.

Monday-morning quarterbacking is a frequent sport in the commercial theater, and the Broadway production of *Execution* received a thorough going-over. Most people blamed the producers for not raising enough money for a reserve that might have kept the production open. Others suggested New York critics rarely awarded kudos to a play anointed in the regions. Some thought the producers should have stuck with Douglas Wager; others, that Mann should not have directed her own play, which Mann took to mean, "The chutzpah of this woman."

Suzy Hunt remembered sizeable audiences and "lots of screams and 'bravos!' and people shouting 'yes!'" In fact, she recalled "it was a huge build-up to that opening night, so when the reviews came out, and our closing notice was listed on the board, I had no clue. I come to the theater and see the closing notice, and I went upstairs to the dressing room and I had to vomit. I was so undone by seeing that. After all our work."

Mark Bly, who thought the production every bit as strong as the one at the Guthrie, reflected years later that moving to a proscenium stage diluted the production's energy and its impact on an audience. Contrary to Hunt, in Bly's memory, "people just sat there politely, watching." Mostly he empathized with Mann during her first Broadway endurance test: directing an enormous production; endeavoring to navigate Broadway's backstage unions; trying to raise money that was not her responsibility to raise; and needing to soothe a cast that included her husband, all worrying if the show would help or hinder their careers. "She had given everything," said Bly.

The play was adapted for television by Michael Butler in 1999 and has continued to be produced, often by college and university theater departments. The British premiere finally took place in 2012 at London's Southwark Playhouse.

It remains at the pinnacle of Mann's documentary plays: for its theatrical pairing of stage action with video and film imagery; for its incisive portrait of the flawed workings of the American judicial system; and for arousing our visceral responses in the face of an imperfect society, including asking us to have pity for Dan White as well as anger at what he represents.

Theater scholars frequently place *Execution of Justice* into the "trial play" category, as Mann herself did initially, and the trial of Dan White is certainly the core of the play's structure. But the "trial play" box diminishes the play's political scope and resonance. Mann, in handwritten notes early in *The Dan White Project*, urged herself to

> Keep in mind. Trial of VALUES. TRIAL a metaphor for
>> city on trial
>> country
>> the times

Mann grasped that the issues which divided the citizens of San Francisco in 1978 were deeply rooted in American society. To quote Sister Boom Boom, "As gay people and as people of color and as women we all know the cycle of brutality which pervades our culture."

11

Transitions
(1986–1989)

Mann worried that the quick closing of her play would discourage people from hiring her. "I took it as an incredible failure," she remembered. "I was beat up pretty badly on that show." Despite her fears, she did receive offers to direct stage plays and assignments to write teleplays ("disease-of-the-week movies," she called them), which earned her more money than she could make directing or writing for the theater, and helped support her family.

The three years between directing *Execution* on Broadway and applying to become head of the McCarter Theatre Center were a transitional period for Mann, although she was only partially aware of it, like an undercurrent tugging at her as she went about her work and her daily life. Nicholas turned three in September 1986, and Emily and Gerry hired an au pair to live with them at Grandview and look after "Nicko" when they were away. Emily's parents visited regularly for the holidays, although in 1987, Arthur was diagnosed with lymphoma and underwent a bout of chemotherapy, and Emily began flying to Chicago as much as possible, to see him. This was also a period when she acknowledged to herself that her relationship with Gerry was no longer as loving as when she married him.

The 1980s saw a backlash against feminism, led, according to the feminist Susan Faludi, by the so-called New Right and expressed by media-spun myths that women's (supposed) financial and sexual independence was causing them extreme unhappiness. In her controversial 1991 best-seller, *Backlash: The Undeclared War Against American Women*,

Faludi wrote that "behind the news, cheerfully and endlessly repeated, that the struggle for women's rights is won, another message flashes. You may be free and equal now, it says to women, but you have never been more miserable." In Faludi's opinion, the struggle for women's rights was not won. She cited statistics that showed job opportunities for women actually declining, and women earning less than men for the same work. Certainly women in the professional theater continued to wrestle with hiring and remuneration inequality. On April 12, 1986, Mann's thirty-fourth birthday, she was the keynote speaker for the fourth annual Women in Theatre Festival, held at Marymount Manhattan College in New York City. She talked about what she considered an absence of political substance in the plays being produced, and the challenges facing women, who, like herself, wanted to make their living in the professional theater.

One of the features of Mann's career during this transitional time is its focus on women. Women are primary figures in the theater productions she was directing and the theatrical writing she undertook: Ibsen's *A Doll House* and *Hedda Gabler* (both adapted by Gerry Bamman and Irene L. Berman); her continuing collaboration on the rhythm-and-blues musical *Betsey Brown*. Women are the subjects of the film and television scripts in which Mann was most absorbed: *Sarafina!*, about a fictional Black South African student who helps lead the legendary Soweto Uprising of 1976; *The Story of Winnie Mandela*, about the wife of South Africa's imprisoned anti-apartheid leader, Nelson Mandela. Mann revisited what was now called *Annulla, An Autobiography* (1985), to which she added a recorded voice representing herself.

From Mann's perspective, the least independent among this array of women were the Ibsen heroines. In contrast to Claire Bloom's portrayal of Nora back in 1973, Mann's highly regarded November 1986 production of *A Doll House*, for the Hartford Stage Company, starred Mary McDonnell as an adorable, sexy, but childlike Nora Helmer. Having played the cute, flirtatious wife for so long, this Nora's exit at play's end was less a defiant slamming of the door than a hurt, frenzied, confused leave-taking. "Ibsen was not writing about a woman who suddenly gets hit by a bolt of lightning and walks out the door a new person," Mann commented for Janice Paran's 1987 article "Redressing Ibsen," in *American Theatre* magazine. "She's not Gloria Steinem. Quite the contrary—she's as much the childish woman as ever."

If Mann had at least some sympathy for Nora, she brought minimal compassion to Hedda for a July 1987 production at La Jolla Playhouse in California. Natalia Nogulich played General Gabler's haughty, sexually stifled daughter, and Emily cast Gerry as the venal Judge Brack. The production received positive reviews, but that did not lessen Mann's fundamental dislike of the play. "It's an awful play," she asserted years later. "There's no release in that play. And at a certain point, if you don't do it right, the audience thinks, 'When the hell is she just going to fucking blow her brains out?' I loathe this woman. So you have to keep all the balls in the air long enough for the audience to care enough or be fascinated enough not to lose patience."

So how did she get past her animus toward the bored and boringly vicious Hedda? Mann finally empathized with Hedda's marital situation. "She'd married the wrong man," Mann declared. "Everything about him drove her crazy. And that's how I got through it, I think. I understood being twenty-nine, the year women often make decisions. I did. And in that culture, she was long past her shelf life. Talk about settling: she was caught in a trap of her own making."

Mann and Winnie Mandela were a surer pairing. A youngster during the Civil Rights Movement, and a teenager when Black Power became a battle cry, Mann was on the outskirts of those struggles, no matter how concerned or engaged she felt. Now, courtesy of producers Camille Cosby and Judy James, who sold the idea for a series called *The Story of Winnie Mandela* to NBC Television, here was an opportunity to write about a ferocious battle for civil rights, led by a woman who appeared to be an unflinching example of self-ownership. She had married Nelson Mandela, one of South Africa's fiercest anti-apartheid leaders, in 1958; in 1962, Nelson was arrested and would remain in prison for twenty-seven years. Winnie Mandela took up the fight.

Mann began accumulating background material about the Man-
delas, assisted by Sara Blecher, who had moved from South Africa to
the United States with her family when she was twelve and was now
preparing to study filmmaking in New York. Mann indicated, however,
that she would not write about fifty-one-year-old Winnie Mandela on
the basis of news clippings. She wanted to talk with her in person.

Camille Cosby put up the money to send Mann to Johannesburg, but
Mann would have to contact Mandela herself. Blecher went on ahead
and arranged for Mann to meet the photographer Peter Magubane, who
was close to Winnie (they had been lovers, so far as Mann knew). When
Mann arrived in Johannesburg in October 1987, she visited Magubane
at his home in a white suburb called Sandton, for this short, stocky
man, whose large hands had trained his camera on people all over the
world, refused to live in a racially segregated township. Mann recollected that he "vetted" her for six hours. Subsequently he introduced
her and Blecher to Winnie, and for about a month he would pick Mann
up at her hotel in the morning and drive her to the reddish-brown brick
house in Soweto that Winnie had shared all too briefly with Nelson, and
to which she had returned after eight years of banishment to a shack in
the town of Brandfort. At the end of each day, Magubane would pick
Mann up and take her back to her hotel. He also made sure that the
women who cleaned Mann's hotel room protected her audio cassettes
when the South African secret police "swept" the rooms, which they
were wont to do on a regular basis.

"I saw [Winnie] nearly every day for four weeks," Mann recalled
fondly, "and when it was too dangerous, Peter did not take me. There
were near-death experiences for her while I was there. Gunfire attacks.
Bomb threats. I was there at a very bad time. As Winnie said, 'One
of the last kicks of the dying horse.' The apartheid government was
going down, and it became more and more cruel." Mann often stood
in Mandela's kitchen, its walls peppered with bullet holes, watching and
listening while Winnie and her friends and, no doubt, members of her
security detail, cooked and ate and talked.

Left to right: Emily Mann, Winnie Mandela, and Sara Blecher in South Africa, 1987
COURTESY OF EMILY MANN

"When I look back at it, as a rather mature adult, I am angry at myself for taking the kind of risks that I took," said Mann. Her father was furious that she had put herself in danger. But Gerry had encouraged her to go, even though it would mean being away from Nicholas for a month. "I was so filled with adrenaline. It was like being a war journalist. I was following a story."

Sometimes Mann and Mandela went to church together or traveled in Mandela's Volkswagen Kombi, or van, and drove around Soweto, past concrete houses with corrugated tin roofs as well as shacks built out of sticks. Photographs among Mann's papers show men tending fruit stands and women carefully balancing tubs laden with goods on their heads. If Mandela, when Mann met her, was already involved in the kidnapping, torture, and murders undertaken by her security detail, reportedly at her orders, Mann said she was unaware of it. Over a year earlier, however, in April 1986, Mandela had given a speech endorsing "necklacing," the practice of placing a tire around a person's neck and setting it on fire.

"She did hate the traitors within the Black community," said Mann, "and she hated the people around them, the whites who were living in privilege. She had a lot of hate in her heart." Mann believed that Mandela had been damaged psychologically, the result of imprisonment, torture, surviving solitary confinement, and banishment from her home. Her husband had been incarcerated for more than twenty years, and she had run a revolution in his absence, "using what was left of herself to continue getting justice for Black people in South Africa." She drank heavily, and Mann observed that "You'd see [Winnie] one day, and she'd be one way, and another day she'd be very different." Mandela owned numerous wigs and "would change according to how she felt that day. She was often unrecognizable from one day to the next."

But, Mann added, Winnie "may be the most naturally charismatic person I've ever met. She would walk into a room, and your back would be to her, and something would make you turn. The air in the room changed when she would enter it. She could dance like nobody's business. Laugh like nobody's business. Cry. Huge, incredible personality. . . . She's a complex figure." The two women established a rapport, largely, Mann believed, because they shared with each other their experiences of being mothers (Winnie had two daughters). Also, Mandela wanted to cooperate for the television project, because she and Magubane wanted her story out in the world.

Mann's teleplay, originally titled *The Story of Winnie Mandela*, is in two parts. Part One, "The Awakening," takes Winnie from her childhood in Pondoland Hills, where she attended an all-Black school headed by her father, through her early career as a social worker, her passionate marriage to Nelson Mandela, and his arrest and imprisonment in 1962. Part Two, "The Challenge," leads us through the next twenty-two years of Mandela's life, as she withstands her own imprisonment, torture, banishment, and illness, yet manages, between arrests, to defy South Africa's racist laws and rally Black Africans, especially women, to battle apartheid alongside her. Part One calls for the sort of visuals of which commercial television was fond: Winnie's father taking her to a store and buying her first pair of shoes; Winnie as a young social worker, helping children suffering from malnutrition; accepting Nelson's marriage proposal, in the front seat of his car; watching Nelson in court. But Part Two is stronger thematically and visually, filled as it is with Mandela's physical and mental struggles, and with images that a commercial television network of the late 1980s probably found too grim: a guard twisting Mandela's arm until we hear it crack; Mandela forced to stand for days on a pile of bricks, until she urinates blood and faints; Mandela sleeping on the dirt floor of the shack in Brandfort.

In scene after scene, Mann builds the horror of what Mandela endured at the hands of South Africa's authoritarian regime, interspersed with scenes involving Mandela's friends and family, who try, as much as the restrictive laws allow, to help her survive. Part Two ends with several fast-moving events: news that on November 21, 1985, in Pretoria's Black township of Mamelodi, white police have fired on thousands of women peacefully marching to present their mayor with a list of grievances; news that Winnie's shack has been bombed; Winnie speaking at the funeral of women and infants slaughtered in Mamelodi; and finally, Winnie pushing away a white policewoman who tries to arrest her, getting into a car, and driving home to Soweto.

"The triumph of the spirit is what I found there," said Mann about her South African journey. "I don't know if, finally, at the end of Winnie's life, you would say that. But I found triumph in the face of horrible oppression. They refused to have their humanity stripped from them." Magubane said Mann had "whispered with history."

Among the women whose stories Mann was exploring during the late 1980s was that of Emily Mann herself. In February 1985, while Arena Stage was pondering whether or not to produce *Execution of Justice*, Mann was at the Repertory Theatre of St. Louis, where Timothy Near, who had shifted from acting to directing, was preparing to stage Mann's play about Annulla Allen. Jacqueline Bertrand would be playing Annulla, in a production slated also for Atlanta's Alliance Theatre. "'I'm going to dare to ask you this,'" Near remembered saying to Mann, "'but I feel that your voice should be in the play.' I didn't really think she'd say okay, but she did. . . . I felt her story, why she wrote the play, was so important," Near explained. "A modern young woman trying to connect to her roots. It was Emily's journey to self-knowledge."

"My initial reaction," Mann recalled, "was 'I don't belong in it.' I wanted the audience to be me, so that they have a direct connection with Annulla. I didn't want to stand in the way of that. And Timi [Near] basically said, 'Well, they can still have that connection. You're not going to be onstage. You're going to be a voice over.' And I said, 'Well, let's see what comes out.'"

In a reversal of roles, Near became the interviewer and Mann the subject, although Mann ultimately selected the new words to be inserted into her play and where to put them. Much in the interviews did not go into the St. Louis revision, because Mann, always protective of her family, was careful about what she wanted to reveal. But the stories and reflections that she did cull for the play are earthy, and they sound colloquial and American in contrast to Annulla's Eastern European inflections and speech rhythms. Near's intuition, that the Young Woman's Voice would add dimension to the play, proved correct. The Young Woman's narrative about how she and a college friend went to Europe in the summer of 1974, first to meet her friend's aunt, then to search for the town where her own ancestors had lived and died, enlarges the play's thematic resonance and provides the conceptual authority missing from the original version. *Annulla, An Autobiography* is not only about survivors such as Annulla Allen and the descendents of Mann's Jewish ancestors, but also about the act of journeying that many of us take, to find where we come from and perhaps where we belong. In addition, as Near anticipated, listening to the Young Woman (Near's voice, recorded) at times allows the audience simply to watch Annulla puttering about in her kitchen. "I wanted to see Annulla not talking," said Near. "I wanted to see her living."

In October 1988, eleven years after first directing the play at Guthrie 2, Mann was asked by Deborah Pope, the artistic director of the New Theatre (TNT) of Brooklyn, to stage the reconceived version in TNT's ninety-nine-seat open-proscenium theater on Dean Street.

Karen Ludwig, an actor with a smooth, warm voice, recorded the Young Woman. Forty-three-year-old Linda Hunt, winner of the 1983 Academy Award for Best Supporting Actress for *The Year of Living Dangerously*, played Annulla.

A videotape of a performance exists in the Theatre on Film and Tape (TOFT) Archive at the New York Public Library for the Performing Arts. Hunt's short, dark hair is slicked back behind her ears, and large eyeglasses dominate her face; she wears a tailored gray jacket over a white blouse and gray skirt. Her Annulla is energetic and sly, outgoing and humorous, but also pained at times by her memories. Hunt gestures theatrically, even when holding a carrot in each hand and making chicken soup.

As in Minneapolis and Chicago, critics focused on the performance, which they extolled, and to a lesser extent on the play and Mann's direction. After all, it was Hunt's celebrity that had drawn more critics than usual to what, for many, were still the wilds of Brooklyn. Most reviewers wrote that the Young Woman's Voice contributed breadth to the play. Even Mel Gussow, who believed the script needed "additional structuring and clarification," wrote in the *New York Times* that "What gives the monodrama unexpected dimension is the narrator." He thought the play would be stronger "if the narrator took an even more active role as counterpoint."

Re-acquainting herself with *Annulla, An Autobiography* in 1988 was a paradoxical event in Mann's life. *Annulla* had not only been her first professionally produced script, but also its production at Guthrie 2 had set her on the dual paths of director and playwright, and during the eleven years since Barbara Bryne bustled onto the stage with Annulla's packages in her arms, Mann had achieved recognition accorded only a few women in post–World War II American theater.

Directing and writing for the theater did not provide a substantial living, however, especially at the regional theaters where Mann was most likely to be hired. Also, whether as director or playwright, she put vast amounts of energy and devotion into projects that sometimes took years to come to fruition, or for one reason or another did not materialize.

She had adapted *Les Nuits et les Jours* (*Nights and Days*) by Pierre Laville, who had translated *Still Life* into French, and on March 1, 1985, she directed a reading at the Public Theater with a cast that included John Spencer, Swoosie Kurtz, Blythe Danner, and Barbara Bryne. A production had been discussed for May 1986, with Danner and possibly Christopher Walken, and Mann held the time open in her schedule. The production never happened. Mann had been working on Shange's *Betsey Brown* for the Public since 1983, directing readings and workshops and preparing for a pre–New York try-out. But the out-of-town production was cancelled, and in 1988, after Mann and Joe Papp butted heads about the musical's next step, Papp cancelled the project.

The film and television industries proved as unpredictable as the theater. Mbongeni Ngema, who had written and staged the musical *Sarafina!*, asked Mann in 1987 to write a film adaptation of the popular show, and she believed she turned out a screenplay in two and a half weeks. Her script was never used. She submitted Part One of *The Story of Winnie Mandela* in January 1988 and Part Two in March, and subsequently made numerous revisions at the request of Cosby, James, and network executives. Then the word came from NBC that the script might be better as a one-shot, made-for-television movie than a series. Finally the network killed the project. Winnie Mandela had been implicated in assassinations carried out by her security detail, a.k.a. the Mandela United Football Club, and American commercial television was not about to invest any further in a film about an African woman associated with torture and murder, no matter how much she had suffered or how brave she had once been. In 1990, Nelson Mandela was released from prison after twenty-seven years and immediately became a more appealing, and marketable, subject than his wife, whom he moved to divorce two years later.

Perhaps Mann would have continued her freelance existence had she and Gerry Bamman remained together. But the marriage had been struggling at least since 1987, when they were both in La Jolla for *Hedda Gabler*. "Gerry and I were not happy," said Mann. "It was a dark time. . . . Gerry explained it to Nick once by saying, 'I guess neither one of us felt loved enough.' I think that's pretty true," said Mann. "It got to a point where the distance between us was so great, and there were long silences, and it was so cold for so many years."

They were spending more and more time apart and by May 1989, had separated. Mann told of going down to Louisville, where Bamman was playing Prospero in *The Tempest* at ATL, and meeting in his bedroom. "I remember sobbing on the bed," she said, "and took off the ring, and I remember thinking 'Am I acting out *Doll House*? Or is this really me?'. . . We had a great few years together. We didn't know how to keep it going." Mann, six-year-old Nicholas, and an au pair remained in the house at Grandview-on-Hudson. Gerry moved out, but lived nearby.

Mann, of course, was more self-sufficient than Ibsen's heroine, but as Susan Faludi and other feminists had noted, their activism had not brought women the equality for which they had strived. "I thought, when we started to make breakthroughs in the '70s, that we would continue," said Mann about women in the professional theater. "The doors would open, and off we'd go, and it would be by merit, not by gender. And I took stock and realized—not." Even if film and television assignments paid well, none of Mann's commissioned scripts had been produced. "With the collapse of the Winnie project and the horrible experience on Broadway, and then not getting *Betsey* off the ground properly, I came to realize I really needed an institution behind me if I were ever going to get my work done in a way that was healthy for me."

Now thirty-seven and a single parent, with whom Nicholas would be living most of the time, while spending several weekends each month with his father, she contemplated two options: teaching at a university or heading a theater. The first might allow her to write, but not to direct as much as she wished; the second conceivably could allow her to write, direct, and build the kind of supportive internal structure she often found lacking as a guest in someone else's theatrical house. But would being responsible for management and artistic decisions even give her time to write and direct?

"I started to talk to people about what it was like to run a theater and stay an artist," said Mann. Often she recounted how Mark Lamos, who had been artistic director at Hartford Stage since 1980, encouraged her, saying in effect "that you will bring to the theater those people whom you think are most important as artists in the country and put that in front of that audience. And you are absolutely built for that. And you'll stay an artist and you'll grow. And the minute you're not growing, leave."

In 1989, the McCarter Theatre Center in Princeton, New Jersey, was looking for a new artistic director. Mann applied for the job.

12

By the Scruff of the Neck
(1989–1994)

THE MCCARTER THEATRE officially opened on February 21, 1930, with a musical item called *The Golden Dog*, performed by sundry members of Princeton University's famed undergraduate drama group, the Triangle Club. Costumed in bonnets, short jackets, and skirts that revealed a lot of leg between hem and shoe, the chorus of men kicked their way across the vast proscenium stage. The show was written and directed by A. Munroe Wade, Class of 1930, and Joshua L. Logan, Class of 1931, who later became a notable Broadway and Hollywood director. One of the men in the chorus that night was reportedly a sophomore by the name of James Stewart.

The millionaire behind the stone, neo-gothic theater building at 91 University Place was one Thomas Nesbitt McCarter, Class of 1888, and he must have wanted the edifice that bore his name to be huge. A tower six stories high contained the dressing rooms. The stage area—wings and all—was exceeded at that time in New York City only by the stages of the Metropolitan Opera House and the Ziegfeld Theatre, where the musical *Showboat* had opened in 1927. The McCarter's orchestra and balcony sat 1,077, more than several Broadway houses.

With amenities like those, the McCarter became both a pre-Broadway stop during the 1930s and 1940s and a destination for touring companies of Broadway hits. But in the 1950s, the quality of the Broadway tryouts diminished, the McCarter lost money, and the university, which had taken ownership of the building from the Triangle Club in 1950, decided to turn the McCarter into a center for the performing

The McCarter Theatre Center long before the Berlind Theatre was added (n.d.)
COURTESY OF THE MCCARTER THEATRE CENTER

arts. Guided by the stage director Milton Lyon, then by the actor and director Arthur W. Lithgow (father of actor John Lithgow) and a young booking director named William Lockwood Jr., the McCarter expanded its music, dance, and film programming. Theater, however, remained its core offering.

Operating expenses rose, and in 1973 the university leased the building to the newly incorporated, not-for-profit McCarter Theatre Center for the Performing Arts, which became responsible for day-to-day operations and fundraising, although the university, as the building's owner, continued to contribute a share and have a say in the McCarter's life. The director Michael Kahn became producing director at the start of the McCarter's 1974–1975 season and took the McCarter into the world of government and foundation grants, forestalling the university's push to close the center completely.

For the next fifteen years, the theater at the heart of the McCarter seemed in search of an identity. Kahn imported well-known actors from New York City, produced American and European classics and usually staged two new plays each season, including the world premieres of Sam

Shepard's *Angel City* and Ann Commire's *Put Them All Together*. But critics started panning McCarter's productions. Subscriptions fell, deficits climbed, and Kahn exited in the spring of 1979, as did his managing director, Edward A. Martenson.

The Board of Trustees turned next to forty-three-year-old Nagle Jackson, who had been artistic director of the Milwaukee Repertory Company for six seasons. Relying on a core group of professional local actors, Jackson set up a version of a resident company, although on occasion he, too, brought actors from New York City. He set up a director exchange with Moscow's Bolshoi Drama Theater, better known as the Gorky; introduced a "Playwrights at McCarter" reading series on Monday nights and his own adaptation of *A Christmas Carol*, which became a December fixture of McCarter's six-production season.

Jackson's tenure coincided with the physical renovation of the McCarter, which was in desperate need of rejuvenation, and during the 1985–1986 season the theater went dark for Phase I of the rehabilitation. The proscenium was rebuilt, the auditorium gutted. A new balcony was constructed, side boxes added, and the ceiling was lowered to improve the acoustics. Air conditioning was installed.

Phase I cost more and took longer than anyone anticipated, and Phase II, for constructing new offices, dressing rooms, rehearsal rooms, and a new shop (the old one was beneath the stage) also threatened to take longer than planned. Managing director Alison Harris, who had been indispensable during the renovations, resigned at the end of the 1986–1987 season rather than endure another round of building. To replace her, the board hired one Robert Altman (not the film director), but he resigned abruptly after six months, and so the board promoted John Herochik, who had been production manager since the 1982–1983 season. Jackson, who maintained that he had promised to stay for only ten years, told the board that he would be leaving after the 1989–1990 season.

"I had gone to other theaters and asked what they thought of McCarter," said Liz Fillo, an actor and McCarter trustee who was on the search committee for a new artistic director. "And the most telling comment

I got was from the managing director of the Old Globe in San Diego. 'I don't think about it,' he said. And I thought, 'Ah, that tells me a lot.' We were just not on the map. He said, 'You are a safe theater that does good work. But it has no excitement, there's no notoriety about it.'" According to Fillo, even the Princeton University students did not pay much attention to the McCarter. "I'd meet students and say, 'Oh, do you go to McCarter?' and they'd say, 'What's McCarter?' I mean, we were right there." Fillo recalled that the board received maybe two dozen applications for the position of artistic director, a small number for an arts center wih a League of Resident Theatres (LORT) contract.

Mann's first interview took place in the early autumn of 1989, in the spacious home of Ruth Wilson, McCarter's board chair and the head of the search committee. Mann's recollection of the meeting was mainly sensory. She had driven an hour and a half from Grandview and arrived on time. It was also lunch time. Unfortunately, nobody offered her anything except iced tea and peanuts, and she felt dizzy from hunger.

The committee responded in varying ways to her proposals. "We liked her idea," said Wilson, "that 'here we are in Princeton, New Jersey, halfway between New York and Philadelphia. We have a lot of professional talent in those places. I intend to bring them down here.'" Mann told the committee that, if she were offered the position, she would not have a resident company and her seasons would be a mixture of classics and new work from around the world. She remembered one woman saying, "Well, you know, we don't use the F-word in Princeton." Mann responded that she guessed she would not be able to bring her friend David Mamet or "a whole lot of plays written in the last fifteen or twenty years," which led others on the committee to jump in and say they would welcome David Mamet or anyone else of his caliber.

One of the committee's primary concerns was whether a person who had practically no administrative experience could be in charge of a performing arts center. Despite the presence of William W. Lockwood Jr., who selected the dance, music, film, and special programs and was widely admired, McCarter's artistic director was in charge of setting artistic policy for the entire center, not just the theater series.

Ruth Wilson remembered that Mann "was very confident in what she could do, and at first we were kind of stunned. You don't know what to believe sometimes when you've just met somebody and they're full of . . . self-confidence," a reaction, had Mann known about it, which might have made her wonder if Wilson and others would have responded similarly to a "very confident" man.

But at least one member of the committee did not share Wilson's concerns. "I was very taken with her," said Joan S. Girgus, who had been dean of the college at Princeton and also the first woman to be a university trustee on the McCarter's board. "I thought she was really smart. I thought she understood universities. She was a 'fac brat,' as we called them here, and that was a plus for McCarter, to have someone who understood universities. I had been a thirty-five-year-old dean of the college, so I was not at all taken aback by the notion of a woman in her late thirties running something. . . . I, in fact, argued, and no one objected, that we were better off finding a young person on the way up, given our situation in the theater world."

According to Liz Fillo, the committee narrowed the list of applicants to three, one of whom was Mann. "The big discussion," said Fillo, "was whether to take this leap of faith and go with, number one, a woman, and number two, a woman who had a real agenda and was going to be controversial, and we knew it. I guess we felt that, after a safe ten years with Nagle, we needed to shake things up a bit. And we thought Emily was the one to do that for us."

On a chilly Monday morning, December 4, 1989, local journalists gathered in the McCarter's lobby while Ruth Wilson introduced Mann, who praised Nagle Jackson's accomplishments and the university with which she planned to establish a new relationship. "The work that I do has political, social and historical implications. I hope to take advantage of the great minds here as resources," the press quoted her as saying. Regarding her plans for upcoming seasons, Mann made it clear that she wanted to "celebrate all that is American. Ethnicity is part of America and will be on our stage."

"Woman Playwright Appointed Director of McCarter Theatre" went one local headline, and "A Mann for (at least) three seasons" chortled another, referring to the new artistic director's three-year contract. The sexist innuendos did not go unnoticed by Mann, but for the moment she basked in the pleasure of her new position, with all the opportunities for change and creativity it promised. She was the first woman to head the McCarter in its nearly sixty-year history. Out of LORT's sixty-eight theaters in 1989, she was the eleventh woman to lead a member theater.

When considering whether to apply for the McCarter position, Mann had been warned that being a liberal in Princeton was like going behind enemy lines. This town, where the first nine presidents of its fabled university had owned slaves, had once been called the most Northern outpost of Southern culture, a description attributed to the actor Paul Robeson, who was born in a segregated Princeton in 1898 and lived there until he was about eight. When Robeson performed *Othello* opposite Uta Hagen at the McCarter for one August night in 1942, in a pre-Broadway touring production directed by Margaret Webster, he would not have been welcome at any inn in white Princeton.

In response to the Civil Rights and Women's Liberation movements, Princeton seemed to change outwardly. In 1969, James Floyd became the first African American elected to the Princeton Township's governing board, which then chose him to be mayor in 1971. The university had begun admitting women in 1969. Even so, conservatism dominated the political outlooks of both town and gown. But why do you want to preach to the choir? Mann's father had asked, and Mann agreed with him. Yet she did not expect the implicit racism, outright anti-Semitism, and sexism that she encountered.

"I didn't realize what a segregated place this was," Mann said about the Princeton to which she moved with Nicholas in 1990. "I felt it when I got here. I was very uncomfortable. I had recently come back from South Africa, and the McCarter board wanted me to come to a gala on June 16 (I was starting July 1). And June 16 is, like, a sacred day in South Africa and in much of the Black community in America, because it is the anniversary of the 1976 Soweto Uprising. And here I was at an all-white gala in the middle of Princeton. There was not one Black person at that gala. It felt like Johannesburg in the late '80s."

The anti-Semitism was not aimed at her directly. "At that time people didn't know I was Jewish, because I can pass," she said. "One of the first cocktail parties I went to, I was in a circle of people talking and making anti-Semitic comments. They were big donors to the theater. And I kept saying to myself, 'Say something, say something, you little coward.' I was so upset with myself, because I shut up. I was crying to my mother on the phone, and she said, 'No, you did the right thing. You find out who's who and don't ever forget it.' And I did. And I haven't."

Mann did take a stand when it came to defying the stone-age rules of the Nassau Club, which had been founded in Princeton in 1889 as a gentlemen's club. The new artistic director of the McCarter had been asked to speak there to a group of Rotarians, and when she went up the front steps, one gentleman told her she had to go around to the back door. Their ensuing tête-à-tête, as Mann recounted it, was scene-worthy dialogue:

"He said, 'Ohnonono, you can't go in the front door.' I said, 'Excuse me?' He said, 'Only the wives of members can go in the front door. All the other women have to go in the back.' And I said, 'Well, I don't go in the back door. That's not my style.' And he said, 'Well, but you're speaking at noon.' And I said, 'Well, I won't be speaking if I don't go through the front door.' He said, 'But what do you mean?' And I said, 'Well, just what I said. I have to go through the front door.'"

So Mann went through the front door. And gave her speech.

The challenges for Mann during her first season at the McCarter came from both outside and inside the arts center. Phase II of the McCarter's physical overhaul was supposed to have been completed in time for Mann to schedule a full season beginning in the fall of 1990. But the approval of Phase II by the Princeton Regional Planning Board had lapsed in 1988 and had to be renegotiated. Then, in spring 1990, James Florio, New Jersey's new governor, cut the state arts budget by more than 40 percent, which sliced grants that had been designated for the renovation. What with one thing and another, ground breaking for Phase II did not begin until July 12, 1990. Mann and her staff were exiled to offices opposite Princeton Airport, about four miles away, and the theater was dark until December, reopening just in time for the traditional holiday-season Nutcracker ballet and *A Christmas Carol*. But those productions, along with the three plays and one musical Mann had slated for January through May 1991, needed to rehearse elsewhere, and sets had to be built in the leaky Armory on the university campus.

Internal mismanagement, according to what Mann wrote her parents at the beginning of October 1990, was causing even more serious problems.

"Unfortunately, I was not properly informed about the state this theater was in. I don't believe it was deliberate misinformation, I think the people here simply do not know what it takes to make theater," Mann wrote. "We had a meeting last night of the Long Range Planning Committee . . . and I outlined in brutal detail what needs to be done. They were shocked at the state of affairs we are in, but at least the board members present now see what the problems are. The question is: is it too late to make the theater what it needs to be this season and next, or can we mobilize the board quickly and raise the money needed to make the plans a reality? Can we recover the lost money and time and sell this season so that we at least can have revenue from the box office? Can we raise money to pay the bills for this season? Can we raise money to back the level of shows I want to do next season?"

In a report Mann submitted to the board's personnel committee, point by damning point she outlined the mismanagement she was encountering. Since March 1990, Mann wrote, she had been asking for a budget update from managing director John Herochik, but had not received it until October. Exorbitant salary increases and artists' fees had been arranged without her knowledge or board approval. As for the sort of advance work necessary to make a season happen, numerous contracts had either been negotiated poorly, sent out late, or not sent at all, resulting in the loss of a choreographer and a musical director for the musical *Betsey Brown*, which Mann was preparing to direct in the spring. Without contracts, designers and actors were threatening to take other jobs. The performance rights for *The Glass Menagerie*, which was going into rehearsal on December 4 for a January opening, had almost not been secured. Fortunately the literary manager, Evangeline Morphos, had discovered the lapse in time.

"This is what I think happened," said Liz Fillo. "John [Herochik] started making mistakes and then he started covering up the mistakes. And once you start covering up the mistakes, . . . you can't get yourself out of it. He didn't come to the board and tell us what was happening."

Mann was a fighter, but she was understandably distressed by the potential calamity facing her. She had moved herself and Nicholas from Grandview-on-Hudson, and had rented a ranch-style house of late-1950s vintage about a mile from the theater. Nicholas, who had just turned seven, was enrolled in a new school. But the McCarter could plausibly collapse around her before she even had a chance to produce her first season.

Mann called Peter Zeisler, the executive director of Theatre Communications Group (TCG), and he put her in touch with William P. Wingate, formerly the general manager of the Mark Taper Forum and at that time a consultant to the National Arts Stabilization Fund. Wingate sat down with Mann and with the business manager, Timothy J. Shields, and at the beginning of December 1990 spent considerable time meeting with department heads, key board members, and key people at the university and local banks.

"[The McCarter] had not raised enough money to complete [the construction], and the banks were reluctant to provide more credit," Wingate explained. "Princeton University was getting cold feet, and the staff Emily inherited from Nagle and the staff she brought in were seriously at odds. The community was taking a wait-and-see attitude. 'What do you mean? We've been here sixty years, and we liked what Nagle did.'" The McCarter, Wingate affirmed, "was on the verge" of closing, "but board members were determined to let Emily have a crack at a first season," although, he said, "they needed somebody besides Emily to tell them that things could work out if they would stand behind her."

John Herochik was asked to resign, and Wingate agreed to be interim executive director on a two-days-a-week basis until a new managing director could be hired. By February, the McCarter had enlisted Abby Evans as associate executive director, to be at McCarter full-time; Timothy J. Shields went from business manager to general manager; and the two presented Wingate with a plan that they thought the university could back financially, including a staff reduction and salary cuts of at least 25 percent. "Emily didn't hesitate to get behind the plan and was the first one to take the cut," said Wingate. "Most agreed with it. A couple left. That was the groundwork for rebuilding. Then I began looking for candidates for a permanent managing director, telling them the theater was shrunk, but there would be a chance to rebuild."

"I slept, like, four hours a night for a year," said Mann.

The Glass Menagerie, Mann's first production as artistic director of the McCarter Theatre Center, opened on January 18, 1991. In keeping with the traumas of the previous months, the opening was not without its snafus. In Mann's memory, the sound technician pushed the "go" button for Mel Marvin's opening music and there was no sound. The production stage manager, Susie Cordon, recalled that the turntable "got screwed up," although an announcement was made, the machinery was fixed, and the performance continued. Adding to the tension, just two days before, the United States and a coalition of thirty-four countries began bombing Iraq in retaliation against Iraq's president, Saddam Hussein, for invading Kuwait, and in one of her first public gestures as leader of the McCarter, Mann made an announcement about the bombing before the start of Wednesday night's preview performance. The war brought renewed poignancy to Tom Wingfield's closing lines: "For nowadays the world is lit by lightning! Blow out your candles, Laura—and so good-bye."

Mann had selected *Menagerie* because it played to her strengths as a director and because her earlier production at the Guthrie had been received so warmly by audiences and critics. Ming Cho Lee essentially recreated his abstract, suggestive set and built a thrust stage out into the audience, and at the McCarter, that thrust, coupled with the McCarter's cavernous proscenium stage, accentuated the enormity of the world beyond the Wingfield family's struggles. Jennifer von Mayrhauser once again designed the costumes, and Mann used the tapes of the music that Mel Marvin had composed for Minneapolis. Lighting designer Robert Wierzel was the only newcomer to the creative team.

Yet Mann was directing actors who brought different qualities and rhythms to the script than the ensemble at the Guthrie. At the McCarter, Shirley Knight played Amanda, according to the critic for the *Philadelphia Daily News*, as "a ripely alive matron . . . who isn't remotely unwilling to come on to the Gentleman Caller as surrogate to the painfully shy Laura." The reviews suggest that this production belonged to Amanda and to Dylan McDermott's vigorous, sardonic Tom, although Judy Kuhn made a poignant, overtly crippled Laura, and Jeff Weatherford, playing Jim O'Connor, the gentleman caller, was appealingly brash and tender during their love scene.

Alvin Klein, the critic for the New Jersey section of the *New York Times*, became a Mann enthusiast with this production. "Unlike the transparent, closed-in representation of an apartment and the tenement exterior that one customarily associates with Tennessee Williams's first masterwork," he wrote, "the vision of Ms. Mann's production is of vastness. . . . she has grasped the play in new—yes, unexpected—and never less than loving ways." Even Mel Gussow praised the production, although he could not resist a gratuitous comment: "With an assurance that partly derives from the fact she has staged the play before . . . Ms. Mann lets 'The Glass Menagerie' unfold with a quiet resonance.'"

Mann's parents flew east for the opening. Arthur Mann, at sixty-nine, was still teaching, but cancer and bouts of chemotherapy had left him thin and frail, and his face looked gaunt. "Now that you have proved you are worthy of McCarter," he wrote his daughter after returning home, "the big question is whether McCarter is worthy of you. I say that not in truculence but as a statement of fact. You might find it helpful to remember as efforts are made to rebuild the theater on sound financial and administrative principles. . . . More plainly, You won a big victory on Friday the 18th, Emily Mann. Enjoy."

Mann often told the story of how, when she was seeking advice about tackling an artistic director post, the British director Peter Hall told her to make a pact with herself: everything she put on the stage should be an event. "Don't go up to your room and pick five titles you like," Hall urged in Mann's telling. "Each play has to have a reason for being, and you build a sense of anticipation and excitement around each piece."

"That became my mantra," Mann said.

Of course, at times a production becomes an event for less-than-de-sirable reasons. The second production of Mann's inaugural season, David Rabe's new play, *Those the River Keeps*, which Rabe himself was directing, ran three and a half hours in rehearsal, with one intermission, and before it opened Mann sent a cautionary letter to subscribers, alert-ing them that the play had tough content and rough language. Mann acknowledged years later that, had the play come to her after she had more experience heading the McCarter, she would have held a work-shop, as she did with *Betsey Brown*, which was an event.

In 1976, *for colored girls who have considered suicide / when the rainbow is enuf*, the first play by the twenty-seven-year-old poet Ntozake Shange, was produced by Joseph Papp at the New York Shakespeare Festival Public Theater. The play, which Shange called a choreopoem, began life in a Lower East Side bar and was first picked up by Woodie King for the New Federal Theatre, and then by Papp. It migrated to Broadway, where it was nominated for a 1977 Tony Award. The writing was fluid and passionate and rhythmic, and defiant in its portrayal of forceful, independent Black women. Shange became a feminist hero. The New York Shakespeare Festival became her theatrical home, and she called Papp one of her "artist daddies."

By 1979, Shange, who was born Paulette Linda Williams in New Jersey, had started to collaborate with the jazz pianist Cecil Taylor on an opera called *Carrie*, based on one of her short stories. The setting is St. Louis, 1957, where Shange moved with her upper-middle-class family when she was eight years old, attending newly integrated schools in one of the most segregated cities in the United States. About a girl's coming-of-age, *Carrie* was semi-autobiographical. The action, as Shange describes it in an early treatment, starts in "a house fulla chirren who was fulla the dickens." Letty, which was Shange's name at camp, is the oldest of four. Other characters include grandma; Letty's father, a staunch believer in integration; her mother, who leaves home for a time; Regina, who helps with the kids but is fired when the grandmother catches her necking with a boy named Roscoe; and Carrie, who is "a big woman." Carrie lives with the family while the mother is away and teaches Letty about becoming a self-respecting young woman. But the mother returns, she and Carrie don't get along, and when Carrie winds up in jail, "cuz i hadta cut this friend a mine," Letty's mother tells Carrie to pack up and move out. Letty sings the final lines: "cdnt see how anybody didnt know carrie wdnt cut nobody less they hurt her a whole lot. not less she hurt a whole lot."

Shange had been enamored of the 1982 production of *Still Life* in Los Angeles and believed that she recommended Mann to Joe Papp for the project. Thus it was that in August 1983, the Public Theater asked Mann to attend a reading, with the idea of hiring her to improve the structure of what was still a stream-of-consciousness riff more than a script, and ultimately direct it. *Carrie* had already undergone several changes. Letty was now Betsy Brown ("Betsy" would eventually become "Betsey"), and there was a new title: *Betsy Brown: A Rhythm and Blues Opera*. Papp had not gotten along with Cecil Taylor, according to Shange, and charming, bearded Baikida Carroll, who played a sensuous trumpet and could compose in a range of styles, from blues to free jazz, was now on board.

"Mr. Papp sent me around to Emily's house on 6th Street with a script in hand to meet her, and express my views on the music and the show," Carroll wrote me in an email in 2015. "It was a steamy summer afternoon. I was clad in shorts, sandals and tee [sic] shirt. Emily opened the door with a radiant smile, an affectionate hello, the glow and stomach of a pregnancy, and the enthusiasm of a powerful director ready to get to work."

In an interview with Nancy Erhard at the University of Minnesota, Duluth, Mann described the early draft of *Betsy Brown* as "this wreck of a script with some of Zake's best poetry in it, but really no structure." The reading she attended had "a great group of people, Ruby Dee, Hattie Winston. . . . But it was a mess. I had no idea what it was really about." Still, she told Erhard, "I thought, you know, it's Zake, this composer's brilliant, Baikida . . . what works is brilliant and totally unique and what doesn't should be fixable."

On September 10, she sent Shange her "impressions of the piece" and ideas for improving it dramaturgically. Mann wrote candidly that the "major structural problem now is that it takes too long to get to Carrie, that once we get to her not quite enough happens (I think there is either a missing scene or we need a stronger dynamic with her and Betsy i.e. that Betsy does NOT trust her at first and that Carrie earns her trust)." She suggested that Betsy's mother, now called Jane, leave home earlier in the action and that Carrie arrive sooner, at the end of Act I. Mann also suggested strengthening the integration theme. Finally she urged Shange to write songs "to build both story and character."

Mann, nine months pregnant, also wrote Shange that "I am due in just a few days and feel quite ready to go, but told the baby that he/she had to hang on until I got my first letter off to you. The baby has complied."

Over the next five years, Mann and Shange, who became co-authors around 1985, birthed at least thirteen drafts of the script, with Mann contributing lyrics as well as whole scenes (Carroll also wrote lyrics). The women's collaboration was by no means problem-free: for reasons ranging from teaching assignments outside of New York, to personal troubles, to frustration with a project that was taking years, Shange apparently had difficulty turning in or responding to rewrites. Mann's own schedule was complicated, for she was everywhere, writing plays, directing plays. "It wasn't a pure process," was ultimately Mann's politic description. "It wasn't totally mine and it wasn't totally hers, and so that's never good. . . . It was very tough." Shange, in 1985, wrote a novel based on the story of the opera, which was often cited erroneously in the press as the musical's source. "We did that to appease her," said Mann, "but the novel's based on the musical."

By contrast, Mann felt that her collaboration with Baikida Carroll was rich and productive. "I describe the score to *Betsey* as: 'Great Black Music,'" Carroll wrote in his email in 2015. "[E]ach song or composition was specifically designed for a particular dramatic moment. However, it was all fashioned from the same 'Great Black Music' fabric. The black music genre embraces a broad spectrum of rhythm and emotion that I felt could effectively paint the entire soundscape of the show. . . . The only recurring theme for an individual in the play was 'Betsey's Theme.' Other characters had stand-alone songs that exemplified different genres. For instance: the Grand-mother [*sic*]; ragtime, The Father; avant-gard[e] jazz and calypso, The Children; rock and roll, and salsa, . . . Carrie; funk, gospel and r&b."

Despite tensions and delays, a workshop at the Public in August 1987 "blew people's minds," according to Mann, and Papp vowed a full production, scheduled for February 1988. But the Public was going through tough financial times, and Papp was struggling with personal ordeals. In April 1987, he had been diagnosed with prostate cancer and underwent chemotherapy, and several months later his son Tony was diagnosed with AIDS. Papp could not raise the money to produce *Betsey Brown* in New York, so he arranged for a production in association with Florida State University (FSU) in Tallahassee, where he had taught, and he planned, after mounting the show in Florida, to bring it either to the Public or Broadway. The idea was to cast the leads with New York actors, use FSU students in subsidiary roles, and musicians from FSU's School of Music.

But when Mann, Carroll, and others went to FSU to audition students and check out the facility, they were uniformly unimpressed. Mann's report to Papp was unsparing: there was no tech director at FSU, no master electrician, no sound designer. The turntable did not work and neither did one-third of the dimmers. She could barely cast from among the students and local actors who auditioned. Carroll thought the musicians no better than adequate.

Papp cancelled the FSU production, publicly blaming problems with the musical's book, a displeasure he also expressed in no-holds-barred language to Mann. "I remember the phone call," said Mann. "Just yelling at me on the phone. . . . It was awful." He wanted her off the project. But Carroll and Shange stood by her. In a letter dated April 11, 1988, Barbara Hogenson at the Lucy Kroll Agency, which was representing Shange, wrote Papp that "each of the collaborators involved in BETSEY BROWN expressed their desire to continue as a team. Speaking for Ntozake Shange, we do not feel that Emily Mann can be removed from the creative development of the play. Emily has worked very closely with Zake and Baikida for many years. Zake does not feel that Emily's participation in the project has been detrimental in any way." In any case, by that time the Public Theater's option had expired.

By 1988, Shange, Mann, and Carroll had transformed the script that Mann first encountered five years before. Now, Carrie arrived onstage earlier. Her imprisonment for attacking another woman with a knife was eliminated; there was only the argument with Betsey's mother, after which Carrie leaves, Betsey runs away, and Carrie finds her and tells her to go back home. Unnecessary characters were cut, scenes shaped. The dominant action was Betsey learning about varieties of love: sexual love; love of oneself; and feelings of both love and anger toward her mother and Carrie.

With the Public Theater out of the picture, both Mann and her agent George Lane scanned the horizon for a not-for-profit theater or commercial producer interested in mounting the show. They met with little success until Gregory Mosher, who had become director of Lincoln Center Theater, recommended the script to Marjorie Samoff, producing director of the American Music Theater Festival in Philadelphia. And there, in the Forum Theater, from March 25 to April 8, 1989, *Betsey Brown* finally had its world premiere.

The budget was tight, so rather than create a realistic set of the interior of the Brown house or use a scene-shifting turntable, scene designer Marjorie Bradley Kellogg painted a vivid collage of furniture, flowers, and household items on the stage floor and on a scrim at the rear of the proscenium stage. Stairs ran up the sides and around the back of the stage, stopping to provide several levels along the way. The only actual furniture onstage was a small dining table with a few chairs. "I love the richness and detail of [the collage]," Mann told Darlene Olson, a graduate student at the University of Minnesota who was writing a PhD dissertation about both Mann and the director Joanne Akalaitis, and was watching rehearsals. "It makes it quick to change scenes," Mann told Olson. "There is a great sense of movement."

The sound system at the Forum, however, was dreadful. This was not a theater at all as it turned out, but a public radio sound stage being used as a theater. Critics complained about lyrics sounding muddy and the eight-piece orchestra drowning out all but the strongest voices, despite body mics. Several critics wondered, understandably, why the producer or the director hadn't addressed these problems before the show opened. Mann's explanation, years later, was that Marjorie Samoff supposedly had a proper theater when contracts were signed, then at the proverbial last minute a lack of funds necessitated the change of venue. The mic problem was eventually fixed, but only after critics had seen the show on opening night. "We felt cursed," said Mann.

Considering the sound handicaps, reviewers were remarkably appreciative of the material and the performances. They complimented the entrancing soprano of Alisa Gyse, who played Betsey's mother, Jane; admired Ann Duquesnay's characterization of Betsey Brown's sometimes comical, sometimes unpleasant grandmother, who carps about light-skinned Jane marrying a dark-skinned man. Michelle Thomas, familiar to television audiences from appearances on *The Cosby Show*, was considered affecting as Betsey, but not equal to the singing or acting of the other leading women, especially twenty-six-year-old Kecia Lewis-Evans, who had played Carrie in the Public Theater's August 1987 workshop. Several reviewers wrote that the production really came alive

*Kecia Lewis-Evans as Carrie in
the 1989 production of* Betsey
Brown, *written by Ntozake Shange
and Emily Mann, and directed
by Emily Mann, American Music
Theater Festival, Philadelphia*
COURTESY OF MARK GARVIN

when Lewis-Evans entered toward the end of Act I, her voice booming
from offstage.

What some critics called a lack of focus, others called an abundance
of riches, both musically (thirty songs in a range of styles) and thematically (Black racism, upper-middle-class snobbery, the joys and trials
of adolescence, book-learning versus life lessons). Mann, Carroll, and
Shange could feel encouraged by the mostly favorable responses to what
was now a new American musical, although structural and thematic
issues still needed to be addressed.

Less than a month after the show closed, Shange sent a script to
Mann and Carroll with an Author's Note: "Please receive this revised
text free of associations to all other versions of this project. In this version, the characters, the timbre of their time, and the manner in which
we are introduced, is independent. . . . It is terribly important that we
shed past impressions of this family and its environs. We must make
sure; they breathe."

Perhaps the most striking new element reflected "the timbre of their time," for in this version, unlike any that came before, Shange forcefully invoked African American worlds beyond the comparatively protected, upper-middle-class realm in which the Brown family lived. Shange has three "Black Girls" beat up Betsey on the street, and one asks, "Cd we get her hair to turn high yellah too?" Jane leaves home and risks her life, presumably in the Civil Rights Movement: "goin' south . . . cuz I cain't sit by and watch all this/ I gotta be on my own personal freedom ride/." Betsey learns about the varieties of love but also that there are goals outside herself. Her last line is "I'm fixin' to change the world."

Conceivably Shange wanted *Betsey Brown* to have more political resonance, while Mann saw the musical as a story about an adolescent girl growing up. "You see," Mann had told Darlene Olson, "this is not a play about being Black. It's about coming of age. Because it's not about revolution, it's not about the usual things Black theatre is supposed to be about—Blacks as victims, Blacks as problems, or Blacks as revolutionaries: it is truly radical. It breaks preconceived notions of Black work. This is an upper-middle-class Black family that is going through turmoil. It's Black people on a stage for once just being people."

For Mann, putting *Betsey Brown* into her inaugural season was an event rife with both risks and possibilities. It was a form of resistance against the white, male-authored repertory that had dominated McCarter's seasons during its entire existence. The current generation of McCarter audiences had seen only one play by an African American about African Americans on the McCarter stage: during the 1970–1971 season, Arthur W. Lithgow had produced Lorraine Hansberry's 1959 drama *A Raisin in the Sun*, and Nagle Jackson had produced *Raisin* in 1985. Michael Kahn had offered up Sheldon Epps' musical revue *Blues in the Night*. *Betsey Brown*, Mann believed, would challenge the willingness of McCarter's subscribers to be engaged with an unfamiliar theater experience . "BETSEY is like a church piece," Mann exclaimed to Darlene Olson. "It gets people clapping and singing and carrying on and crying."

Mann also hoped she could bring audiences of color to the McCarter for *Betsey Brown*, and if she did that, conceivably she could encourage a broad-based audience for other productions. As Shirley Satterfield, a guidance counselor and historian who had grown up in Princeton, wrote me, "I remember when I was a child, our teachers took us to several plays at the McCarter Theatre, but I never saw anybody who looked like me. Many years later I saw *Betsey Brown*, and the theme related to my years of growing up in a segregated Princeton. . . . I finally saw a play at McCarter that was 'real,' one where people looked like me!"

Baikida Carroll and Emily Mann in rehearsal for Betsey Brown, *written by Ntozake Shange and Emily Mann, directed by Mann, McCarter Theatre Center, 1991*

Mann directed a workshop of the musical in New York City during August of 1990. Eight months later, on April 2, 1991, with Mann directing and George Faison choreographing, the show opened at the McCarter.

David Mitchell's scenery design at the McCarter relied on pastel-colored projections to create the exterior of the Brown home and the various worlds of St. Louis. The only set pieces were a stair unit and a tree downstage left for Betsey to climb, and as in Philadelphia, the only furniture was a dining table. Mitchell also created a three-part scrim downstage, and when the central panel was flown out and disappeared, the remaining stage-left and stage-right scrims helped focus the action and the dancing at the center of the McCarter's wide proscenium.

Kecia Lewis-Evans once again played Carrie, and she entered with bravado, swinging down the house-left aisle, singing to cheers from the audience. Ann Duquesnay recreated her portrait of Betsey's snobbish grandmother, and Raquel Herring made a feisty, strong-voiced Betsey Brown. Betsey's father was sung by robust, dignified Tommy Hollis, and Pamela Isaacs gently sang Betsey's mother. Twenty-eight-year-old Harold Perrineau charmed as the basketball-playing teenager who dribbles and dances his way into Betsey's heart.

Mann and Baikida Carroll had worked intensively on the script, and in two significant ways it reflected the changes Shange had sent her colleagues after Philadelphia. Now the musical included a scene at Betsey's newly integrated school, where she recites a poem written by Harlem renaissance luminary Paul Laurence Dunbar, to the laughter of her white classmates and the disbelief of the white teacher, a woman, who reprimands Betsey for not selecting "an American poet" and exclaims, "What you were reciting isn't even English!" In the other new scene, white students (they and the white teacher were portrayed in the production by Black actors wearing white masks), chase and surround Betsey after school, shout racist slurs, and beat her up.

These new scenes strengthened the conflict between the father's pro-integration outlook and the risks to African Americans who were on the front lines of school integration during the 1950s, making this

Betsey Brown more politicized than most of its earlier incarnations. "The scenes," wrote Shirley Satterfield "were particularly relevant for audiences old enough to remember integration coming to Princeton's public schools, in 1948." Black children lost their caring teachers, and the white teachers basically communicated that Black children couldn't learn as well as white kids.

The second act still seemed to be more about Carrie and her conflicts with Betsey's mother and grandmother than about Betsey, although Kecia Lewis-Evans noted that, "Without Carrie, [Betsey's] life would have been very much what her mother and especially her grandmother wanted for her. The working versus the upper class, racism within the black community—all of that was wrapped up in this story—and Carrie was a lightning rod for Betsey to come into her maturity about these issues."

"It needs one more complete overhaul," Mann reflected. "I think you need a whole lot less exposition. You should start with the house in chaos, but get to Carrie sooner. I think Baikida didn't want to lose some of the songs, and I think we can lose some of the songs. This is me thirty years later knowing a whole lot more than I did. There's a lot of good stuff in there, but it needs to be unified in one style. I'm hearing different styles of writing. I can hear it's not as seamless to my ear."

Bob Campbell, reviewing for the *Star-Ledger*, summed it up this way: "The eagerly awaited show has all the adolescent symptoms. It's alternately sophisticated and childish, purposeful and disorganized, brash and demure. Sometimes it springs into glorious handstands. Sometimes it just stands around, bashful and tongue-tied."

Reviews were mixed, but according to information the McCarter released to the press, box office receipts for *Betsey Brown* were among the highest in the theater's history. Nonetheless, Campbell at the *Star-Ledger* noted that the show's "raucous energy seemed to nonplus the McCarter's genteel audience." For audiences wondering what sort of productions the McCarter's new artistic director would stage, *Betsey Brown* either thrilled them with its vibrant score, vivacious characters, and political implications, or sent them scurrying up the aisle, vowing never to return.

Mann, in her conversations with doctoral candidate Darlene Olson, attributed such audience responses to a mixture of racism and sexism. "No one who would reject the play would ever say that's why," Mann stated. "They would be horrified because on a conscious level . . . they think they're beyond racism and sexism. The point is for some reason they cannot connect to these people without barriers because they do have problems with race, they do have problems connecting to the internal world of women. Often they're just plain not interested. There is nothing you can do about that. That's the nature of our culture and our society. You just have to keep working despite it."

Mann's inaugural season closed with *The Film Society* by Jon Robin Baitz, a shrewd choice stylistically for audiences flummoxed by the boldness of *Betsey Brown*, but a selection that made similar political points. Baitz's 1985 play, his first, is set in a bankrupt private school for boys in Durham, South Africa, in 1970, and is a study of varying personalities and political outlooks, from colonialist to anti-apartheid. The deteriorating school is a metaphor for South Africa's decay. Douglas Hughes directed, and Alvin Klein, in his complimentary review in the New Jersey section of the *New York Times*, wrote that, "If you have given up on finding a stimulating contemporary play, elegantly written, sensitively directed and distinctively acted, attend the McCarter's 'Film Society' to reclaim the faith."

A few months later, in an article about New Jersey's major theaters, Klein singled out the McCarter for producing "the most stimulating" plays, despite suffering funding cutbacks and "managerial gaps." The McCarter season was "flawed," he wrote, "[b]ut Ms. Mann delivered the season's singular creative spark, if only because she restored a sense of adventure to theatergoing."

"I thought, artistically, we did wonderful work," said Mann, reflecting on her first season. "I thought *Glass Menagerie* was a very good way to lead off. I felt that *Betsey Brown* mattered and set a new tone of who we were and what we were doing. I got flu during *Those the River Keeps* . . . and it was chaos. But I let the artists go and fulfill their vision, and it was not right, but I thought—three out of four. . . . I also thought it was interesting to have chosen that play, to give people a sense of this is a new day. We're going to do hard-hitting new plays, we're going to do classic work, we're going to do work by people of color. I felt I made a statement."

Mann had survived her first season as artistic director, but the McCarter still needed to raise $4.5 million to complete the Phase II construction, erase the deficit, and pay for Mann's second season. In her diaries, Mann made lists of possible plays for her second go-round, in a personal style of short-hand: "Of Mice and Men, Our Town, ?All My Sons, Cat, Salesman, [Eccentricities?]" and wrote notes to herself: "Get one blockbuster" and "3 + 4 should be audience pleasers - NUMBERS!" One item definitely on her to-do list was replacing the tired *A Christmas Carol* with a new edition, adapted by David Thompson with a set by Ming Cho Lee that captured the gray, chimneyed buildings and cobbled streets of Dickens' London.

Although the McCarter's finances were still shaky, the theater was climbing out of its administrative morass. For a new managing director, Wingate recommended balding, bespectacled Jeffrey Woodward, managing director of the Northlight Theatre in Evanston, Illinois, and before that, general manager at Hartford Stage. He joined McCarter in June 1991. As for the board of trustees, Ruth Wilson completed her three-year term, and the board elected Liz Fillo president. Fillo, ready and able to fight for the theater, raise money, and provide the stronger oversight that was necessary, essentially told uncommitted board members to find themselves another organization. "We got rid of a lot of dead wood," she quipped.

The second phase of the McCarter construction was completed in time for Mann's second season with seconds to spare. Audiences now mingled in two spacious side lobbies, where they could purchase food and drink before a performance. Downstairs were new administrative offices, an enlarged rehearsal room, a green room, and new dressing rooms. Gone were the days when actors had to climb flights of stairs to reach archaic dressing rooms in the McCarter's tower. Mann's office was scarcely large enough for a round table that could sit four, a few bookshelves, and a built-in desk, but she decorated the walls with photographs of her family, theater posters, and production photographs. Woodward's similarly spare office was only a few feet away.

Grace Shackney, who often joked that she came to the McCarter in the fall of 1991 as a forty-one-year-old intern, observed that, for a time, Mann and Woodward metaphorically tip-toed around each other, even though they had known each other from when Mann directed at Hartford Stage. But gradually they began to trust each other. "Emily has a lot of respect for people who she knows can do the things she can't do, and Jeff is very astute artistically," said Shackney. Mann began to select a young, dedicated staff of artists with whom she wished to work: Loretta Greco, a directing intern the previous season, was now her assistant, and Janice Paran, literary manager for the New Theatre of Brooklyn, was on board as McCarter's literary manager and dramaturg. At the end of the 1991–1992 season, after a gala Tony Bennett concert, Shackney remembered that the staff gravitated to the stage for a party. Mann and Woodward danced together, and soon everyone was dancing. "Everybody relaxed after that," said Shackney, who had become an administrative assistant that season to both Mann and Woodward. "I always felt that was a turning point for the staff and for Emily and Jeff's relationship. It was like this circle of trust developed, and we knew we had these leaders."

In January 1992 Mann directed Anton Chekhov's *Three Sisters*, the production, she always believed, that brought McCarter out of its crisis.

Mann chose playwright Lanford Wilson's translation because of its conversational, contemporary language, and with the help of casting directors Elissa Myers and Paul Fouquet, gave the play, and herself, a remarkable troupe. As much as possible, she wanted to bring well-known

Left to right: Josef Sommer, Linda Hunt, Mary Stuart Masterson, and Frances McDormand in Three Sisters, *directed by Emily Mann at the McCarter Theatre Center, 1992*
PHOTO: © T. CHARLES ERICKSON

actors to the McCarter, and she endowed *Three Sisters* with Linda Hunt as Olga, the oldest of the Prozoroff sisters; Mary Stuart Masterson, who was starring at the time in the new film *Fried Green Tomatoes*, played the youngest sister, Irina, who works in the local telegraph office; and Frances McDormand, recently of the film *Mississippi Burning*, was cast as unhappily married Masha. Edward Herrmann, best known to television audiences for his portrayal of Franklin D. Roosevelt, played the unhappily married Colonel Vershinin, with whom Masha is in love. The rest of the cast were equally skilled: Myra Carter, Paul McCrane, John Christopher Jones, Peter Francis James, Laura San Giacomo of *Pretty Woman* and *Sex, Lies and Videotape*, and Josef Sommer of just about any play, film, or television series anybody had ever seen. Michael Yeargan designed a spare interior setting, with a row of French doors upstage and tantalizing vistas of the world beyond, the world of far-away Moscow, where the sisters desperately wish to live. It was an ideal play for Mann's preferred directing style. This family could be playful, as in Act I, when Irina twirled about like a delighted child, or when the sisters teased their love-addled brother Andrei (McCrane) and chased him around a corner of the room. This family struggled with underlying tensions: the sexual tension between Masha and Vershinin; the sisters' irritation aroused by Andrei's disruptive wife (San Giacomo) and their new baby; the nearly uncontrollable desire of Solyony (Peter Francis James) for Irina, which in Mann's interpretation led almost to rape. Under her direction, Chekhov's play exposed different shades of love and, all too often, love's absence.

On opening night, Mann sat next to her father, and they held hands, perhaps suspecting that this was the last production of Emily's that Arthur would see. The reviews were mixed. *The New York Times* critics— Alvin Klein for the New Jersey section, David Richards in the New York edition—complained: it was not the Chekhov they knew and esteemed; the sisters did not look as though they were related; Mann had no unifying concept. But other reviewers, notably Michael Sommers at the Newark-based *Star-Ledger*, savored what he called Mann's "memorable, quirky, flawed but often quite lovely production." In Sommers' view, Mann had staged each act in a distinct manner, from "classical American resident theatre style" to "more reflective and introspective" in the dark, Russian manner, to what he called "haute-Broadway," and finally an "elegiac" last act during which the sisters, who will never get to Moscow, are left "huddling together like refugees." In that last act, Michael Yeargan's set displayed only a corner of the house in which the sisters had romped in Act I. The view upstage was of a dismal horizon, against which Andrei pushes a baby carriage, in a prosaic, even ironic, end to his sisters' dreams.

Three Sisters played to capacity audiences, but Mann was learning that an artistic revolution at the McCarter would have to proceed more slowly than she had hoped, especially with a still-jittery budget. Kathleen Nolan, who became the new general manager during Mann's second season, described an environment that "was about Jeff and Emily, and the whole team—the marketing team, the production team—all of us together putting the pieces into place. And while [Emily] may have had to take a step back from scope and scale, that doesn't mean you have to take a step back artistically."

Mann tried to put one overtly political play in the mix each season, not always successfully; Arthur Kopit's *Indians* in October 1991 was decidedly unpopular with subscribers. Alternatively she experimented within the productions themselves, through contemporary translations and interpretations of European and American classics. Following *Three Sisters*, Stephen Wadsworth staged the American premiere of Marivaux's eighteenth-century comedy *The Triumph of Love*, in a version Wadsworth adapted from his own translation with Nadia Benabid. This delightful artifact from 1732, in which women disguise themselves as men, and everyone is enamored of someone else, became the critical success of McCarter's 1991–1992 season.

Mann also invited well-known playwrights to use the McCarter as a theatrical home, whether to revisit previous work or introduce new plays. Thus, in a co-production with the Alley Theatre, Mann brought Edward Albee to direct the East Coast premiere of *Marriage Play*, with Shirley Knight and Tom Klunis as a long-married couple. If subscribers ultimately were bored by Albee's verbiage, they apparently were eager to be among the first audiences to see a play by the author of *Who's Afraid of Virginia Woolf?* and *A Delicate Balance*, directed by the author himself. The production was victorious at the box office.

Through it all, Grace Shackney remembered, Mann smoked packs of cigarettes, swigged copious amounts of coffee, and somehow managed, late at night when Nicholas was asleep, to finish a teleplay, *The Greensboro Massacre*, for NBC Television. She pressured herself and those around her to keep working, and at times those dearest to her suffered from her determination not to fail. Stephen Wadsworth remembered that after Mann watched a run-through of *Triumph of Love*, the first non-operatic theater piece he ever directed, her notes, given to him in person, were brief and curt.

"She is capable of hurting me, and I didn't particularly know that until we got into work situations," said Wadsworth. "Either by things she said obliviously or, when I'd bring it up, she'd contest it and fight back." After that *Triumph of Love* rehearsal, he wrote Mann at length about his hurt, acknowledging at the same time that "I would never write this note to someone I didn't love."

"My first two years here, I think the lord was testing me," said Mann. "If I could live through it, then I would have what I needed to go on. . . . And if I failed, I was afraid I might never get another offer as a woman, right? Women don't get second chances. So I was sleeping very little and working around the clock, making sure I got home to Nicholas for dinners and making sure, when I wasn't in tech for my own shows or previews for others, that I was home with him."

"She lives to get over whatever is blocking her," said Grace Shackney. "Whatever she feels she has to do or needs to do."

The McCarter reportedly had gone into Mann's second season with a $900,000 deficit, but by season's end had balanced the books, helped by a 30 percent increase in its subscription base. "I definitely lost most of the old, established Princeton audience during my first few seasons," said Mann. "It wasn't for them. And I was very happy to wave goodbye. And a new group did come in." At the end of the 1991–1992 season, the board renewed her contract ahead of schedule, for four years. Managing director Jeffrey Woodward would later say that Mann took the McCarter and pulled it up by the scruff of its neck.

Late in January of 1993, Emily flew to Chicago to be with her father, who was at the University of Chicago Medical Center. In her diary, Emily described "a nightmare" during which her mother, usually so stalwart, could barely cope with the prospect of Arthur dying. She and Emily would hold each other and cry. Emily remembered everyone, including her father, telling her to go back to Princeton, because she had a job to do and a play to direct. Instead of obeying her instinct to stay, she flew back for tech rehearsals of *Miss Julie*. "I re-teched the entire show," Mann remembered, "and it was excellent, and I woke up the next morning, and my brother-in-law called me." It was Sunday, February 7, and that morning Arthur Mann had died at the age of seventy-one. "And I went really crazy. I got up and I got myself together and said,

'Okay, I'm going to go to the funeral.' But they said come the next day. So then I was going to go to the theater and do a rehearsal. And I never made it. Grace found me staring at the wall in my living room, in total shock. Just sitting there."

On April 3, Emily spoke at her father's memorial service, in the University of Chicago's Bond Chapel. She described the man who had most influenced her life, whom she loved, with whom she fought, and with whom she had much in common:

> Many people who knew him have described him as a gentleman—a real one—a gentleman scholar—a man of dignity, charm, learning and quality. A man of high standards. That's all true.

> But he was also a street fighter, a man of passions and anger, a fierce competitor, a genius on the squash or tennis court, a man repelled by vulgarity as much as by injustice. A man prone to seething tempers as well as cool rationale. It is these contradictions in him I have loved and fought in him, and now I can say happily I might have inherited.

"Her dad was a take-no-prisoners intellect, with take-no-prisoners expectations of those two girls," said Stephen Wadsworth, who got to know Arthur after becoming Emily's close friend. "They felt the pressure. A very intense pressure from his direction. They better get out there and excel and produce and . . . do something useful and well. . . . I've actually seen over the years, I've seen more of that pressure, that Arthurian pressure in Emily to achieve. . . . And to do something meaningful. . . . He was a lovely man. You wanted to hug him if you knew him. But he could be very forbidding."

Sorrow at losing her father, and the stress of running the McCarter, seemed to catch up with Mann in the spring of 1993, when she prepared to fly to Los Angeles to rehearse and direct the world premiere of Anna Deavere Smith's solo performance, *Twilight: Los Angeles, 1992,* scheduled to begin previews on May 23 at the Mark Taper Forum. During the weeks before she left for California, Mann was having trouble walking and in considerable pain. Grace Shackney accompanied Mann to a local neurologist, who examined her, recommended tests, and urged her to cancel the trip. But Mann ignored the advice. She had not directed at a theater other than the McCarter since staging *Betsey Brown* in Philadelphia in 1989, and the invitation from Gordon Davidson appealed to her. Smith's subject was the vicious beating in 1992 of Rodney King by Los Angeles police officers; the trial of only four of the fourteen officers at the scene, none of whom were convicted of either assault or excessive force; and the ensuing riots that engulfed downtown L.A., all of which resonated with Mann's own focus on violence and racism. Mann also anticipated that *Twilight* would receive national attention. Just the year before, Smith had been acclaimed for her *Fires in the Mirror: Crown Heights, Brooklyn and Other Identities*, a series of monologues drawn from her interviews with numerous people whose words, speech rhythms, attitudes, and mannerisms Smith assumed during her performances. Mann arranged with the Taper and Smith for *Twilight* to come to the McCarter during the 1993–1994 season, anticipating that it would move to New York.

Gordon Davidson probably thought that pairing a dramatist and director known for her documentary plays with an actor creating a verbatim performance piece would be an excellent match: two theater artists with similar artistic and political bents; two women. But Judy James, with whom Mann had become good friends while writing the Winnie Mandela teleplay, knew that Mann "was having a hell of a time with Anna Deavere. Anna didn't want to be directed," said James. "Her ego, her creative spirit. She didn't think she needed anybody else. She made it hell for Emily. What are you, a white girl, doing with me, [a] Black actress?" The production opened on June 13, 1993, and Smith's and Mann's working relationship was not helped by a controversial review in the *Los Angeles Times*, where Jan Breslauer wrote that Smith had been "masterfully directed by one of the American stage's best, Emily Mann," but "Ultimately, there's less to this one-woman show than meets the eye."

More distressingly for Mann, the physical problems she suffered in New Jersey flared in Los Angeles. She was staying in downtown L.A., near the Taper, and one morning she called Judy James in a panic. "She could not get out of bed," James remembered. "I said, 'Get in the car and come here.' She said, 'I can't stand up. I can't do anything.' I took her to a doctor friend of mine, and he knew something was really wrong, but he couldn't figure it out. She got better at walking, but we both knew something had hit her."

Once back home in New Jersey, Emily tried to restore herself physically and emotionally. Carol Mann and her husband, Howard Helene, invited Emily to spend the July 4 weekend with them in Claverack, New York, where Howard's frequent tennis partner, a fifty-one-year-old lawyer named Gary Mailman, had a second home. Howard thought that Emily and Gary might get along. Carol remembered her reaction: "I was, like, *Gary?* No." Gary was a litigator, Emily was in the theater. Gary had grown up on the Lower East Side of Manhattan, Emily was raised amid academia. Gary tried to approach the world in logical ways, while Emily dramatized life.

Howard, Carol, and Emily drove up to Gary's, and pretty soon Gerry showed up and dropped off Nicholas, to spend the weekend with his mother. Recalling this meeting, Gary remembered that he had seen Emily at least once before at a party in the area and was attracted to her. Emily remembered that, on this long weekend, she and Gary assiduously ignored each other until one day Gary loudly asked if anyone was interested in going to the movies, and Emily slowly raised her hand.

"Tomorrow is my 42nd birthday!!" Mann wrote to a friend on April 11, 1994, "And, oh, how much happier I am this year than last!"

It had been her fourth season as artistic director of the McCarter, a season that included a play by the novelist Joyce Carol Oates, who was on the Princeton faculty; Athol Fugard directing his 1965 play *Hello and Goodbye*; and *Changes of Heart: (The Double Inconstancy)*, another Marivaux comedy translated and directed by Stephen Wadsworth. The production that received the most attention, however, was the fall presentation of *Twilight: Los Angeles, 1992*, although Mann, reportedly per Anna Deavere Smith's wishes, had nothing to do with the show once Smith arrived at the theater. "She didn't want to go back to the McCarter if Emily was involved," said Judy James.

"Evidently, the collaboration came to a halt," wrote Alvin Klein in the New Jersey section of the *New York Times*. "There were reports of a rift between Emily Mann . . . and Ms. Smith, who made no comments, gave no interviews and declined to participate in the McCarter's customary post-performance discussion." Smith did not want reviews of the McCarter production, and so critics were not officially invited. Later that season, when the Public Theater produced *Twilight* before moving it to Broadway, George C. Wolfe directed the production.

By the end of the 1993–1994 season, Mann told friends that she had put the Anna Deavere Smith episode behind her. It was much better to enjoy the positive things in her life. She embarked on a new project for the McCarter: adapting the bestselling book *Having Our Say: The Delany Sisters' First 100 Years*, an oral history voiced by Sarah Louise ("Sadie") and Annie Elizabeth ("Bessie") Delany, two African American centenarians, with the journalist Amy Hill Hearth. And on May 16, Mann, her staff, and her board learned to their elation, that, on the recommendation of the American Theatre Critics Association (ATCA), the McCarter would receive the 1994 Special Tony Award for Continued Excellence in Regional Theater.

At home, after months of sadness following his grandfather Arthur's death, Nicholas was "on an even keel," and Emily, who had been talking with a therapist, felt on more of an even keel herself. "This Gary Mailman, the lawyer, is very good to and for me," she wrote her friend Louise Grafton. "I am content. Things seem in balance. I have, I realize, grown to really love him. And <u>trust</u> him. My, my . . . what a marvelous trait in a man - <u>trustworthiness</u>. Highly under-rated. He's funny and warm and loving and smart and he tells me he isn't going anywhere. That is, he's in it for the long haul. . . . So we're taking it slowly and slugging it out;

as the demons emerge, we battle them. I've never fought so much with anyone and enjoyed it so much."

Gary was not completely without his own connections to the theater: his cousin Bruce Mailman was an off-Broadway theater owner and producer. Bruce was dying of AIDS, and on the Friday night before the 1994 Memorial Day weekend, Gary and Emily visited Bruce at his home in Manhattan. Then they began the two-and-a-half-hour drive up the Taconic Parkway to Claverack. Gary had finally convinced Emily to take golf lessons, and they planned to hit the golf course Saturday morning to give her a chance to play. "I loved spending time with her," said Gary, "and I loved golf."

But on the drive to Claverack, Gary recalled, "Emily started getting numbness in the face. I said we shouldn't go. She said, 'No, it will be fine.' And it subsided, and she was okay. Then, Saturday morning, instead of playing golf, we ended up going to Kingston Hospital, which was the nearest hospital with a neurology department, because it was clear she had some kind of neurological thing." At the hospital, Mann had a CAT scan. To Gary's and Emily's mutual irritation, the diagnosis was "women's anxiety," because the symptoms had disappeared, as they had Friday night. Sunday she was fine, and either on Sunday or Monday they drove back to the city. On Tuesday, May 31, Gary remembered, Emily went shopping in Manhattan with Jennifer von Mayrhauser for a gown to wear to the Tony Awards. Gary went to his office.

While trying on a dress at Saks Fifth Avenue, Emily fell, and she called Gary for help. A colleague put him in touch with "a head guy" in neurology at the Hospital for Special Surgery in New York City, and that afternoon the neurologist interviewed Emily, with Gary present. "He asked me some questions about what I had observed and then he told Emily to go into a room and change into a gown, and he was going to examine her. But he told me, when Emily left, that from what he had been told before the examination, he thought it was MS. In those days. . . . He might have told me she was going to die, or at least be paralyzed." That afternoon she underwent an MRI, and because she was in meetings the next day, June 1, Gary's fifty-second birthday, they agreed that Gary would call for the results. The MRI confirmed the diagnosis of multiple sclerosis.

Even years afterward, when recounting how he sat in their living room later that day and told Emily the results, Gary cried. "It might be the most difficult moment of my life, telling her," he said.

"I went from shock to sobs," Emily remembered. "I thought, 'My life is over.'"

Mann did not immediately tell her mother; Sylvia's cousin who suffered from MS had existed in a wheelchair until she died. But Mann did tell McCarter's board president, Liz Fillo, and offered to resign. Fillo and the board turned her offer down.

The 48th Annual Tony Awards took place at the Gershwin Theatre on the night of June 12, 1994. The actor Jane Alexander, who was also at that time executive director of the National Endowment for the Arts (NEA), welcomed Mann, Jeffrey Woodward, and Liz Fillo onto the stage to accept the McCarter's Tony Award and a $25,000 grant from the Clairol Foundation. Mann wore a long-sleeved, scoop-necked black gown, and what looked like short, flat, black boots. She walked from stage left slowly and carefully, holding tightly to Woodward's left arm, and Fillo walked a few steps behind them until they reached the center of the stage and faced the audience. "I couldn't walk that day," Mann recalled. Her dark hair was swept up in a mass of elegant curls. Makeup accentuated her high cheekbones, and her dark eyes looked directly at the camera as she thanked, first, the New Jersey State Council on the Arts, then the NEA, Princeton University, and lastly the McCarter's subscribers. "One cannot have an adventurous theater without an adventurous audience," she said. The camera focused on her face and cut away when she turned slowly and reached out to Fillo for help walking offstage.

Alvin Klein wrote in the *New York Times*:

[T]he McCarter's Tony, many theatergoers feel, might as well be dubbed the Mann award. It wasn't until the 1990–91 season, the first under the artistic direction of Emily Mann, that a consistent sense of occasion marked productions in the McCarter's theater series. To many, the arrival of Ms. Mann was tantamount to a wake-up call for a theater that had lapsed into complacency. To others with a wait-and-see attitude, Ms. Mann had to prove she had the goods to hold on to a tried—or perhaps tired—and true audience and to attract a new one. In just four seasons, she proved it.

13

Having Her Say
(1994–2000)

In the world of the McCarter Theatre, morale was high as the 1994–1995 season began. The Tony Award stood prominently in the McCarter lobby for audiences to admire. Come February, Mann would direct her adaptation of *Having Our Say: The Delany Sisters' First 100 Years*, and everyone understood that the production would go to Broadway. Mann was also writing a documentary play about a murderous attack in 1979 by the Ku Klux Klan in Greensboro, North Carolina.

But inside Mann's private world, she was suffering. Multiple sclerosis attacks the myelin, or sheaths, which insulate the nerves, particularly the nerves controlling motor and cognitive functions. For Mann, walking became difficult at times, and she was afflicted with what she termed "foggy brain." She was often in pain.

Mann was trying to keep the knowledge of her diagnosis within the McCarter, a few close friends, and her family. Sylvia Mann, remembering how her cousin Rosalind had suffered with the disease, urged Emily to give Gary the chance to decide if he wanted to remain in the relationship. "Tell him to take two days to think about it," Sylvia advised. So Emily did. And Gary thought. And he told Emily he was not going to leave her. He was, in fact, spending more and more time at Emily's home in Princeton, and essentially they were living together.

Emily confided about her illness to Camille Cosby, who recommended a healer in Los Angeles. Gary was skeptical, but Camille told Emily that she "must see" this woman René Espy, and at some point Emily and Gary flew to L.A. "I had to drive Emily," he remembered, "and when we got to the office building, I needed to get a wheelchair from the custodian, and so I wheeled her into this guru's office, and she told me—this was maybe late morning—she told me to come back at five o'clock, or whatever, and 'she'll be walking.' I came back, and she was walking. So Emily was completely sold, and I was certainly sold temporarily."

Mann seemed to improve under the healer's guidance, mostly because she embarked on a regimen of physical exercise, massage, and a healthful diet. Yoga helped minimize spastic movements, and self-hypnosis helped clear her brain so she could focus on her work. In an interview about her illness for the online "Theatre Commons" HowlRound, conducted in 2017 by the dramaturg and arts administrator Sara Brookner, who herself has MS, Mann said, "I felt better physically and emotionally when I was working. It's when the work ended that I had to deal with some depression and pain and the real disability. I learned from my healer that depression was part of the disease."

"She gave it all to the theater," Mann's thirty-six-year-old son, Nicholas, who became a lawyer, recalled in 2019. Eleven years old when his mother was diagnosed with MS, he described how, at night, "When she came back [home], she was exhausted. But we always ate dinner together. . . . Without that job, she would have been really depressed. The job saved her. It gave her something she was very dedicated to, although at the same time it wore her out." Nicholas remembered helping his mother walk, especially at airports, when she needed to use a wheelchair.

In November of 1994 Mann went to Greensboro, North Carolina, to interview people for her new play, spend a day with the English director Mark Wing-Davey, who would be staging *Greensboro (A Requiem)* at the McCarter, and introduce him to survivors of the Ku Klux Klan attack. Ned Canty, a McCarter intern that season, was designated to accompany her on the plane, drive her to meetings, and help her walk if she was unsteady or her legs felt numb. Two months later, when Mann was in rehearsal for *Having Our Say*, "I had horrible MS," Mann recalled. "They had to carry me out after every rehearsal." Canty frequently would pick her up in his arms, carry her to a car, drive her home, and carry her into the house. "That isn't something that I talked about," he said, "because I don't think that was an easy thing, needing that kind of assistance. It felt like a very private thing that I could do for Emily. It was nothing shameful, but it felt at the time like a small thing that I could do to help at that point, when she was still figuring out what the limits were."

Canty went on to direct opera and in 2010 became general director of Opera Memphis in Tennessee. Looking back, he felt that Mann's multiple sclerosis "did inform the year," in the sense that the staff, while completely supportive of Mann and her needs, also wondered, "What does this mean? What does it mean going forward? Is it going to get worse, is it going to get better? Do we adapt to that? I feel I was in the thick of people grappling with those questions, sometimes to the extent it was replacing what might have been the vibe the year after the Tony."

Adapting *Having Our Say* for the stage had come about from a fortuitous meeting of minds. In 1993, Carol Mann sent her sister an advance copy of the book by Amy Hill Hearth, Annie Elizabeth ("Bessie") Delany, and Sarah ("Sadie") Louise Delany (it would become a *New York Times* bestseller). Mann loved it, but did not recall thinking of it in terms of a play. Then Judy James visited her in Princeton, read *Having Our Say*, called Camille Cosby, who just happened to have finished reading the book herself, and within twenty-four hours, according to James, they were contacting the William Morris Agency for the rights. Before Mann had even written a word, the McCarter had announced *Having Our Say* for the 1994–1995 season.

At first she did not know how to dramatize the Delanys's oral history, Mann told the *Washington Post* theater critic David Richards. Then she visited Bessie Delany and Sadie Delany at their home in Mount Vernon, New York. She and Bessie behaved amicably with each other, Mann told Richards,

> but Sadie and I fell in love. Maybe it's because I always wished I were more like Sadie, a woman so at peace with herself. While we

were talking, she hiked up her skirt and said, "Emily, I've got to show you something." She had just had hip surgery six months earlier, and I expected to see this gash. The scar was pencil-thin, barely a teeny white line. She had been treating it with vitamin E oil. And she said, "One thing you have to understand in life, Emily, is that you have to love your wounds."

By the end of the visit, the two women had forged the sort of warm connection usually relished by people who have known each other for years. Mann left the Delanys' home wanting to evoke a similar relationship between the sisters and audiences at the McCarter.

The play's galvanizing event became the dinner the sisters prepared every February 5, to celebrate their father, who was born on that day in 1858. Henry Beard Delany had come into the world as a house slave in Georgia, but his owners taught him and his family to read and write, and with freedom after the Civil War, the Delany family built a house, and Henry became a skilled mason. When Henry was in his twenties, a white Episcopal priest helped enroll him in what was then called St. Augustine's Normal School, in Raleigh, North Carolina, and after graduating in 1885, Delany joined the faculty. He was consecrated an Episcopal Bishop in 1918, the first African American bishop in the Episcopal Church.

In Mann's play, the audience in effect becomes the Delanys' guests—invited first for tea and then, because everyone is enjoying themselves so much, staying on while the sisters prepare dinner and, finally, participating in the birthday celebration. "I knew from *Annulla*," Mann wrote me, that "sitting in the kitchen, smelling the smells of fresh food being prepared and cooked, is a wonderful experience for an audience." For Emily personally, it brought back memories of sitting in the kitchen with Gussie, of the closeness she felt watching her grandmother cook and listening to her talk. There was also sadness, for Henry Delany's February birth date and the date of Arthur Mann's death were only two days apart. The play's central event recreated both the joys and the sorrows of family.

Using text from the book for dialogue, Mann wrote the first drafts of her script at Gary's house in Claverack, New York, during the summer of 1994. In its affectionate portraits of two exceptional women, and its unfiltered jabs at white America, *Having Our Say* was material to which Mann gravitated. The dialogue, replete with personal recollections and snappish retorts, asked for the kind of realistic performances Mann delighted in drawing from actors, and at the same time it was theater of testimony. "Almost the definition of it," Mann observed to me, because "they're having their say."

Having Our Say is also a feminist play. Rather than allowing themselves to be marginalized because they are African American and women, Bessie Delany, the second African American woman to become a licensed dentist in the state of New York, and Sadie Delany, the first African American to teach home economics in New York City's public schools, have resisted the white America that would deny them training and employment in their chosen fields. They have also resisted marriage, preferring life-long independence. They are heroic women—quietly revolutionary women—and their armaments are humor, determination, collaboration, love of family, and an unclouded view of white racism. If audiences found the play healing, as many apparently did, that was in part because the two sisters, in actuality and as Mann portrayed them in her play, preferred to overcome their foes firmly yet peacefully.

Adaptations were becoming another feature of Mann's repertory. In college she had helped a boyfriend adapt Euripides' *Medea*, and in 1984 she adapted Pierre Laville's *Nights and Days* from a literal translation. But "I really hate working that way," she told Geraldine Brodie and Emma Cole for their book *Adapting Translation for the Stage*, published in 2017. Mann's preference was to sit side by side with a translator and a script in the original language, "talk about the lines one by one," and then write her own version (she has referred to such scripts as "translation/adaptations."). A literal translation, she told Brodie and Cole, "becomes less faithful, I think, to the original because you are two steps removed. . . . It doesn't really tell you much in terms of what you need to put in your mouth as an actor and how you are going to construct character out of it and how you are going to get the necessary action of a line on a stage." Beginning with *Miss Julie*, which she adapted for the 1992–1993 season with the help of a bilingual Swedish student, Mann would write ten adaptations while at the McCarter, although not all of them were produced there. They ranged from *Having Our Say* (1995) to *The House of Bernarda Alba* (1997), which she later revised for a 2012 London production set in Iran, to her riff on Chekhov, *A Seagull in the Hamptons* (2013).

"Adaptation is so fluidly used as a term that I suppose I don't particularly love it," she reflected more than two decades after writing *Having Our Say*. "[The term] can diminish the work of the playwright when working with an existing source . . . diminish the creativity of the playwright-author."

Judy James and Camille Cosby, who were providing enhancement money for the McCarter production, were envisioning a script for a cast of ten or more, reflecting the many persons whom the sisters speak about in their oral history. But Mann wanted a tour-de-force for two women. James, who believed that a "two-hander" would be risky on a stage as wide as the McCarter and most Broadway houses, had to be convinced. "But we did a reading," she remembered, "and it was great."

Gloria Foster was cast as 103-year-old Sadie Delany, and Mary Alice as 101-year-old Bessie Delany. Mann held auditions, but according to Judy James, "there was no question we'd have Gloria, and we came to Mary Alice soon after. Holy shit they were difficult!" During rehearsals, Mann spent precious time and energy soothing the egos of the two actors, who had no qualms about bringing their rivalry into the rehearsal room. "I can remember days when one note would take an hour and a half," said Janice Paran, who worked with Mann as a dramaturg on the script and in rehearsals. But, said Paran, "[Emily] maintained her patience with them. She knew how to give them their due. She knew how to work with divas. I feel that *Having Our Say* was a real love story for Emily from the get-go. She was in seventh heaven."

Left to right: Gloria Foster and Mary Alice in Having Our Say: The Delany Sisters' First 100 Years, *written and directed by Emily Mann, McCarter Theatre Center, 1995*
PHOTO: © T. CHARLES ERICKSON

Sitting in the audience at the McCarter, the first image one saw was the exterior of the sisters' brick Mount Vernon home, projected onto scrim, part of which then rose to reveal Thomas Lynch's set: a comfortable but unprepossessing sitting room of low bookshelves, a drop-leaf table, and two modestly upholstered armchairs. A smiling Gloria, as Sadie, began the play by talking to the audience, as though to a group of friendly strangers, and then Mary Alice's Bessie entered. She was gruffer than her more soft-spoken older sister, or as Bessie puts it, "If Sadie is molasses then I am vinegar." For the second and third acts, Lynch's set revolved to reveal a dining area and nearby kitchen, where the sisters prepare their late father's favorite five-course dinner. Through it all, Bessie and Sadie not only talk about themselves and banter with each other, they also tell numerous stories about their family, so that the stage at times feels populated with Delanys. Photographs of the family were projected onto scrim surrounding the action, leading William McCleery to write in the New Jersey newspaper *Town Topics*, "Ms. Mann, as she has done so successfully for other small-cast plays, cuts the mighty McCarter stage down to size by wooden-picture-framing at its center a small acting area, which the two sisters can fill."

Critics were unanimously enthusiastic, as were audiences. One reviewer wrote that from time to time the audience sitting around him simply began applauding spontaneously, whenever they approved of a saucy Delany retort or an actor's particularly affecting moment. Whatever difficulties Gloria Foster and Mary Alice had with each other during rehearsals, audiences saw two actors at the top of their game. Box office sales were the highest for any theater production in the McCarter's history.

Still, according to Judy James, "Where [the play] really belonged was the Booth," the theater with the smallest house on Broadway (it sat 783). "And miracle of miracles," she recalled, "something at the Booth moved, and we went in." There, on April 6, 1995, a cool Thursday night in New York City, *Having Our Say* opened to critical cheers for the actors, the play, and the lives of the two women being celebrated. Sitting with Nicholas, her mother, and Gary during the opening night party at the Laura Belle Supper Club, on West Forty-Third Street, Mann savored her winning return to Broadway nine years after the collapse of *Execution of Justice*. She had felt "pretty much in exile from New York. Smashed by the mainstream press on *Still Life*. And I got smashed on

Execution and smashed on *A Weekend Near Madison*." Vincent Canby at the *New York Times*, who was a playwright as well as a film and theater critic, led his review with, "The most provocative and entertaining family play to reach Broadway in a long time has a cast of two." He wrote that Emily Mann "has shaped the material so that the tales flow easily one into another . . . 'Having Our Say' is not a conventional, well-made play, though it has the effect of rich theater."

The play was nominated for a 1995 Tony Award, Mann was nominated for Best Director of a play, and Mary Alice for Best Actress in a play, reportedly to Gloria Foster's annoyance. Neither Mary Alice nor Mann nor the play won a Tony Award (the Tony for Best Play went to Terrence McNally's *Love! Valour! Compassion!*). But of all Mann's plays, *Having Our Say* proved to be one of the most frequently produced and critically applauded. The Broadway production played 317 performances, and the producers sent out a national tour staged by Loretta Greco, who had left the McCarter at the end of the 1994–1995 season to pursue a directing career. Greco also directed a production of *Having Our Say* in 1998 at South Africa's revered Market Theatre.

Mann subsequently wrote the teleplay "Having Our Say," which aired on CBS in 1999, with James and Cosby as executive producers. The one-hour-and-forty-minute drama is constructed around flashbacks, as the elderly sisters talk about their lives to the co-author of their book, Amy Hill Hearth, played by Amy Madigan. The verbal descriptions in the book and the stage play become visualized scenes of Sadie and Bessie as children, then as young, professional women, and finally centenarians. Lynne Littman's direction veers toward the sentimental, and the effect of making Diahann Carroll's Sadie look elderly by using a prosthesis is excruciating, but Ruby Dee's portrayal of Bessie is exquisitely detailed and stirring.

Mann received a Peabody Award and a Christopher Award for the teleplay, and a Writers Guild of America nomination. "I did well by it," she said. "I was proud of the script. It was the one TV script I wrote that got made, and I was glad it was that one."

Shortly after the Broadway opening, Mel Gussow interviewed Mann for the *New York Times*, and for the first time she spoke publicly about being diagnosed with multiple sclerosis. Gussow wrote, "With the show open, Ms. Mann has returned to her duties at the McCarter. Undaunted by a diagnosis of multiple sclerosis, she continues to lead an extremely active life as playwright, director and artistic director." As in Princeton, the New York rehearsals for *Having Our Say* had been challenging physically. At the beginning of the day, she usually could walk into the rehearsal room, but by the end of a rehearsal she often would have to be carried out or need two people supporting her when she walked. "I didn't want people wondering, you know, 'Is she drunk?' or 'What's wrong with her?'" she told Sara Brookner, "so I decided to come clean, and said, 'I'm doing all my work, I'm able to get it all done. I'm feeling positive and good and I'm seeing someone who I think is helping me a great deal. I have multiple sclerosis.'"

Grace Shackney remembered feeling relieved that the staff could now acknowledge what their artistic director was going through. "I was just so glad we didn't have to keep it a secret anymore," she recalled. Mann had cut back on public commitments to conserve her energy, and "When that article came out," said Shackney, "I thought, now people will understand."

In retrospect, Mann was not sure the theater community did understand. "I didn't get many directing offers for quite a few years outside of my own theatre after the Gussow article," she told Brookner, "though who knows if it's because of the MS." She also told Brookner that, especially for actors suffering with MS, her advice was not to let anyone in the profession know. "People don't understand the disease. If you feel you can work, it's your private business. If you're working with colleagues who are really good friends you can tell them, but it can sometimes get in the way of being hired."

Despite her struggles with illness that 1994–1995 season, and despite the energy required not only to run the McCarter but also to write and direct *Having Our Say*, Mann found the physical resources to work on her script about the slaughter known as the Greensboro Massacre.

In Greensboro, North Carolina, shortly before eleven o'clock on the morning of November 3, 1979, protesters from the Communist Workers Party (CWP) congregated to demonstrate against white supremacists of the Ku Klux Klan. Communist Workers Party members had come to North Carolina during the 1970s to organize white textile workers, and when that failed, they turned their attention to African American textile workers. The CWP's efforts resulted in clashes with a local KKK chapter and the American Nazi Party (ANP), and Communist Workers Party members, now calling themselves members of the Communist Workers Organization (CWO), scheduled what they billed as a "Death to the Klan March" for Saturday, November 3. At least one of the protesters was armed, and news reports later indicated that marchers had "beat on" passing cars.

Yet none of the protesters expected the assault that ensued. They had received a permit from the Greensboro Police Department to assemble at a largely Black housing project called Morningside Homes and then walk to the Greensboro City Hall. But no police were on the scene, despite the department's knowledge, through an informant, that the Klan was planning an attack, and despite the awareness of the FBI and the Bureau of Alchohol, Tobacco and Firearms (ATF). Members of the Klan and the American Nazi Party arrived at Morningside Homes in an armada of vehicles. They unloaded shotguns, rifles, handguns, and an AR 180, a semi-automatic weapon resembling a machine gun. They opened fire and, within eighty-eight seconds, killed five protesters and wounded seven more before speeding away. One Klan member was wounded.

The assault should have been the stuff of extensive news coverage. But the next day, November 4, 1979, Iranian demonstrators entered the American embassy in Tehran and took more than sixty hostages, sweeping other news off the front page. In 1980 and 1984, state and federal prosecutors brought criminal charges against the Klan and ANP members who participated in the attack, but the defendants were acquitted in both trials. A $48 million civil suit, filed in 1980 and settled in 1985 after a three-month trial, ultimately revealed that the Greensboro Police Department had conspired with the Ku Klux Klan, and jurors found them jointly liable. The City of Greensboro consented to pay $351,500 to the surviving marchers and their families, but never turned over the full amount. The Klan paid no damages at all. The verdict was nonetheless deemed a victory, as a slide at the play's end explains: "In 1985, for the first time in American legal history, local police and the Ku Klux Klan were found jointly liable in a wrongful death."

Mann's introduction to the Greensboro massacre occurred around 1990, when Brandon Tartikoff, chairman of the NBC Entertainment Group, announced that NBC would commission a select group of American dramatists to write two-hour teleplays for the network. Tartikoff hired the theater producer James B. Freydberg and the television and film producer Michael Manheim to deal directly with the playwrights. According to Freydberg, Manheim was particularly enamored by the idea of a teleplay based on the massacre and the civil trial that ensued in 1985. Freydberg said he recommended Mann, at the same time alerting Manheim that Emily was "what I define as an independent thinker" who might not see the project the way Manheim did.

The commission did not go smoothly. As Mann described the situation in one of our interviews, "I was trying to serve two masters . . . I had the survivors [of the massacre] on the one hand and I had the network on the other hand, and the network wanted me either to turn it into a love story or a buddy picture." The teleplay Mann finally wrote, titled "The Greensboro Massacre," was both courtroom drama and romance, and according to Mann, the survivors whom she had interviewed, and to whom she felt beholden, hated it. "They loved me, they loved my plays, they didn't love this," she said. "They wanted me to take it back from the network and make a play of it." In the event, Tartikoff left NBC in 1991 to become chairman of Paramount Pictures, and Freydberg and Manheim departed as well. The NBC project evaporated. Mann set about writing a stage play.

One of Mann's devices in the teleplay had been for the survivors to talk to an unseen camera, as though being interviewed. In her stage play, she made the interviewing mechanism visible, initially by putting Emily Mann, playwright, as a character in the script, but eventually simply calling her "Interviewer." The Interviewer becomes one of the structural threads holding the play together, and at times, when the Interviewer is not onstage asking questions, a TV camera is visible. The sense is that all the figures in this drama, whether the massacre's survivors or their antagonists, are providing testimony. Unlike the teleplay, this is no longer a literal courtroom drama, despite a few scenes where Lewis Pitts, the attorney for the survivors in their civil case, questions witnesses. This is a trial play in a figurative sense, displaying good versus evil for the world to see through the memories of the participants/testifiers and their responses to the Interviewer.

Mann originally called her new play *To Know a Monster*, a title derived in part from an observation made by the psychiatrist Dr. Paul Bermanzohn, who was shot in the head and an arm on November 3 and partially paralyzed. "You know, the biggest mistake the post-war generation made, I think," Paul says in the script, "was teaching their kids the Nazis were monsters, like they were a different species from us. The Nazis weren't 'monsters.' They were people. That's the problem. . . ."

Mann decided to track down and speak with those people, especially with a person who had become a national standard-bearer for white supremacy in the United States: a former Grand Wizard of the Ku Klux Klan and the founder of the National Association for the Advancement of White People, Louisiana native David Duke.

The task of locating Duke and getting him on the phone fell to Grace Shackney. "[Emily will] say, 'This is what I want.' 'This is what I want.' And she gets results," said Shackney. Finding Duke proved surprisingly easy. "I just made cold calls to people, and they'd say, 'Oh, he's not here now, but you might be able to reach him there. And this is the number.' When Shackney did reach Duke, "I told him Emily was making this play, and she wanted to interview him for a statement in the play, and he said 'fine.'" In 1995, Mann and the former Ku Klux Klan leader spoke at length on the phone. Transcribed by hand, the conversation runs twenty-six pages, evidence of Mann's ability for eliciting "the spill." The monologue Mann subsequently crafted from the conversation runs nearly seven pages in the published script and includes a startlingly pre-scient description of racism cloaked in the language of America's right-wing politics, as voiced in the second decade of the twenty-first century:

> I think the people of the world are turning
> conservative and I think the European-Americans
> and European-Europeans for that matter
> are starting to realize like every culture and every
> heritage they have a right to preserve what's theirs
> and their way of life.

"It was like sitting in the room with the devil," said Mann.

As Janice Paran observed in her notes after an in-house reading at the McCarter in April 1995, the most monstrous people tended to be the most vivid onstage. In addition to Duke, there is Virgil Griffin, the Grand Dragon of the Invisible Knights of the Ku Klux Klan, a violent racist and proud of it. There is Roland Wayne Wood, who astounds Lewis Pitts in court by singing an anti-Semitic rendition of "Jingle Bells" with gusto. And there is Edward ("Eddie") Dawson, a smarmy fellow whose schooling never went beyond the sixth grade and who moved from New Jersey to Greensboro, where he joined the KKK. He became a paid Klan mole for the FBI until he and the Bureau parted company, and then he became a Klan informant for the Greensboro Police Department. He was at the head of the Klan's armada on November 3, but claimed he skedaddled before anyone got shot. "I didn't see nobody point a gun at anybody," he tells the Interviewer in the play.

By contrast, those on the side of the anti-Klan marchers do not have distinctive personalities or voices. Lewis Pitts, the attorney, gets angry on occasion but sounds lawyerly most of the time. The Interviewer assumes an objective stance. "I didn't want me to be an important character,"

Mann said. "I just wanted to be a facilitator, a texture rather than a motor." The self-described survivors are sympathetic and earnest, but on the page and on the stage their monologues tend to sound like speeches rather than organic expressions of what they think and feel. The exception is Nelson Johnson, an African American civil rights activist who later became a minister serving the poorest in Greensboro's Black community. His is an angry energy at the start of the play, then a sad but determined force at the end, when, at a ceremony dedicating the ground on which the five anti-Klan marchers died, he calls for reconciliation between Black people and white people.

Mann had intended to direct her new documentary play herself. Janice Paran, in March 1994 notes for an early draft, asked how Mann imagined staging a particular scene, and whether she planned to have the whole company onstage throughout the production.

But three months after Paran asked those questions, Mann had been diagnosed with MS, and she stepped back as director after "a big discussion in-house," during which, in her recollection, "people convinced me it would be wise to have another director." By the time she visited the city of Greensboro in November 1994, the English director Mark Wing-Davey, best known in the New York theater world for directing Caryl Churchill's *Mad Forest* off Broadway, had accepted the offer to stage Mann's new play.

They were not a good match. His theater background was the Joint Stock Theatre Company, founded in London in 1974 and based on the concept that plays would emerge from workshops during which actors, playwright, and director brought together ideas and research. Out of that mixture of materials, the playwright wrote her script. "The Joint Stock process," Wing-Davey explained during our interview, "is that [the playwright] can't have anything written. You're not supposed to at all. And so therefore what you're doing is you're responding to what you get right there, then and there."

But Mann had already written a script, although according to Janice Paran's notes throughout 1995, the script still needed textual work.

Presumably that would be a focus of the workshop scheduled to take place from October 2 through 15, 1995, in a room at a childcare center in Princeton, for what she now titled *Greensboro (A Requiem)*.

"The way I do a workshop is very loose," said Wing-Davey, interviewed in 2018 at New York University's Tisch School of the Arts, where he was chairman of the Graduate Acting Program. "I get people to give talks, they give lectures, they research stuff, we learn songs. We kind of work basically around the edges of whatever it is we're doing, so that it becomes a kind of mulch. This is absolutely not the way Emily worked." Production stage manager Cheryl Mintz's written account of one particular day noted that "we wrapped up our oral reports." John Spencer, who was playing Eddie Dawson in the workshop, gave an oral report on "History & Efforts of the KKK," and Brian Stokes Mitchell, who was portraying Nelson Johnson, gave a report on racism. Wing-Davey read the Billboard Top 20 Hits and Top 10 Country Hits from 1979, and the company apparently tried to sing as many of the songs as they knew. The company then watched a portion of *The Birth of a Nation*, D.W. Griffith's 1915 silent film in which the Ku Klux Klan is portrayed heroically. They finished by reading Mann's new rewrites.

Wing-Davey was right: that was not the way Mann worked. She wanted the sort of workshop where actors receive rewrites each day, get on their feet, and work through the changes, allowing Mann to sit with her script, observe how new lines work or don't, and make notes to herself for more rewrites when she returns home. "He didn't really want me in rehearsal," Mann asserted. "He did a whole lot of theater games rather than working on the scenes themselves." In her memory, Wing-Davey and the actors did little except toss Koosh balls back and forth (he used some Koosh ball-tossing as a warm-up). He did block a staged reading for the final day of the workshop, which was a presentation for an invited audience, and according to Cheryl Mintz's report, the presentation was "quite a wonderful in-house event for us." But Mann was furious. She thought two weeks had been wasted and communicated as much to Wing-Davey.

From Mann's point of view, the situation did not improve during rehearsals for the February 1996 opening. She felt she was being sidelined. "The thing is," she said, "you finish a play in rehearsal. I do anyway. So when I'm working on a play of mine with actors, I'm constantly analyzing whether a moment works or doesn't work. Is it the writing, is it the directing, is it the actor? Or is it the design? I'm constantly doing that, . . . I just keep honing a text while I'm working on it, when I'm directing it. That's why I like directing the first productions of my plays."

"My sense of why they didn't get along," said Janice Paran, "was that Mark's aesthetic was so different from Emily's. He's not sentimental, he likes the rough and tumble of ideas on the stage, and she's more a humanistic director, interested in emotional content, which interested Mark less. Interpretive differences, and because Mark was the director and not Emily, made it difficult for them to come to a consensus." It did not lessen the tension that the three days allotted for technical rehearsals proved insufficient. Mara Isaacs, newly on board at the McCarter as staff producer, believed "there were some decisions made about the physical production that were made to look simple, but actually were quite complicated and were perhaps overly ambitious for the technical schedule."

The look of Robert Brill's revolving sets was another contentious point. The sets presented several unadorned interiors downstage, backed by low walls painted a light institutional green or gray, with chairs and the occasional table the only furniture. While in Greensboro with Mann in November 1994, Wing-Davey had accompanied her to a community center and was impressed by its sparseness. "What struck me," he said, "was the ordinariness of it all. The circumstances. We were in classrooms. Or we were in a community center. It wasn't some kind of heightened environment in which we were meeting people . . . there weren't any rays of sunshine that came in. It was just as plain as could be." Wing-Davey was pleased with Brill's design, which he thought "moved a bit towards a kind of Fritz Lang *Metropolis*," the 1927 silent film about a futuristic, dysfunctional city. Mann hated it. "It looked so grim," she said. "There was no color. It looked like Poland. Somebody said to me it was what the DMV might have looked like in Warsaw."

Whatever was going on between Mann and Wing-Davey, one afternoon he walked out of a technical rehearsal, and Mann temporarily took over the directing. Wing-Davey took a walk in the snow, smoked a cigarette, and came back to rehearsal, and in his recollection "they were all fairly apologetic about stuff." The first preview was cancelled to allow for one more day of tech.

Snow covered the ground in Princeton on Friday night, February 9, 1996, when *Greensboro (A Requiem)* opened at the McCarter. An exceptional cast included Michael Countryman, Jon DeVries, Deborah Hedwall, Myra Lucretia Taylor, and Carol Woods, most of whom played several parts. A relatively unknown Philip Seymour Hoffman played sundry Klansmen and a scurrilous FBI agent, among other roles.

Left to right: Jon DeVries, Michael Countryman, Philip Seymour Hoffman, and Deborah Hedwall in Greensboro (A Requiem), *written by Emily Mann and directed by Mark Wing-Davey, the McCarter Theatre Center, 1996*
PHOTO: © T. CHARLES ERICKSON

John Spencer, to Mann's distress, had bowed out after the workshop to make a film, but by all accounts Jeffrey DeMunn portrayed the racist informant Edward Dawson vividly. Brian Stokes Mitchell was also no longer in the cast, but Stanley Wayne Mathis was commendable as Nelson Johnson, the Communist-protester-turned-minister. Angie Phillips gave a sly, understated performance as the Interviewer.

Critics were respectful: of the subject, of what Mann was attempting, of the production. They were not exuberant, but neither were they discouraging. Vincent Canby crossed the Hudson to review it for the *New York Times* and wrote that Mann had built a "canny collage of a script," which revealed "a situation that is far more complex and melancholy than that found in agitprop literature. What emerges is a mare's-nest of evil, innocence, fury and sometimes fatally misguided impulses to do good. In short, a particularly all-American tragedy." Like other critics, he recognized that "the text seems still to be in the process of shaking down. . . . Coherence isn't the problem so much as the occasional lack of dramatic emphasis."

More than twenty years later, Wing-Davey said, "I'm actually rather proud of the piece. Because I'm interested in a play as an event, which stands on its own. If people like it, that's great. But to a certain extent, I'm less concerned about that. . . . There's a dialectic between the audience and the piece, there's a tension about what they expect and who they are, watching this piece. What their expectations are and what they see—that's where the vibrations, if you like, occur." He acknowledged that *Greensboro* was "a kind of set of events, a set of statements. . . . Which add up or don't add up. And it may be that Emily wanted a more passionate event. But I don't think the play was that."

"I don't feel like I got to finish the play," said Mann, who, more than two decades later, spoke regretfully, even angrily, about Wing-Davey's production. As of 2020, she has never directed the play herself. In 1999, to mark twenty years since the massacre, San Francisco's Unconditional Theatre staged the play, as did students at the University of North Carolina, Greensboro (UNCG). Michael Scott Pryor, in his MA thesis, "The Matter of Memory: Visual and Performative Witnessing of the

Greensboro Massacre," credited the production with being "a critical turning point in the grassroots struggle to help Greensboro come to terms with the history of November 3, 1979."

"This lineage is important," Pryor wrote, "because it highlights the way in which Mann's play haunts the truth process. While other artworks likely would have emerged without the precedent of 'A Requiem,' the play did so much to . . . to reinvigorate the memory of November 3 within the local consciousness that it must be thought of in terms of an originary [*sic*] work that helped pave the way for the art that came afterward." Not only the art, but also the Greensboro Truth and Reconciliation Commission, formed in 2004, which held hearings and released its Report in 2006, condemning the behavior of Greensboro police and city officials.

It is constructive to compare *Greensboro (A Requiem)* with *Execution of Justice*. They are Mann's most complex documentaries up to that time, and each uses interviews, testimony, photographs, and film clips, among other materials. But in terms of Mann's dramaturgy, the earlier play is more theatrical than *Greensboro*. *Execution* contains a central conflict: a battle of words, character, and shrewdness between a deft defense attorney and a frustrated prosecutor. The back-and-forth with witnesses is stimulating, entertaining, and happens in front of us as though in the present. The characters are distinctive, and Mann brings the various threads to an intricate and affecting climax. Two murders have been committed, and the murderer and the ideologies he stands for and against are being judged by us, the audience, as we watch a trial move to its conclusion.

In *Greensboro (A Requiem)*, Mann does not achieve the same degree of theatricality, perhaps because she introduces extensive background information during the first half of the play, and because the action is basically a retelling or explaining of events in the past. Broadly speaking, there are two groups of people in the play— Communist protesters and racist Klansmen—and members of each group give their testimonies, which are often recollections or, in the case of the survivors, expressions of mourning. Referring to the play's title, Mann said that *Greensboro*

(A Requiem) "was in some ways a memorial service," not only for those killed on November 3, 1979, but also because "there was a great loss in our country for those who have fallen at the hands of white supremacists. . . . And there was that sense of recognition of the dead." That concept, more than anything else, explains the play's form, which at times feels like a succession of eulogies.

The violent events of *Execution of Justice* and *Greensboro (A Requiem)* took place only a year apart, although the plays were written more than a decade apart. Dan White murdered Mayor George Moscone and Harvey Milk in November 1978; the Klan and the American Nazi Party attacked and murdered Greensboro protesters twelve months later. The facts differ, but the conflicts that ignited each assault are comparable. The assailants in each case were defending their own kind and ridding America of those they considered "the other": gays and political liberals in San Francisco; Communists, African Americans, and civil rights activists in Greensboro.

In *Execution*, however, Mann asks us to look at Dan White with pity as well as anger, and because of White's suicide, there is a kind of closure. In *Greensboro (A Requiem)*, there are only monsters and their victims (the play barely cites the marchers' militancy). The play's warning is unambiguous, or as Signe Waller, whose husband Jim was murdered on November 3, says in the script:

> once there are categories of people who do not qualify as having full
> human stature–whether they are gays or black people or communist
> or whoever they are–I mean, once you can separate humanity that
> way, then you have already created an entire framework in which
> you can practice all kinds of oppression on people.

The only hope Mann leaves us with is the possibility of Black people and white people forging some kind of reconciliation, or as the Reverend Nelson Johnson says at the end of the play, "I wrote a letter to the white clergy here. I told them: I made the first step. Now it's up to you–up to all of us–we got to turn these people, your people, *around*."

In contrast to the note of possible Black–white reconciliation with which *Greensboro* ends, on June 26, 1996, the playwright August Wilson stood on the McCarter stage and delivered his polemical speech, "The Ground on Which I Stand," to an audience of theater artists and administrators. The occasion: the keynote at Theatre Communications Group's 11th Biennial Conference. The effect: akin to "blowing up the conference," according to the director Benny Sato Ambush.

"I have come here today to make a testimony," Wilson said, "to talk about the ground on which I stand and all the many grounds on which I and my ancestors have toiled, and the ground of theatre on which my fellow artists and I have labored to bring forth its fruits, its daring and its sometimes lacerating, and often healing, truths." He noted that, of what at that time were sixty-six LORT theaters, only one, Crossroads Theater Company in New Brunswick, New Jersey, "can be considered black"—a situation, he stressed, due not to a lack of Black artists, but an absence of funding. Citing his personal history as a disciple of the Black Power Movement of the 1960s, he passionately urged African Americans to start their own theaters, write their own plays, direct and perform their own plays. He also urged Black theater artists to avoid what he considered racist contrivances such as all-Black productions of *Death of a Salesman.* He derided "colorblind casting," which he called "an aberrant idea that has never had any validity other than as a tool of the Cultural Imperialists who view American culture, rooted in the icons of European culture, as beyond reproach in its perfection. . . . For a black actor to stand on the stage as part of a social milieu that has denied him his gods, his culture, his humanity, his mores, his ideas of himself and the world he lives in, is to be in league with a thousand naysayers who wish to corrupt the vigor and spirit of his heart."

Wilson's speech provoked a cascade of responses, including virulent exchanges between him and Robert Brustein, the founder and artistic director of the American Repertory Theatre in Cambridge, Massachusetts, and the theater critic for *The New Republic.* Three years earlier, Wilson said, Brustein had decried "funding agencies" for "substituting sociological criteria for aesthetic criteria in their grant procedures," or as Wilson interpreted it, presuming "inferiority of the work of minority artists." On January 27, 1997, there would be standing-room-only in New York City's Town Hall for "On Cultural Power: The August Wilson-Robert Brustein Discussion," moderated by Anna Deavere Smith.

Mann could not endorse the artistic separatism that Wilson seemed to be calling for. She had challenged theatrical convention by casting Black actors in traditionally white roles; co-written and directed a Black musical; written and directed a play about two Black American women. She had served on the Directors Committee of the Non-Traditional Casting Project, which Actors' Equity Association (AEA) co-founded in 1986 to address that the majority of AEA productions were being cast with white actors. She did not stand to applaud at the end of Wilson's speech.

Mann does not remember exactly when her health began to decline steadily, but in an interview she referred to the summer of 1996 as a time when she was horribly ill. The season that just ended had been grueling, what with *Greensboro*; directing her third incarnation of *A Doll House*, starring Cynthia Nixon as a seductive, giggling, but finally sad and dignified Nora; and hosting the TCG Conference. She spent July at Gary's house in Claverack, lying on their bed and unable to do much except read Isaac Bashevis Singer, one of her father's favorite authors, and search for a novel or story she could transform into a play.

In this search, she was helped by Charles McNulty, who had been hired as a part-time literary manager in Janice Paran's department. "Emily and I spent the summer reading all of I.B. Singer's works," McNulty wrote me in an email. "The two of us divided up his corpus and reported back to each other at regular intervals on what we thought would work onstage. It was a dream summer for me."

Mann particularly was drawn to Singer's short, semi-autobiographical novel *Meshugah*, which the author had serialized as *Lost Souls* in the popular Yiddish newspaper, the *Jewish Daily Forward*. She decided to dramatize it. Set in Manhattan in the early 1950s, *Meshugah* (Yiddish for "crazy") is a love triangle with complications both humorous and dark, and a bitter ending. Aaron Greidinger, a forty-seven-year-old editor and writer for the *Forward*, and Miriam, a twenty-seven-year-old Holocaust survivor with a tarnished past, fall in love. But Miriam is also having an affair with Aaron's elderly friend Max, and at the same time she is married to a psychotic American poet whom she hates.

Aaron and Miriam overcome the obstacles to their relationship, but then Aaron learns that Miriam survived her incarceration in a Nazi concentration camp by becoming a "kapo," a prisoner assigned to supervise and punish other prisoners. Aaron is horrified, yet he is still enthralled by Miriam. They marry, but Aaron refuses to have children with her. "You and I, we are like mules," he tells her in the novel's final lines. "The last of a generation."

"I read it," McNulty recalled, "and saw what she loved in the novel. But I had reservations. I thought the story might be too episodic, and hence better suited to television than the theater. . . . My challenge as a dramaturg was to support her choice by heightening her awareness of some of the challenges with the material. I worried principally about the storytelling. The conflict in the novel isn't calibrated as it would be in a traditional drama. Singer's gifts for scene-setting and humorous character observation can only be exploited so far onstage. What was driving the action? How could the tensions among the characters be concentrated?"

McNulty eventually became wary of giving substantial notes, or as he put it, "As the script evolved, it became more difficult to give structural notes. Emily was more open to small-scale revisions at a certain point than in a more fundamental reordering of the work. It's a delicate line as a dramaturg, and I wasn't all that experienced in working so closely with a writer who was also my boss."

Yet if McNulty experienced Mann's resistance to his suggestions, he also experienced what he and other colleagues described as her thoughtfulness and caring. In January 1998, the McCarter was co-producing Mark Lamos's revival of *Cymbeline* with Hartford Stage, and the meet-and-greet was held in the McCarter's theater. "I tended to avoid these kinds of introductions," McNulty explained in his email, "because I stutter and saying my name in a large group can be difficult for me. But

I felt I had to be there, and when my turn came, I slammed into the initial consonant and my face probably turned red. A moment later, I noticed that Emily, who was sitting on the aisle not too far from me, made eye contact with me. She saw me suffering and subtly raised her shoulders and lifted her head to me as if to say, 'You carry yourself with the dignity and pride you deserve.' It was the simplest of gestures and yet to me it was the most profound. In that moment, I experienced in a deeply personal way her inspirational example as an artist."

By the end of the summer of 1996, Mann seemed to have rallied physically. McNulty observed that "she worked from home a good deal of the time, but when she came in, the only sign of her condition was when she had to get up out of her chair and walk across the room. Her gait was impaired but her energy was as unflagging as her determination." Nicholas would turn thirteen on September 15, and Emily organized a bar mitzvah for him on August 24 at the Jewish Center on Nassau Street in Princeton, saddened that her father was not there to witness it. Nicholas remembered being less than enthusiastic about the ceremony, but loving the party afterward at Liz Fillo's house, which had a swimming pool.

During the 1997–1998 season, Mann directed two readings of *Meshugah*, and that summer she traveled to the Sundance Institute in Utah for a workshop of the play, with Gary accompanying to help her walk. She had rallied, but Gary was alarmed. "Once Emily started going downhill," he recalled, "I very quickly, in my opinion, recognized René as not a guru. But Emily understandably was very, very resistant to absorbing that, believing that. So it took a while. And I knew Emily quite well by then. If I said to her, 'You're leaving [René] and going here,' that was the surest way it wasn't going to happen. So I tried to be gentle about it, but also insistent, and finally we went to a doctor in New York. He put her on a trial. The idea was, you put myelin into the body—the disease is the immune system attacking this—and you fool the body into attacking what you've added. Theoretically it made perfect sense," Mailman explained haltingly. "It didn't work. . . . She was continuing to go downhill."

On October 23, 1998, *Meshugah* opened to positive reviews, but not the rapturous responses which would lead a commercial producer to take the production to New York, as Mann had hoped. In February 2000, Oskar Eustis directed a production at Rhode Island's Trinity Repertory Company, where he was now artistic director, and in 2001 Boston Theatre Works presented a workshop production directed by Jason Slavick. Ultimately, in 2003, Loretta Greco would stage an intense, slimmed-down version off Broadway at Naked Angels. As with *Annulla*, the first of Mann's plays to address the Holocaust, *Meshugah* is a portrait of survival. But it goes beyond *Annulla* to grapple with the moral implications of being a Jew and surviving the annihilation of 6,000,000 other Jews, especially, as in Miriam's case, when you have survived by doing the bidding of a lethal enemy.

Despite her disappointment that the McCarter production did not go to New York, Mann wrote a friend at the end of the run that "it was a gorgeous, absolutely satisfying closing—also very tight . . . and had deepened enormously through my adjustments but also simply by playing it. I was very happy with it." She had to admit, however, that directing *Meshugah* had exhausted her and that she was not improving. "When I get busy," she wrote, "I feel better. When I crash, it is disaster physically and emotionally. Opening this show really did me in. All the emotions went right to my body—lots of pain, numbness, but I walked. I never lost the ability to walk."

A friend recommended Mann see Dr. Saud A. Sadiq, who in 1998 had become Director of the MS Research and Treatment Center at St. Luke's-Roosevelt Hospital in Manhattan. "A wonderful man," said Gary, who was with Emily when Sadiq examined her. He told her that, had she waited even a few more months, the disease might have progressed to where remission was no longer possible. Eventually she responded to a regimen he prescribed: she learned to give herself daily injections and to be alert for factors that could bring about symptoms, such as sudden changes in temperature, outdoors or indoors. She gave herself a new exercise routine, which included leading actors in a half hour of yoga before each of her rehearsals. "She started improving," Gary recalled in

2018. "Never did either of us imagine that she would be where she is today, given where she was."

On a sunny Sunday afternoon, June 4, 2000, Emily Mann and Gary Mailman were married in Princeton, on the grounds of an estate loaned to them for the occasion. Gary donned a yarmulke in honor of the

Emily Mann and Gary Mailman at their wedding, Princeton, New Jersey, June 4, 2000
COURTESY OF EMILY MANN

event. Emily wore a strapless, gold-tinged ball gown with a matching stole to cover her shoulders. On a green lawn, underneath a white chuppah, Rabbi Jennifer E. Krause performed the ceremony, while family and dozens of friends watched, sitting in canvas chairs arranged in rows on the lawn; photographs capture Emily and Gary after the ceremony, arm in arm and beaming ecstatically. Mann relished that memory of her renewed health. "I danced at my wedding," she said.

14

Rebel Artist
(2001–2013)

Tuesday morning, September 11, 2001, was sunny and pleasantly cool in the New York metropolitan area. The sky was an early autumn blue and nearly empty of clouds. Then, at 8:46:40 a.m., American Airlines Flight 11 plunged into the North Tower of the World Trade Center in lower Manhattan, and at 9:02:57 United Airlines Flight 175 struck the South Tower. By 10:30 that morning, both towers had collapsed, leaving ruins, dense gray smoke, and death and fear in their wake.

That Tuesday evening Mann cancelled the first preview performance of her production of *Romeo and Juliet*. Actors coming from New York City could not get to Princeton, and besides, everybody, from performers to staff to audience, was too stunned to do anything except sit in front of a television and watch the horrifying images, broadcast again and again. A number of Princeton residents had worked at the World Trade Center, and Jeffrey Woodward would remember seeing the same cars parked for weeks at the Princeton and Princeton Junction train stations, where their owners had left them before the early morning commute to the office.

Mann decided there had to be a performance of *Romeo and Juliet* on Wednesday evening, September 12. Commemorative candles burned in the front lobby, and before the audience began to arrive, the staff and the cast stood in a circle outside the main building and held lighted candles while Mann acknowledged their sorrow. Audience members later thanked her for letting them come together and express their grief through watching a play, one which posed a young couple's joyous love against the irrational hatred between their families. "The current production at the McCarter," wrote Alvin Klein in the *New York Times*, "is indisputably a tragedy, but it could have been divinely chosen for the moment, for it fulfills the highest purpose of theater—to enlighten and to purge, to create order out of chaos."

After consulting with her staff, Mann did cancel the season's next scheduled production, Richard Nelson's *The Vienna Notes*, a political satire about a self-involved U.S. senator who comes under siege by terrorists in Austria. "We are a country in pain," Mann stated for a press release. "As a theater dedicated to serving our community, we want to remind everyone of what is best in humanity in the face of evil. 'The Vienna Notes' is a brilliant and timely political drama . . . but it would be insensitive of us to present the play at this moment in our history." She filled the slot with *Lackawanna Blues*, a reminiscence written and performed by Ruben Santiago-Hudson, about his childhood and the woman who raised him. He had begun working on the play at the McCarter, and under Loretta Greco's direction, the play and the gentle performance tried to heal the shock and the loss people were experiencing.

But healing would be slow in coming. Mann and her administrative staff observed that the terrorist attacks had affected theater-going. People seemed less inclined to go out, to leave the protection of their homes. Fear became an undercurrent in Americans, lives, as did war. Shortly after 9/11, the United States invaded Afghanistan, and two years later, Iraq.

Despite the pervasive anxiety, Mann was experiencing renewed autonomy. On April 12, 2002, she turned fifty, and physically she was feeling stronger than she had in years. She could walk and drive without assistance. Her stamina had improved.

Freedom from pain and fatigue translated into artistic experimentation of the sort she pursued when first at the McCarter. In October 2002, the McCarter, in association with Manhattan's Second Stage Theatre, produced a rousing combination of theater and gospel music called *Crowns*, based on photographs and interviews in the book *Crowns:*

Portraits of Black Women in Church Hats by Michael Cunningham and Craig Marberry. In 1999, Marberry had introduced himself to Mann in North Carolina, when both were attending events related to the twentieth anniversary of the Greensboro Massacre. "There was a Town Hall for the whole community to get together to talk about what had happened," Mann recalled. "Craig was there. . . introduced himself and gave me an envelope of pictures and testimonies, saying—'I think this should be your next play." Mann was intrigued, but believed that someone who had grown up in the Black church would be better qualified than she to adapt and stage it. Mann invited the actor and playwright Regina Taylor to theatricalize the material and direct, and the result—the first project to be developed in what was called the McCarter Lab—was a joyous paean to African American women and the glorious hats they often wore to church. It was a celebration that drew African American audiences, including some of the splendidly hatted women who had appeared in Cunningham and Marberry's book, who traveled to Princeton to see the show.

In March of that 2002–2003 season, Mann upended convention by directing Shakespeare's *The Tempest* with Blair Brown playing the exiled duke, Prospero, as the exiled duchess Prospera. King Alonzo, one of the victims shipwrecked by Prospera's tempest, was now Queen Alonsa, and the shipwreck seemed to happen in the auditorium, where actors clung to the slender, brass-colored metallic posts in the side boxes overhanging the orchestra and also staggered down the aisles, a bit of directorial rebellion against the McCarter theater's staid ambience and its audience's ingrained habit of facing front.

The opening in September 2003 of the McCarter's new performance space, the Roger S. Berlind Theatre, further liberated Mann as a producer and director.

She had wanted an additional performance space ever since she first walked into the McCarter's auditorium. "I certainly remember her interest in a second space from the very beginning," said McCarter trustee Joan Girgus. "She looked at the theater and said 'Oh, my god.' Nine-hundred-plus seats in a room that's narrow and rectangular, and where the people sitting in the back connecting to the actors onstage is going to be impossible. . . . It took her maybe three seconds—maybe five minutes—to start talking about a smaller space." Athol Fugard called it "that coffin of an auditorium."

What with the McCarter's financial woes, building a new theater during the first decade of Mann's tenure was not feasible. Lacking an additional performance space, Mann and her staff improvised when it came to playwrights whose work they admired, but were unable to produce in the subscription season. For a festival called Winter's Tales '94, in January of Mann's fourth season, the McCarter commissioned twelve brief plays and one full-length work, arranged 150 chairs on the McCarter stage, and reserved the rest of the stage for minimally blocked performances, script-in-hand staged readings, and readings at music stands. Then in 1995, as Alvin Klein wrote in the *New York Times*, this new play series was "placed as epilogue in the McCarter subscription season, not as an interrupter," renamed Random Acts '95, and scheduled for June. That year the series' centerpiece was *A Park in Our House* by Nilo Cruz, with whom Janice Paran, the festival's dramaturg, was trying to establish an artistic relationship. In 1996, when the festival was redubbed Second Stage Onstage, it included Cruz's play for radio, *Two Sisters and a Piano*, which Brian Kulick would direct on the main stage in February 1999.

The McCarter's goal, according to Paran, was to find alternative ways to nourish playwrights who were embarking on fresh projects. They did not want, as she put it, "to contribute to a developmental treadmill." They did not want to produce a reading series, as so many theaters did, with no commitments to playwrights and no effort toward some sort of production. "What we were trying to do," said Mara Isaacs, "was really link whatever you called development as the early stages toward production. It was a continuum, not a separate program." In fact, said Paran, they tried to stop using the terms "play development" and "new-play development," and instead "to actually sit down with the writer and say, where do you think you are with this piece, what's helpful, how do you want to move forward?"

"We were a really good team," said Isaacs, speaking about how she, Paran, and Mann worked together. The three women would try to meet weekly, usually around the table in Mann's office, to share opinions about plays and playwrights, and plan seasons. Isaacs described a scenario where Mann would bring her wish-list, Paran might generate ideas for classics, and Isaacs would suggest director-driven projects that would not necessarily be Mann-directed projects. Kathleen Nolan, who was general manager through the 2001–2002 season, dubbed them "the art tarts." Said Isaacs, "We wore that badge proudly. At that time it was very unusual to have the three top artistic leaders of a theater be all women. Particularly in an institution of that size."

As the millennium approached, however, the McCarter's finances were stable enough to initiate a capital campaign for a new theater. The prominent theater architect Hugh Hardy, Princeton '54, designed the new space. The McCarter, Princeton University, and the Broadway producer Roger S. Berlind, Princeton '52, divided up the $14.1 million cost, with Berlind contributing $3.5 million. Princeton University students would share the use of the theater.

A second theater, but not a secondary one. "We talked about a second stage," said the McCarter's Director of Production David York, who had worked at the McCarter since before Mann took over in 1990, "and many people envision that as doing smaller, audience-demand work. But we decided to split the main stage season between two theaters. We wanted to make sure we equipped it as such. . . . It matches smaller Broadway playhouses." The back wall of the new stage abutted the exterior back wall of what was now known as the Marie and Edward E. Matthews Theater. The Berlind was also a proscenium, but its dimensions were less overwhelming than those of the Matthews. The Berlind's proscenium opening was thirty-seven feet, seven inches wide, and twenty-two feet high—nearly four feet narrower than the Matthews—and the stage was twenty-nine feet deep (the depth of the Matthews stage was forty-three feet and four inches). But the new theater's most endearing feature from Mann's point of view as a director was that it sat 360 in a comparatively intimate house. Actors could make eye contact with members of the audience, nearly to the back of the house. The audience could feel connected to the action onstage.

The inaugural production was Nilo Cruz's romantic and sensual *Anna in the Tropics*, which had been awarded the Pulitzer Prize for Drama the previous spring, the first time a Latino playwright had won the coveted prize. Mann directed, and local critics relished the Berlind, the play, and the production, which reportedly sold out even before it opened. Courtesy of Roger Berlind and co-producer Daryl Roth, *Anna* went directly to Broadway's Royale Theater, although it closed after only 115 performances.

"It was ten years overdue, but it was like night and day," Mann exclaimed about the Berlind. "Suddenly three out of the five shows were in a theater that was friendly to new work and the twentieth- and twenty-first-century repertoire. It was a sea change." In contrast to Mann's pre-Berlind years, the McCarter was now hiring more women and people of color to direct, a shift Mann also attributed to the new space. "Women and people of color had very little opportunity to work in a house as big as the Matthews," she averred. "I didn't want people drowning up there. I trained at the Guthrie, so at least I knew about big houses, and I directed on the Guthrie main stage and I directed at BAM and I directed on Broadway. I was one of the few women who had done that. [The Berlind] opened up a lot."

She would have been glad never to direct in the Matthews again. "I've only gone back to the Matthews a handful of times since the Berlind opened," she calculated. "Thirteen years was enough in that space." In the Berlind she returned to the subject of the Vietnam War, which felt disturbingly apt after the United States invaded Iraq in March 2003 and toppled Saddam Hussein, despite worldwide protests against the invasion. Steven Deitz's *The Last of the Boys*, which received its world premiere in September 2004, with Mann directing, was a drama about the Vietnam War's collateral human damage. Except now the Vietnam veterans are thirty years older, and one of them lives in an abandoned trailer park atop toxic waste, Dietz's metaphor for a country of ruins.

In the Berlind, in 2007, Mann also staged her new play *Mrs. Packard*, inspired by the life of a mostly forgotten American reformer for women's rights.

Elizabeth Parsons Ware had been born in Ware, Massachusetts, in 1816 to a Congregational minister and his wife and was educated at Amherst Female Seminary. At the age of twenty-three, probably because she was approaching what was then considered old-maidhood, her parents strongly urged their daughter to marry a thirty-seven-year-old Calvinist minister named Theophilus Packard, whom she hardly knew. She married him, bore six children, and apparently lived compliantly with her husband for about twenty years.

Then, to her husband's displeasure, Elizabeth rebelled publicly against his Calvinism, his punitive approach to rearing their children, and his condoning of slavery. Theophilus resented her objections and outspokenness, which he believed cost him his position at more than one church. In Illinois, where they had moved in 1854, a man could commit his wife to an insane asylum any time he wished, her consent be damned. And so in 1860 Theophilus did just that. Elizabeth spent three years in Illinois' Jacksonville Insane Asylum, beaten and tortured alongside women who, like herself, were incarcerated by dissatisfied husbands and had no recourse. Finally, she was deemed incurable and was released to Theophilus, who imprisoned her in their home. She escaped with the help of a sympathetic neighbor, and a jury of men subsequently found her sane. But in the meantime, Theophilus had sold their house and moved away with the children. Elizabeth spent the rest of her life trying to regain custody (she did, after nine years); writing about a system that allowed a disgruntled husband to brand his wife insane if she displeased him; and fighting for legislation that would give anyone accused of insanity a public hearing. She died in 1897, at the age of eighty-one.

Mann first waded into this hellish tale of a woman's oppression around 2005, alerted to it by a friend in Princeton. "I was looking for my next story," she said, "and sometimes I just put that out into the world: 'If you hear of a great story, let me know.'" She did not know that "a woman could be thrown into an insane asylum basically on the whim of her husband. . . . I thought she was an unsung heroine, with all of her flaws, which made me all the more interested. She was beautiful and she was brilliant, and she had so much to give, and she married a man who wasn't up to her."

Mrs. Packard is feminist theater wrought darkly. Like many women who began careers during the Women's Liberation Movement of the 1970s, Mann had ultimately realized that the recognition and parity for which her generation fought had yet to be achieved. Any supposition on that score was knocked off its pedestal in 1991, when the lawyer Anita Hill testified about being sexually harassed by Supreme Court nominee Clarence Thomas. Feminists reacted with dismay when Hill's testimony could not sway a majority of the senate, which voted 52–48 to confirm Thomas as an associate justice. In her 1992 article for *Ms.* magazine, "Becoming the Third Wave," Rebecca Walker enjoined women to "Let Thomas' confirmation serve to remind you . . . that the fight is far from over. Let this dismissal of a woman's experience move you to anger. Turn that outrage into political power." By the time Mann was writing *Mrs. Packard*, a backlash against second-wave feminism had been superseded by third-wave feminism, which aimed, among other goals, to end violence against women, whether as rape, domestic abuse, or psychological or physical harassment.

In this context, *Mrs. Packard* is Mann's definitive feminist play up to that time. Although Mann herself makes a feminist statement in *Still Life* by conveying that the Vietnam veteran's wife and lover are caught in a social construct that still privileges men, the two women never really confront their situations, even in the face of physical abuse.

Elizabeth Packard, by contrast, actively resists a patriarchal system that grants her no legal rights as a wife or mother, or as a human being who refuses to be silenced. In Mann's dramatization of the conflict between Elizabeth and the patriarchy, there is no gray area. She could divorce Theophilus, but then she would lose custody of her children. She is the victim of a system that allows her to be incarcerated against her will, abused physically and mentally, and manipulated sexually. Mann has said that the British director David Leveaux, after reading a draft

Dennis Parlato and Kathryn Meisle in Mrs. Packard, *written and directed by Emily Mann, McCarter Theatre Center, 2007*
PHOTO: © T. CHARLES ERICKSON

of the play, suggested a love affair between Mrs. Packard and the asylum's superintendent, Dr. McFarland, but Packard's own writings also imply she was in love with McFarland. Whatever the inspiration, Mann invented a sexually charged encounter between Elizabeth and the doctor, who, under the pretext of calming his new patient, strokes her back, neck, and breasts and brings her to orgasm. Elizabeth believes McFarland cares for her, only to discover that when she speaks her mind, as she did with her husband, the doctor also retaliates. He confines her in "the 8th ward," a place of filth and mayhem.

The word "invented" is significant, for the play is closer to historical fiction than documentary theater. The characters are drawn from Elizabeth Packard's own writings and accounts of Packard's life, including Barbara Sapinsley's 1991 biography *The Private War of Mrs. Packard*. But in a departure from her documentaries, Mann imagined the pleadings and angry words between Elizabeth and Theophilus Packard, imagined the sexually taut dialogue between Mrs. Packard and the doctor, and made up both the abusive language of the asylum's matron and the supportive conversations among the incarcerated women. That said, Mann does not romanticize history. Elizabeth Packard ultimately defeats the institutions which existed to contain and own and silence her. She manages to persuade a court to exonerate her. Yet she nearly loses her life in the process, and Mann makes it clear that many women at the time would be unable to fight the awful circumstances to which husbands and existing laws could condemn them.

The form is realistic drama with aspects of Victorian melodrama, except that in this battle between good (Mrs. Packard) and evil (Theophilus), no male hero swoops in to save the heroine. The doctor proves as ill-intentioned as the husband, and in the end Mrs. Packard essentially rescues herself. Rather than a "happily-ever-after" finish, a few lines describe how Elizabeth Packard worked tirelessly to protect other women from the fate to which Theophilus tried to sentence her.

Within the body of the play, Mann uses the intercutting technique of *Still Life* and *Execution of Justice*. On Eugene Lee's grim set, a bridge above the Berlind stage became the locus for characters testifying about Mrs. Packard's sanity, and the action on the stage below stopped while Jeff Croiter's lighting focused on the bridge. Only at the end of the play, however, does Mann break the fourth wall, when each character except Mrs. Packard turns to the audience and tells their fate in the third person, Mann's reminder that the characters were "real" and that, in most respects, this awful story actually happened:

THEOPHILUS: Theophilus Packard remained a minister, but never again had his own church.
DR. McFARLAND: Dr. McFarland and Mrs. Packard never saw each other again. In 1891, Dr. McFarland . . . hanged himself.

Mrs. Packard opened at the Berlind on May 4, 2007, and traveled in June to the John F. Kennedy Center for the Performing Arts in Washington, D.C., courtesy of a grant awarded by the Fund for New

American Plays. Reviews in both Princeton and Washington unanimously praised Kathryn Meisle's portrayal of Elizabeth. Otherwise the critical response was mixed. Some reviewers recognized the feminist issues Mann raised and applauded that she raised them; others objected that the play dragged at times, or that the clash between good and evil lacked subtlety.

The play has been produced by not-for-profit theaters, but it really found a life in colleges and graduate theater programs, where student actors, directors, and audiences apparently cared less about supposed dramaturgical flaws than the messages about women's rights and women's empowerment. Between 2013 and 2018, there were at least four college and university productions, and directors experimented with the script. At the University of California, Riverside, in 2015, Professor Bella Merlin cast actors of diverse races and, before the action of the play started, she lined her actors up on the stage as though they were a church choir, and had them sing hymns. She placed the judge presiding over Elizabeth Packard's sanity trial at a judge's bench in the middle of the stage and hung prison doors above the stage. "In a play about what is sanity and insanity, and attempting to figure out who you can trust, [Mrs. Packard] certainly is a woman of conviction," Merlin told a journalist at UC Riverside's newspaper the *Highlander*. "Mrs. Packard's greatest quality is her adherence to truth, and to the truth about what her story teaches society: That women deserve much better than simply being seen as objects to be owned."

While the opening of the Berlind was a high point in Mann's artistic life at the McCarter, the next ten years would alternate between pride and anxiety. Mann and her McCarter family celebrated the election of Barack Obama, the country's first Black president. Arthur Mann, she knew, would have seen this election as one of the long-sought outcomes of the Civil Rights Movement for which he had marched.

Yet the Great Recession, which the new president inherited from President George W. Bush's administration, affected the sources of monetary support on which the McCarter, like other not-for-profit theaters, relied. "Our Lehman Brothers gifts and our Merrill Lynch gifts—they went away overnight. From the corporations and then from the individuals who worked at all those companies," said Kathleen Nolan, who had resigned as general manager after the 2001–2002 season, but served briefly as managing director when Jeffrey Woodward went to Syracuse Stage in 2008.

However, unlike the theater Mann inherited in 1990, the McCarter now had reserves in place for a financial emergency. Mann and Woodward had built a rainy-day fund and set it up in something called "the Board Designated Fund," invested over at the university, according to Nolan. That helped ease the pain, but pain there was, Nolan said. "Staff was laid off, salaries were frozen. Positions were combined. Pension contributions were put in abeyance." For several seasons, Mann mostly scheduled small-cast productions or productions that did not require elaborate sets. As for the corporate money lost in the wake of the recession, Nolan predicted it "was not going to come back. Not in the same way."

On April 12, 2010, the McCarter's staff, the board, and their guests stopped fretting about budgets for one night to celebrate Mann's twentieth season at the McCarter, and her fifty-eighth birthday. Sylvia, who was ten days shy of turning eighty-nine and would soon move from Chicago to an assisted-living residence in Princeton, joined the festivities. Dinner at the Matthews was followed by toasts and speeches, including one from Gary, who described "Emily intermittingly squeezing my hand so tightly on opening nights that I start to think about securing medical attention at intermission." An announcement was made about "Emily's Fund for Artistic Exploration," established to honor Mann and be used at her discretion for the "development and production of new work and other artistic priorities." A jazz band played. Guests danced. Mann received a book of photographs and tributes, including this from staff producer Mara Isaacs:

> Perhaps the most important moment in our 15-year collaboration was during Emily's own Greensboro (A Requiem). I couldn't be

more proud of this fierce and important play that documented a nearly-forgotten travesty in modern American history. Personally, it was my initiation into Emily's unyielding commitment to giving voice to the voiceless. . . . The production experience itself was a wild emotional ride for both of us—full of triumphs and disappointments—but, at the end of the day, I consider it an immense success.

Beginning in the early 1990s, Mann had relied on a close-knit group of artists and administrators, but her McCarter family was breaking up. Since 2005, Mann had lost Janice Paran, Jeffrey Woodward, and Grace Shackney. Mara Isaacs was the last of Mann's team to depart, at the end of the 2012–2013 season, to be an independent theatrical producer. Mann herself had looked beyond the McCarter during the spring of 2012, to direct a multiracial Broadway revival of *A Streetcar Named Desire*, with Nicole Ari Parker as Blanche DuBois; Daphne Rubin-Vega as her sister, Stella; Blair Underwood as Stella's husband, Stanley; and Wood Harris as Mitch.

The history of African American and multiracial productions of Williams's plays goes back to the 1940s. In 1947, two years after *The Glass Menagerie* opened on Broadway, the Howard Players at Howard University, in Washington, D.C., produced the play with a Black cast, and since then, according to theater scholar Philip C. Kolin, who has delved into the history of Williams's plays performed by casts of color, there had been other Black and multiracial productions, both amateur and professional. One of the more notable was Tazewell Thompson's production at the Arena Stage in 1989, with Ruby Dee playing Amanda.

For *A Streetcar Named Desire*, the first production with an entirely Black cast took place in 1953 at Lincoln University in Jefferson City, Missouri. The first professional production with a Black cast happened two years later at Los Angeles's Ebony Showcase Theater, which was owned by the actor Nick Stewart and his wife, Edna. Stewart's agent happened to be Audrey Wood, who also represented Williams, and Stewart told Philip Kolin that "Audrey Wood saw what I was doing at the Ebony to uplift the image in our community, to do humanitarian things, and she helped me in this respect." During the 1970s and 1980s there were several productions of *Streetcar* with casts of color, including one from the Dashiki Project Theatre in New Orleans, where *Streetcar* is set. But there had been no such production of the play on Broadway.

Enter Stephen C. Byrd and Alia M. Jones, who in 2008 had been the lead producers of a Broadway revival of *Cat on a Hot Tin Roof* with a Black cast, staged by an African American director, Debbie Allen. Mann "had not put together who [Byrd and Jones] were" when, in 2011, she learned that they were going to produce *Streetcar* on Broadway and were looking for a director. She had yearned to stage the play for years, had in fact imagined a production with a cast of color, and she asked her agent to arrange a meeting. "I didn't know that the producers were African American," said Mann, "and I got there, did my whole idea of making it a Black *Streetcar*. . . . So I started pitching this, and they were smiling and nodding, and I said, 'You know, New Orleans is a Creole city, and this is a no-brainer really.' And they said, 'Well, what's so amazing is that's what we want to do.'"

The Williams estate had no objection to a production with actors of color. On the other hand, *New Yorker* magazine theater critic John Lahr, possibly aware of the upcoming Broadway production, begged "Santa, baby," in a December 2011 blog, for "no more infernal all-Black productions of Tennessee Williams plays unless we can have their equal in folly: all-white productions of August Wilson." When asked about such complaints, Blair Underwood, who was playing Stanley, wrote in a Facebook post:

> Once you know your history and know that there was indeed a cul-
> ture of people (in the 1700s), endemic to Louisiana called the "gens
> de colour libre," or "free people of color," and that these owned
> plantations & some actually owned their own slaves, there is no
> basis to dismiss the backstory of our DuBois sisters who hail from
> their family owned plantation called Belle Reve; Or to dismiss the
> part of the story where Blanche DuBois pines for an oil millionaire

called Shep Huntleigh. If these dismissive Nay Sayers knew their history, they would know that there were a number of black people that owned oil wells in the 30s & 40s.

Mann's script changes, made with the permission of the Williams estate, mainly excise "Kowalski" and any lines about Stanley being Polish. By casting Underwood, who was dark-skinned in comparison to Parker and Rubin-Vega, Mann gave this Blanche the ammunition to criticize her sister's husband for belonging to another, supposedly lower, class of people, a form of class- and color-consciousness that audiences of color knew and probably had experienced.

The production that opened at the Broadhurst Theater on April 22, 2012 received an amalgam of positive and negative reviews. By most accounts it was a highly sexualized production, and David Rooney in the *Hollywood Reporter* wrote that "what distinguishes [Mann's] production . . . is the evocative atmosphere of a milieu in which sex, death and violence perfume the sweaty air. Spiced by the jazzy strains of Terence Blanchard's original score, this *Streetcar* smolders."

At the outset Blanche and Stanley recognized each other's sexuality, and Rooney wrote that this Blanche's "dealings with a crudely antagonistic hulk like Stanley suggest she knows her way around guys like him. Or at least thinks she does." *Streetcar* brought forth Mann's commitment to portraying physical violence, in this case against Blanche. "Stanley is a great life force," Mann said during a lengthy WNYC Radio interview with her and the four leading actors. "But he's also her executioner." Marilyn Stasio in *Variety* wrote that "Mann's blunt staging of the rape scene blows away another conventional view of the play; namely, that refined Blanche and barbaric Stanley are two sides of the sexual coin, involving Blanche as a semi-complicit partner in her own rape. In this production, rape means rape."

The positive reviews did not help the production outweigh the negative ones, especially in an environment where substantive theater criticism was becoming rare, whether in print or on the Internet. Michael Musto in the *Village Voice* damned with minimal praise, writing that

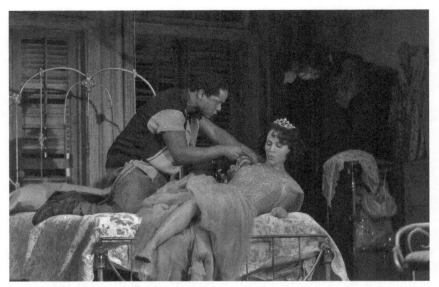

Blair Underwood threatens Nicole Ari Parker in A Streetcar Named Desire, *written by Tennessee Williams and directed by Emily Mann, the Broadhurst Theater, 2012*
PHOTO: © KEN HOWARD

the production's "straightforward approach deprives us of a central battle royale—or of crackling electricity—but whose affection for the text still merits the kindness of strangers." Ben Brantley in a brief review for the *New York Times* dismissed the production as "mostly an exquisite snooze." The producer Stephen Byrd had claimed that his production of *Cat on a Hot Tin Roof* was one of the highest grossing productions of the 2007–2008 season; *Streetcar* did not meet that standard and closed after 105 performances. There had once been talk of taking the production to London, but that possibility evaporated.

The McCarter's theater series had not fared well in Mann's absence that spring of 2012. Knowing she would be away for March and much of April in rehearsals for *Streetcar*, Mann left the theater in the hands of the new managing director, Timothy J. Shields, and Mara Isaacs. But problems arose during the rehearsals of John Guare's *Are You There, McPhee?* which was being directed by Sam Buntrock for a May premiere, and given Mann's rehearsal schedule, she could not give the play or production the attention they evidently needed. Reading Charles Isherwood's review for the *New York Times* it is hard to tell if he is laughing or crying about the chaos he witnessed on the Berlind stage.

"I came home to a mess," Mann remembered. "John Guare's play nearly cost me my job. It was a complete and total wreck. I had to decide whether to stay and fight for my job, or not." As a result of the Great Recession, the McCarter was still having economic problems, which had not been helped by the disastrous reviews for *McPhee* and, at the beginning of the season, mixed reviews for Marina Carr's play *Phaedra Backwards*, which Mann directed. As January 2013 approached, the board president, Brian MacDonald, told Mann that her contract would only be renewed for one year.

"That was a really difficult season," said Kathleen Nolan, who was now on the board. "That season it was like the perfect storm, and, yes, the board was unhappy. Because it was not just that she was gone, it was that the board felt that attention hadn't been paid to two new plays that required more time and attention. And you know, she's the artistic leader. She's where the artistic buck stops. I think some people overreacted, but I do think it was a proper reaction. It's not like the artistic house was not in order. It was in order. But maybe we just needed more time and attention. I think Emily heard the message loud and clear. And that was one season and done."

Mann was angry. "I made a choice to stay and fight," she recalled, "but I will never forget what happened. And it made me think, 'Well, okay, what are my other options?'" Mann's friend Faye M. Price, the co-artistic producing director of the Pillsbury House and Theatre in Minneapolis, urged her to apply to be artistic director of the Guthrie; Joe Dowling, who had headed the theater since 1995, and oversaw the Guthrie's move to new quarters by the Mississippi River, announced in April 2014 that he would be retiring after the 2014–2015 season. "I tried to strong-arm her," said Price, who knew Mann from the Lab School, the Guthrie of the 1970s, and had acted in *Execution of Justice* at the Guthrie. "I really wanted her to apply. I felt with her experience, her sensibility, her sense of equity and social justice—all the things I think that board was looking for—her ability to lead an institution out of fiscal trouble. I thought she was so right for that job. I really wanted to see her in that job."

But Mann did not need to return to what she described as "a toxic institution. . . . It's an unhappy place, and that seeps deep into an institution. I decided to make a theater that was the opposite of that. It was in reaction to my years at the Guthrie to make McCarter the way it is." She believed there were still goals for her to achieve at the McCarter, and for the time being, she chose to stay where she was.

By the end of the 2012–2013 season, the board's displeasure had mostly evaporated, diffused by the success of Christopher Durang's new comedy, *Vanya and Sonia and Masha and Spike*, which the McCarter had commissioned and nurtured. Nicholas Martin directed the play in the Berlind in September 2012, to acclaim from audiences and critics. In October, the production transferred to the Mitzi E. Newhouse Theater at Lincoln Center and in March 2013 headed to Broadway. Play, production, and actors received six Tony Award nominations, and *Vanya* won the Tony Award for Best Play. The surge of theater awards, in fact, made Durang's comedy the most honored production that the McCarter had generated to that point. It also did not hurt Mann's standing with the board that, two years later, she won the 2015 Margo Jones Award, given to "that citizen-of-the-theatre who has demonstrated a significant impact, understanding and affirmation of the craft of playwriting, with a lifetime commitment to the encouragement of the living theatre everywhere."

15

The Political Is Personal

(2013–2019)

ALMOST ONE YEAR after receiving the board's warning, Mann wrote the trustees an explanatory, deferential, but canny email about how Gloria Steinem, Lincoln Center Theater, and the producer Daryl Roth had asked her to write "a stage event" for Steinem to perform. Her email was gauged to alert the board to the project's benefits for the McCarter, to assure the board that the project would not interfere with her duties as artistic director, and by the way remind the board about her professional reputation:

> It is a spectacular opportunity and honor, as you can imagine, for me to continue my life's work as the pioneer in this country of documentary theater, and to be asked to create a new form within that form—a documentary piece with the iconic subject herself on-stage—and to do this with the premiere theater in NY, our newest partners, Lincoln Center; and to continue my partnership with Daryl Roth who produced ANNA IN THE TROPICS on Broadway.

> In terms of the amount of work it will take, I judge it to be about the same amount of work it has taken me to write the other 15 or so plays, screenplays and adaptations I've written during my 23+ years at McCarter Theater [sic] to date. I have always written late at night, early mornings, weekends and holidays, never allowing it to get in the way of my McCarter administrative and artistic duties. . . . I

wish to assure you that I have been writing the entire time I've been
at McCarter and it has never interfered with my function as artistic
director. And of course I am also the resident playwright. I have
always made the time to write. I will as always be available to Tim
[Shields], Brian [MacDonald], the Board and the staff as needed.

From the time Mann received her warning from the board at the
end of 2012, she worked intensely to consolidate what she had built
artistically and ensure that, going forward, the McCarter would have a
sturdy foundation financially. For months, she recollected, "It was like
when I came here. I was in the office at ten in the morning, leave at six
sometimes, meet Gary for dinner, then go into the city or back to the
theater." Beginning with the 2013–2014 season, for the first time she
had an associate artistic director, Adam Immerwahr, who had started at
the McCarter as an intern. At his urging, she acquiesced to producing
middle-brow plays in the Matthews, to fill the house: plays like Ken
Ludwig's *Baskerville: A Sherlock Holmes Mystery* and Ludwig's adaptation of the Agatha Christie mystery *Murder on the Orient Express*, which
Mann directed at both the McCarter and Hartford Stage Company. The
Campaign for McCarter, launched in 2015, added $10 million to the
endowment, bringing the endowment to $25 million.

During this period, her own writing, as she had explained to the
board, generally happened before and after working at the theater, even
though, as she noted in her letter to the board, she was McCarter's
Resident Playwright and could have taken time to write whenever she
wished. She fashioned a colloquial, American-friendly script for Ivo Van
Hove's stage adaptation of the Ingmar Bergman teleplay *Scenes from a
Marriage*, which Van Hove directed at New York Theatre Workshop in
September 2014. With Pierre Laville she adapted his French stage rendition of Tennessee Williams's film *Baby Doll* and directed it in the Berlind in September 2015. *Hoodwinked (A Play Inspired by Real Events)*,
Mann's first documentary play since *Greensboro (A Requiem)*, received a
staged reading at the McCarter in January 2016, with Mann directing.

After *Greensboro (A Requiem)*, Mann had vowed never to write another documentary. "I do this every once in a while—I make these global statements and then I break [them]," she confessed with some amusement. "[Documentaries] take so much time, energy, research, agony, transcribing. It takes years and years and years to write a documentary . . . and yet when I think about the most important contributions I'm going to make, if I make any, they are with my documentary plays."

Mann's immediate motivation for writing *Hoodwinked (A Play Inspired by Real Events)* was U.S. Army Major Nidal Malik Hasan's lethal assault on soldiers and civilians at Fort Hood, Texas, in November 2009. The thirty-nine-year-old Hasan was an American and a devout Muslim, born to Palestinian parents who had emigrated to the United States. He had joined the United States Army right after high school and subsequently acquired a medical degree, completed a residency in psychiatry at Walter Reed Army Medical Center, and was assigned to Fort Hood. There, at around 1:30 on Thursday afternoon, November 5, Hasan shot and killed thirteen people and wounded thirty-two others. He was taken into custody and eventually tried in a military court, and in 2013 he was sentenced to death. As of September 2020, he was still imprisoned at Fort Leavenworth, in Kansas, awaiting execution.

Hasan's assault was the impetus for Mann's new play, but her concern dated back to 9/11, when the tension and confusion surrounding political and religious extremism had risen dramatically around the world. The play's title comes from a comment made by a former jihadi (Muhammad in the play) who says, "I witnessed a senseless murder of a Christian student at my school, committed by a fellow jihadi. It woke me up. I realized Radical Islamism is a perversion of my faith. I'd been hoodwinked."

In a draft dated "March 2010," the play, then simply called *Hoodwinked*, began dramatic life as a mysterious, fear-inducing series of conversations involving "HE," a Muslim searching for his wife, who may or may not have become a radical Islamist. Tightly written and suggestive of current events, the one-act ends with HE locating his wife, who triggers a bomb that kills him and possibly kills her as well.

But Mann wanted to explore the sources and political ramifications of radical Islam, and a draft dated "November 2010," which received a workshop at the McCarter, reveals that in the intervening months she transformed the play into a documentary. She delved into newspaper and Internet articles, watched and acquired video clips of Congressional investigations, and interviewed a Muslim cleric. She wanted to visit Fort Hood, but her request was turned down. Act I of the script, which finally received five partially staged readings at the McCarter, focuses on a female Student, a stand-in for Mann, as she interviews the cleric; a counter-terrorism expert; the former jihadi, Muhammad; and sundry academics. Video and film clips provide visual background. Act II is designated to be "discussion and conversation," and after each staged reading, held from January 28 through 31, 2016, and directed by Mann in the Berlind Rehearsal Room, two specially invited guests held forth on the political, religious, and ethical issues that have roiled the world since Al Qaeda attacked the United States on September 11, 2001.

Ultimately *Hoodwinked (A Play Inspired by Real Events)* is more symposium than play. Unlike Mann's strongest plays of testimony, *Hoodwinked* lacks dramatic drive, and only a couple of the figures are characterized in any dimensional way. The Student in particular lacks a distinctive personality or even a life apart from her quest, or as Mann explained, "She's the investigative reporter. . . . You learn from her." Her function, Mann has said, "is for the audience to learn as I did." The Student does ask questions and elicit information, but she is a flat character, akin in that respect to the Interviewer in *Greensboro (A Requiem)*.

Hoodwinked is, finally, a work by someone who wants to reveal and discuss the motivations and beliefs underlying Radical Islam in particular and fanaticism in general, and perhaps even warn about the global spread of Radical Islam. The play is didactic in the best definition of that word, in that it wants to elucidate and teach. Mann has called it "an ideas play." But as Brecht wrote, "Theatre remains theatre even when it is instructive theatre, and in so far as it is good theatre it will amuse."

Hoodwinked, instructive but not theatrical, represents the sort of play-writing Mann always said she wished to avoid and raises the issue, often broached by scholars of documentary theater, of the relationship between the genre's political uses and its aesthetics. Mann herself said during one of our interviews, "I think of myself as a political playwright . . . but I don't want to be put off into that category that leaves out the human story behind it. There are many political playwrights who are writing simply to make a political point, and I'm doing that *and*," she emphasized. "It's still very much involved with the human heart and soul as much as the politics."

Hoodwinked draws on Mann's research abilities and her skill at positing and intercutting a variety of perspectives, yet it does not draw on her ability to transform testimony into dramatic dialogue. Nor does it draw on her capacity to embed moral arguments within a character's internal conflicts, as happened with the Vietnam veteran in *Still Life* and Dan White in *Execution of Justice*. *Hoodwinked* is a play by a dramatist who perhaps needs to experiment once again with the documentary form, or find a subject that touches her more fiercely and personally.

As it happened, opportunities for both came Mann's way. In 2017, the theater producer Michael Wolk, who knew Mann from the University of Minnesota, asked her to write a play inspired by *The Pianist*, Wladyslaw Szpilman's memoir of his escape from the Nazis in Warsaw, Poland, during World War II (the memoir had been the basis for the 2002 film *The Pianist*). She was already writing a documentary play about Gloria Steinem.

It began as a play that Gloria Steinem herself would perform. "Kathy Najimy—who is an actor, writer, director and also a friend—said that I should do a one-woman show about my life," was how the revered feminist remembered it in an email she sent me. "It seemed both completely impossible," she wrote, "yet also not completely different from the lectures and talking circles I was already doing. . . . I was touched and honored that she would say this, but I just assumed it would never happen." Najimy, however, was determined. She and the filmmaker

Amy Richards brought the idea to Daryl Roth, who was on the Lincoln Center Theater (LCT) board at the time, and Roth suggested taking the project to André Bishop, LCT's artistic director.

"We thought it would be fascinating and we thought this would be a fabulous piece," said Anne Cattaneo, LCT's dramaturg and the creator and head of the Lincoln Center Theater Directors Lab. Bishop and Cattaneo imagined Sunday and Monday night performances in the 1,200-seat Vivian Beaumont Theater, the same schedule LCT had arranged for Peter Parnell's *QED*, produced during the 2001–2002 season with Alan Alda giving a solo performance as the American physicist Richard Feynman. According to Cattaneo, she and Bishop believed that Steinem, if her schedule permitted, could fill the house. "We batted around who would write this material," said Cattaneo during our interview, "and I think Emily was my idea. It seemed relatively obvious."

Mann was walking on the Princeton campus one day in 2013 when Kathy Najimy called her. "How would you like to write a play about Gloria?" Mann remembers Najimy asking. In Mann's telling, it took her "two seconds" to say yes.

Despite her schedule at the McCarter, and the recent reprimand from the board, Mann delved into the project. She read Steinem's books, watched two documentary films, and interviewed Steinem at her New York City apartment twice in December 2013, for several hours each time. Transcripts of the conversations reveal two women who admire each other but are also attempting to discover common ground, initially in lighthearted fashion: they both love elephants; neither has the time to cook and so they perpetually order out; they both have difficulty remembering names.

But during these early conversations they also shared memories and personal experiences. They talked about their mothers: Steinem's mother, Ruth, gave up a career as a journalist in Toledo, Ohio, to marry the wrong man. They talked about growing up in white America. Steinem remembered that there was not one woman of color in her class at Smith College (in the final script, Gloria naively expresses her concern about this to the Dean of Admissions), and Mann described her family's road trip through the American South. Steinem had an abortion when she was twenty-two, yet did not talk about it publicly for a number of years. Mann had never spoken publicly about being raped and wanted to know if having an abortion was "like that." Definitely not, Steinem averred, and in the final script Gloria thanks the English doctor who asks her to promise, if he refers her for an abortion, that she will do what she wants with her life. Steinem is a feminist; Mann described herself during their conversations as a humanist. "That makes us disappear," Steinem responded.

In January 2014, Mann wrote André Bishop and Adam Siegel, LCT's managing director:

> I plan to write a highly theatrical documentary with Gloria herself performing herself. It is an evening for the audience to meet and spend time with Gloria Steinem in the spirit of HAVING OUR SAY except you are actually meeting the real person! Gloria's reminiscences and present thoughts will comprise 2/3 of the 80 minute evening, I think. A full 1/3 of the evening will be video and documentary footage of both her, her times, and the movement, or that is what I am thinking now.

"Gloria is fully on board. She and I agree about the form," Mann continued in her letter. "I plan to construct it in blocks of monologues, punctuated and framed by visuals—stills and video—and music."

Gloria Live at Lincoln Center was the working title of the one-woman documentary. An early draft, dated October 16, 2014, calls for the performance to open with video clips of male newscasters spouting condescendingly about Women's Liberation, and clips of antifeminist Phyllis Schlafly and of "a young" Gloria. Then Gloria Steinem herself enters, greets the audience, and takes us back to the 1950s, when "We were all educated to be wives ('housewives') and mothers." She admits ruefully that, "When I came to NY in the early 60's, I'm not sure I even knew what feminism was."

Mann's script takes us through Gloria's early career as a journalist, including her legendary undercover assignment in 1963 for *Show* magazine, when she did a stint as a Playboy Bunny in Manhattan. Then the documentary moves to events that solidify her feminist consciousness and lead to friendships with Black activists Dorothy Pitman Hughes and Florynce ("Flo") Kennedy, and the feisty Congresswoman Bella Abzug. Gloria disparages the "false imaging" and ridiculing of feminism in the press and describes the public accomplishments which gave her the most pride: co-founding *Ms.* magazine in 1970 and speaking at the National Women's Conference in Houston, Texas, in 1977. Interspersed are stories about her personal life: the abortion, when she was twenty-two; memories of her father, from whom she inherited her love of "the road"; and conflicted recollections of her depressive, unfulfilled mother, whom Gloria essentially looked after from the age of eleven, in Toledo, until she left home at seventeen to go to Smith. She tells the audience of her bout with breast cancer and, at the age of sixty-six, falling in love with David Bale and marrying him (Bale died three years later). Her last story in this early draft involves a visit to Zambia, where women tell her they continually lose their maize harvest to marauding elephants, and Gloria returns to the States and raises money for an electrified fence.

"I want to ask one thing of you before we all go home tonight," she says in the script after the lights come up. "Promise me you will commit one outrageous act in the cause of simple justice tomorrow."

A workshop presentation of the play took place in LCT's large rehearsal room, on Friday, January 8, 2016, for an invited audience. Graciela Daniele directed. The eighty-two-year-old Steinem, slim and blonde, wore her signature black pants and long-sleeved black top. She mostly stood behind a music stand to read the script, but sometimes she moved to an armchair downstage left. Video clips played at intervals upstage. "Everyone was as spellbound as we were with her story," said Cattaneo. "We all realized there was huge interest in this. And people would be eager to see it."

Clearly, however, Steinem was not at ease. "I realized I just couldn't do it," she explained in her email for this biography. "I'd finally learned to speak in public as long as it was spontaneous, but theatre is an art form in which actors miraculously perform a play every night as if it were for the first time. I not only realized that I couldn't do that, but also that I'd never even had to be in the same place at the same time every day. I was always a freelance writer, or an editor at a magazine where we made our own schedule, or traveling and speaking on the road. Even as a child, I didn't go to school regularly. I not only couldn't do the content of a play, I couldn't even do the form. . . . I worked up the courage to go to lunch with Daryl and Andre, and tell them I just couldn't do it."

Mann was reluctant to talk on the record about the intricacies of dealing with Steinem's entourage, who often plied her with reams of notes. Cattaneo had no such reticence. "We had to say, 'that's not how we work at Lincoln Center . . . and we're not going to put any writer through this process.'" But Cattaneo could not control what happened outside her purview, which is perhaps why the script that was read for an invited audience on April 14, 2017, for the moment called

GLORIA at LINCOLN CENTER
Look Out

was "by Emily Mann and Gloria Steinem."

In addition to Steinem stepping back from giving a solo perfor-mance, much had changed in the year and three months since the first reading. Diane Paulus, artistic director of the American Repertory The-ater in Cambridge, was now directing. Graciela Daniele, according to Cattaneo, had directed the first reading "to help us, because she likes us. But too many cooks in the stew."

The form of the play had also changed. "It turned out that Gloria was uncomfortable with it being a one-woman show," Mann said. "And she didn't really know how to articulate it. She kept saying, 'I don't want it to be all about me,' so in the writing I would make sure she was always giving credit to other people. I didn't realize it was the form, the actual form, that was bothering her and her friend Kathy Najimy." In Mann's account, Paulus suggested including a chorus of young people, of different ethnicities, who would be a part of Gloria's life. "I said, 'Well, yeah, sounds like it's a new play.' And Diane said, 'No no no. It doesn't have to be a new play.' I said, 'Uh hunh, I don't know how to do it. You can't just chop the play up into different voices.' And she said, 'Well, let me sit down with my assistant and do a few pages, like I might address you, like she's telling a story. There are some lines that are already there, but you have the other person say them.' And I said, 'I don't want to be difficult, but I just don't truly see how to do it unless I reconceive the whole piece.'"

According to Mann, by the first day of the new workshop, Monday, April 10, 2017, "Diane had broken some of it down. It was very, very clunky, but a few things worked." Mann went back to her room at the Beacon Hotel on Manhattan's Upper West Side and applied herself to the script until 3 a.m., got up at 6:00 a.m. or so on Tuesday, April 11, went to the workshop, and had a meltdown. "I came to Diane and said, 'You know, it just sounded so bad to my ear yesterday, I don't know how to make it better.' We had a really great talk, and once we finished our talking, I went off and started writing." Except for going to a small dinner hosted by Nadine Strossen, to celebrate Mann's sixty-fifth birthday on Wednesday, April 12, Mann hunkered down for three days, during which she wrote, went to rehearsals, returned to her hotel, and resumed writing.

"I've met my match," was how Mann described working with Diane Paulus. "That woman has more energy than I do. I push people really hard and go really fast, but she doesn't take a lunch break. She doesn't take a break ever. The actors do, but then she turns to the writer, me, and her staff, and says, 'Okay, here's what I think we should do now.'. . . And I finally said, 'No, I'm going to take a breath of air.'"

The reading of the expanded script, again for an invited audience, took place at 3 p.m. on Friday, April 14, in a small, packed rehearsal room at LCT that Mann likened to a "bunker." Tall, lean, blonde Jan Maxwell stood behind a music stand and read Gloria, and an ensemble of three women and two men read various people in Gloria's life. Mann sat in the center of the second row, the three-ring binder containing her typescript upright on her lap as she turned pages and scrawled notes.

Mann had reconceived the play. Now Gloria acknowledged the audience in a direct, inclusive way, and the ensemble provided a performative energy that the play had not possessed as a monologue. After Gloria welcomed the audience, a woman in the ensemble stepped forward and started a Call & Response: "We are here America, at last," she called out, and the rest of the ensemble, and even the small audience that afternoon, answered back: "We are here America, at last." At the end, for the first time, Mann's script indicated there would be an Act II, consisting of a talking circle, Steinem's favored way of bringing people together to share experiences and learn from each other. As conceived by First Nations leaders, the talking circle allowed all the tribal council's leaders to have a say. Sitting in a circle, they would pass around a sacred object—a stick perhaps, or feather—and whoever held this Object of Power could speak as freely as they wished. Act II, involving the entire audience, would be a less formal version of this talking circle.

The aim of the play had changed. Previously, Mann had written a somewhat introspective story: personal testimony along with the recognizable accoutrements of documentary theater, such as projected photographs, video, and film clips. "I loved the one-woman," Mann said during a conversation in her office, six days after the April 14 reading. Jan Maxwell reading the one-woman script at the start of the workshop, before the "broken-down version" went into effect, was "so elegant and moving and funny," said Mann. Now the play was acquiring a more overt political aim. As Gloria tells her listeners, "Today, by sharing my story, I want to demystify how to become an activist. I want this movement to continue through you."

The shift in tone, toward reconceiving the play as an activist event, was partly due to an earthquake rumbling through American society.

On November 8, 2016, Donald J. Trump was elected the forty-fifth president of the United States. The Democrats' candidate, Hillary Rodham Clinton, had won the popular vote but lost the electoral college, a loss that brought sorrow to feminists who had hoped to elect the first woman to the American presidency. For those feminists, Trump embodied the political inequities, and the sexual abuse and assaults they had fought for centuries to eradicate. In a conversation videotaped on a hot mic in 2005 and published by the *Washington Post* on October 7, 2016, Trump boasted to *Access Hollywood* anchor Billy Bush about grabbing women's genitals: "When you're a star, they let you do it. You can do anything." His first wife, Ivana Trump, had once accused him of rape, and numerous women publicly accused him of making unwanted sexual advances or aggressively invading their privacy. During the campaign, he promised to appoint Supreme Court justices who would overturn *Roe v. Wade*.

Clinton losing, and Trump winning despite his harassing behavior and abusive language, energized women to call for a worldwide protest. On Saturday, January 21, 2017, the day after Trump's inauguration, the Women's March became one of the largest protests in United States history to take place on one day. More than 3 million women, men, and children gathered in over three hundred cities and towns, "to send a bold message to our new administration on their first day in office, and to the world that women's rights are human rights," as the organizers stated. In Washington, D.C., numerous celebrities, including Honorary Co-Chair Gloria Steinem, spoke to a crowd estimated at more than 200,000, many of them bedecked in pink "pussyhats," which had become a symbol of solidarity. Steinem, wearing a red scarf draped over her black jacket, stood on a platform and told the marchers that, "We are here and around the world for a deep democracy that says we will not be quiet, we will not be controlled."

"It's a new world," Mann said to me shortly after the Women's March, "and a lot of *Gloria* is probably going to have to do with what just happened."

Nine months after the march, in October 2017, the *New York Times* and the *New Yorker* magazine reported in separate articles that, over three decades, numerous women had either been raped, sexually assaulted, or sexually harassed by the American film producer Harvey Weinstein. As those accusations came to light, more and more women came forward publicly with stories of rape, assault, and harassment. Adopting Me Too—the movement started in 2006 by the African American activist Tarana Burke—in 2017 the actress Alyssa Milano added a hashtag and posted a #MeToo message on her Twitter account, urging women to share their experiences of sexual harassment. #MeToo became an international movement and a platform, enabling women and men not only to voice their feelings but also to call out their abusers.

The movement touched Mann more deeply than she anticipated. From June 13 to 16, 2018, she attended Theatre Communications Group's national conference in St. Louis, Missouri. One afternoon, a session was scheduled to allow people, without naming names of abusers, to testify about their experiences of sexual assault and harassment. Mann was in her room writing when Lisa Portes, head of the MFA directing program at the Theatre School of DePaul University, texted Mann that she should come to this, because this was "major." As Mann told me,

> So I thought, "Oh, yeah, this might be useful for the play." So I come down with my notebook, thinking I'm doing research. I want to hear what people are saying and how they're saying it. The place is packed. Hundreds of people. The full conference showed up, in this huge hall. And first a young African American man gets up, and he said "eight years ago I was an intern and I went to a theater," and basically the artistic director assaulted him. And I was very moved and I had tears in my eyes, and I also began to feel I couldn't breathe very well and I began to remember all kinds of things in my life. And then a young woman got up and she gave a very moving testimony, and somebody else got up and read an Audre Lorde poem about a bruised daughter. And so I am crying. And another woman gets up, and she's written a poem, and a woman in her fifties probably, Black woman, talking about taking her power back. Beautiful poem, and it was so beautifully read, and all of a sudden I can't breathe and I'm sobbing, all at the same time, and it was a

combination of being moved by everything, but something broke inside of me. That was a physical break, and suddenly I was racked with sobs. I couldn't stop. Lisa saw me and she came racing over and said "Are you okay?" and I said, "I don't think so. I can't stop crying." And she said, "Have you been raped?" and I said "Yes," and she said, "Okay, we're here for you. We're going to get you a counselor." I couldn't walk. I couldn't do anything. So we waited until everyone left, and they shielded me from people seeing me, and they got me to a little room, and it took almost forty minutes to help me stop sobbing.

Back home in Princeton, she told Gary what had happened and made an appointment with a therapist whom she had not seen in ten years. On both occasions, she again began sobbing almost uncontrollably. The therapist was supportive and encouraging: Mann's volcanic response to the #MeToo revelations at the conference had provided a release for decades of pent-up hurt and anger. "[The therapist] was happy for me," Mann said. "You were ready," he told her. "It's time."

During the summer of 2018, Mann worked on both *The Pianist* and *Gloria*, part of trying to recover from her volcanic emotional response in St. Louis. She spent hours on the phone with Diane Paulus and Christine Lahti, who had been cast to play Gloria Steinem. Paulus, Mann thought, was inspiring but fanatical about script work, often going through the text with Mann word by word. *Gloria: A Life*, as the play was now called, was heading for a two-week workshop in New York City in August, followed by rehearsals in September for an October 2018 opening off Broadway at the Daryl Roth Theater, just east of Union Square. The new draft called for seven actors: one to play Gloria, and six others, all women, to play other women and any men in the script. Lincoln Center Theater was no longer in the picture, as LCT apparently did not have an available theater of the size the production now required. Also, according to Anne Cattaneo, "Daryl came to tell us it needed to be an all-female producing name. . . . We were told we were a male producing organization."

The workshop and the rehearsals were collective efforts to form a final script. Paulus involved everyone in the room, including Steinem when she could be there. Mann, used to controlling her script, pushed back on occasion, but usually joined with her customary intensity in what became a shared creative process. Paulus created an environment in which anyone could suggest changing a line, taking out or adding a scene. Members of the ensemble urged Mann to cut the scene where Gloria meets with the Zambian women and ultimately provides them with an electrified fence. "They thought it was too much the rich American white woman condescending to poor Africans," said Mann, and she removed it. "As an actress," said Christine Lahti during our telephone interview, "I've never been allowed, invited, to participate in the actual creation of the play. [Here] I was able to offer ideas. . . . Emily and Diane were so open. And if something felt too long or wordy, Emily would change it. Or Diane weighed in. It felt so fluid."

"The contribution I made that I treasure the most," said Lahti, "was digging deep into the relationship with [Gloria's] mother." When Gloria was about ten years old, her mother, Ruth, suffered what, in the 1940s, was called a nervous breakdown. Gloria's father and older sister were apparently no longer around, and at home Gloria tended to her mother and tried to study for school at the same time. Said Lahti, "The story about taking care of her mother and trying to read *A Tale of Two Cities*, and her mother suddenly wakes up out of a bad dream and pushes her hand through a glass window. And Gloria tries to finish her homework and keep her mother quiet. I don't know where I found that. Maybe Gloria told me. Maybe in one of [her] books. But I suggested it, and Emily put it in."

The fluid approach to Mann's script would continue even after the production opened. After the midterm elections of November 2018, which brought an additional 117 women to Congress, Mann wrote new lines for Lahti about the women's electoral victories, and Mann, Paulus,

and Lahti continued to update the text as local and national political events warranted.

By the time the off-Broadway production went into previews, few of Gloria's monologues from Mann's earlier drafts remained, and those that did now resembled conversations Gloria was having with the audience. Mann frequently broke up the stories that Gloria once told and turned them into sequences acted by Gloria and the ensemble. The description of Gloria's incognito experience as a Playboy Bunny became a scene in which Gloria and other Bunnies-in-training walk about in a circle, holding trays of drinks high above their heads, then practice the special "dip," a supposedly enticing, thoroughly uncomfortable, way of leaning over, to display breasts and serve drinks without touching the men ogling them. A memory of America's pre–*Roe v. Wade* world, in which Gloria hears women speaking publicly about their illegal abortions, became a scene during which members of the ensemble stood at different places onstage and told Gloria and the audience about the physical and emotional suffering they had endured.

In a sense, many of the play's scenes became "talking circles," an impression heightened in performance by Paulus's staging, and by the intimacy of the Daryl Roth Theatre, where audiences sat around the oval stage, close by the actors. In Act II, which followed the scripted part of the production after a brief pause, the audience participated in a contemporary form of talking circle, led either by a guest, including Steinem herself on occasion, or Christine Lahti and the cast. This felt like a natural outcome of the scenes which the audience had just watched and heard. Steinem also noted this. "I'm especially glad that Act II is a talking circle," she wrote in her e-mail to me, "so that each group of people will be creating their own play, telling their own stories."

The production opened on October 18, 2018, and reviews were mixed. But people's responses to each performance and to the talking circle afterward suggested that reviews had little to do with why audiences, mostly of women, were coming to *Gloria: A Life*. To be there was to participate in an event more than attend a play, to be part of a feminist community and draw sustenance from shared anger and frustration. Audience members often joined hands and sang "We Shall Overcome" along with a projected film clip of Coretta Scott King singing the hymn at the 1977 National Women's Conference in Houston. The first half of the play ended with Gloria urging the audience to take political action, no matter how small. Heeding that encouragement, people took the mic during the talking circle and asked what they could do to change the inequities suffered by women, people of color, people in the LGBTQ community. By any group that has been labeled "other."

Mann asserted that the play "totally goes with my whole body of documentary and testimony. She's telling her life story. It's autobiography, like *Annulla*. It is eventized, for sure, but is still within that same genre, using a lot of the same techniques as *Execution*, as *Greensboro*, with the media and the cameras and the visuals and the music." It was not, however, a nuanced portrayal like *Annulla, An Autobiography* or *Still Life* or even the script Steinem read in 2014 to the invited audience at Lincoln Center Theater. Perhaps nuance was not possible, given the adulation that surrounds Steinem and given Paulus's concept for the production.

But as a feminist occasion in the theater *Gloria* was lively and provocative, loud and proud. Descriptions and images of violence that Mann in the past had brought to her documentary plays are practically absent, as though Mann for the moment had shed her experience of a threatening world and was celebrating a brave new one. On the stage of the Daryl Roth Theater, Gloria Steinem was unquestionably a feminist hero: she defines herself, professionally and politically; she resists the stereotypical assignments that male editors once fed female journalists; she co-founds a magazine that rejects the woman-as-sex-object and woman-as-homemaker tropes. She stands with other women, especially women of color and young women, to resist racism and sexism.

As documentary theater, the relationship of *Gloria: A Life* to headlines and current events evokes the Living Newspapers of the 1930s, in which a fact-based script was centered around a contemporary political issue, and performers addressed the audience directly. The play's call to action stirred the kind of fervor aroused by Clifford Odets's *Waiting for Lefty* in 1935, when, at the end, actors playing the underpaid taxi drivers

Left to right: Joanna Glushak, Fedna Jacquet, Francesca Fernandez McKenzie,
Christine Lahti, Patrena Murray, DeLanna Studi, and Liz Wisan in Gloria: A Life,
written by Emily Mann and directed by Diane Paulus, the Daryl Roth Theatre, 2018
PHOTO: © JOAN MARCUS

yelled "STRIKE, STRIKE, STRIKE!!!" and famously drew cheers from
the audience. At one point Gloria and the ensemble of women marched
arm in arm, carrying a banner and chanting, "Sisterhood is powerful—
we demand equality."

Ironically, Mann said that at first she "sort of fought against that. I
said this is old agitprop style, and Diane said, 'Oh no, it's part of the
drama.'" And Paulus was right. At that moment, with the actors holding
that banner high, members of the audience might well have linked arms
and marched over to Union Square, voices raised, and fists defiantly
punching the air.

Epilogue
Seasons of Reckonings

ON A COOL WEDNESDAY evening in November 2018, the McCarter Theatre, collaborating with the Ghostlight Project, held a Community Play Reading on the Matthews stage. The play was Emily Mann's *Greensboro (A Requiem)*, and the community was anyone in and around Princeton who wanted to read a part cold. The staff placed copies of *Testimonies: Four Plays* by Emily Mann, containing the published script, on a table in the lobby, and by 6:30 p.m. readers and their friends were sitting in a huge circle on the stage, behind the massive closed curtain, fortified by soda and grapes and chocolate chip cookies. For the next three hours, more than fifty women, men, and children, some of whom knew each other, many of whom did not, read a play out loud.

The event was evidence of an artistic director's vision that an engaged, inclusive theater brings people together, both in a formal way, in an auditorium, and informally, sitting in a circle to share the telling and hearing of a story. The evening was evidence of Mann's power as a dramatist who has chiefly used people's own words—their testimonies, as the South African director Barney Simon described it—to engage audiences emotionally and intellectually. Thirty-nine years after the murders that formed the background for the play, the words based on that history felt current to the readers on the Matthews stage. There had been a resurgence of overt white supremacist fervor, and on August 12, 2017, at a "Unite the Right" rally in Charlottesville, Virginia, a self-proclaimed white supremacist drove his car at top speed into a throng of counter-protesters, killing one, a woman named Heather Heyer. On the

Matthews stage, people read the script, shook their heads, and exclaimed at how little had changed in thirty-nine years, let alone since the country's founding. Mann's documentary plays, particularly *Still Life, Execution of Justice*, and *Greensboro (A Requiem)*, speak about the urge to violence, and hatred of the "other," that remain ugly truths in American society. She asks us to confront these aspects of American society that, sadly, endure.

Why Emily Mann turned her gaze to these issues is a question that has no definitive answer. She learned about or was exposed to a variety of public traumas while growing up. She heard about the Holocaust and its terrors as a youngster, and came of age in a decade that witnessed a contrived war's awful toll, the assassinations of political and religious leaders, and blood spilled in American streets. Privately, physical violence touched Mann in frightening ways.

The wellsprings that feed an artist's imagination are mysterious, and Mann is protective of the deepest sources of her creativity. Charles McNulty, the dramaturg for *Meshugah* and later chief theater critic for the *Los Angeles Times*, offered that, "Emily is a storyteller drawn to characters who can rouse us from the darkness that is always threatening, even if by only making us more conscious of the nature of the threat."

Mann's view of the world has never been one-sided, however. She is devoted to the theater as a source of understanding, enlightenment, and healing. Mann has needed to fight for her devotion, because at the time when she entered the professional theater, women were rarely sought after as directors and playwrights. She rebelled against the naysayers and headed for the Guthrie Theater and then to New York, where she encountered both success and failure but not defeat. At the McCarter Theatre Center her tenacity helped salvage that institution, and transformed a respected but insular theater into a venue recognized nationally for challenging, diverse, meticulously produced work. When she took the McCarter position, she worried that she would not be able to continue her own directing and playwriting. Instead she succeeded at heading a theater and expanding her careers of director and dramatist, a triple play that few have made in the American theater. All this, while prevailing over a debilitating disease.

In addition, she raised a son and made a home. That career, and that mingling of career with private life, have been models for women at the McCarter and women across the country who have met her, heard her speak, or worked side by side with her in the rehearsal room. Her mentoring and behind-the-scenes advocacy have helped bring a new generation of women to directing, playwriting, and producing. Women have by no means reached parity with men in terms of the number of plays produced or directed at not-for-profit regional theaters, although the percentages are higher than when Mann entered the fray at the Guthrie in 1974. Similarly, a higher percentage of women lead LORT theaters than when Mann took over the McCarter. But there is not the parity which Mann and so many other women in the American theater sought to achieve. Sometimes, being a rebel simply means staying the course.

The Community Play Reading that November evening in 2018 showed the distance the McCarter had traveled politically and aesthetically since Mann became artistic director. The audiences who watched *Betsey Brown* during her first season were unaccustomed to seeing a musical by and about Black Americans on the McCarter stage. They probably could not have imagined coming together to read a play out loud, let alone a play about white racists targeting Communist protesters. The Reverend Willie J. Smith, upon Mann receiving an Honorary Doctor of Arts degree from Princeton University, in 2002, wrote that, "She places on stage individuals working through great difficulties, then coming together across racial, religious, age, class and gender lines. Shattering the wrongs of arrogance and pretense in our society, she brings us, much as Dr. King did, to the altar of repentance for neglecting the call to make this world better."

One month after the *Greensboro* reading, on December 19, 2018, Emily Mann delivered a letter to Reginald M. Browne, the interim president of the McCarter Theatre Center's Board of Trustees: she would be stepping down as artistic director of the McCarter at the end of the 2019–2020 season, her thirtieth, after her sixty-eighth birthday.

She wrote to the board:

> It has been an extraordinary tenure, and I want to pass my torch to the next generation of artistic leaders, many of whom I have mentored, as I continue my own directing and writing opportunities. . . . Thank you for supporting what is on our stages and the extraordinary work we have done in the community and in the schools. Thank you for supporting both the emerging artists we produce and the legends—thank you for supporting my backing of the work of women and people of color—way before it was fashionable. Thank you for supporting me in sickness and in health . . . You supported a young female artist when most of America scoffed at women writing and directing in the American theater.

"You gave me my life," she wrote toward the end of her letter, "and I gave you my all."

Mann's closest friends knew that she had been weighing how much longer to remain at the McCarter. "For many years," said the lawyer Nadine Strossen, "she and I have talked about wanting to step away and focus more and more on our own voices. Before the last contract renewal, it was up in the air whether she wanted to have the contract renewed for another term." Anyone who had observed Mann since the McCarter board issued its warning in 2012 would have noticed she was accepting projects which had the potential for taking her from the McCarter for periods of time: writing *Gloria: A Life*; directing Susan Miller's play *20th Century Blues* off Broadway in the fall of 2017; writing a stage version of Wladyslaw Szpilman's memoir, *The Pianist*, which the producers who commissioned it from her hoped to take directly to Broadway. Anyone who knows Mann's history or has observed her for any stretch of time realizes that she is always moving forward, always searching for her next project, her next story. Certainly her health was not preventing her. The multiple sclerosis had been in remission for years. "It doesn't define me anymore," she said. "It's just one more thread in the weave."

Family, too, was drawing her away from the McCarter. On June 10, 2017, her son Nicholas's wife, June Kyuha Lee, gave birth to Oliver Arthur Bamman. The family lived in Washington, D.C., where both June and Nicholas worked as attorneys, and Mann, enthralled with her grandson, wanted time and freedom to visit them as much as possible. (June would have a second child, a girl whom she and Nicholas named Claire, on March 25, 2021.)

Yet the choice to leave the McCarter had not come easily. "I wake up one day and say, 'It's time,'" she revealed in the month before finalizing her decision, "and then I wake up the next day going, 'But why? I have so much to give and do as a leader, not just as a director and writer.' So I go back and forth, literally, every morning. I started to write it down. Because I have a really good reason to say, 'Let's go on and move on and see what else is out there for me without an institution on my back.' And then the next morning I'm, 'But I have an artistic home and I worked so hard, and it's so fantastic and I love it. I love my staff . . . how can I live without coming to the theater and making theater every day?' And then at the end of the day, I'm like, 'Oh, really I just want to spend time traveling.' It's emotional whiplash."

In response to the announcement of her departure from the McCarter, the national theater community saluted her, as did her immediate New Jersey community. The *Trenton Times* ran an editorial: "To Emily Mann, we'd like to say, thank you for being Emily Mann. As the artistic director and resident playwright of the McCarter Theatre Center in Princeton, you lifted a small regional theater to national and even world recognition." On June 7, 2019, at its National Conference in Miami, Theatre Communications Group presented her with its Visionary Leadership Award, the fourth woman to be honored since TCG established the award in 2009. On November 18, 2019, Mann was inducted into the Theater Hall of Fame. The McCarter planned to celebrate Mann throughout her final season, which opened with Mann directing *Gloria:*

A Life in the Berlind and reuniting with Mary McDonnell, who played Steinem to huzzahs from New Jersey critics.

As was the ironic pattern during her own life, public acclamation coincided with private sorrow. On Tuesday morning, January 15, 2019, Sylvia Blut Mann died at the age of ninety-seven. She went peacefully, Mann wrote in an email. "I was with her for her final hours. Nothing was left unsaid between us. Still—I am heartbroken."

Emily Mann and her mother, Sylvia Mann
COURTESY OF EMILY MANN

Mann could not have foreseen that her final season would be truncated by a pandemic that infiltrated the world in the late winter and early spring of 2020, infecting and killing millions of people. In the United States, almost any venue that offered live performances closed. On March 23, the McCarter Theatre Center suspended all performances through June 30 and soon laid off the majority of its staff, even as it announced, on April 23, that Sarah Rasmussen had been selected as the McCarter Theatre Center's new artistic director (the McCarter eventually canceled all indoor performances until Fall of 2021). The forty-year-old Rasmussen, formerly the artistic director of the Jungle Theater in Minneapolis, would be the second woman to lead the McCarter.

Emily stayed home with Gary. As an antidote to the absence of live theater, the McCarter streamed videos of past productions. A gala honoring Mann's three decades at the McCarter was live-streamed via Zoom, the Internet tool of choice for millions during the pandemic. And under McCarter's aegis, in June 2020 she led a four-week, virtual Documentary Theatre Workshop, out of which emerged Fly Eyes Playwrights, a group formed by women in the workshop who wanted to continue making documentary theater.

To Mann's surprise, the anxiety surrounding her decision to resign from the McCarter dissipated while self-isolating at home and gradually returning to the freelance life. She led a virtual directing workshop sponsored by La MaMa Umbria International. Sitting at the desk in her study, at her computer, she worked on the book for a new Lucy Simon musical based on the romance *Our Souls at Night*, by the American novelist Kent Haruf. And she continued to revise *The Pianist*, preparing to direct a virtual reading in October 2020.

The Pianist is a capstone to Mann's previous plays involving the Holocaust. Unlike *Annulla, An Autobiography* or *Meshugah*, where the Holocaust serves as backdrop to the survival of Annulla Allen and Miriam respectively, *The Pianist* is a tension- and horror-building testimony to the Nazis' annihilation of Szpilman's Polish-Jewish family, the Jews of Warsaw, and Warsaw itself. Szpilman, who wrote the first version of his memoir in 1945, put his narrative in the past tense. Mann credits the Irish playwright Marina Carr with urging her to put Szpilman's monologues in the present. He speaks directly to the audience, taking us on an increasingly terrifying journey of loss, near-starvation, and escape.

The monologues alternate with scenes and conversations between Szpilman and his loving family, vicious German soldiers, generous Polish friends who risk their own lives to hide the pianist—scenes, dialogue, and characters that Mann imagined, based sometimes on mere mentions in Szpilman's text. Music functions as yet another character.

But finally *The Pianist* feels like a morality play, with Szpilman an Everyman, an artist enduring a harsh moral and physical journey, and surviving. "That he can find a glimmer of life at the end," Mann said to me, "is a triumph."

As with Mann's personal explorations prior to writing about Annulla Allen, in 2017 she flew to Poland, to meet Szpilman's ninety-two-year-old widow and their sixty-one-year-old son, Andrzej. With Andrzej, Mann went to Treblinka, the extermination camp where Wladyslaw Szpilman's family died, and there, among hundreds of rough engraved stones she found one engraved with "Ostrołęka," memorializing victims of the Holocaust who had been transported to Treblinka from the shtetl of her mother's ancestors.

There had been an instant of doubt about accepting the Szpilman project. Mann recalled that, in August of 2017, "I said to myself, 'Does anyone want to hear about the Holocaust, again?' And I looked up and it was Charlottesville on the television, and I saw the neo-Nazi flags. And at that moment, I thought, 'Yeah, I should be doing this.'" A little more than a year later, on October 27, 2018, her decision was reinforced when a man armed with an assault rifle and handguns invaded the Tree of Life Synagogue in Pittsburgh, Pennsylvania, killing eleven people and wounding six.

These were moments in time when, quite possibly, theater of testimony was needed more than ever.

Plays by Emily Mann

(Unless otherwise noted, dates refer to first production or first public reading.)

Amy (1971) (Unproduced)

Annulla Allen: The Autobiography of a Survivor (1977, Guthrie 2, Minneapolis, MN)

Annulla Allen: an Autobiography of a Survivor (1978, Earplay Radio Drama, National Public Radio)

Still Life (1980, Goodman Theatre, Stage 2, Chicago, IL)

Execution of Justice (1984, Actors Theatre of Louisville, Louisville, KY)

Nights and Days (1984, translation/adaptation, reading at The Public Theater, New York City)

Annulla, An Autobiography (1985, Repertory Theatre of St. Louis, St. Louis, MO)

Betsey Brown (1989, Ntozake Shange and Emily Mann, American Music Theater Festival, Philadelphia, PA)

Miss Julie (1993, translation/adaptation, McCarter Theatre Center)

Having Our Say: The Delany Sisters' First 100 Years (1995, McCarter Theatre Center)

Greensboro (A Requiem) (1996, McCarter Theatre Center)

The House of Bernarda Alba (1997, adaptation, McCarter Theatre Center)

Meshugah (1998, adaptation, McCarter Theatre Center)

The Cherry Orchard (1999, adaptation, McCarter Theatre Center)

Uncle Vanya (2003, adaptation, McCarter Theatre Center)

Antigone (2005, adaptation, Ten Thousand Things Theater Company, Minneapolis, MN)

Mrs. Packard (2007, McCarter Theatre Center)

A Seagull in the Hamptons (2008, a free adaptation of Chekhov, McCarter Theatre Center)

The House of Bernarda Alba (2012, revised adaptation, Almeida Theatre, London)

Scenes from a Marriage (2014, English version, New York Theatre Workshop, New York City)

Baby Doll (2015, Pierre Laville and Emily Mann, adaptation, McCarter Theatre Center)

Hoodwinked (A Play Inspired by Real Events) (2016, staged reading, McCarter Theatre Center)

Under the Liberty Trees (2017, reading, McCarter Theatre Center)

David Duke (2017, Theatre for One, Lewis Arts Complex, Princeton, NJ)

Still Life Today: La Guerre à Domicile (2018, Théâtre Les Déchargeurs, Paris)

Gloria: A Life (2018, Daryl Roth Theatre, New York City)

The Pianist (A Play with Music) (2018, staged reading, McCarter Theatre Center)

It Could Be You (July 20, 2020, The 24 Hour Plays: Viral Monologues)

Staying Home (Monologue) (August 26, 2020, "OVER & ABOVE: Women over 55 speak," Zoom presentation, Brave New World Rep, Brooklyn, NY)

Big Country (working title). Musical adapted from the novel *Our Souls at Night* by Kent Haruf. Book by Emily Mann, music by Lucy Simon, lyrics by Susan Birkenhead.

Acknowledgments

THIS BIOGRAPHY could not have been written without the generous cooperation of Emily Mann, who was unstinting in giving of her time for interviews about her life and her life's work. In addition, she graciously allowed me to pore through drawers and boxes and shelves, a cornucopia of letters and diaries, drafts of scripts, collections of theater reviews, and family documents and photographs, all of which have been invaluable resources for writing this biography.

The McCarter Theatre Center's fine staff of artists and administrators were always considerate and helpful. I particularly thank Thomas Miller, who at that time was director of public relations, for alerting me to the film *Saigon: Year of the Cat* and a glimpse of Emily Mann's acting, and for retrieving photographs of Emily Mann's McCarter productions. I reserve a special thank you for Manda Bliss, Emily Mann's exceptionally organized and dedicated executive assistant, who somehow always found time on Mann's schedule for us to meet.

I am especially grateful to my agent Philip Turner, for his superior editing, his patience, and his commitment to finding the ideal home for this book, which has been so beautifully produced by the editors and designers at Rowman & Littlefield/Globe Pequot.

I want to thank my late aunt, Anita Zacharias, for her munificent gift. I also thank Preston M. Torbert, lecturer at the University of Chicago Law School and visiting professor at the Peking University School of Transnational Law, for his generous gift of several days at the University of Chicago's Quadrangle Club, while I researched the Arthur

Mann Papers at the university's Joseph Regenstein Library. Biographers could not exist without knowledgeable librarians, and those at the Regenstein, Harvard University's Houghton Library, the Brooklyn College Library, the Barnard Library at Barnard College, and the Seeley G. Mudd Manuscript Library at Princeton University allowed me to sit for hours, sometimes days, and sift through files. I am particularly grateful to Rebecca Bramlett, Research Services Coordinator for the Special Collections Research Center of the George Mason University Libraries, and Delinda Stephens Buie at the University of Louisville Libraries for their assistance and guidance.

My friends Martin Cohen, Cynthia Cooper, Cathy Hemming, Michal Kobialka, and Elizabeth Swain were always there to provide advice and encouragement, as was my generous stepson Benjamin Hough. No words can express my gratitude to my husband, Gordon Hough, for his patience, encouragement, and his love.

A. G.

Notes

Arthur Mann (AM)
Emily Mann (EM)
Sylvia Mann (SM)
Typescript (TS)

Prologue: Emilyville

ARCHIVES: Emily Mann Papers, Private Collection.

INTERVIEWS BY AUTHOR: EM

Chapter 1: Family

ARCHIVES: Arthur Mann Papers, University of Chicago Library, Department of Special Collections, Accession No.: 93–101; Arthur Mann Papers, Private Collection; Emily Mann Papers, Private Collection; Sylvia Blut Mann Papers, Private Collection.

INTERVIEWS BY AUTHOR: EM; George Mann.

NOTES: (Numbers refer to page numbers.)

    5 *Jargon of exile*: Joel Conarroe, "'The World Is One Vast Madhouse,'" *New York Times* on the Web, April 10, 1994. http://movies2.nytimes.com/books/98/01/25/home/singer-meshugah.html.
    5 *Most profound wisdom*: Alexis Greene, "Emily Mann," in *Women Who Write Plays* (Hanover, NH: Smith and Kraus, 2001), 306.

9 *By reason of scholarship*: Certificate, Brooklyn College Department of Athletics. n.d. Arthur Mann Papers, Private Collection.

12 *Histories of the 89th Infantry*: "The 89th Infantry Division," United States Holocaust Memorial Museum, https://www.ushmm.org/wlc/en/article. php?Moduled=10006140.

12 *Coming home*: AM to SM, January 14, [1946]. Arthur Mann Papers, Private Collection.

Chapter 2: Beloved Second Born

ARCHIVES: John Hope Franklin Papers, Duke University; Arthur Mann Papers, University of Chicago Library, Department of Special Collections, Accession No.: 93–101; Arthur Mann Papers, Private Collection; Sylvia Blut Mann Papers, Private Collection; Emily Mann Papers, Private Collection; Forbes Library, Northampton, MA.

INTERVIEWS BY AUTHOR: EM; Marilyn August; John Whittington Franklin; Carol Mann; William Leuchtenburg; Nancy Weiss Malkiel; Jean McLure Mudge; Reverend Jane Rockman; Ruth Becker-Painter (née Weinstein).

NOTES:

25 *Philosopher Martha Nussbaum*: Martha Nussbaum, *Not for Profit*, 95.

28 *Her operation*: AM to Howard Rabinowitz, April 18, 1966, Arthur Mann Papers, University of Chicago Library.

28 *Arthur had been considering*: AM to John Hope Franklin, March 9, 1962. John Hope Franklin Papers, Duke University.

29 *You must have divined*: AM to John Hope Franklin, February 6. 1966. Arthur Mann Papers, University of Chicago Library.

Chapter 3: Living the Sixties, Discovering Theater

ARCHIVES: John Hope Franklin Papers, Duke University; Arthur Mann Papers, University of Chicago Library; Arthur Mann Papers, Private Collection; Emily Mann Papers, Private Collection; Sylvia Blut Mann Papers, Private Collection.

INTERVIEWS BY AUTHOR: EM; Ralph Austen; Karl Bortnick; Lorraine Ann Bowen; Polly Bruno; Susan Fiske; Richard Flacks; Louise Grafton; Gina

Heiserman; Robert Keil; Carol Mann; Michael Rosenberg; Loren Sherman; Stuart Sherman.

NOTES:

33 *I've been in many demonstrations*: Ron Grossman, "Flashback: 50 years ago: MLK's march in Marquette Park turned violent, exposed hate," *Chicago Tribune*, July 28, 2016, https://www.chicagotribune.com/news/opinion/ commentary/ct-mlk-king-marquette-park-1966-flashback-perspec-0731-md-20160726-story.html"

34 **Lab School proved an ideal place**: University of Chicago Laboratory Schools, Wikipedia, https://en.wikipedia.org/wiki/ University_of_Chicago_Laboratory_Schools.

35 *An entry about Keil*: U-High Yearbook, 1969. Emily Mann Papers.

35 *Emily . . . described Keil*: David Savran, *In Their Own Words*: 147.

39 **On January 30, 1968**: Julian E. Zelizer, "How the Tet Offensive Undermined American Faith in Government," *Atlantic*, January 15, 2018, https://www.theatlantic.com/politics/archive/2018/01/how-the-tet-offensive -undermined-american-faith-in-government/550010/.

40 *Violence*: Todd Gitlin, *The Sixties: Years of Hope, Days of Rage*, 316.

40 *It was as if the assassinations*: Todd Gitlin, *The Sixties: Years of Hope, Days of Rage*, 316.

41 *Martin Luther King Jr.*: "Beyond Vietnam," Stanford University, The Martin Luther King, Jr. Research and Education Institute, https://kinginstitute.stanford.edu/king-papers/documents/beyond-vietnam.

42 *Marlene Dixon*: Marlene Dixon, "The Rise and Demise of Women's Liberation: A Class Analysis," 1977, https://www.marxists.org/subject/ women/authors/dixon-marlene/rise-demise.htm"

42 *The radicalization*: Supriya Sinhababu, "The sit-in-40 years later," *Chicago Maroon*, December 2, 2008, https:///www.chicagomaroon. com/2008/12/02/the-sit-in-40-years-later/

42 *The radicalization*: Carrie Golus, "Which Side Are You On?" *The Core*, Winter 2010, http://thecore.uchicago.edu/winter2010/which-side.shtml.

43 *Dealing with a very tiny minority*: AM to Jean Mudge, April 24, 1969. Arthur Mann Papers, University of Chicago Library.

44 *Dear Mommy and Daddy*: EM to AM and SM, August 8, 1969. Emily Mann Papers.

44 *Four Days of Rage*: Todd Gitlin, *The Sixties: Years of Hope, Days of Rage*, 393.

47 *Processional*: Emily Mann Papers.

Chapter 4: Radcliffe Days, Harvard Plays

ARCHIVES: Arthur Mann Papers, University of Chicago Library; Arthur Mann Papers, Private Collection; Emily Mann Papers, Private Collection; William Alfred Papers, Brooklyn College Library; Houghton Library, Harvard University.

INTERVIEWS BY AUTHOR: EM; Jamie Bernstein; Irene Dische; Peter Frisch; Jack Gilpin; David Gullette; Gina Heiserman; Marianna Houston; Vesna Neskow; Stephen Wadsworth; Ed Zwick.

NOTES:

49 *Really the work here*: EM to "Mom and Dad," September 11, 1970. Emily Mann Papers.

50 *Rapist was in our dorm*: EM to "Mom and Dad," October 27, 1970. Emily Mann Papers.

51 *Crying now*: EM to "Mom and Dad," November 10, 1970. Emily Mann Papers.

51 *It's nonsense*: AM to EM, November 1970. Emily Mann Papers.

52 *I like my life and work here*: EM to SM, December 8, 1970. Emily Mann Papers.

52 *Innovative theater designer*: George C. Izenour, *Theater Design*, 250–251; 294–295.

53 *The British Feminist*: Michelene Wandor, *Look Back in Gender*, 13.

54 *Emily Mann . . . is great*: Review, unidentified publication, March 1971. Emily Mann Papers.

54 *Three-act play called Amy*: *Amy*, reel-to-reel audio tape, 1971. Arthur Mann Papers, University of Chicago. Emily Mann reads all the parts in this recording of her first play.

57 *Her old-time friends*: EM to "Mom and Dad," February 26, [n.d.]. Emily Mann Papers.

57 *He left a note on my bicycle*: EM to "Mom and Dad," n.d. Emily Mann Papers.

58 *I keep wondering*: EM to "Mom and Dad," n.d. Emily Mann Papers.

58 *Shallow, transparent, self-indulgent*: EM to "Mom and Dad," May 10, 1971. Emily Mann Papers.

58 *I want to give you*: EM to AM, Father's Day, 1971. Emily Mann Papers.

59 *I am . . . realizing*: EM to "Mom and Dad," July 19, 1971. Emily Mann Papers.

59 *And this is the perfect script*: EM to "Mom and Dad," July 19, 1971. Emily Mann Papers.

59 *Had torn bits of him*: Tennessee Williams, *Suddenly Last Summer*, in *The Theatre of Tennessee Williams*, Vol. 3 (New York: New Directions Books, 1990): 422.

59 *To cut this hideous story*: Tennessee Williams, *Suddenly Last Summer*, in *The Theatre of Tennessee Williams*, Vol. 3 (New York: New Directions Books, 1990): 423.

59 *Seeing the core of the play*: Emily Mann, "Directorial Comments on a Production of Suddenly Last Summer," English 1752, January 9, 1972. Emily Mann Papers.

60 *Massive tree-flowers*: Tennessee Williams, *Suddenly Last Summer*, in *The Theatre of Tennessee Williams*, Vol. 3 (New York: New Directions Books, 1990): 349.

60 *Like the plague*: Antonin Artaud, *The Theater and Its Double*, translated by Mary Caroline Richards (New York: Grove Press Inc., 1958): 31.

61 *Director Emily Mann's idea*: Richard Bowker, "Suddenly Last Summer," *Harvard Crimson*, November 13, 1971.

61 *If I must slave*: EM to Mom and Dad, May 2, 1972. Emily Mann Papers.

62 *Neither adaptation*: "Author's Note." Robert Montgomery, *Subject to Fits* (New York: Samuel French, 1972).

63 *The contortions*: Michael Sragew, *Harvard Crimson*, December 2, 1972.

63 *William A. Henry III*: *Boston Globe*, December 2, 1972.

65 *I still think nothing comes close*: EM to "Mom and Dad," June 1973. Emily Mann Papers.

65 *She is lovely but*: EM to "Mom and Dad," June 1973. Emily Mann Papers.

65 *You may not believe this*: EM to "Mom and Dad," June 29, 1973. Emily Mann Papers.

65 *I don't know how I had the nerve*: EM to "Mom and Dad," June 29, 1973. Emily Mann Papers.

66 *Not 2 weeks*: EM to "Mom and Dad," June 29, 1973. Emily Mann Papers.

66 *Richardson still has not*: EM to "Mom and Dad," July 1973. Emily Mann Papers.

66 *I have finally reached*: EM to "Mom and Dad," July 1973. Emily Mann Papers.

66 *V. Redgrave*: EM to "Mom and Dad," July 1973. Emily Mann Papers.

67 *I returned to a building*: EM to "Mom and Dad," September 17, 1973. Emily Mann Papers.

68 *I am not confident*: EM to "Mom and Dad," October 12, 1973. Emily Mann Papers.

68 ***Strangely life confirming***: EM to "Mom and Dad," October 29, 1973. Emily Mann Papers.

68 ***The play is going superbly***: EM to "Mom and Dad," October 29, 1973. Emily Mann Papers.

69 ***I come to know***: EM to "Mom and Dad," October 29, 1973. Emily Mann Papers.

70 ***Director Emily Mann***: "'Macbeth': Quality varies in quantity," Stephen Gray, *Christian Science Monitor*, December 4, 1973.

70 ***Bold and strong but careful***: "Snares of Watchful Tyranny," Phil Patton, *Harvard Crimson,* December 1, 1973.

73 ***We are all clowns***: Jacques Lecoq, *The Moving Body*, 154.

73 ***The smallest mask***: Jacques Lecoq, *The Moving Body*, 154.

73 ***When the actor comes onstage***: Jacques Lecoq, *The Moving Body*, 155.

74 ***I am quiet, stupid***: This quote and others related to Mann's clown work were found in a notebook labeled "Clowns." Emily Mann Papers.

75 ***Rehearsal Process***: Mann's notes on Peter Frisch's suggestions for a rehearsal process. Emily Mann Papers.

76 ***NEWS***: EM to "Mom and Dad," March 8, 1974. Emily Mann Papers.

76 ***I feel great***: EM to "Mom and Dad," April 14, 1974. Emily Mann Papers.

77 ***I didn't want Allen***: "Elliot Richardson Will Be Speaker at Commencement," by Nicholas Lemann, *Harvard Crimson*, May 7, 1974, http://www.thecrimson.com/article/1974/5/7/elliot-richardson-will-be-speaker-at/.

77 ***Equal Opportunity for Women***: Unattributed photograph, *Boston Herald American.* June 14, 1974.

Chapter 5: Annulla Allen

ARCHIVES: Emily Mann Papers, Private Collection.

INTERVIEWS: By author: EM; Irene Dische; Stephen Wadsworth. Interview with EM by Sara Blecher; "Emily on Annulla with Sara," 1988.

NOTES:

80 ***We may develop a script***: EM to "Mom and Dad," n.d. Emily Mann Papers.

81 ***I am not in the rain***: Red Memo Book, Emily Mann Papers.

82 ***Amazing 12 hr. drive***: Red Memo Book, Emily Mann Papers.

83 ***The memory of slaughtered Jews***: Red Memo Book, Emily Mann Papers.

Chapter 6: Portrait of a Survivor

ARCHIVES: Emily Mann Papers, Private Collection; McCarter Theatre Archives, McCarter Theater, Princeton, NJ; New York Public Library for the Performing Arts, Billy Rose Theater Division.

INTERVIEWS BY AUTHOR: EM; David Ball; Martha Boesing; Barbara Bryne, Michael Casale; Jon Cranney; Thomas Dunn; David Feldshuh; Barbara Field; Susan Galbraith; Mark Lamos; Carolyn Levy; Mary McDonnell; James Morrison; Janice Paran; Jack Reuler; Barry Robison; Phyllis Jane Rose; Bruce Siddons.

NOTES:

87 *What has __made__ the apartment*: EM to SM, September [?], 1974. Emily Mann Papers.

88 *Minneapolis is a marvelous city*: EM to "Mom and Dad," September 24, 1974. Emily Mann Papers.

88 *Excellent voice*: Ibid.

91 *__Annulla__ is going nowhere*: EM to SM, October 1,1974. Emily Mann Papers.

92 *I'm so happy for you*: AM to EM, January 13, 1975. Emily Mann Papers.

92 *Her first major*: Peter Altman, *Minneapolis Star*, February 21, 1975.

93 *Lop-sided work*: Ibid.

93 *Provocative chamber play*: Mike Steele, "Matrix," *Minneapolis Tribune*, February 22, 1975.

93 *Either the play has to be unfamiliar*: *Minneapolis Star*, March 19, 1975.

93 *Unbroken by walls or pillars*: *Minneapolis Star*, July 30, 1975.

95 *Sly and sweet*: Peter Altman, "Cast treats 'Magistrate' well," *Minneapolis Star*, July 21, 1975.

95 *Dear Annulla*: EM to Annulla Allen, September 22, 1975. Emily Mann Papers.

96 *I can well understand*: AM to EM, October 5, 1975. Emily Mann Papers.

96 *Apologetic letter*: EM to Annulla Allen, October 8, 1975. Emily Mann Papers.

98 *Put me straight*: EM to Mom and Dad, October 28, 1975. Emily Mann Papers.

98 *Clubbed in the stomach*: EM to "Mom and Dad," "6 Jan." [1976]. Emily Mann papers.

98 *Funkily unrestored*: "Guthrie 2 will juxtapose new plays and old Minneapolis memorabilia," Don Morrison, *Minneapolis Star*, January 7, 1976.

100 *Mick has gotten to the essence*: Carole Nelson, "Marilyn: Her Life Revisited," *St. Paul Sunday Pioneer Press*, April 1976.

101 *Unmemorable evening of theatre*: *Variety*, April 7, 1976, 84.

101 *Brilliant script*: EM to AM, January 19, 1975. Emily Mann Papers.

101 *Heavy-handed*: Peter Vaughn, "Sledge-Hammer Interpretation Leaves 'Summer Folk' in Ruins," *Minneapolis Star*, March 25, 1976.

101 *Missed on this one*: Mike Steele, "Summerfolk' Is Presented by Theatre in the Round," *Minneapolis Star Tribune*, March 22, 1976.

102 *I get in:* Unpublished Nancy Erhard interview with Emily Mann, Draft #1, June 23–26, 1988, 22. Emily Mann papers.

106 *Going to help me*: EM to "Mom and Dad," September 4, 1976. Emily Mann Papers.

107 *Never having stage-managed*: EM to AM, December 26, 1976. Emily Mann Papers.

110 *Here, Mann's playwriting*: This and the following paragraphs about the Guthrie 2 production refer to the draft playscript *Annulla Allen: Autobiography of a Survivor* by Annulla Allen and Emily Mann, Emily Mann Papers. Mann's agreement with Annulla Allen initially required them both to be listed as authors.

111 *This is supposed to be a review of* **Annulla Allen**: Mike Steele, "Barbara Bryne Triumphs in Role as Annulla Allen," *Star Tribune*, March 18, 1977.

112 *If Miss Mann*: John H. Harvey, "One-Woman Show Bubbles, Philosophizes about Life," *Pioneer Press*, March 17, 1977.

112 *Faithfully recording*: Rees, "Annulla Allen," *Variety*, March 23, 1977.

112 *Broke the ground*: Philip Weiss, *Metropolis*, March 28, 1977.

113 *Superb theater*: AM to EM, March 21, 1977. Emily Mann Papers.

113 *Hard to have this show close*: EM to Mom and Dad, March 31, 1977. Emily Mann Papers.

113 *I would like to do the show*: EM to Mom and Dad, October 16, 1977. Emily Mann Papers.

113 *Shrewdly constructed*: Richard Christiansen, "'Annulla': One Woman, One History," *Chicago Tribune*, March 21, 1978.

114 *Half-baked*: David Elliott, "'Annulla Allen'—Portrait of a Survivor," *Sun-Times*, March 20, 1978.

114 *Legendary Chicago theater critic*: Claudia Cassidy, WMFT, March 19, 1978.

114 *Men have strong feelings*: *Annulla Allen, an Autobiography of a Survivor* by Annulla Allen, adapted for radio by Emily Mann. Emily Mann Papers.

Chapter 7: Woman of the Theater

ARCHIVES: Emily Mann Papers; New York Public Library for the Performing Arts, Billy Rose Theatre Division.

INTERVIEWS BY AUTHOR: EM; Gerry Bamman; Martha Boesing; Mel Marvin; Jennifer von Mayrhauser; Duane Schuler.

NOTES:

117 *Gifted and dedicated artist*: Michael Langham, Artistic Director, to "To whom it may concern:" April 22, 1977.

117 *Highly critical of Emily's talents*: Stephen Kanee, Associate Director, to "To whom it may concern:" April 20, 1977. Emily Mann Papers.

118 *Get a season from the Guthrie*: EM to AM, November 4, 1977. Emily Mann Papers.

119 *Right timing*: David Hage, "Deceptively Simple," *Free Press Review* [n.d.].

119 *Mann's direction is relaxed*: Peter Vaughn, "'Roads in Germany' Avoids Ruts, Follows Route of Wistful Nostalgia," *Minneapolis Star*, April 24, 1978.

120 *Don and Alvin*: Emily Mann Papers.

120 *Look forward*: EM to "Mom and Dad," July 9, 1978. Emily Mann Papers.

121 *Most consistent characterization*: "Guthrie 2 Presents Ibsen's 'Little Eyolf,' *Star Tribune*, February 7, 1979.

121 *Directed with quiet dignity*: Mike Steele, "'Mount Chimborazo' Is Most Fascinating of Guthrie 2 Plays," *Star Tribune*, October 25, 1978.

122 *Is this what I am worth?*: Emily Mann Papers.

123 *Corny headline*: "Mann to be 1st woman directing at the Guthrie," *Minneapolis Star*, February 2, 1979.

123 *Ming Cho Lee and I*: EM to AM, December 31, 1978. Emily Mann Papers.

123 *You, Ming, made me an artist*: "Ming Cho Lee." Speech delivered at New York City celebration of Lee's career, January 19, 2018. Emily Mann Papers.

124 *Duane Schuler's*: Mike Steele, "Like Play, Guthrie's 'Menagerie' Is Ethereal, Brittle, Sentimental," *Star Tribune*, June 21, 1979.

128 *Unforced and airy production*: Mike Steele, *Star Tribune*, June 21, 1979.

128 *Depicting the fragility*: AM to EM, June 1979. Emily Mann Papers.

130 *One of the first to enter the halls*: Mike Steele, "Emily Mann Seeks Repute as Director, Not Woman Director," *Star Tribune*, July 15, 1979.

130 *Gloria Steinem*: AZ Quotes, https://www.azquotes.com/quote/1149466.

130 *Pushed aside Tom's centrality*: Peter Vaughn, *Minneapolis Star*, June 21, 1979.

130 *Explore some unexamined focuses*: Don Morrison, *Minneapolis Star*, June 21, 1979.

131 *Of course I'm a feminist*: Mike Steele, "Emily Mann Seeks Repute as Director, Not Woman Director," *Star Tribune*, July 15, 1979.

Chapter 8: *Still Life*

ARCHIVES: Emily Mann Papers Leon Levy BAM Digital Archive; NYPL for the Performing Arts, Billy Rose Theatre Division.

INTERVIEWS BY AUTHOR: EM; Charleen Bacigalupo; Nancy Bagshaw-Reasoner; Gerry Bamman; Laurie Kennedy; Steve Marcus; Mary McDonnell; Joe Morton; Gregory Mosher; Timothy Near; Richard Nelson; Nadine Strossen; Liz Woodman.

NOTES:

140 *There isn't any choice, Tom*: He and She, 928.

140 *Old New York cliché*: Emily Mann Papers.

141 *Race for skyscrapers*: Emily Mann Papers.

141 *Superb - alive, fun*: Emily Mann Papers.

142 *Now*: Emily Mann Papers.

142 *Big scene*: Emily Mann Papers.

142 *Women wandering silently*: Steve Lawson, "Women Now and Then," *The Soho Weekly News,* June 4, 1980.

142 *Triumph*: Marilyn Stasio, "Splendid 'He/She' at BAM, *New York Post*, May 30, 1980.

142 *Soggy*: Edith Oliver, "Crothers and Sisters," *The New Yorker*, June 9, 1980.

143 *Production sparkles*: David Sterritt, "A Strikingly Modern Look at Feminism—in a 1910 Drama," *Christian Science Monitor*, June 5, 1980.

143 *John Simon dismissed everything*: John Simon, *New York Magazine*, June 16, 1980.

143 ***BAM's most successful ensemble***: Steve Lawson, "Women Now and Then," *Soho Weekly News*, June 4, 1980.

143 ***Busy***: Mel Gussow, "Theater. 'He & She' Of 1911 in Brooklyn, *New York Times*, May 30, 1980.

143 ***The guys at the BAM Theater***: Erika Munk, "A Frieze Grows in Brooklyn," *Village Voice*, June 9, 1980.

144 ***Jolted***: Emily Mann Papers.

145 ***What's a Marine?***: Transcripts, Vietnam veteran. Emily Mann Papers.

146 ***I want it to come off the way it is***: Transcripts, Vietnam veteran. Emily Mann Papers.

147 ***THEY COME ALIVE***: Emily Mann Papers.

150 ***Roxane Gay***: Deirdre Sugiuchi, "Hurt People Hurt People: An Interivew with Roxane Gay," *Electric Literature*, June 2, 2014. electricliterature.com/hurt-people-hurt-people-an-interview-with-roxane-gay/

154 ***Talking about a traumatized victim***: Marilyn Stasio, "'Still Life' a Moving & Harrowing Drama," *New York Post*, February 20, 1981.

155 ***The characters***: Jeremy Gerard, "Threnody," *Soho News*, February 25, 1981.

155 ***Fuzzy-headed***: Frank Rich, "'Still Life' by Emily Mann at American Place," *New York Times*, February 20, 1981.

155 ***Point which seems to have bypassed***: Michael Feingold, "Home Fronts," *Village Voice*, February 25, 1981.

157 ***We can't be silent!***: Athol Fugard, Introduction, *Testimonies: Four Plays by Emily Mann* (New York: TCG. 1997).

158 ***Red-lit palms***: Melinda Guttman, *STAGES*, September 1984.

159 ***Museum pieces***: "Repertory," *The New Yorker*, January 21, 1980.

160 ***Taking critical opinion a while:*** Jerry Adler, "All the World's a Stage," *New York Sunday News*, May 25, 1980.

160 ***Stilted Lysander of Joe Morton***: John Simon, "Bard in Brooklyn," *New York Magazine*, January 26, 1981.

160 ***Problem of the chorus***: Emily Mann interview by Roger Oliver, "The Need to Know," BAM *INSIDE* (The BAM Theater Company, 1980).

163 ***To be pitied***: Eileen Blumenthal, "With a BAM? With a Whimper," *The Village Voice*, April 29, 1981.

163 ***Emily Mann's treatment of the Greek wonderwork***: Walter Kerr, "An 'Oedipus' Fatally Flawed," *New York Times*, May 3, 1981.

163 ***Ragged creation***: Marilyn Stasio, "Pale Shades of Oedipus," *New York Post*, April 24, 1981.

164 ***Received a letter from Jones***: "Dear Emily," n.d. Emily Mann Papers.

164 ***Variety pegged***: "Curtain Falls on BAM Theatre," *Variety*, June 3, 1981.

164 *Cartoonist in crisis*: Richard Christianson, "Dwarfman, Master of a Million Shapes," *Chicago Tribune*, May 29, 1981,

165 *Once the tension*: AM to "Gerry and Emily," January 1, 1981. Emily Mann Papers.

165 *My father and I were especially close*: AM to "Emily and Gerry," "The week that was, 1981." Emily Mann Papers.

Chapter 9: *The Dan White Project*

ARCHIVES: Emily Mann Papers; NYPL for the Performing Billy Rose Theatre Division; University of Louisville Libraries.

INTERVIEWS BY AUTHOR: EM; Julie Crutcher; Oskar Eustis; Mark Lamos; Paul Owen; Carlotta Schoch; Tony Taccone; André Gregory.

NOTES:

170 *There is a real connection*: Unpublished Emily Mann interview by Michael Murphy, February 1983. Emily Mann Papers.

170 *Career side*: Emily Mann Papers.

170 *Not ready yet for children*: EM to SM, May 13, 1982. Emily Mann Papers.

171 *Lovable dimwit*: Roger Downey, "Dinner with Andre in a Portland 'Doll House,'" *The Weekly*, August 9, 1982.

172 *How do you tell just the story*: Emily Mann Papers.

172 *Trial on Stage*: Emily Mann Papers.

173 *First draft done*: EM to Liz Coe, December 18, 1982. Emily Mann Papers.

173 *Brilliant lawyer*: Emily Mann Papers.

174 *Possibly start layering or juxtop*: Emily Mann Papers.

175 *Spine of the play is the trial*: Emily Mann interview by Michael Murphy, February 1983. Emily Mann Papers.

176 *Where to start with Harry?*: Ibid.

176 *Freitas wanted to spill his guts*: Ibid.

178 *I am still examining*: EM to Harry Britt, January 8, 1983. Emily Mann Papers.

179 *Just now coming up out of the haze*: EM to AM, October 15, 1983. Emily Mann Papers.

180 *Afraid of being murdered*: Emily Mann Papers.

183 *Dark grey, nearly circular stage*: William Kleb, "You, The Jury: Emily Mann's Execution of Justice," *Theater 16*, Fall/Winter 1984, 55–60.

183 *Feature article*: Mel Gussow, "Women Playwrights: New Voices in the Theater," *New York Times*, May 1, 1983.

183 *'Execution of Justice'... is not about families*: Mel Gussow, "9 New Plays at Louisville Festival," *New York Times*, March 29. 1984.

Chapter 10: *Execution of Justice*

ARCHIVES: Emily Mann Papers; Arena Stage collection and Zelda Fichandler collection, Special Collections Research Center, George Mason University Libraries; NYPL for the Performing Arts, Billy Rose Theatre Division.

INTERVIEWS BY AUTHOR: EM; Gerry Bamman; Mark Bly; David Copelin; Suzy Hunt; James C. Nicola; Tara Rubin; Douglas Wager; M. Burke Walker.

NOTES:

185 *Very much want to direct the play*: EM to Gordon Davidson, July 23, 1984. Emily Mann Papers.

186 *Think it hits a good note*: Zelda Fichandler collection, GMU Libraries.

188 *The play presents*: Douglas Wager, April 12, 1985, Arena Stage collection, GMU Libraries.

189 *Landmark production*: Roger Meersman, "'Justice' royally executed in stunning Arena production," *The Journal* [n.d.].

189 *It's absorbing, it's riveting*: Judy Green, "'Execution': An engrossing saga of murder," *Bowie Blade-News*, May 23, 1985.

190 *Deeply disturbing*: David Richards, "'Justice' for All,'" *Washington Post*. May 17, 1985.

190 *Doug—congratulations*: Handwritten note from Zelda Fichandler to Douglas Wager, GMU Libraries.

190 *You are a Treasure*: Handwritten note from Zelda Fichandler to EM on Arena Stage stationery, GMU Libraries.

190 *Thank you*: EM to Zelda Fichandler, GMU Libraries.

191 *Riveting journey*: Elinor Fuchs, "Capital Gains," *Village Voice*, June 11, 1985.

191 *Structural problems*: Mel Gussow, "STAGE: IN WASHINGTON, 'EXECUTION OF JUSTICE,'" *New York Times,* May 29, 1985.

192 *Osterman suggested*: Nan Robertson, "Broadway," *New York Times*, August 16, 1985.

194 *Shimmering, plasticized*: Mike Steele, *Star Tribune*, October 21, 1985.

197 *Watched several productions*: Mike Steele, "Playwright Reaches Goal in 'Execution,'" *Minneapolis Star and Tribune*, October 13, 1985.

198 *Bertolt Brecht taken into the electronic age*: Mike Steele, *Star Tribune*, October 21, 1985.

198 *Stunning piece*: David Hawley, "Breathtaking Size, Acting Turn Guthrie Play into Epic," *St. Paul Pioneer Press Dispatch*, October 20, 1985.

198 *Superbly crafted*: Tim Campbell, *GLCVOICE*, October 21, 1985.

198 *Exceeding projections*: "Well-executed," *Star-Tribune*, November 29, 1985.

198 *He had rolled up the windows*: Jay Mathews, *Washington Post*, October 22, 1985.

199 *Dan White was found dead*: *Execution of Justice* script, October 23, 1985, Emily Mann Papers.

199 *Suicide announcement*: Mike Steele, "White Suicide Meant Fast Revision of Guthrie Play," *Star Tribune*, October 23, 1985.

200 *I would have been the secretary*: Tara Rubin email to author, February 3, 2019.

200 *According to a letter*: Letter from Douglas Wager to Benjamin Zinkin of Cohen, Grossberg and Zinkin, December 31, 1985. Zelda Fichandler collection, George Mason University Libraries.

201 *Mann's lawyer, George Sheanshang*: Letter from George Sheanshang to Benjamin Zinkin, misdated January 15, 1985 instead of January 15, 1986. Emily Mann Papers. According to this letter, it was written in response to a December 27, 1985, letter from Douglas Wager to Emily Mann. I could not locate the December 27, 1985, letter among Emily Mann's papers.

202 *crying so profusely*: Susan Letzler Cole, *Directors in Rehearsal*, New York: Routlege, 1992, 61.

202 *Variety's final tally*: Richard Hummler, "Poor Notices Bounce 'Execution,'" *Variety*, March 26, 1986.

202 *Mel Gussow*: "Stage: Emily Mann's Execution of Justice," *New York Times*, March 14, 1986.

203 *Agreed to loan*: Letter to "Dear Emily" from THE JUSTICE COMPANY LIMITED PARTNERSHIP, Lester Osterman, General Partner, March 27, 1986. Emily Mann Papers.

203 *I felt a lot of the New York notices*: Richard Hummler, "Poor Notices Bounce 'Execution,'" *Variety*, March 26, 1986.

203 *We're all really proud of the work*: George Richardson III, "Justice, Change and Optimism," *St. Louis Post-Dispatch*, April 9, 1986.

205 *Keep in mind*: Trial of VALUES: Emily Mann Papers.

205 *Sister Boom Boom*: Emily Mann, *Testimonies: Four Plays* (New York: Theatre Communications Group, 1997).

Chapter 11: Transitions

ARCHIVES: Emily Mann Papers; NYPL for the Performing Arts, Billy Rose Theatre Division; NYPL for the Performing Arts, Theatre on Film and Tape.

INTERVIEWS BY AUTHOR: EM; Judy James; Timothy Near; Deborah Pope.

NOTES:

208 *Behind the news*: Susan Faludi, *Backlash: The Undeclared War Against American Women.* New York: Crown Publishing Group, ix.
209 *She's not Gloria Steinem*: Janice Paran, "Redressing Ibsen," *American Theatre*, 4, 8, November 1987, 14–20.
215 *Videotape of a performance*: "Annulla, an autobiography" [videorecording], Brooklyn, 1988. New York Public Library for the Performing Arts.
215 *Even Mel Gussow*: Mel Gussow, "Testimony of a Survivor," *New York Times*, November 2, 1988.
216 *Film adaptation*: Mann, Emily, and Mbongeni Ngema, *Sarafina!* Second draft, October 29, 1988.
216 *She submitted Part I*: *The Story of Winnie Mandela.* Part One, "The Awakening." January 5, 1988.

Chapter 12: By the Scruff of the Neck

ARCHIVES: Emily Mann Papers; Mudd Library, Princeton University

INTERVIEWS BY AUTHOR: EM; Baikida Carroll; Susie Cordon; Liz Fillo; Joan Girgus; Alison Harris; Judy James; Kecia Lewis-Evans; Gary Mailman; Carol Mann; Kathleen Nolan; Shirley Satterfield; Grace Shackney; Ntozake Shange; Stephen Wadsworth; Ruth Wilson; William Wingate.

NOTES:

219 *Broadway tryouts diminished*: Herbert McAneny, "McCarter Theatre in the 1960s," *The Princeton University Library Chronicle*, 48, 1 (Autumn 1986), 42–57.
223 *Celebrate all that is American*: *Town Topics*, December 6, 1989.
223 *The work that I do*: Caroline Reitz, "A Mann for (at least) Three Seasons," *Princetonian*, December 7, 1989.

226 *Unfortunately, I was not properly informed*: EM to "Mom and Dad," October 2, 1990. Emily Mann Papers.

228 *For nowadays the world is lit by lightning!*: Tennessee Williams, *The Theatre of Tennessee Williams*, Vol. I (New York: New Directions, 1971).

229 *Shirley Knight played Amanda*: Nels Nelson, "A Fresh 'Menagerie,'" *Philadelphia Daily News*, January 21, 1991.

229 *Unlike the transparent*: Alvin Klein, "An Unexpectedly Moving 'Menagerie,'" *New York Times*, January 27, 1991.

229 *With an assurance*: Mel Gussow, "The Limits of Love and Little Glass Animals," *New York Times*, January 21, 1991.

229 *Now that you have proved*: AM to EM, January 24, 1991. Emily Mann Papers.

230 *Artist daddies*: Upham, Emily W., and Linda Gravenson, eds, *In the Fullness of Time: 32 Women on Life After 50* (New York: Simon & Schuster, 2010).

231 *Cuz i hadta cut this friend a mine*: CARRIE, an opera by Ntozake Shange and Cecil Taylor, TS, 1979. Emily Mann Papers.

232 *This wreck of a script*: Nancy Erhard, unpublished Emily Mann Interview, June 23-26, 1988, Draft #1. Emily Mann Papers.

232 *Major structural problem*: EM to Ntozake Shange, September 10, 1983. Emily Mann Papers.

232 *I am due in just a few days*: Ibid.

233 *I describe the score to Betsey*: Baikida Carroll in email to author, March 29, 2015.

234250 *Each of the collaborators*: Barbara Hogenson to Joseph Papp, April 11, 1988. NYPL.

235 *I love the richness and detail*: EM interviewed by Darlene Olson. Emily Mann Papers.

236 *Please receive this revised text*: "FROM: Ntozake Shange, May 31, 1989. RE: (Version A: Post AMTF) Betsey Brown." Emily Mann Papers.

237 *You see*: EM interviewed by Darlene Olson. Emily Mann Papers.

237 *BETSEY is like a church piece*: Ibid.

239 *What you were reciting isn't even __English!__*: 23 Revised 3/24/91. Emily Mann Papers.

240 *The eagerly awaited show*: "Betsey Bown," *Star-Ledger*, April 10, 1991.

240 *Raucous energy*: Ibid.

241 *If you have given up*: Alvin Klein, "Film Society,' a Good Play Improved," *New York Times*, May 26, 1991.

241 *The most stimulating*: Alvin Klein, "New Season Invites Optimism," *New York Times*, September 1, 1991.

242 *In her diaries*: Emily Mann Papers.

245 *Memorable, quirky*: Michael Sommers, "'Three Sisters' at McCarter Is 4 Stagings in 1," *Star-Ledger*, January 14, 1992.

247 *30 percent increase*: Evelyn Apgar, "McCarter Theatre Director Inks New Pact," *Home News*, June 16, 1992.

247 [P]ulled it up: Alexis Greene, "Emily Mann: The Quiet Radical," American Theatre, June 26, 2015

248 *Many people who knew him*: DADDY'S MEMORIAL. Emily Mann Papers.

249 *Masterfully directed*: Jan Breslauer, "One Woman Takes on a City's Voices," *Los Angeles Times*, June 15, 1993.

250 *Tomorrow is my 42nd birthday!!*: EM to Louise Grafton, April 11, 1994. Emily Mann Papers.

251 *The collaboration came to a halt*: Alvin Klein, "Confusing Start for the Theater Season," *New York Times*, January 2, 1994.

251 *This Gary Mailman*: EM to Louise Grafton, April 11, 1994. Emily Mann Papers.

253 *The 48th Annual Tony Awards*: The 48th Annual Tony Awards [video recording], New York, 1994. NCOX1056, Performing Arts Research Collection-TOFT.

253 *[T]he McCarter's Tony*: Alvin Klein, *New York Times*, June 13, 1994.

Chapter 13: Having Her Say

ARCHIVES: Emily Mann Papers; NYPL for the Performing Arts, Billy Rose Theatre Division; McCarter Theatre Archives.

INTERVIEWS BY AUTHOR: EM; Nicholas Bamman; Gary Mailman; Ned Canty; James Freydberg; Mara Isaacs; Judy James; Charles McNulty; Janice Paran; Grace Shackney; Mark Wing-Davey.

NOTES:

256 *I felt better physically*: Sara Brookner and Emily Mann, "Chronic Theatremakers: Emily Mann on Mindset and Living with Multiple Sclerosis," *HowlRound*, September 11, 2017.

257 *But Sadie and I*: David Richards, "The Delany Sisters, Having Their Day," *Washington Post*, May 14, 1995.

262 *As she has done so successfully*: William McCleery, "Mann's 'Delany Sisters' at the McCarter An Entertaining & Heart-Opening Occasion," *Town Topics*, February 15, 1995.

263 ***The most provocative***: Vincent Canby, "A Visit With 2 Indomitable Sisters," *New York Times*, April 7, 1995.

264 ***Mel Gussow interviewed Mann***: Mel Gussow, "A Good Listener Who Writes Plays on Social Justice," *New York Times*, April 18, 1995.

270 ***Cheryl Mintz's report***: "Greensboro Workshop, Sunday [October 15, 1995]." McCarter Theatre Archives.

273 ***Canny collage of a script***: Vincent Canby, "When Communists Clashed With Nazis and the Klan," *New York Times*, February 12, 1996.

274 ***Critical turning point***: Michael Scott Pryor, "The Matter of Memory: Visual and Performative Witnessing of the Greensboro Massacre," MA Thesis, University of Texas, Austin (2012), 15.

274 ***This lineage is important***: Ibid.

275 ***Once there are categories***: Emily Mann, *Greensboro (A Requiem)*, in *Testimonies: Four Plays by Emily Mann*, 277.

276 ***Blowing up the conference***: https://www.centertheatregroup.org/news-and-blogs/news/2016/september/the-ground-on-which-i-stand/

276 ***I have come here today to make a testimony***: August Wilson, "The Ground on Which I Stand," *American Theatre* magazine, https://www.americantheatre.org/2016/06/20/the-ground-on-which-i-stand/.

280 ***It was a gorgeous***: Unidentified email, November 11, 1998. Emily Mann Papers.

Chapter 14: Rebel Artist

ARCHIVES: Emily Mann Papers; NYPL for the Performing Arts, Billy Rose Theatre Division; McCarter Theatre Archives.

INTERVIEWS BY AUTHOR: EM; Anne Cattaneo; Joan Girgus; Christine Lahti; Kathleen Nolan; Faye M. Price; Gloria Steinem; David York.

NOTES:

284 ***The current production at the McCarter***: Alvin Klein, "Finding Hope in the Timeless Tale of 'Romeo and Juliet,'" *New York Times*, September 23, 2001.

284 ***We are a country in pain***: Emily Mann Papers.

286 ***That coffin of an auditorium***: Alexis Greene, "The Quiet Radical," *American Theatre*, July/August 2015.

287 ***The Berlind's proscenium***: Dimensions from Dixie Uffelman, Director of Production, McCarter Theatre, email to author, May 30, 2019.

289 *Elizabeth Parsons Ware*: Elizabeth Packard, Wikipedia, https://en.wikipedia.org/wiki/Elizabeth_Packard.

290 *Let Thomas' confirmation*: "Becoming the Third Wave," January 1992, *Ms.*, 39–41.

292 *Theophilus Packard remained a minister*: *Mrs. Packard,* in Front Lines (New York: The New Press, 2009), 285.

293 *Play about what is sanity and insanity*: Nathan Swift, "'Mrs. Packard': How a Single Woman's Story Transcends Time." *HIGHLANDER*, April 28, 2015.

294 *Mann's twentieth season at the McCarter*: All the quotations for this section are from documents among the Emily Mann Papers.

294 *Perhaps the most important*: McCarter Theatre Archives.

295 *The history of African American*: The source relied on here is "Black and Multi-Racial Productions of Tennessee Williams's *The Glass Menagerie,*" Philip C. Kolin, *Journal of Dramatic Theory and Criticism* (Spring 1995).

295 *Audrey Wood saw*: "A Streetcar Named Desire"—on Broadway, by Guava Puree, guavapuree.wordpress.com/2012/05/17/a-streetcar-named-desire-on-broadway/.

296 *No more infernal*: John Lahr, December 2011, newyorker.com/culture/culture-desk/the-best-theatre-of-the-year.

296 *Once you know your history*: "Blair Underwood and Nicole Ari Parker Address *Streetcar* Critics, *Playbill,* http://www.playbill.com/article/blair-underwood-and-nicole-ari-parker-address-streetcar-critics-com-193579.

297 *What distinguishes [Mann's] production*: David Rooney, "A Streetcar Named Desire: Theater Review," *Hollywood Reporter*, April 22, 2012. www.hollywoodreporter.com/review/a-streetcar-named-desire-theater-314871

297 *Mann's blunt staging of the rape scene*: Marilyn Stasio, "A Streetcar Named Desire," *Variety*, April 22, 2012. variety.com/2012/legit/reviews/a-streetcar-named-desire-2-1117947418/.

297 *Damned with minimal praise*: Michael Musto, "Streetcar of Color Opens: My Review," *The Village Voice,* April 22, 2012.

298 *An exquisite snooze*: Ben Brantley, "Hey, Stella! You want to Banter?" *The New York Times*, April 22, 2012.

Chapter 15: The Political Is Personal

ARCHIVES: Emily Mann Papers; NYPL for the Performing Arts, Billy Rose Theatre Division.

INTERVIEWS BY AUTHOR: EM; Anne Cattaneo; Christine Lahti; Kathleen Nolan; Gloria Steinem.

NOTES:

301 *Spectacular opportunity*: "FOR THE BOARD: THE GLORIA STEINEM PROJECT," December 2013. Emily Mann Papers.

304 *Brecht wrote*: Dukore, *Dramatic Theory and Criticism*, 852.

307 *I plan to write a highly theatrical documentary*: "The Gloria Steinem Project," Emily Mann email to Andre Bishop and Adam Siegel, January 12, 2014. Emily Mann Papers.

307 *Gloria Live at Lincoln Center*: The following quotations and description are from Emily Mann's draft dated October 16, 2014. Emily Mann Papers.

309 *GLORIA at LINCOLN CENTER Look Out*. GLORIA at LINCOLN CENTER *Look Out*, Lincoln Center Workshop April 2017. "Final Draft (4/14/17)".

311 *We are here America, at last*: Ibid.

312 *Washington Post*: On October 7, 2016, during the 2016 United States presidential election, the *Washington Post* posted a video and accompanying article about then-presidential candidate Donald Trump and television host Billy Bush having "an extremely lewd conversation about women" in 2005. Trump and Bush were in a bus on their way to film an episode of *Access Hollywood*, a show owned by NBCUniversal. In the video, Trump described his attempt to seduce a married woman and indicated he might start kissing a woman that he and Bush were about to meet. He added, "I don't even wait. And when you're a star, they let you do it. You can do anything. Grab them by the pussy. You can do anything." en.wikipedia.org/wiki/Donald_Trump_Access_Hollywood_tape.

312 The Women's March was a worldwide protest on January 21, 2017, the day after the inauguration of President Donald Trump. According to organizers, the goal was to "send a bold message to our new administration on their first day in office, and to the world that women's rights are human rights." en.wikipedia.org/wiki2017_Women%27s_March.

312 *We are here and around the world*: The entire transcript of Gloria Steinem's speech in Washington, D.C., on January 21, 2017, can be found at www.elle.com/culture/news/a42331/gloria-steinem-womens-march-speech/.

317 *STRIKE, STRIKE, STRIKE!!!*: *Waiting for Lefty*, in *Six Plays of Clifford Odets* (New York: Grove Press, 1979), 31.

318 *At that moment*: *Gloria: A Life*, Final Draft, October 16, 2018, 25.

Epilogue: Seasons of Reckonings

ARCHIVES: Emily Mann Papers.

INTERVIEWS BY AUTHOR: EM; Charles McNulty; Nadine Strossen.

NOTES:

321 ***LORT Theatres***: Porsche McGovern, "Who directs in LORT Theatres by gender: positions & people, averages, & prolificity," *howlround.com* https://howlround.com/who-designs-and-directs-lort-theatres-gender-4. HowlRound

321 ***She places on stage***: The Rev. Willie J. Smith, "Mann, What a Difference She Has Made," *Times*, June 12, 2002.

322 ***It has been an extraordinary tenure***: "Dear McCarter Board of Trustees," December 18, 2018. Emily Mann Papers.

324 ***To Emily Mann***: https://www.nj.com/opinion/2019/01/pioneering-theater-director-is-retiring-to-do-more-work-we-cant-wait-to-see-what-comes-next-op. Posted January 17, 2019.

Selected Filmography

Butler, Michael. *Execution of Justice.* Adapted from the play by Emily Mann. Directed by Leon Ichaso. Aired November 28, 1999, on the Showtime Networks.

Hare, David. *Saigon: Year of the Cat.* Directed by Stephen Frears. Aired November 29, 1983, on Thames Television,

Mann, Emily. *Having Our Say: The Delany Sisters' First 100 Years.* Directed by Lynne Littman. Aired April 18, 1999, CBS.

Selected Bibliography

For the convenience of the reader, I have divided the selected bibliography into two sections. The first includes works by and related to Emily Mann, the second includes additional resources on which I drew while researching and analyzing Emily Mann's life and work. TS indicates the document is a typescript.

1. Emily Mann

Allen, Annulla, and Emily Mann. *Annulla Allen: Autobiography of a Survivor.* 1976. Emily Mann Papers.

Allen, Annulla. *Annulla Allen: an Autobiography of a Survivor.* Adapted for radio by Emily Mann. Emily Mann Papers.

Betsko, Kathleen, and Rachel Koenig, eds. "Emily Mann." In *Interviews with Contemporary Women Playwrights.* New York: Beech Tree Books, 1987.

Brodie, Geraldine, and Emma Cole. "Multiple roles and shifting translations." In *Adapting Translation for the Stage.* London: Routledge, 2017.

Brookner, Sara. "Emily Mann on Mindset and Living with Multiple Sclerosis," HowlRound.com/chronic-theatremakers, Sept. 11, 2017.

Cole, Susan Letzler. "Emily Mann Directs Execution of Justice." In *Directors in Rehearsal: A Hidden World.* New York: Routledge, 1992.

Dixon, Michael Bigelow, and Liz Engelman. "Emily Mann," in *The Playwright's Workout.* Hanover, New Hampshire: Smith and Kraus, Inc., 2009.

Eichenbaum, Rose. "Emily Mann." In *The Director Within: Storytellers of Stage and Screen.* Middletown, CT: Wesleyan University Press, 2014.

Fliotsos, Anne, and Wendy Vierow. *American Women Stage Directors of the Twentieth Century.* Champaign, IL: University of Illinois Press, 2008.

Greene, Alexis, ed. "Emily Mann." In *Women Who Write Plays.* Hanover, NH: Smith and Kraus, Inc., 2001.

————, ed. *Women Writing Plays: Three Decades of the Susan Smith Blackburn Prize*. Austin: University of Texas Press, 2006.

Harris, Roy. *Eight Women of the American Stage: Talking about Acting*. Foreword by Emily Mann. Portsmouth, NH: Heineman, 1997.

Laville, Pierre. *Nights and Days*. Adapted by Emily Mann from a literal translation by Peregrine Whittlesey. TS, 1984. Emily Mann Papers.

———— *Nights and Days,* adaptation by Emily Mann, *Avant-Scène* (July 1984).

Laville, Pierre, and Emily Mann. *Baby Doll*. TS, January 7, 2014. Emily Mann Papers.

Mann, Arthur. *Growth and Achievement: Temple Israel 1854–1954*. Cambridge, MA: The Riverside Press, 1954.

————. *Yankee Reformers in the Urban Age*. Cambridge, MA: The Belknap Press of Harvard University Press, 1954.

————, ed. *The Progressive Era*. New York: Holt, Rinehart and Winston, 1963.

————. *La Guardia: A Fighter Against His Times, 1882–1933*. Chicago: The University of Chicago Press, 1959.

————. *La Guardia Comes to Power: 1933*. Philadelphia: J.B. Lippincott Company, 1965.

Mann, Emily.

————. *The Pianist*. TS, January 15, 2021. Emily Mann Papers.

————. *Gloria: A Life*. New York: Theatre Communications Group, 2019.

————. *Gloria, A Life*. Master Script. January 3, 2019. Emily Mann Papers.

————. *Still Life*. TS, 2018. Emily Mann Papers.

————. *Gloria, A Life*. TS. October 16, 2018. Emily Mann Papers.

————. *Gloria, A Life*. Pre-rehearsal draft. August 18, 2018. Emily Mann Papers.

————. *The Pianist*. TS, July 10, 2018. Emily Mann Papers.

————. GLORIA at LINCOLN CENTER: *Look Out,* Final Draft, April 14, 2017.

————. *David Duke One on One*. TS, 2017. Emily Mann Papers.

————. *Under the Liberty Trees*. TS, Nov. 28, 2016. Emily Mann Papers.

————. *Hoodwinked*. TS, Jan. 26, 2016. Emily Mann Papers.

————. *Gloria Live at Lincoln Center*. TS, Oct. 16, 2014. Emily Mann Papers.

————. *Scenes from a Marriage*. TS, Final Draft, Sept. 22, 2014. New York Theatre Workshop.

————, *A Seagull in the Hamptons*, adaptation from the play by Chekhov. New York: Broadway Play Publishing, 2013.

————. *Mrs. Packard*. In *Front Lines*, edited by Alexis Greene and Shirley Lauro. New York: The New Press, 2009.

————. *Antigone*, adaptation from the play by Sophocles. Woodstock, Illinois: The Dramatic Publishing Company, 2006.

————.*Uncle Vanya*, adaptation from the play by Chekhov. Woodstock, IL: The Dramatic Publishing Company, 2005.

————. *Meshugah*. New York: Dramatists Play Service, 2004.

————, and David Roessel, eds. *Political Stages; Plays that Shaped a Century.* Preface by Emily Mann. New York: Applause Theatre & Cinema Books, 2002.

————. *The Cherry Orchard*, adaptation from the play by Chekhov. New York: Dramatists Play Service, 2000.

————. *The House of Bernarda Alba*, adaptation from the play by Federico García Lorca. New York: Dramatists Play Service, 1998

————. *Execution of Justice*. In *Testimonies: Four Plays*. Also includes *Annulla, An Autobiography*; *Still Life*; *Greensboro (A Requiem)*. New York: Theatre Communications Group, 1997.

————. *Having Our Say: The Delany Sisters' First 100 Years.* New York: Dramatists Play Service, 1996.

————. *Miss Julie*, translation/adaptation from the play by Strindberg. 1993. Unpublished.

————. *The Greensboro Massacre*, a screenplay. TS, 1992. Emily Mann Papers.

————. *The Story of Winnie Mandela*. Part One: "The Awakening." TS, Jan. 5, 1988. Emily Mann Papers.

————. *The Story of Winnie Mandela*. Part Two: "The Challenge." TS, March 5, 1988. Emily Mann Papers.

————, and Mbongeni Ngema. *Sarafina!* Screenplay. TS, Second Draft, Oct. 29, 1988. Emily Mann Papers.

————. "The Clinic." TS for television episodes, 1987. Emily Mann Papers.

————. *Execution of Justice*. TS, October 23, 1985. Emily Mann Papers.

————. *Execution of Justice*. TS, August 1, 1985. Mark Bly Papers.

————. *The Dan White Project*. TS, September 17, 1982. Emily Mann Papers.

————. *Fanny Kelly*, a screenplay. TS, 1982. Emily Mann Papers.

————. *Odor of Chrysanthemums by D. H. Lawrence*. Filmscript, n.d. Emily Mann Papers.

————. "Pinter's Party: No Answers." November 1975. Emily Mann Papers.

————. *Amy*. Reel-to-reel audio tape, 1971. Arthur Mann Papers, University of Chicago.

Nevin, Stan, and Emily Mann. *Medea*. TS, n.d. Emily Mann Papers.

Olson, Darlene Faye Poppe. "A Comparative Study of Joanne Akalaitis and Emily Mann: Playwrights and Directors." PhD diss., University of Minnesota, n.d.

Pryor, Michael Scott. "The Matter of Memory: Visual and Performative Witnessing of the Greensboro Massacre." MA thesis, The University of Texas at Austin, August 2012.

Rand, Ronald. *Create! How Extraordinary People Live to Create and Create to Live*. Deadwood, Oregon: Wyatt-MacKenzie Publishing, 2017.

Sapinsley, Barbara. *The Private War of Mrs. Packard*. New York: Kodansha International, 1995.

Savran, David, ed. "Emily Mann." In *In Their Own Words*. New York: Theatre Communications Group, 1988.

Shange, Ntozake. *Betsey Brown*, a novel. New York: St. Martin's Press, 1985.

——, and Cecil Taylor. *Carrie, an Opera*. TS, 1979. Emily Mann Papers.

——. *Carrie: A Rhythm and Blues Opera*. TS, 1981. Emily Mann Papers.

Shange, Ntozake, and Emily Mann. *Betsey Brown*. TS, 1991. Emily Mann Papers.

——, and Emily Mann. *Betsey Brown: The Colored World in a Whirl/At Least a New Direction*. A drama with music. TS, May 1989. Emily Mann Papers.

——, and Emily Mann. *Betsey Brown*. TS, Version J, Nov. 23, 1987. Emily Mann Papers.

Szpilman, Wladyslaw. *The Pianist*. London: Victor Gollancz, 1999.

2. Theater Texts and Criticism, Feminism, American Political History

Aronson, Arnold. *Ming Cho Lee: A Life in Design*. New York: Theatre Communications Group, 2014.

Ball, David. *Summerfolk (through October 16)*. TS, 1976. Emily Mann Papers.

Bentley, Eric. *Are You Now or Have You Ever Been*. New York: Harper & Row, 1972.

Boyer, John. *The University of Chicago: A History*. Chicago: The University of Chicago Press, 2015.

Canning, Charlotte. *Feminist Theaters in the U.S.A.:* New York: Routledge, 1996.

Coe, Liz. *The Bull Gets the Matador Once in a Lifetime*. TS, 1972. William Alfred Papers, Brooklyn College Library.

Colleran, Jeanne, and Jenny S. Spencer, eds. *Staging Resistance: Essays on Political Theater*. Ann Arbor: The University of Michigan Press, 1998.

Crothers, Rachel. *He and She*. In *Representative American Plays*, edited by Arthur Hobson Quinn. New York: Appleton-Century-Crofts, Inc., 1953.

Daniels, Rebecca. *Women Stage Directors Speak*. Jefferson, NC: McFarland & Company.

Dawson, Gary Fisher. "American Documentary Theatre: In Content, Form and Stagecraft Since Martin Duberman's *In White America: A Documentary Play*." PhD diss., School of Education, New York University, 1996.

Delany, Sarah L., and A. Elizabeth Delany, with Amy Hill Hearth. *Having Our Say: The Delany Sisters' First 100 Years*. New York: Dell Publishing, 1994.

Dolan, Jill. *Utopia in Performance: Finding Hope at the Theater*. Ann Arbor: University of Michigan Press, 2005.

Duberman, Martin B. *In White America*. In *Best American Plays*, Sixth Series 1963–1967, John Gassner and Clive Barnes, eds. New York: Crown Publishers, 1971.

Dukore, Bernard F. *Dramatic Theory and Criticism*. New York: Hold, Rinehart and Winston, Inc., 1974.

———. *Documents for Drama and Revolution*. New York: Holt, Rinehart and Winston, Inc., 1971.

Duplessis, Rachel Blau, and Ann Snitow, eds. *The Feminist Memoir Project*. New York: Three Rivers Press, 1998.

Epstein, Helen. *Joe Papp: An American Life*. Boston: Little, Brown and Company, 1994.

Faludi, Susan. *Backlash: The Undeclared War Against American Women*. New York: Crown Publishing Group, 1991.

Field, Barbara. *Matrix*. In *Collected Plays Volume One*. New York: On Stage Press, 2008.

Flacks, Richard. *Making History*. New York: Columbia University Press, 1988.

Franklin, John Hope. *A Mirror to America*. New York: Farrar, Straus and Giroux, 2005.

Freed, Donald. *Inquest*. In *Voicings: Ten Plays from the Documentary Theater*, Attilio Favorini, ed. Hopewell, NJ: The Ecco Press, 1995.

Gitlin, Todd. *The Sixties: Years of Hope, Days of Rage*. New York: Bantam Books, 1987.

Guilfoyle, Peg. *The Guthrie Theater*. Minneapolis: Nodin Press, 2006.

Haas, Jeffrey. *The Assassination of Fred Hampton*. Chicago: Lawrence Hill Books, 2010.

Isser, Edward R. *Stages of Annihilation*. London: Associated University Presses, 1997.

Izenour, George C. *Theater Design*. New York: McGraw-Hill Book Company, 1977.

Lecoq, Jacques, in collaboration with Jean-Gabriel Carasso and Jean-Claude Lallias. *The Moving Body*. London: Bloomsbury Methuen Drama, 2009.

McAneny, Herbert. "McCarter Theatre in the 1960s." *The Princeton University Library Chronicle*, 48, 1 (Autumn 1986): 42–57.

Madden, Paco José. "A Feminist Manifesto for Playwrights," howlround.com. December 11, 2016.

Mamet, David. *Reunion* and *Dark Pony*. New York: Samuel French, 1979.

Marivaux. *Three Plays*. Translated and Adapted by Stephen Wadsworth. Hanover, NH: Smith & Kraus, Inc., 1999.

Martin, Carol. "Bodies of Evidence," *TDR 50*, 3 (2006): 8–15.

Mastrosimone, William. *A Tantalizing*. New York: Samuel French, 1985.

Montgomery, Robert. *Subject to Fits*. New York: Samuel French, 1972.

Morgan, Robin. *Sisterhood Is Forever*. New York: Washington Square Press, 2003.

Ndlovu, Duma, ed. *Woza Afrika! An Anthology of South African Plays*. New York: George Braziller, 1986.

Nolte, Charles. *The Roads in Germany*. TS, n.d. Emily Mann Papers.

Nussbaum, Martha C. *Political Emotions*. Cambridge, MA: The Belknap Press of Harvard University Press, 2013.

———. *Not for Profit*. Princeton: Princeton University Press, 2010.

O'Brien, Mark, and Craig Little, eds. *Reimaging America: The Arts of Social Change*. Philadelphia: New Society Publishers, 1990.

Parkison, Aimee. "Women Writing Violence," *The Writer's Chronicle 49*, 2 (October/November 2016): 110–120.

Pierpont, Claudia Roth. *Passionate Minds*. New York: Vintage Books, 2000.

Primus, Francesca. "Indomitable Women Making Indelible Marks," *Backstage*, August 3, 1990.

Reinelt, Janelle G. "Toward a Poetics of Theatre and Public Events: In the Case of Stephen Lawrence," *TDR: The Drama Review* 50, Number 3 (Fall 2006), 69-87.

———. "Feminist Theory and the Problem of Performance," *Modern Drama 32* (1989): 48–57.

Sartre, Jean-Paul. *No Exit and Three Other Plays*. Vintage Books, Inc., 1958.

Shilts, Randy. *The Mayor of Castro Street*. New York: St. Martin's Press, 1982.

Singer, Isaac Bashevis. *Meshugah*. New York: Farrar Straus Giroux, 1994.

Solga, Kim. *theatre & feminism*. New York: Palgrave MacMillan, 2016.

Stuller, Jennifer K. *Ink-Stained Amazons and Cinematic Warriors*. London: I. B. Tauris & Co., 2010.

Sweet, Jeffrey. *The Value of Names*. New York: Dramatists Play Service, 1997.

Tolan, Kathleen. *A Weekend Near Madison*. New York: Samuel French, Inc., 1984.

Tremblay, Michel. *La Duchesse de Langeais and Other Plays*. Vancouver: Talonbooks, 1976.

Wandor, Michelene. *Look Back in Gender*. London: Methuen London Ltd., 1987.

Watterson, Kathryn. *I Hear My People Singing*. Princeton: Princeton University Press, 2017.

Weiss, Peter. "Fourteen Propositions for a Documentary Theatre." In *Voicings: Ten Plays from the Documentary Theater*, Attilio Favorini, ed. Hopewell, NJ: The Ecco Press, 1995.

———. *The Investigation*. In *Voicings: Ten Plays from the Documentary Theater*, Attilio Favorini, ed. Hopewell, NJ: The Ecco Press, 1995.

Weller, Michael. *Dwarfman: Master of a Million Shapes*. TS, n.d. Emily Mann Papers.

Wilkerson, Isabel. *The Warmth of Other Suns*. New York: Random House, 2010.

Wishna, Victor. *In Their Company: Portraits of American Playwrights*. Brooklyn, NY: Umbrage Editions, 2006.

Index

Note: Page references for photographs are italicized.

Northampton, Massachusetts, 1, 13, 15–29, 31; African American community and racism, 15–16; Jewish families, 16–17, 21; Mann's childhood, 1, 15–29; Smith College, 13, 15, 23, 28
Northlight Theatre (Evanston, Illinois), 242
Nosanow, Barbara. *See* Field, Barbara
not-for-profit theater, 85, 203–4, 220, 234, 293, 321
The Nuclear Family, 113, 118
Nussbaum, Martha, 25–26

Oates, Joyce Carol, 250
Obama, Barack, 293
Obie Awards (*Village Voice*), 155, 164
O'Brien, Irene, 100, 101
Odets, Clifford, 317
Oedipus the King, 154, 160–64, *162;* BAM Theater production, 154, 160–64, *162;* casting, 160, 163–64; Lee's set design, 160, 161–62, 163; Mann's chosen translation, 160–61; Mann's preparatory trip to Greece, 153–54, 161; Mann's reflections on, 163–64; reviews, 160, 163
The Old Globe (San Diego), 222
Oliver, Edith, 142
Oliver, Roger, 160, 161, 162
Olson, Darlene, 235, 237, 241
"On Cultural Power: The August Wilson-Robert Brustein Discussion" at New York City's Town Hall (January, 1997), 277
Ondaatje, Michael, 99
O'Neill Playwrights Center (Waterford, Connecticut), 121
On Mount Chimborazo, 121

Oregon Contemporary Theatre (OCT), 164, 170–71
Osborne, John, 52, 53
Osterman, Lester, Jr., 192, 199–201, 202–3
Osterman, Marjorie, 192
Ostrołęka, Poland, 3–5, 81, 82–83, 326
Othello, 224
The Other Place (Minneapolis), 86–87
Our Souls at Night (Haruf), 325
Owen, Paul, 182–83

Packard, Elizabeth Parsons Ware, 289–92. See also *Mrs. Packard*
Palinski, Maurice, 100
Paone, Gerry, *189*
Papp, Joseph, 179, 216; and *Betsey Brown*, 230–32, 233–34; and Shange, 230–32
Paran, Janice: *American Theatre* article "Redressing Ibsen," 209; and *Greensboro (A Requiem)*, 268, 269–70, 271; on *Having Our Say* rehearsals, 260; on Mann's empathic directing, 103; as McCarter's literary manager, 103, 243, 277, 286–87, 295
Parker, Nicole Ari, 295, 297, *298*
A Park in Our House, 286
Parlato, Dennis, *291*
Parnell, Peter, 306
A Party for Two, 106
Patterson, Jay, *194*
Paulus, Diane, 309–10, 314–16, 317, 318
Peabody Awards, 263
people of color in the theater: and Mann's production of *Betsey Brown*, 237–41, 242;